BEYOND COPING

BEYOND COPING: MEETING GOALS, VISIONS, AND CHALLENGES

Edited by

ERICA FRYDENBERG

University of Melbourne, Australia

OXFORD
UNIVERSITY PRESS

OXFORD

UNIVERSITY PRESS

Great Clarendon Street, Oxford OX2 6DP

Oxford University Press is a department of the University of Oxford.
It furthers the University's objective of excellence in research, scholarship,
and education by publishing worldwide in

Oxford New York
Auckland Bangkok Buenos Aires Cape Town Chennai
Dar es Salaam Delhi Hong Kong Istanbul Karachi Kolkata
Kuala Lumpur Madrid Melbourne Mexico City Mumbai Nairobi
Sao Paulo Shanghai Taipei Tokyo Toronto

Oxford is a registered trade mark of Oxford University Press
in the UK and in certain other countries

Published in the United States
by Oxford University Press, Inc., New York

A catalogue record for this title is available from the British Library.

Library of Congress Cataloging in Publication Data
(Data available)

ISBN 0 19 850814 X (Pbk)

10 9 8 7 6 5 4 3 2 1

Typeset by Newgen Imaging Systems (P) Ltd., Chennai, India
Printed in Great Britain
on acid-free paper by
T. J. International Ltd, Padstow

FOREWORD

Beyond Coping provides a solid foundation of significant theory and research on coping with stress in the 21st Century. The topics considered in this volume represent the next phase of research on stress and coping, and provide an excellent sequel to *Learning to Cope*, edited by Erica Frydenberg and published in 1999 by Oxford University Press. The author(s) of each chapter are distinguished contributors to theory and research on coping as a vital process that not only helps people to deal effectively with stress, but also motivates them to engage in self-actualizing behaviors that contribute to meeting life's challenges.

Interest in coping was stimulated in the 1960s by Richard Lazarus' classic book, *Psychological Stress and the Coping Process*. Since that time, most research on coping has focused on dealing with the effects of stress on negative emotions, such as anxiety, anger, and depression. A unique feature of *Beyond Coping* is the emphasis given by the contributing authors to positive emotions. Positive psychology helps people to use their strengths and values to thrive and flourish in seeking self-fulfillment and achieving important life goals.

The chapters in this volume clearly demonstrate that effective coping is a multidimensional process that encompasses both individual adjustment and group or communal adaptation to stressful, demanding, and complex situations. Individual coping, as discussed by Schwarzer and Taubert, can be reactive to past events that involve compensation for loss or harm, or anticipatory and preventive in helping people deal with imminent threats and the management of risks that might occur in the future.

Individual coping can also be proactive by activating self-regulatory goal attainment processes that motivate people to strive to improve themselves and their environment while seeking self-fulfillment. The Proactive Coping Inventory (PCI) developed by Greenglass, Schwarzer, and Taubert was designed to assess the positive aspects of coping that are related to autonomous goal-setting and self-regulatory striving to achieve value-oriented goals. Greenglass reports impressive research findings with the PCI in this volume.

In the context of understanding human resiliency and personal mastery, Hobfoll presents an interesting comparison between individualistic and communal coping. His research indicates that being socially connected can be highly beneficial to communal coping, and that gender is often a source of important individual differences in the coping process. Burke observes that the hardiness of workers and the resources available to them are critical variables in coping with occupational stress. Positive coping strategies that have the potential for reducing the impact of stress on health are investigated by Moore, who cogently points out that health is not merely the absence of illness, but also involves striving toward self-actualization.

Special attention is given to coping by young people in the five chapters that comprise Parts II and III of this volume. It is especially interesting to note the emphasis given to positive psychology by Boekaerts and Pekrun et al., and by Frydenberg and Lewis. The role of positive psychology and self-regulation in goal setting is emphasized by Boekaerts from the perspective of educational psychology. The impact of positive emotions on self-regulation, learning and student achievement is also emphasized by Pekrun et al. Frydenberg and Lewis note the progression of research on coping, from previous concerns with dysfunction to the current focus on optional functioning. Johnson and Johnson point out that in order to be effective in dealing with stress and adversity in the classroom, coping processes must be developed in the context of cooperation, shared values, and constructive conflict resolution.

While the contributions of each chapter to *Beyond Coping* are substantive and important in their own right, the theoretical insights and research of the authors have had a very positive impact on one another. The long-term interaction among the contributors to this volume has benefited from their past participation in the annual meetings of the Society for Stress and Anxiety Research (STAR). As one of the founders of STAR and an active participant in most of the meetings of this Society over the past 20 years, I was especially pleased to note how the work of my colleagues has developed and expanded, and has focused on previously neglected aspects of coping. I would like to congratulate Professor Frydenberg and the contributors to this volume for a work well done!

Charles D. Spielberger, Ph.D.
September, 2002

PREFACE

As we entered a new century Martin E. P. Seligman and Mihaly Csikszentmihalyi (2000) have called for a positive psychology that moves away from a model of human behaviour which identifies inadequacies to one which helps us to move to a 'good life' in which actions lead to 'well-being, positive individuals, and thriving communities'. Since the Second World War psychology has become a science largely about healing, repairing damage associated with disease and human functioning. This emphasis on pathology has overlooked the circumstances under which people thrive and flourish. As Seligman and Csikszentmihalyi point out the field of positive psychology is 'valued subjective experiences: well-being, contentment and satisfaction (in the past); hope and optimism (in the future); and flow and happiness (in the present) (Seligman and Csikszentmihalyi 2000, p. 5). It is expected that Beyond Coping: Meeting Goals, Visions and Challenges will contribute to our understanding of the circumstances under which people thrive and flourish as they call on their strengths and virtues and move to systematically build competency rather than correcting weakness.

While the genome and other related projects tell us about our shortcomings or potentialities it will be psychology that will continue to focus on *how* we maximize human potential. Genetics may make us better human animals but the promise of positive psychology is that it will make us better human beings.

There are many who emphasize the part that positive psychology can play in overcoming psychology's reductionist epistemological perspectives by studying human motives, potentialities and capacities (e.g. Sheldon and King 2001). Focusing on human strengths is about flexibility, variability and having goals. Goal frames that focus on approaching positive states are functionally superior to goal frames that are focused on avoiding negative states (Schneider 2001). Furthermore, Csikszentmihalyi (1997) points out that *happiness* for people depends to a large extent on their engagement in task and working towards goals. 'People are not happy because of what they do but because of how they do it (Csikszentmihalyi 1999, p. 826)'.

There has been an emphasis in the literature on attributions, that is, whether the causes of events are internal or external. Is it some characteristic of the individual or a demand of the environment? This is now seen as a false dichotomy, since it is generally an interaction between the two (Schneider 2001). There is an interdependence between individual and environmental constraints and the important part that emotions play. Additionally self-regulation is associated with positive emotions and self-control with negative emotions (see Chapters 7 and 8 in this volume).

This volume has the purpose of bringing together key researchers in the field of coping whose contributions come from a range of perspectives including health, workplace and education. What is striking is that regardless of diversity of approaches they converge towards a collective vision and understanding. Hobfoll (Chapter 4) champions communal mastery over an individualistic perspective, at the same time appreciating individual effort and control. In taking a historical perspective he also points out that individualism and collectivism are on a continuum. When we attempt to separate them we lose a great deal that pertains to the 'fabric of self-in social context'. While there is no definitive study that measures the relative merits of communal over individualistic coping, it is by taking the best elements of each that helps individuals to thrive.

Case studies show that even if we only have scant knowledge about schoolroom experiences, whether the culture was collectivist or individualistic there are core elements over and above talent that explain how individuals thrive and achieve success. Boekaerts (Chapter 7) in considering students in the learning context emphasizes individual effort and control. She explores the issue of why curiosity diminishes at the age of eight when it is understood that effort will not yield results. Chapters 7 and 10 demonstrate that cooperation promotes greater effort to achieve. They emphasize evidence based classroom applications of cooperative learning, conflict resolution and peer mediation as ways in which to promote optimum development in the classroom.

Perhaps Hobfoll's question 'how did the social unit to which I belong benefit?' is achieved by Johnson and Johnson's approach. Johnson and Johnson have spent many years of fruitful research in the educational context demonstrating that collaborative work in the classroom leads to better outcomes. In a similar vein, Chapter 8 in this volume highlights the benefits that positive social environments along with positive emotions can contribute to enhancing the learning experience.

In moving beyond coping to examine how people flourish and succeed, several of the contributors use as their starting point recent publications in the area of positive psychology. They go on to review the literature in the field of coping in order to demonstrate the process and the progress that has been made since the stress and coping paradigms have been first documented. Burke does this in Chapter 5 on the workplace as does Shwarzer and Taubert in their Chapter 2 on proactive coping. Shwarzer and Taubert in their review integrate the major theories such as those of Lazarus (1991) and Hobfoll (1988, 1998). They also go on to identify extensions of the coping construct to include positive strivings which were hitherto in the domain of motivation. This is not reflected in proactive coping, a relatively new concept. As is pointed out in Chapters 2 and 3, reactive coping is about risk management and proactive coping is about goal management. It is about self-initiating rather than about self-defeating practices. This is again picked up by Boekaerts when she focuses on the educational context where goal identification and attainment are all important. She describes self-regulated learning as a form of proactive coping. Greenglass in Chapter 3 demonstrates the validity and the utility of an instrument to assess proactive coping and the implications of this for the workplace. Burke reviews the field as it relates to the organizational setting and considers ways in which occupational stress can be reduced or minimized.

Several of the contributors have chosen as their starting point to review the relevant literature in the field. This allows the reader to see their individual contributions as part of a continuum in the field of stress, coping and beyond. Individually they represent one part of the jigsaw. The first chapter is an introductory one and is included not merely as another review but rather an opportunity to introduce and sometimes elaborate on theory that complements those presented in subsequent chapters.

Since research in the adult arena has led the field, the major theoretical, conceptual, and research advances in the adult arena are presented in Part I. The domain of young people is presented in Part II. In that section, following the work of Boekaerts, and Johnson and Johnson, there is a review by Frydenberg and Lewis of factors associated with well-being and some insights into how it might be achieved. This complements the chapter by Moore (Chapter 6), in the adult section, who points out that health is not merely the absence of illness but to take a term from Maslow (1954), the striving towards self-actualization. Chapter 8 addresses the all important challenge of understanding the part that emotions play in serving the individual or inhibiting their pursuit of potential. The final chapter attempts to bridge the divide between childhood and adulthood by illustrating the impact of childhood experience on outcomes in adulthood. In presenting the life trajectories of high achievers in the arts, commerce and sporting arenas, the stories illustrate how the interplay between talent and ability, along with personality and the experience of childhood through to adulthood, account for individual success and achievement in a diverse range of settings.

While there is a view held by some, that coping research has failed to achieve its promise from such a vast body of research, there are others such as the contributors to this volume, who see that we have come a long way, and are taking a leap forward beyond the models that focus on adaptation to those that contribute to our understanding of well-being and success.

An edited volume such as this provides the opportunity for a range of experts to reflect on their work and on the field in general. Each chapter has been written as a resource in its own right. At the same time each of the chapters contribute to an integrated whole that advances our understanding of how people thrive and flourish in their environments. We have endeavoured to provide the reader with the most outstanding theoretical and conceptual formulations provided by key researchers in the field and at the same time it is intended to present a coherent and integrated body of work that allows us to move forward in our research and understanding of how people flourish to achieve success that is beyond just coping.

July 2002   Erica Frydenberg

References

Csikszentmihalyi, M. (1997). *Finding flow*. New York: Basic Books.

—— (1999). If we are so rich why aren't we happy? *American Psychologist*, **54**, 821–7.

Hobfoll, S. E. (1988). *The ecology of stress*. Washington, DC: Hemisphere.

—— (1998). *Stress, culture, and community. The psychology and philosophy of stress*. New York: Plenum.

Lazarus, R. S. (1991). *Emotion and adaptation*. London: Oxford University Press.

Maslow, A. H. (1954). *Motivation and personality*. New York: Harper & Row.

Seligman, M. E. P. and Csikszentmihalyi, M. (2000). Positive psychology. *The American Psychologist*, 55, 5–14.

Schneider, S. L. (2001). In search of realistic optimism: Meaning, knowledge and warm fuzziness. *American Psychologist*, 56(3), 250–63.

Sheldon, K. M. and King, L. (2001). Why positive psychology is necessary. *American Psychologist*, 56(3), 216–17.

CONTENTS

Young people's worlds

Impact of childhood on adulthood

Dedication

This book is dedicated to the contributors. A team of colleagues with whom it has been a privilege to work and advance our understandings, Esther, Monique, Kate, David, Roger, Ralf, Reinhard, Ron, and Stevan. May we each continue to draw inspiration from the work of the other.

Acknowledgements

This volume is the outcome of collaboration between a large number of people, many of whom are active members of Stress Anxiety Research Society (STAR). Their energy and commitment to advancing the field of stress and coping has made it a privilege to collaborate with them. The organization of STAR with its annual scientific meetings, has challenged our thinking and inspired us to push boundaries that otherwise we may not have done. But above all it has been the commitment of the individuals to the achievement of the whole that has made the volume possible. In particular Esther Greenglass has provided the encouragement and support for the project through all its stages. For that I am truly appreciative.

The support of the University of Melbourne, which has provided me with an academic environment that both encourages and makes possible scholarship and collaboration in a borderless world is gratefully acknowledged. The staff at Oxford University Press in Oxford, particularly Martin Baum the commissioning editor and his team, have been instrumental in bringing the project to fruition. It has been a pleasure to work with such a truly professional team.

My final note of appreciation goes to my partner Harry and our children Joshua and Lexi. They have shown by example that our lives are enriched by moving beyond adaptation towards fulfilment and satisfaction through endeavour and achievement, and above all through a contribution to the wellbeing of humankind.

LIST OF CONTRIBUTORS

Monique Boekaerts Leiden University, The Netherlands

Ronald Burke Schulich School of Business, York University, Canada

Erica Frydenberg University of Melbourne, Carlton, Australia

Thomas Goetz University of Munich, Germany

Esther Greenglass York University, Canada

Stevan Hobfoll Kent State University, Kent Hall, USA

David Johnson Department of Educational Psychology, College of Education and Human Development, Minneapolis, USA

Roger Johnson Department of Educational Psychology, College of Education and Human Development, Minneapolis, USA

Ramon Lewis Institute of Education La Trobe University, Melbourne, Australia

Kathleen Moore Deakin University, Burwood, Australia

Reinhard Pekrun Institute of Educational Psychology, University of Munich, Germany

Raymond Perry Department of Psychology, Center of Higher Education Research and Development, University of Manitoba, USA

Ralf Schwarzer Gesundheits Psychologie, Freie Universität Berlin, Germany

Steffen Taubert Freie Universität Berlin, Psychologie Habelschwerdter Allee 45, 14195 Berlin, Germany

Wolfram Titz University of Munich, Germany

CHAPTER 1

BEYOND COPING: SOME PARADIGMS TO CONSIDER

ERICA FRYDENBERG

Coping research evolved from stress research and so moved from a deficit model of adaptation to exploring people's capacity to deal with life's circumstances. The relationship to health, well-being, and productive coping has recently become of interest. The next phase in coping research is an exploration of how people attain goals, achieve success, and meet challenges. Diverse but compatible theories of coping, along with theories of temperament, optimism, hope, emotions, attributional style, and the way to avoid burnout, contribute to our appreciation of how individuals thrive in their efforts to achieve success.

There are many challenges to be faced in contemporary society including the stresses of everyday living in the technological age and changes in patterns of employment and family life. Despite the technological advances in our communities and the lifestyle benefits that accrue from progress, depression is being experienced in 'epidemic' proportions in many Western communities, and in particular amongst young people. The search for effective ways to reverse this trend has resulted in a significant shift in psychological approach from a focus on helplessness and pathology to a more positive orientation that emphasizes health and well-being. This shift is evident in the literature. The fostering of personal agency is an important component in 'inoculating' both young people and adults against depression and freeing them to achieve success.

There is a close relationship between general adaptation and coping. While there are those who emphasize positive affect as the other side of coping (e.g. Folkman and Moskowitz 2000), it is helpful to construe coping as a continuum that extends from the management of stress and adaptation to achieving success and flourishing in the pursuit of goals. Accomplishment and thriving, typically involves seeing circumstances as opportunities rather than a burden or problem.

A review of coping research to date reveals that while the transactional model of stress and coping has been widely adopted there are important developments such as proactive and communal coping. (See Chapters 2 and 3 in this volume for proactive coping and Chapter 4 for communal coping). In general coping can be construed as a multidimensional process, a multi-system series of events that continue throughout the life span and to which the interplay of many determinants contributes. It is essentially a dynamic interaction between persons and their environments. A number of heuristic devices and empirically supported models have been developed which describe the process. Recently, terms such as communal coping and proactive coping have entered the literature. The way in which these models can be integrated, and the way in which there can be a synthesis of theories promises to move us forward in understanding human endeavour.

Stress research

Stress and coping are arguably the most widely researched area in psychology (Hobfoll *et al.* 1998). Some people would claim that this vast body of research has been disappointing in its outcomes in that it has failed to deliver clear definitions as to what works and what does not work in terms of human adaptation (see Chapter 5 in this volume). Nevertheless, there is a great deal that we know about coping and the gains in the stress and coping field have enabled us to move beyond understanding human adaptation to examining how people succeed in meeting their goals and challenges. A review of coping provides us with a springboard from which to examine how people achieve success and flourish. This is done in Chapter 2 (in this volume) as it demonstrates the progression from stress research to recent additions of communal and proactive coping and in Chapter 5 (in this volume) as it makes the historical links between coping and the workplace.

Early interest in the adaptational process dates back to the nineteenth century with the work of Sigmund Freud (1894–1964) and the work he did on psychological defences in an attempt to understand how people manage anxiety. Whenever these unconscious defence processes have proven difficult to assess, psychologists have turned to objective laboratory studies of stress (Selye 1950) or used checklists of life events (Holmes and Rahe 1967).

Historically, the human stress response has been characterized metaphorically as fight-or-flight in the face of threat (Cannon 1932). Recently, there has been a major challenge to this theorizing by the work of Shelley Taylor and her colleagues (Taylor *et al.* 2000) who point out that the evidence for fight-or-flight has largely been derived from work with male subjects, both human and animal, and has not adequately taken into account the typical responses of females. According to Taylor and others, the biobehavioural female stress response can be more accurately construed as tend-and-befriend (Taylor *et al.* 2000). This response is directed at maximizing the survival of the self and the offspring through nurturing, protecting the offspring from harm, and affiliating with others to reduce risk. This work throws into question much of our understandings about the gender-neutrality of responses in the stress and coping area. Tend-and-befriend is not likely to replace the fight-or-flight metaphor, since both males and females respond in the same way to situations of extreme stress, but rather, it adds another dimension to our understanding of how people respond to environmental demands.

Selye (1976) described stress as 'the non-specific response of the body to any demands' (p. 472). Selye makes the distinction between stress which mobilizes the individual to effective performance 'eustress', such as when there is heightened performance during a competition, and stress which is more negative and has been labelled 'distress'. Lazarus (1991) describes stress as the mismatch between the perceived demands of a situation and the individual's assessment of his or her resources to deal with these demands. Stresses can be physical such as those pertaining to the environment, like extreme heat or cold, psychosocial stresses such those experienced when relationships are not working, and daily hassles, such as having a quarrel with a friend. It is eustress that energizes and maximizes the achievement of potential. Furthermore, it is both the presence of resources, alongside the positive appraisal of events that are required to maximize success.

Much of the theorizing on coping which followed stress research is reviewed and expounded in subsequent chapters. However, two bodies of literature, outside the traditional coping area, inform us about success and challenge. The first is the work of Carol Dweck and her associates which illustrates how our attitudes are formed at an early age and how school experience plays an important part. The body of work relates to children's theories of intelligence and mindset towards either mastery or helplessness orientation. The second relates to the part that emotions play. A crucial factor in achievement is the ability to cope with challenges and setbacks. Are people who love challenges willing to take risks? Do those who achieve beyond their apparent potential thrive when they hit obstacles?

Mastery-orientation

Two decades ago, in their work on learned helplessness, Hiroto and Seligman (1975), Miller and Seligman (1975), and Diener and Dweck (1978, 1980) spelled out two different reactions to failure. There are those who are helpless (give up and show deterioration in performance) and there are those who are mastery-oriented (take action to surmount problems). It is not a matter of ability, but of mindset. In a series of experiments by Diener and Dweck (1978, 1980) students were given concept formation problems on which they initially succeeded but failed on subsequent more difficult tasks. An attribution questionnaire determined how they would attribute failures. It was predicted that those who would attribute failures to lack of effort were likely to display a mastery-oriented response. The researchers were also interested in students' thoughts, feelings, and behaviours when confronting failure. Those in the helpless group denigrated their intellectual competence. Those in the mastery-oriented group did not analyse reasons for their failure, but gave themselves instructions on how to improve their performance by concentrating harder or reviewing the feedback. Everyone expressed positive emotions when succeeding. The helpless group expressed sadness and boredom when failing while the mastery group continued to enjoy the problems. Some displayed increased positive affect in face of adversity 'I love a challenge', 'mistakes are our friends'. The helpless group deteriorated in problem-solving while the mastery group continued to improve (Dweck and Sorich 1999).

In another study, Licht and Dweck (1984) gave fifth graders new material to master. The students were ascribed to mastery and helpless groups and half in each group were given a confusing passage. Seventy per cent of the mastery-oriented group successfully completed the task and only one-third of the helpless group was able to learn material when preceded by a confusing paragraph.

Elliot and Dweck (1988) established that the goals students set themselves gave rise to helpless or mastery-oriented responses. They identified three types of goals, performance goals (aim to gain favourable judgement of his or her own competence, and avoid unfavourable judgements, that is, look smart) versus learning goals (where aim is to increase competence, that is, to get smarter) (p. 237). 'Both sets of goals are natural, necessary, and pretty much universal' (p. 238). Everyone wants their ability to be esteemed by others and everyone wants to learn new things. They repeatedly observed that performance goals, where students were focused on measuring their ability by their performance, made them vulnerable to a helpless pattern in the face of failure. In contrast, learning goals that involved focusing on the effort and strategies students need for learning, fostered a mastery-oriented stance toward difficulty (Ames and Archer 1988; Dweck and Leggett 1988; Pintrich *et al.* 1994) (also see Chapters 7 and 11 in this volume).

Students' theories of intelligence are associated with their goals. That is, those with performance goals see intelligence as static while those with mastery goals see that intelligence can be developed. These two theories of intelligence have been called entity and incremental theories (Dweck and Sorich 1999). In a series of studies they showed that different theories of intelligence set up different goals (Dweck and Leggett 1988; Zhao *et al.* 1998). Entity theory fosters performance goals and helpless responses to failure, and incremental theory fosters learning goals and a mastery response to failure. Entity theorists feel that if you have to work hard (show effort) you risk showing that you do not have ability.

The impact of mindset on achievement was examined in Dweck's study of transition to junior high school. Students' theories of intelligence were the best predictors of their seventh grade results. Entity theorists remained low achievers with a helpless pattern of response while incremental theorists showed a mastery-oriented pattern. Another study (Sorich and Dweck 1997) found that both learning and performing were important goals, but when goals were placed in conflict (as in real life), incremental theorists were far more interested in learning than simply performing well. They wanted to meet challenges and acquire new skills rather than just have easy work to make them look smart. Entity theorists wanted to minimize effort. They had conflicting interests. They wanted to do well, but had an aversion to the effort required. Incremental theorists believed that effort was a key ingredient to success. The mastery-oriented approach by incremental students yielded better results intellectually and emotionally.

These patterns begin as early as the preschool years, with at least one-third of the students showing helpless response when experiencing failure (Cain and Dweck 1995; Herbert and Dweck 1985; Dweck 1991). In kindergarten, helpless children felt 'not good' and 'not nice'. In their role play, they showed more criticism and more punishment. Furthermore, helpless young children (Heyman *et al.* 1992) see badness as a stable trait. It is socialization that makes a difference.

Socialization

Adult feedback in the form of criticism that reflected on the child's traits fostered a stronger helpless reaction in response to later setbacks, as well as negative emotions, self-blame, and feelings of badness (Mueller and Dweck 1998). Criticism which indicated that more effort was required, or a new strategy was needed, set up a mastery-oriented reaction (feedback that criticized the behaviour but not the child was in between).

In the study with kindergarteners and fifth graders, it was found that when praise was given for the child as a whole and praise was given for the child's traits (e.g. intelligence) after a job well done, a significantly greater helpless response was created when the child failed (Mueller and Dweck 1998). It was the strategy of praise for effort that created the most mastery-oriented coping response. There were three responses: the intelligence praise group, 'You got it right you must be smart', the effort praise group, 'You got it right. That's a good score and you must have tried hard' and the control group, 'You got it right. That's really good'. The intelligence praise group fell apart after failure. They also showed less enjoyment of the task after failure. They lied about their scores. The effort group felt that they needed to try harder. The effort praise group did best on the last task. After feedback was given and a choice of performance or learning goals made, the intelligence praise group just wanted to keep looking smart, with the majority choosing performance tasks.

Labelling children as gifted or bright promotes the entity theory of intelligence. Giving young people a gifted status can make them sensitive to failure, that is, vulnerable and helpless. They show enthusiasm for the product rather than enthusiasm for the process. Those who believe in fixed traits differ from those who believe in malleable qualities, not only in the way that they judge themselves, but also in the way in which they judge others. The fixed entity theorists tend to stereotype others more than do the increment theorists.

It is clear then, that a helpless mindset leads to a host of maladaptive thoughts, including fear of challenge and avoidance of effort, while the mastery-oriented young people focus on effort. They think about how to accomplish things, how to surmount challenges to achieve their goals, and to increase their abilities. Children with an incremental theory of intelligence were more successful in negotiating transitions while children with entity theory performed less well. If we give messages explicitly or implicitly that ability is fixed and ability can be measured from performance, we are very likely to undermine mastery-oriented inclinations and promote helplessness, even when the message is couched in praise. The indications are, that to maximize success we need to socialize young people to see their ability as malleable and that there is a reward for effort.

Martin Seligman has spent much of his career moving from a study of learned helplessness to understanding how people develop a positive explanatory style (Shatte *et al.* 1999). He describes such a style as fixed from an early age, unless there are attempts at intervention. While there is strong evidence that a positive explanatory style is helpful under adversity (Carver *et al.* 1993; Fitzgerald *et al.* 1993; Scheier *et al.* 1986, 1989), it would seem that a positive explanatory style is also a dominant quality in high achievers (see Chapter 11 in this volume).

Coping and emotions

The relationship between coping and emotion is important in that emotions have been generally seen as interfering with cognitions and coping. Often, emotions appear to dominate and the individual can be described as floundering in a sea of emotions. Historically, coping has been viewed as a response to emotion. In more recent years, there has been a shift where the two are understood to be in a reciprocal dynamic relationship (Folkman and Lazarus 1988*a*). Just as emotion determines how an encounter is appraised, so the outcome in turn determines the individual's emotional state both in the ongoing interaction and in-future interactions. Folkman and Lazarus (1988*a*) distinguish this from the Darwinian approach, where emotions like fear and anger are thought to come to the aid of the organism in the face of threat and also from the ego psychological approach which includes reference to cognitive processes like denial, repression, suppression, intellectualization, and problem-solving in an effort to reduce stress and anxiety. Although there is no readily agreed definition of emotion, there is general agreement that emotions comprise an experiential (affect, appraisal), physiological, and behavioural (action for readiness) component (Izard 1993; Frijda 1993) and these are expressed through separate systems such as the verbal report of feelings, overt behaviour, and expressive physiology (Lang 1984). The metaphors of negative emotions generally portray them as an irresistible force. Thus, in the coping literature much of the emotion-focused conceptualization of coping has focused on the maladaptive. A more recent perspective of emotions has focused on the adaptive nature of emotion and how individuals can organize social communication, goal achievement, and cognitive processes from an early age (Mahoney 1991; Thompson 1994; Ekman 1994; Greenberg and Safran 1987; Izard 1993; Smith 1991). (See also Chapter 8 in this volume.) Thus, emotions are a major organizing force with intra- and interpersonal regulatory effects. Three theoretical constructs exemplify a functionalist view of emotion in personality research, emotional competence (Saarni 1990), emotional intelligence (Salovey and Mayer 1990), and emotional creativity (Averill and Thomas-Knowles 1991). All contribute to healthy inter- and intrapersonal functioning. Emotional competence is essentially self-efficacy in the context of 'emotion-eliciting social transactions' (Saarni 1997, p. 38). The concept of emotional intelligence has integrated the literature from multiple intelligences (Gardner 1983) and can be construed as a subset of social intelligence. Emotional creativity is about creation of emotions that are novel.

Individuals differ in how they perceive, express, understand, and manage emotional phenomena. Essentially, emotional intelligence is the ability to monitor one's own and others' feelings and emotions, as well as having the ability to regulate and use emotion-based information to guide thinking and action. Traditional intelligence is considered to be about reasoning and analytic abilities. Emotions are adaptive and functional and they serve to organize cognitive activities (Leeper 1948; Mowrer 1960). It was first argued by Charles Darwin in 1872 in *The expressions of emotions in man and animal* (Salovey and Mayer 1990) that emotions are a higher order of activity. Darwin claimed that emotions energize and signal in a way that helps other members of the species.

A tripartite model of cognitive activity has been proposed as a way of conceptualizing emotions (Folkman and Lazarus 1988a). The first part is cognitive activity that influences deployment of attention and includes vigilant strategies that neutralize the distress, such as jogging or taking a holiday, and what Folkman and Lazarus label 'escape-avoidance' which is characterized by strategies such as wishful thinking, and tension reduction activities, such as eating, drinking, or sleeping too much. These very strategies can be both adaptive and maladaptive depending on the circumstance. Next, there are the cognitive activities that alter the subjective meaning of an encounter, such as the use of humour and denial. Similarly, in some circumstances, these strategies can be both helpful in the release of tension or in preventing the catastrophizing of events, while in other circumstances they can deny the severity of a problem and avoid engaging in appropriate action. These strategies can also be utilized to remain on task and enhance performance. Included, are those actions that alter the person–environment interaction such as standing one's ground, getting someone to change their mind, or getting more information. Changes in the emotional response depend on whether the desired outcome is achieved, on how an individual evaluates his or her own response, and what the implications are of the present encounter for future events. Gender is considered to be a moderator of emotional coping and adaptive outcomes. One explanation may be that girls are exposed by caretakers from an early age to a wider range of emotions. Physical and mental health comes from neither emotional inhibition nor exhibition *per se*, but from flexibility (Averill 1994, p. 102). Furthermore, enhanced performance requires not only the capacity to deal with demands flexibly, but the capacity to utilize those strategies to forge ahead.

Consistent with a call for a focus on preventive coping in the educational sphere (Snyder 1999), a framework of coping represented by the Adolescent Coping Scale (Frydenberg and Lewis 1993, 1996) and the Coping Scale for Adults (Frydenberg and Lewis 1997) has been used to develop programs in school settings (Cohen and Frydenberg 1995; Bugalski and Frydenberg 2000; Cotta *et al.* 2001; Frydenberg and Brandon, 2002). The evaluation of these programmes is promising. Coping actions are determined in part by one's belief that certain consequences are possible (Hock 1999). This belief in one's control over internal states which means having control over one's thoughts, feelings, and behaviours, together with a positive attributional style is associated with the use of more positive coping responses. There is also emerging evidence that what makes the difference is coping efficacy, that is, the belief that one has the strategies to cope (Cunningham 2002). These findings, along with the clear-cut evidence that non-productive coping is associated with depression and other forms of emotional and social malfunctioning (Chan 1998; Lewis 1999), has informed what to teach and when to teach coping skills to young people (see also Chapter 9 in this volume).

Personality

There has been a strong re-emergence of interest in the role that personality traits play in coping and adaptation (Costa *et al.* 1996; Suls *et al.* 1996; Watson and Hubbard 1996), although situational measures have dominated coping for 20 years (Lazarus and Folkman 1984). In line with this interest in personological factors, several dispositional measures of coping have been developed (Ayers *et al.* 1996; Carver *et al.* 1989) which assess that what people typically do in response to stressful events is substantially stable over time and broadly consistent in different situations. This is in contrast to situational measures like the *Ways of Coping Checklist* (Folkman and Lazarus 1988b). There are also measures which take account of the person and the situation by gauging the General and Specific coping of individuals (Frydenberg and Lewis 1993). There is evidence for cross situational consistency of coping and temporal changes (Frydenberg and Lewis 1994, 2000). Research over past decade has shown that coping behaviours are heavily influenced by the characteristics of the individual, especially personality traits (Bolger 1990; Costa *et al.* 1996; Watson *et al.* 1999). What people do in response to stress and in dealing with their lives is largely determined by who they are and by their enduring dispositions. Personality traits are not easily changed, so coping and the achievement of success will always be easier for some than for others.

The role of temperament is often cited as an important determinant of coping responses (e.g. Kagan 1983; Rutter 1981). It is also the foundation of what was later called personality. Temperament generally refers to an individual's stable and consistent dispositions, the usual style of emotional and behavioural responses of an individual that are predictable. Rutter and Rutter (1992) define temperament as 'those aspects of behaviour that reflect the intrinsic non-maturational stylistic qualities that the individual brings to any particular situation' (Rutter and Rutter 1992, p. 185). Rutter argues that these intrinsic qualitites have a biological basis that includes a genetic component, although these qualities or traits are tempered and influenced by experiences.

In the theory of temperament put forward by Buss and Plomin (1984), three broad dimensions of personality are considered to be present in an individual's early years and continue to be relatively stable throughout later life. These dimensions are emotionality (the tendency to be easily distressed), activity, and sociability. It is suggested that these dimensions may play an important role in moderating the effects of stress during childhood and adolescence. Hauser and Bowlds (1990), for example, argue that temperament influences the available range of coping strategies an individual may draw on in stressful situations, and at the same time temperament affects the type of events that are recognized as being stressful by an individual. Ebata and Moos (1994) used a longitudinal and cross-sectional study of 315 adolescents and found that adolescents who reported greater distress were more likely to use cognitive avoidance, resigned acceptance, and emotional discharge as coping strategies (avoidance methods). In contrast, those who were more active used more positive reappraisal, guidance/support, problem-solving and alternative rewards (approach methods). The findings from other studies of adolescents support these results (e.g. Kurdek and Sinclair 1988). The Australian Temperament Project which followed 2000 young people through each developmental stage of their life (Prior *et al.* 2000) found that easy temperament as rated by teachers, the warmth of the mother–child relationship and the level of stress as perceived by the child was the best predictor of coping.

It is clear that neither nature nor nurture has an exclusive effect on temperament (and hence coping), since most traits rely upon the interaction of both genes and the environment. It has long been accepted, based on studies of twins, that shared family experiences play a role in personality development. For example, in a study of 7144 adult twin pairs drawn from a Finnish cohort, the relative contribution of genetic influences along with common experience were clearly affirmed in relationship to personality (extraversion and neuroticism) as measured by the Eysenck personality inventory (Rose *et al.* 1988). The delineation of the relative contribution of nature and nurture to the coping process is awaiting clarification.

Analyses of an Australian data set attempted to shed light on the role of biology in the development of coping skills. A study using the 18 strategies identified by the Adolescent Coping Scale (ACS) with a sample of 1035 monozygotic and 1229 dizygotic twins, aged 12–24 years (Tat 1993) found that the biologically identical twins used more work-hard and achieve strategies than their non-identical counterparts. An argument can be mounted for the role of the environment, as monozygotic twins may need to work harder to distinguish themselves as individuals, thereby avoiding the inevitable comparison of one twin against the other.

An analysis of the same data provided an insight into the association between personality and coping in adolescence (White *et al.* 1995). Personality traits were identified and subjects were grouped as being extroverted, neurotic, or psychotic. The strategies used to cope with situations were analysed. As one might expect, extroverted adolescents cope more positively and successfully than do the other two groups. They work hard, remain positive and relax, fit in with friends, and utilize social support.

Hope

A related approach to considering the positive cognitions is the research in the area of hope. Hope can be construed as a consolation for other troubles in life. It can also be construed as a sense that something desired might happen. According to Snyder, Cheavens, and Michael (1999) since the late 1950s and in the 1960s psychiatrists (Frank 1968; Frankl 1992; Melges and Bowlby 1969; Menninger 1959; Schachtel 1959) and psychologists (Cantril 1964; Farber 1968; Mowrer 1960, Schamale and Iker 1966; Stotland 1969) have engaged in systematic studies of hope. It is generally agreed that hope taps the positive expectations for goal attainment. In the mid 1970s there was renewed interest in examining stress coping and illness (Smith 1983) and the part that negative and positive thoughts could play. It was found that negative thoughts and emotions could block recovery and positive processes such as hope could promote it (Frank 1975; Simonton *et al.* 1978; Cousins 1976; Mason *et al.* 1969). Generally, perceptions of control or mastery are positively related to psychological well-being (Snyder 1989, 1994; Taylor 1989; Taylor and Brown 1988, 1994 for reviews). In the 1980s and 1990s specific theoretical viewpoints about coping benefits that flow from positive cognitive and emotional motivational states were being discussed as a thought process in which people have a sense of agency and pathways for goals (Snyder 1994, 1998; Snyder *et al.* 1996, 1997). Together, goals, pathways, and agency form the motivational concept of hope.

Goal pursuit thoughts drive emotional experiences. In the context of hope theory, successful coping rests on thinking so as to achieve one's desired goals. 'The more adaptive positive emotional response occurs because higher-hope people can generate additional, alternative paths when blocked via the original route' (Snyder 1994, p. 208). Higher hope helps people deal more successfully with the stress in their lives (p. 209). According to Snyder *et al.* (1997) basic components of hope should be established by age three (p. 209). High hope is positively correlated to competency in life areas, that is, a perception of scholastic competence, social competence, athletic ability, physical appearance, and an increased feeling of self-worth. In adults, this adds up to an increased feeling of self-worth (Curry *et al.* 1997; Snyder *et al.* 1996), self-esteem (Snyder *et al.* 1999) and lower depression (Snyder *et al.* 1997). This may be due to a different attributional style (depressive attributional style is more internal, stable, and global for bad events and external, stable and global for good events) (Kaslow *et al.* 1978). While high hope is not related to intelligence, Snyder *et al.* (1997) suggest that high-hope college students have increased success in the academic realm (Snyder *et al.* 1999). High hope was positively related to problem-solving (see Snyder *et al.* 1991 for a review). Hope is a significant and unique predictor of problem-related coping when controlling for negative affectivity, and optimism. Neither negative affectivity nor optimism added any significant unique predictive value above that of hope. High-hope people focus on success rather than failure when pursuing goals and use adaptive coping strategies (Snyder *et al.* 1991). Furthermore, there is a positive relationship between hope and increased perceived problem-solving ability (Snyder *et al.* 1999).

Engagement in the workplace

The question of how relatively successful women and men cope with the demands in their busy lives is addressed by Burke (see Chapter 5 in this volume) whose research samples have typically involved professionals and managers or MBA students. Burke's most recent work has examined the ways in which control (active) and escapist (passive) coping function in a complex module of stress and health. Studies have been undertaken among police officers and nursing staff in hospitals undergoing dramatic restructuring and downsizing (see Chapter 5 in this volume). Burke emphasizes the part that organizational level interventions can play in enhancing employee performance.

Organizational levels in interventions are also reflected in the work of Mashlach and her colleagues which is the leading work in the field of stress and burnout in the workplace. Their research has also been extended to consider issues of engagement and positive functioning. Burnout is one end of a continuum in the relationship people establish with their jobs (Mashlach and Leiter 1997). As a syndrome of exhaustion, cynicism, and ineffectiveness, it stands in contrast to the energetic, involved, and effective state of engagement with work. Recently, the multidimensional model of burnout has been expanded to include the other end of the continuum, engagement. Engagement is defined in terms of the same three dimensions as burnout, but the positive end of those dimensions rather than the negative one. An important implication of the burnout–engagement continuum is that strategies to promote engagement may be just as critical for burnout prevention as strategies to reduce the risk of burnout.

Thus, the new model of the burnout–engagement continuum focuses on the match, or fit, between the worker and the workplace. It proposes that the greater the match, the greater the likelihood of engagement; conversely, the greater the mismatch, the greater the likelihood of burnout. This framework builds on prior theories of job–person fit, but its unique contribution is the specification of six areas in which this match or mismatch can take place: workload, control, reward, community, fairness, and values. This model focuses attention on the relationship between the person and the social environment, rather than either one or the other in isolation. It provides a new way of identifying the sources of burnout and engagement in any particular job context, and of designing interventions that will actually incorporate situational changes along with personal ones. Furthermore, the recognition of six areas of job–person mismatch expands the range of options for intervention.

We know that personality plays a part, as does experience to shape our perceptions as learners. Emotions act as regulators, along with a sense of hope and optimism. Nevertheless, in order to promote optimum performance, organizations need to change what they do as much as do the individuals within them. Beliefs about the self and notions of emotional intelligence exist and promise to take us forward in our pursuit of positive helpful conceptualizations of human advancement, both for individuals and for collectives.

While the complexity of the task of making research applicable is a challenge which has been recognized by many (e.g. Somerfield and McCrae 2000), the chapters that follow review theory and research, and consider the implications for practice. In particular, the chapters address how what we know helps us to move forward in the pursuit of success.

References

Ames, C. and Archer, J. (1988). Achievement goals in the classroom: Students' learning strategies and motivation processes. *Journal of Education Psychology*, **80**, 260–7.

Averill, J. R. (1994). Emotions are many splendored things, in P. Ekman and R. J. Davidson (eds.), *The nature of emotion: Fundamental questions*, pp. 99–102. New York: Oxford University Press.

—— and **Thomas-Knowles, C.** (1991). Emotional creativity, in K. T. Strongman (ed.), *International Review of Studies on Emotion*, Vol. 1, pp. 269–99. New York: Wiley.

Ayers, T. S., Sandler, I. N., West, S. G., and Roosa, M. W. (1996). A dispositional and situational assessment of children's coping: Testing alternative models of coping. *Journal of Personality*, **64**, 923–58.

Bolger, N. (1990). Coping as a personality process: A prospective study. *Journal of Personality and Social Psychology*, **59**, 525–37.

Bugalski, K. and Frydenberg, E. (2000). Promoting effective coping in adolescents 'at-risk' for depression. *Australian Journal of Guidance and Counselling*, **10**, 111–32.

Buss, A. and Plomin, R. (1984). *Temperament: Early developing personality traits*. Hillsdale, NJ: Erlbaum.

Cain, K. and Dweck. (1995). The development of children's achievement, motivation patterns and conceptualisation of intelligence. *Merrill-Palmer Quarterly*, **41**, 24–52.

Cannon, W. B. (1932). *The wisdom of the body*. New York: Norton.

Cantril, H. (1964). The human design. *Journal of Individual Psychology*, **20**, 129–36.

Carver, C. S., Pozo, C., Harris, S. D., Noriega, V., Scheier, M. F., Robinson, D. S. *et al.* (1993). How coping mediates the effect of optimism on distress: A study of women with early stages of breast cancer. *Journal of Personality and Social Psychology*, **65**, 375–90.

—— **Scheier, M. F.,** and **Weintraub, J. K.** (1989). Assessing coping strategies: A theoretically based approach. *Journal of Personality and Social Psychology*, **56**, 267–83.

Chan, D. (1998). Stress, coping strategies, and psychological distress among secondary school teachers in Hong Kong. *American Educational Research Journal*, **35**(1), 145–63.

Cohen, L. and Frydenberg, E. (1995). *Coping for capable kids*. Waco: Prufrock Press.

Costa, P. T. Jr., Somerfield, M. R., and McCrae, R. R. (1996). Personality and coping: A reconceptualisation, in M. Zeidner and N. M. Endler (ed.), *Handbook of coping*, pp. 44–61. New York: Wiley.

Cotta, A., Frydenberg E., and Poole, C. (2001). Coping skills training for adolescents at school. *The Australian Educational and Developmental Psychologist*, **17**(2), 103–16.

Cousins, N. (1976). Anatomy of an illness (as perceived by the patient). *New England Journal of Medicine*, **295**, 1458–63.

Cunningham, E. (2002). *Developing coping resources in early adolescence: Mediational and latent curve analyses of programme effects*. Doctoral Thesis, University of Melbourne, Melbourne.

Curry, L. A., Snyder, C. R., Cook, D. L., Ruby, B. C., and Rehm, M. (1997). The role of hope in academic and sport achievement. *Journal of Personality and Social Psychology*, **73**, 1257–67.

Diener, C. and Dweck, C. S. (1978). An analysis of learned helplessness: Continuous changes in performance, strategy, and achievement cognitions following failure. *Journal of Personality and Social Psychology*, **36**, 451–61.

—— —— (1980). An analysis of learned helplessness: II. The processing of success. *Journal of Personality and Social Psychology*, **39**, 940–52.

Dweck, C. S. (1991). Self-theories and goals: Their role in motivation, personality, and development, in R. Dienstbier (ed.), *Nebraska Symposium on motivation, perspectives on motivation. Current theory and research in motivation*, Vol. 38, pp. 199–255. Lincoln: University of Nebraska Press.

Dweck, C. S. and **Leggett, E.** (1988). A social-cognitive approach to motivation and personality. *Psychological Review*, **95**, 256–73.

—— and **Sorich, L.** (1999). Mastery-oriented thinking, in C. R. Snyder (ed.), *Coping: The psychology of what works*, pp. 205–27. Oxford: University Press.

Ebata, A. T. and **Moos, R. H.** (1994). Personal, situational, and contextual correlates of coping in adolescence. *Journal of Research on Adolescence*, **4**(1), 99–125.

Ekman, P. (1994). All emotions are basic, in P. Ekman and R. J. Davidson (eds.), *The nature of emotion: Fundamental questions*, pp. 15–19. New York: Oxford University Press.

Elliot, E. and **Dweck, C.** (1988). Goals: An approach to motivation and achievement. *Journal of Personality and Social Psychology*, **54**, 5–12.

Farber, M. L. (1968). *Theory of suicide*. New York: Funk and Wagnall's.

Fitzgerald, T. E., **Tennen, H.**, **Affleck, G.**, and **Pransky, G. S.** (1993). The relative importance of dispositional optimism and control appraisals in quality of life after coronary artery bypass surgery. *Journal of Behavioural Medicine*, **16**, 25–43.

Folkman, S. and **Lazarus, R.** (1988*a*). The relationship between coping and emotion: Implications for theory and research. *Social Science Medicine*, **26**(3), 309–17.

—— —— (1988*b*). *Ways of coping questionnaire test booklet*. Palo Alto: Consulting Psychological Press.

Folkman, S. and **Moskowitz, J. T.** (2000). Positive affect and the other side of coping. *American Psychologist*, **55**, 647–54.

Frank, J. D. (1968). The role of hope in psychotherapy. *International Journal of Psychiatry*, **5**, 383–95.

—— (1975). The faith that heals. *The John Hopkins Medical Journal*, **137**, 127–31.

Frankl, V. E. (1992). *Man's search for meaning: An introduction to logotherapy*, 4th edn. Boston: Beacon.

Freud, S. (1964). The neuro-psychoses of defense, in J. Strachey (ed. and translator), *The standard edition of the complete psychological works of Sigmund Freud*. London: Hogarth (Originally published in 1894).

Frijda, N. H. (1993). Moods, emotions, episodes and emotions, in M. Lewis and J. M. Haviland (eds.), *Handbook of emotions*, pp. 381–403. New York: Guilford.

Frydenberg, E. (1997). *Adolescent coping: Theoretical and research perspectives*. London: Routledge.

—— and **Brandon, C.** (2002). *The best of coping: Developing coping skills*. Melbourne: OzChild.

—— and **Lewis, R.** (1993). *Manual: The adolescent coping scale*. Melbourne: Australian Council for Educational Research.

—— —— (1994). Coping with different concerns: Consistency and variation in coping strategies used by adolescents. *Australian Psychologist*, **29**, 45–8.

—— —— (1996). The Adolescent Coping Scale: Multiple forms and applications of a self report inventory in a counselling and research context. *European Journal of Psychological Assessment*, **12**(3), 216–27.

—— —— (1997). *Coping scale for adults*, pp. 60. Melbourne: Australian Council for Educational Research.

—— —— (2000). Coping with stresses and concerns during adolescence: A longitudinal study. *American Educational Research Journal*, **37**, 727–45.

Gardner, H. (1983). *Frames of mind*. New York: Basic Books.

Greenberg, L. S. and **Safran, J. D.** (1987). *Emotion in psychotherapy: Affect, cognition, and the process of change*. New York: Guilford.

Hauser, S. T. and **Bowlds, M. K.** (1990). Stress, coping and adaptation, in S. S. Feldman and G. R. Elliott (eds.), *At the threshold: The developing adolescent*, pp. 388–413. London: Harvard University Press.

Herbert, C. and **Dweck, C.** (1985). *Mediators of persistence in preschoolers: Implications for development*. Harvard University (unpublished manuscript).

Heyman, G., **Dweck, C.**, and **Cain, K.** (1992). Young children's vulnerability to self-blame and helplessness. *Child Development*, **63**, 401–15.

Hiroto, S. S. and **Seligman, M. E.** (1975). Generality of learned helplessness in man. *Journal of Personality and Social Psychology*, **31**(2), 311–27.

Hobfoll, S. E., **Schwarzer, S.**, and **Chon, K.** (1998). Disentangling the stress labyrinth. Interpreting the meaning of stress as it's studied in the health context. *Anxiety Stress and Coping*, **11**, 181–212.

Hock, R. R. (1999). *Forty studies that changed psychology: Explorations into the history of psychological research*. New Jersey: Prentice Hall.

Holmes, T. H. and **Rahe, R. H.** (1967). The social readjustment rating scale. *Journal of Psychosomatic Research*, **11**(2), 213–18.

Izard, C. E. (1993). Organizational and motivational functions of discrete emotions, in M. Lewis and J. Haviland (eds.), *Handbook of emotions*, pp. 631–41. New York: Guilford.

Kagan, J. (1983). Stress and coping in early development, in N. Garmezy and M. Rutter (eds.), *Stress, coping and development in children*, pp. 191–216. New York: McGraw-Hill.

Kaslow, N. J., **Tanenbaum, R. L.**, and **Seligman, M. E. P.** (1978). *The KASTAN-R: A children's attributional style questionnaire (KASTAN-R-CASQ)*. University of Pennsylvania (unpublished manuscript).

Kurdek, L. A. and **Sinclair, R. J.** (1988). Adjustment of young adolescents in two-parent nuclear, stepfather, and mother-custody families. *Journal of Consulting and Clinical Psychology*, **56**(1), 91–6.

Lang, P. J. (1984). Cognition in emotion: Concept and action, in C. Izard, J. Kagan, and R. Zajonc (eds.), *Emotions, cognition and behaviour*, pp. 192–226. Cambridge: Cambridge University Press.

Lazarus, R. S. (1991). *Emotion and adaption*. New York: Oxford University Press.

—— and **Folkman, S.** (1984). Stress, appraisal and coping. New York: Springer.

Leeper, R. W. (1948). A motivational theory of emotions to replace 'emotions as disorganised response'. *Psychological Bulletin*, **55**, 5–21.

Lewis, R. (1999). Teachers coping with the stress of classroom. *Social Psychology of Education*, **3**, 1–17.

Licht, B. and **Dweck, C.** (1984). Determinants of academic achievement: The interaction of children's achievement orientations with skill area. *Developmental Psychology*, **20**(4), 628–36.

Mashlach, C. and **Leiter, M. P.** (1997). *The truth about burnout: How organisations cause personal stress and what to do about it*. San Francisco, CA: Jossey-Bass.

Mason, R. C., **Clark, G.**, **Reeves, R. B.**, and **Wagner, B.** (1969). Acceptance and healing. *Journal of Religion and Health*, **8**, 123–42.

Melges, R. and **Bowlby, J.** (1969). Types of hopelessness in psychopathological processes. *Archives of General Psychiatry*, **20**, 690–99.

Miller, W. and Seligman, M. (1975). Depression and learned helplessness in man. *Journal of Abnormal Psychology*, **84**, 228–38.

Mowrer, O. H. (1960). *The psychology of hope*. San Francisco: Jossey-Bass.

Mahoney, M. J. (1991). *Human change processes: The scientific foundations of psychotherapy*. New York: Basic Books.

Menninger, K. (1959). The academic lecture on hope. *The American Journal of Psychiatry*, **116**, 481–91.

Mueller, C. and Dweck, C. (1998). Praise for intelligence can undermine children's motivation and performance. *Journal of Personality and Social Psychology*, **75**, 33–52.

Pintrich, P., Roeser, R., and DeGroot, E. (1994). Classroom and individual differences in early adolescents' motivation and self-regulated learning. *Journal of Early Adolescence*, **14**, 139–61.

Prior, M., Sanson, A., Smart, D., and Oberklaid, F. (2000). *Pathways from infancy to adolescence: Australian temperament project 1983–2000*. Australian Institute of Family Studies.

Rose, R. J., Koskenvuo, M., Kaprio, J., Sarna, S., and Langinvainio, H. (1988). Shared genes, shared experiences, and similarity of personality: Data from 14,288 adult Finnish co-twins. *Journal of Personality and Social Psychology*, **54**(1), 161–71.

Rutter, M. (1981). Stress, coping and development: Some issues and some questions. *Journal of Child Psychology and Psychiatry*, **22**(4), 323–56.

—— and Rutter, M. (1992). *Developing minds: Challenge and continuity across the life-span*. London: Penguin.

Saarni, C. (1990). Emotional competence: How emotions and relationships become integrated, in R. Thompson (ed.), *Nebraska symposium on motivation: Socio-emotional development*, Vol. 36, pp. 115–82. Lincoln N.E: University of Nebraska Press.

—— (1997). Emotional competence and self-regulation in childhood, in P. Salovey and D. Sluyter (eds.), *Emotional development and emotional intelligence: Educational implications*, pp. 35–66. New York: Basic Books.

Salovey, P. and Mayer, J. D. (1990). Emotional intelligence. *Imagination, Cognition, and Personality*, **9**, 185–211.

Schachtel, E. (1959). *Metamorphosis*. New York: Basic Books.

Scheier, M. F., Matthews, K. A., Owens, J. F., Magovern, G. J., Lefebvre, R. C., Abbott, R. A., and Carver, C. S. (1989). Dispositional optimism and recovery from coronary artery bypass surgery: The benefits on physical and psychological well-being. *Journal of Personality and Social Psychology*, **57**, 1024–40.

—— Weintraub, J. K., and Carver, C. S. (1986). Coping with stress: Divergent strategies of optimists and pessimists. *Journal of Personality and Social Psychology*, **51**, 1257–64.

Schmale, A. H. and Iker, H. P. (1966). The affect of hopelessness and the development of cancer. *Psychosomatic Medicine*, **28**, 714–21.

Selye, H. (1950). *The physiology and pathology of exposure to stress*. Montreal: Acta.

—— (1976). *Stress in health and disease*. Reading, Massachusetts: Butterworth.

Shatte, A. J., Reivich, K., Gilham, J. E., and Seligman, M. E. P. (1999). Learned optimism in children, in C. R. Snyder, *Coping: The psychology of what works*, pp. 165–81. Oxford University Press.

Simonton, O. C., Matthews-Simonton, S., and Creighton, J. L. (1978). *Getting well again*. New York: Bantam Books.

Smith, M. B. (1983). Hope and despair: Keys to the socio-psychodynamics of youth. *American Journal of Orthopsychiatry*, **53**(3), 388–99.

Smith, C. A. (1991). The self, appraisal, and coping, in C. R. Snyder and D. R. Forsyth (eds.), *Handbook for social and clinical psychology: The health perspective*, pp. 116–37. Elmsford, New York: Pergamon.

Snyder, C. R. (1989). Reality negotiation: From excuses to hope and beyond. *Journal of Social and Clinical Psychology*, **8**, 130–57.

—— (1994). *The psychology of hope: You can get there from here*. New York: Free Press.

—— (1998). A case for hope in pain, loss and suffering, in J. H. Harvey, J. Omarzu, and E. Miller (eds.), *Perspectives on loss: A sourcebook*, pp. 63–79. Washington DC: Taylor and Francis.

—— (1999). Coping: Where are you going?, in C. R. Snyder (ed.), *Coping: The psychology of what works*, pp. 324–33. New York: Oxford University Press.

—— Cheavens, J., and Micheal, S. T. (1999). Hoping, in C. R. Snyder (ed.), *Coping: The psychology of what works*, pp. 205–27. Oxford University Press.

—— Harris, C., Anderson, J. R., Holleran, S. A., Irving, L. M., Sigmon Yoshinobu, L., Gibb, J., Langell, C., and Harney, P. (1991). The will and the ways: Development and validation of an individual difference measure of hope. *Journal of Personality and Social Psychology*, **60**, 570–85.

—— Hoza, B., Pelham, W. E., Rapoff, M., Ware, L., Danovsky, M. *et al.* (1997). The development of and validation of the Children's Hope Scale. *Journal of Paediatric Psychology*, **22**, 399–421.

—— Sympson, S. C., Ybasco, F. C., Borders, T. F., Babyak, M. A., and Higgins, R. L. (1996). Development and validation of the State Hope Scale. *Journal of Personality and Social Psychology*, **70**, 321–35.

Somerfield M. R. and McCrae, R. R. (2000). Stress and Coping research: Methodological challenges, theoretical advances and clinical applications. *American Psychologist*, **55**, 620–25.

Sorich, L. and Dweck, C. (1997). *Psychological mediators of student achievement in transition to junior high school*. Columbia University (unpublished manuscript).

Stotland, E. (1969). *The psychology of hope*. San Fransisco: Jossey-Bass.

Suls, J., David, J. P., and Harvey, J. H. (1996). Personality and coping: Three generations of research. *Journal of Personality*, **64**, 711–35.

Tat, F. E. (1993). *The use of coping strategies and styles in 2,264 Australian adolescent twins*. unpublished masters' thesis, University of Melbourne, Melbourne.

Taylor, S. E. (1989). *Positive illusions: Creative self-deception and the healthy mind*. New York: Basic Books.

—— and Brown, J. D. (1988). Illusion and well-being: A social psychological perspective on mental health. *Psychological Bulletin*, **103**, 193–210.

—— —— (1994). Positive illusions and well-being: Separating fact from fiction. *Psychological Bulletin*, **116**, 21–6.

—— Klein, L., Lewis, B. P., Gruenwald, T. L., Gurung, R. A., and Updegraff, J. A. (2000). Biobehavioural responses to stress in females: tend-and-befriend, not fight-or-flight. *Psychological Review*, **107**, 411–29.

Thompson, R. A. (1994). Emotion regulation: A theme in search of definition. *Monographs of the Society for Research in Child Development*, **59**, 25–52.

Watson, D., David, J. P., and Suls, J. (1999). Personality, Affectivity, and Coping, in C. R. Snyder (ed.), *Coping: The psychology of what works*, pp. 119–40. New York: Oxford University Press.

—— and Hubbard, B. (1996). Adaptional style and dispositional structure: Coping in the context of the five-factor model. *Journal of Personality*, **64**, 734–74.

White, V., Hill, D., Hopper, J., and Frydenberg, E. (1995). *Personality and coping: A longitudinal study of the association between personality and coping among a sample of Australian adolescent twins.* Australian Psychological Society Conference, Perth, Australia.

Zhao, W., Dweck, C., and Mueller, C. (1998). Implicit theories and vulnerability to depression-like responses. Manuscript submitted for publication.

ADULT WORLD

CHAPTER 2

TENACIOUS GOAL PURSUITS AND STRIVING TOWARD PERSONAL GROWTH: PROACTIVE COPING

RALF SCHWARZER AND STEFFEN TAUBERT

Trends in stress and coping theory: resources, goals, and positive emotions

Researchers disagree about the definition of stress. In the biomedical sciences, stress is understood as an organism's response to adverse stimulation. In psychology, however, stress is usually the process where a person and the environment interact, whereby research sometimes focuses on the nature of the stressor. Health psychologists study the joint effects of the person and environment on pathology, along with mediating and moderating factors, such as coping and social support (Hobfoll *et al.* 1998). Basically, three broad perspectives can be chosen when studying the stress process: (a) response-based, (b) stimulus-based, and (c) cognitive-transactional. We will briefly address this distinction in order to provide a better understanding of the history and scope of the topic. We will mention the theories of Selye (1956), Holmes and Rahe (1967), Lazarus (1966, 1991), and Hobfoll (1998) and will conclude with our Proactive Coping Theory (Chapter 3, this volume; Schwarzer 2000).

The response-based perspective

When people say, 'I feel a lot of stress', they are usually referring to their response to an adverse situation. The focus is on the way their body reacts. Selye (1956) has distinguished between a stressor (the stimulus) and stress (the response). Selye was not interested in the nature of the stressor, but rather in the physiological response and the development of illness. This response to a stimulus follows the same typical three-stage pattern in humans and animals, called the general adaptation syndrome (GAS). According to the GAS, the body initially defends itself against adverse circumstances by activating the sympathetic nervous system. This has been called the *alarm reaction*. It mobilizes the body for the 'fight-or-flight' response, which can be seen phylogenetically as an adaptive short-term reaction to emergency situations. In many cases, the stress episode is mastered during the alarm reaction stage.

Often, however, stress is a longer encounter, and the organism moves on to the *resistance stage*, in which it adapts more or less successfully to the stressor. Although the person does not give the impression of being under stress, the organism does not function well and eventually becomes sick. According to Selye, the immune system is compromised, so some typical 'diseases of adaptation' develop under persistent stress, such as cardiovascular diseases.

Finally, in the *exhaustion stage*, the organism's adaptation resources are depleted, and a breakdown occurs. This is associated with parasympathetic activation that leads to illness, burnout, depression, or even death.

This response-based perspective of stress has its merits, and it is still dominant in the biomedical sciences. However, it is no longer supported in psychology, mainly because Selye has disregarded the role of emotions and cognitions by focusing solely on physiological reactions in animals and humans. Selye (1956) claimed that all these organisms show a nonspecific response to adverse stimulations, regardless of how the situation appears. In contrast, modern psychological theories highlight the individual's interpretation of the situation as a major determinant of a stressful encounter.

The stimulus-based perspective

When someone says, 'I have a stressful marriage', they refer to a trying situation, not to their response to that situation. The stimulus-based perspective takes this approach, paying more attention to the particular characteristics of the stressor. It is argued that each critical episode has its unique demands, be it physical, social, role, or task, that specifically tax the individual's coping resources, thus triggering a particular stress response. The research question is how to establish relationships between a variety of distinct stressors and outcomes, including illness.

This line of research emerged when Holmes and Rahe (1967) attempted to measure life stress by assigning numbers, called life-change units, to critical life events. They assumed that the average amount of adaptive effort necessary to cope with an event would be a useful indicator of the severity of such an event. Dohrenwend and Dohrenwend (1974) subsequently edited a publication that was another milestone of the stimulus-based perspective of stress. Today, research in this tradition continues, but it is often flawed by several problems. One basic shortcoming is the use of average weights for events, neglecting the fact that different individuals may perceive the same kind of event differently. Also, studies rely too often on retrospective reports of previous challenges that might not be remembered correctly, or that are distorted as a result of defense mechanisms. In addition, coping processes and changes in social support are often insufficiently examined. The degree to which the objective nature of the stressor should be emphasized in contrast to its subjective interpretation is still undergoing debate (Hobfoll 1998; Schwarzer and Schulz, in press).

Cognitive-transactional theory of stress

The *cognitive-transactional* paradigm sees stress as an on-going process, initiated and maintained by the cognitive appraisal of demands and resistance resources. It is the standard paradigm in the field of psychology. The present section summarizes this approach. This cognitive-transactional theory of stress emphasizes the continuous, reciprocal nature of the interaction between the person and the environment. Since its first publication (Lazarus 1966), it has not only been further developed and refined, but it has also been expanded to a meta-theoretical concept of emotion and coping processes (Lazarus 1991). Stress is defined as a particular relationship between the person and the environment that is appraised by the person as taxing or exceeding his or her resources and endangering his or her well-being.

Within a meta-theoretical system approach, Lazarus (1991) conceives the complex processes of emotion as being composed of causal antecedents, mediating processes, and effects. *Antecedents* are personal resources, such as wealth, social networks, competencies, commitments or beliefs, on the one hand, and objective demands, critical events, or situational constraints on the other. *Mediating processes* refer to cognitive appraisals of such resources and demands as well as to coping efforts. The experience of stress and coping bring along *immediate effects*, for example affect and physiological changes, and *long-term effects* concerning psychological well-being, somatic health, and social functioning.

There are three meta-theoretical assumptions: *transaction*, *process*, and *context*. It is assumed, first, that emotions occur as a specific encounter of the person with the environment, and that both exert a reciprocal influence on each other; second, that emotions and cognitions are subject to continuous change; and third, that the meaning of a transaction is derived from the underlying context, that is, various attributes of a natural setting determine the actual experience of emotions and the resulting action tendencies.

Research has mostly neglected these meta-theoretical assumptions in favour of unidirectional, cross-sectional, and context-free designs. Within methodologically sound empirical research, it is hardly possible to study complex phenomena such as emotions and coping without constraints. Also, because of its complexity and transactional character leading to interdependencies between the variables involved, the meta-theoretical system approach cannot be investigated and empirically tested as a whole model. Rather, it represents a heuristic framework that may serve to formulate and test hypotheses in selected subareas of the theoretical system only. Thus, in practical research, one has to compromise within the ideal research paradigm. Researchers have often focused on *structure* instead of *process*, measuring single states or aggregates of states. Ideally, however, stress has to be analysed and investigated as an *active, unfolding process*. Cognitive appraisals comprise two component processes, namely (primary) *demand appraisals* and (secondary) *resource appraisals*. Appraisal outcomes are divided into the categories challenge, threat, and harm/loss. First, demand appraisal refers to the stakes a person has in a stressful encounter. A situation is appraised as challenging when it mobilizes physical and mental activity and involvement. In the evaluation of *challenge*, a person may see an opportunity to prove herself or himself, anticipating gain, mastery, or personal growth from the venture. The situation is experienced as pleasant, exciting, and interesting, and the person feels ardent and confident in being able to meet the demands. *Threat* occurs when the individual perceives danger, anticipating physical injuries or blows to one's self-esteem. In the experience of *harm/loss*, some damage has already occurred, for instance injury or loss of valued persons, important objects, self-worth, or social standing.

Second, resource appraisals refer to one's *available coping options* for dealing with the demands at hand. The individual evaluates his or her competence, social support, and material or other resources that can help to readapt to the circumstances and to reestablish an equilibrium between person and environment.

Antecedents of stress and coping: demands and resources

To characterize *demands* or situational stressors, Lazarus (1991) describes formal properties, such as novelty, event uncertainty, ambiguity, and temporal aspects of stressful conditions. For example, demands that are difficult, ambiguous, unexpected, unprepared, or prolonged under time pressure, are more likely to induce threat than easy tasks that can be prepared for thoroughly and solved at a convenient pace without time constraints. The work environment can be evaluated with respect to the stakes inherent in a given situation. For example, demanding social situations imply interpersonal threat, the danger of physical injury is perceived as physical threat, and anticipated failures endangering self-worth indicate ego threat. Lazarus additionally distinguishes between task-specific stress, including cognitive demands and other formal task properties, and failure-induced stress, including evaluation aspects, such as social feedback, valence of goal, possibilities of failure, or actual failure. In general, unfavourable task conditions combined with failure-inducing situational cues are likely to provoke stress.

Personal resources refer to the internal coping options that are available in a particular stressful encounter. Competence and skills have to match the work demands. Individuals who are affluent, healthy, capable, and optimistic are seen as resourceful and, thus, are less vulnerable toward stress at work. Social competence, empathy, and assertiveness might be necessary to deal with specific interpersonal demands. It is essential to feel competent to handle a stressful situation. But actual competence is not a sufficient prerequisite. If the individual underestimates his or her potential for action, no adaptive strategies will be developed. Therefore, perceived competence is crucial. This has been labelled 'perceived self-efficacy' or 'optimistic self-beliefs' by Bandura (1997). Perceived self-efficacy and optimism are seen as a prerequisite for coping with all kinds of stress, such as job loss, demotion, promotion, or work overload.

Social resources refer to the environmental options that are available to a person in a stressful encounter. Social integration reflects the person's embeddedness in a network of social interactions, mutual assistance, attachment, and obligations. Social support reflects the actual or perceived coping assistance in critical situations (for a review, see Schwarzer and Rieckmann, in press). Social support has been defined in various ways, for example as a resource provided by others, coping assistance, or an exchange of resources the provider or the recipient perceives to be intended to enhance the well-being of the recipient. Among the types of social support that have been investigated are, instrumental (e.g. assist with a problem), tangible (e.g. donate goods), informational (e.g. give advice), and emotional support (e.g. give reassurance).

Dimensions of coping

Many attempts have been made to reduce the universe of possible coping responses to a parsimonious set of coping dimensions. Some researchers have made two basic distinctions, such as instrumental, attentive, vigilant, or confrontative coping, as opposed to avoidant, palliative, and emotional coping (for an overview, see Schwarzer and Schwarzer 1996).

A well-known approach is that by Lazarus (1991), who separates *problem-focused* from *emotion-focused* coping. Another conceptual distinction has been suggested between *assimilative* and *accommodative* coping, whereby the former aims at modifying the environment and the latter at modifying oneself (Brandstädter 1992). This coping pair has also been coined '*mastery* versus *meaning*' (Taylor 1983) or '*primary control* versus *secondary control*' (Rothbaum *et al.* 1982). These coping preferences may occur in a certain time order, for example, when individuals first try to alter the demands that are at stake, and, after failing, turn inward to reinterpret their plight and find subjective meaning in it.

The number of dimensions that have been established theoretically or found empirically also depends on the level within a hierarchy of coping concepts. Krohne (2001), for example, distinguishes between a behavioural level and a conceptual level, each consisting of two subclasses:

1. Reactions and acts constitute the behavioural level at the bottom of this hierarchy. A coping *reaction* is considered as a single behavioural element, for instance tuning in to a music channel instead of an information channel during a laboratory stress experiment. Several similar reactions can be grouped into an *act*, such as executing a specific problem-solving behaviour.

2. At the conceptual level, researchers can identify a set of acts reflecting a particular *strategy*, for example, making use of social resources or turning to religion. Strategies, in turn, can be grouped into dispositional *superstrategies*, two of which are vigilance and cognitive avoidance (similar to monitoring and blunting; Miller 1987).

Theoretical advancements in the field

Hobfoll (1988, 1998) has expanded stress and coping theory with respect to the conservation of resources as the main human motive in the struggle with stressful encounters. Resources have also been an important ingredient in Lazarus' theory. The difference between the two theories lies mainly in the status of *objective and subjective resources*. Lazarus sees objective resources only as antecedents that may have an indirect effect, whereas subjective resources (resource appraisals) represent the direct precursors of the stress process. Actually, the simultaneous appraisal of demands and resources constitutes the beginning of a stress episode. In contrast, Hobfoll, considering both objective and subjective resources as components, lends more weight to the former than Lazarus does. Thus, the difference between the two theories, in this respect, is a matter of degree, not a matter of principle. Hobfoll tends to interpret Lazarus' approach as a highly subjective 'appraisal theory' and argues that objective resources are more important. This reinterpretation does not do justice to the comprehensive model of a stress episode that starts with objective antecedents, includes appraisal as well as coping, and ends with more or less adaptive outcomes, such as health, well-being, or social harmony. Viewed from a process perspective, Lazarus deals more with initial appraisal, whereas Hobfoll deals more with prior objective resource status and subsequent coping. Thus, his model could also be labelled 'resource-based coping theory'.

Resource loss is central to Hobfoll's theory. He distinguishes the categories (a) *resources threatened with loss*, (b) *resources actually lost*, and (c) *failure to gain resources*.

This loss/gain dichotomy, and in particular the resource-based loss spirals and gain spirals, shed a new light on stress and coping. The *change* of resources (more so, the loss than the gain) appears to be particularly stressful, whereas the mere lack of resources or their availability seems to be less influential.

Failure to gain resources following an investment is another unique feature. Hobfoll argues that burnout and ill health might be consequences of such a detrimental motivational state. In a similar vein, Siegrist (1996) has suggested that 'effort–reward imbalance' may compromise the health of employees. This is a highly attractive concept that enriches stress and coping research.

Extensions of the coping construct

In general, there is a trend to broaden stress and coping research by including *positive strivings* that were formerly domains of motivation and action theories. The notions of mastery, optimization (Baltes 1997; Freund and Baltes 2000), challenge and benefit (Lazarus 1991), and resource gain (Hobfoll 1998) are in line with proactive coping theories (e.g. Aspinwall and Taylor 1997; Schwarzer 2000). People strive for more resources, desire to maximize gains, and build up resistance factors either to ward off future crises or to grow and cultivate their capabilities for their own sake. This forward-time perspective opens new research questions and helps to overcome traditional coping models that overemphasize the reactive nature of coping.

The broadening of stress and coping research has also included the search for *meaning* in stressful encounters (Folkman and Moskowitz 2000; Janoff-Bulman 1992; Schwarzer and Knoll, in press; Taylor 1983; Tennen and Affleck, in press). Researchers have further subdivided the construct. Davis *et al.* (1998) suggest a two-dimensional construal of meaning as 'sense-making' and meaning as 'benefit-finding'. Sense-making relates to finding a reason for what happened, integrating it into existing schemata, such as religion, knowledge about health, or consequences of life stress. Benefit-finding, on the other hand, pertains to positive implications of a negative event or the pursuit of the silver lining of adversity.

Baumeister (1991) has proposed four needs for meaning: (a) purpose (objective goals and subjective fulfillment), (b) efficacy and control, (c) value and justification, and (d) self-worth. Each of these can be regarded as general goals of coping with life stress. Specific coping strategies in certain stress situations can be evaluated with respect to the degree that they serve such higher-order goals in life. Examples of psychological markers of 'efficacy and control' are, (a) perceiving a link between present behaviours and future outcomes, (b) maintaining 'illusions of control' over uncontrollable events, or (c) reporting success in overcoming difficult obstacles in one's past. This need, as Baumeister (1991) calls it, is in line with proactive coping (see Table 2.1).

A different approach at this general level of meaning in life has been taken by Wong (1998), who proposes five dimensions that reflect meaning, namely cognitive, motivational, affective, relational, and personal. The motivational dimension includes coping characteristics, such as 'pursues worthwhile goals', 'seeks to actualize one's potential', and 'strives toward personal growth'. Again, these represent proactive coping (see Table 2.2).

The recent broadening of coping theory might be a reaction to earlier conceptualizations of coping that neglected goals, purpose, and meaning. As these become more salient and

Table 2.1 Four needs for meaning and their psychological markers (Baumeister 1991)

Need	Psychological markers
Purpose: Objective goals and subjective fulfillment	Forming new goals when old goals are reached; linking negative events to future, positive fulfillment states—such as greater appreciation for life; reflecting on one's accomplishments.
Efficacy and control	Perceiving a link between present behaviors and future outcomes; maintaining 'illusions of control' over uncontrollable events; reporting success in overcoming difficult obstacles in one's past.
Value and justification	Downplaying the consequences of, or externalizing responsibility for, immoral or hurtful actions; reporting good and admirable intentions; claiming the victim status.
Self-worth	Comparing the self with less fortunate others; reiterating one's appeal to others; relegating personal failures to the past; assuming credit for success but not failures; asserting superiority over others.

Table 2.2 Dimensions of the conceptualization of a meaningful life (Wong 1998)

Cognitive	Believes that there is an ultimate purpose in life Believes in moral laws Believes in an afterlife
Motivational	Pursues worthwhile goals Seeks to actualize ones potential Strives toward personal growth
Affective	Feels content with who one is and what one is doing Feels fulfilled about what one has accomplished Feels satisfied with life
Relational	Is sincere and honest with others Has a number of good friends Brings happiness to others
Personal	Likes challenge Accepts ones limitations Has a healthy self-concept

explicit in the current thinking, it is appropriate to redesign coping theory in order to extend it into volition and action theory. The present approach makes a systematic distinction between proactive coping and three other kinds of coping that might shed more light on some previously neglected aspects.

Proactive coping theory

This section provides a further perspective that stems from a time-related classification of coping modes and proposes a distinction between reactive coping, anticipatory coping, preventive coping, and proactive coping.

Stressful demands can either reflect a distressing loss in early life or an ongoing harmful encounter. They can also exist in the near or distant future, creating a threat to someone who feels incapable of matching the upcoming tasks with the coping resources at hand. In light of the complexity of stressful episodes in social contexts, human coping cannot be reduced to primitive forms, such as fight-and-flight responses or relaxation. Besides other factors, coping depends on the time perspective of the demands and the subjective certainty of the events.

The temporal aspect of coping has often been neglected. One can cope before a stressful event takes place, while it is happening (e.g. during the progress of a disease), or afterwards. Beehr and McGrath (1996) distinguish five situations that create a particular temporal context: (a) *preventive coping*, long before a stressful event occurs or might occur (e.g. a smoker might quit well in time to avoid the risk of lung cancer); (b) *anticipatory coping*, when the event is expected soon (e.g. someone might take a tranquillizer while waiting for surgery); (c) *dynamic coping*, while it is ongoing (e.g. diverting attention to reduce chronic pain); (d) *reactive coping*, after it has happened (for example, changing one's life after a limb has been amputated); and (e) *residual coping*, long afterwards, by contending with long-term effects (e.g. controlling one's intrusive thoughts years after a traumatic accident has happened).

To introduce an alternative perspective, we distinguish between reactive, anticipatory, preventive, and proactive coping. Reactive coping refers to harm or loss experienced in the past, whereas anticipatory coping pertains to imminent threat in the near future. Preventive coping refers to an uncertain threat potential in the distant future, whereas proactive coping involves upcoming challenges that are seen as potentially self-promoting (see Fig. 2.1).

Reactive coping can be defined as an effort to deal with a past or present stressful encounter or to compensate for or accept harm or loss. Examples of harm or loss are

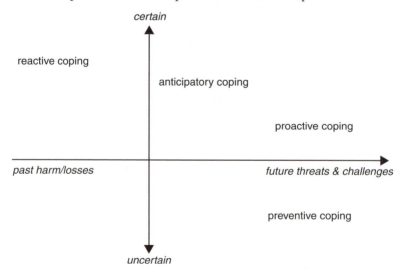

Figure 2.1 Outline of proactive coping theory.

marital dissolution, being criticized by parents or friends, having an accident, doing poorly at a job interview, being demoted, or losing one's job. All of these events happened in the past with absolute certainty. Thus, the individual has to either compensate for the loss or alleviate harm. Another option is to readjust goals, find benefit, or search for meaning to reconceptualize one's life. Reactive coping may be problem-focused, emotion-focused, or social-relation-focused. For coping with loss or harm, people need to be resilient. Because they aim at compensation or recovery, they need 'recovery self-efficacy', a particular optimistic belief in their capability to overcome setbacks (Schwarzer 1999).

Anticipatory coping is fundamentally different because the critical event has not yet occurred. It can be regarded as an effort to deal with impending threat. In anticipatory coping, individuals face a critical event that is certain or fairly certain to occur in the near future. Examples are speaking in public, a dentist appointment, adapting to parenthood, an exam, a job interview, increased workload, promotion, company downsizing, retirement, etc. There is a risk that the upcoming event may cause harm or loss later on, thus the person has to manage this perceived risk. The situation is appraised as either threatening or challenging, or is associated with benefiting, or some of each. The function of coping may lie in solving the actual problem at hand, such as increasing effort, enlisting help, or investing other resources. Another function may lie in feeling good in spite of the risk, for example by redefining the situation as less threatening, by distraction, or by gaining reassurance from others. Thus, anticipatory coping can be understood as the management of known risks, which includes investing one's resources to prevent or combat the stressor or to maximize an anticipated benefit. One of the personal resource factors is situation-specific 'coping self-efficacy' (Schwarzer and Renner 2000), an optimistic self-belief of being able to cope successfully with the particular situation at hand.

Preventive coping can be seen as an effort to prepare for uncertainty in the long run. This is contrary to anticipatory coping, which is a short-term engagement with high-certainty events. The aim is to build up general resistance resources that result in less strain in the future by minimizing the severity of the impact, with less severe consequences of stress, should it occur, or a less likely onset of stressful events in the first place. In preventive coping, individuals consider a critical event that may or may not occur in the distant future. Examples of such events are job loss, forced retirement, crime, illness, physical disability, disaster, or poverty. When people carry a spare key, lock their doors twice, have good health insurance, save money, or maintain social bonds, they cope in a preventive way and build up protection without knowing whether they will ever need it. The perception of ambiguity need not be limited to single events. There can be a vague wariness that 'something might happen', which motivates one to prepare for 'everything'. The individual anticipates the nonnormative life events that are appraised as more or less threatening. Coping, here, is a kind of risk management because one has to manage various unknown risks in the distant future. The perceived ambiguity stimulates a broad range of coping behaviors. Because all kinds of harm or loss could materialize one day, the individual builds up general resistance resources by accentuating their psychological strengths and accumulating wealth, social bonds, and skills—'just in case'. Skill development, for example, is a coping process that may help to prevent possible trouble. Preventive coping is not born out of an acute stress situation. It is not sparked by state anxiety, rather by some level of trait worry, or at least some reasonable concern about the dangers of life. General 'coping self-efficacy' seems to be a good personal prerequisite to plan and initiate successfully multifarious preventive actions that help build up resilience against threatening non-normative life events in the distant future.

Proactive coping is not preceded by negative appraisals, such as harm, loss, or threat. Proactive coping can be considered as an effort to build up general resources that facilitate promotion toward challenging goals and personal growth. In proactive coping, people have a vision. They see risks, demands, and opportunities in the far future, but they do not appraise them as a threat, harm, or loss. Rather, they perceive demanding situations as personal challenges. Coping becomes goal management instead of risk management. Individuals are not reactive, but proactive in the sense that they initiate a constructive path of action and create opportunities for growth. The proactive individual strives for life improvement and builds up resources that assure progress and quality of functioning. Proactively creating better living conditions and higher performance levels is experienced as an opportunity to render life meaningful or to find purpose in life. Stress is interpreted as 'eustress', that is, productive arousal and vital energy.

Preventive and proactive coping are partly manifested in the same kinds of overt behaviours, such as skill development, resource accumulation, and long-term planning. However, motivation can emanate either from threat appraisal or from challenge appraisal, which makes a difference. Worry levels are higher in the former and lower in the latter. Proactive individuals are motivated to meet challenges, and they commit themselves to personal quality standards.

Self-regulatory goal management includes ambitious goal setting and tenacious goal pursuit. The latter requires 'action self-efficacy,' an optimistic belief that one is capable of initiating and maintaining difficult courses of action. The role of beliefs in self-regulatory goal attainment has been spelled out in more detail in a different theory that was designed to explain health behaviour change, the health action process approach (HAPA; Schwarzer 1992, 1999; Schwarzer and Renner 2000). Further amplification of the terms involved is given below, in the context of assessment procedures.

The distinction between these four perspectives of coping is advantageous, because it moves the focus away from mere responses to negative events toward a broader range of risk and goal management that includes the active creation of opportunities and the positive experience of stress. Aspinwall and Taylor (1997) have described a proactive coping theory that is similar, but not identical, to the present one. What they call proactive coping is mainly covered by the term preventive coping in the current approach (see also Greenglass *et al.* 1999).

Proactive coping: assessment and findings

Coping has usually been measured by questionnaires, for instance checklists or psychometric scales. In a review chapter, Schwarzer and Schwarzer (1996) describe 13 conventional inventories that were designed to assess numerous aspects of coping. These measures include various subscales that cover a broad area of coping behaviours, such as problem-solving, avoidance, seeking social support or information, denial, reappraisal, and others. One conclusion is that it will continue to be difficult to measure coping in a satisfactory manner because it is highly idiosyncratic and determined jointly by situational and personality factors. Nevertheless, theory-based psychometric scales can assess an important part of the coping process if repeatedly administered. Approaches that try to tap innovative aspects of positive coping are, for example, the mastery of future threats and challenges, as reflected by preventive or proactive coping.

Preventive coping aims at dealing with uncertain threatening events that will occur mainly in the distant future. People accumulate resources and take general precautions to protect themselves against a variety of critical events. A preventive coping subscale is included in the Proactive Coping Inventory (PCI; Greenglass *et al.* 1999). Typical items are, 'I plan for future eventualities', and 'I prepare for adverse events'. Encouraging empirical evidence is available for the PCI (see Chapter 3).

Proactive coping aims at uncertain challenging goals. People accumulate resources and develop skills and strategies in their pursuit. The PCI includes the Proactive Coping subscale (see Chapter 3) that has been tested in various samples and that is available in several languages. In the Proactive Coping subscale, there are 14 homogeneous items that form a unidimensional scale. It has satisfactory psychometric properties, and there is growing evidence of its validity. Several studies in Canada, Poland, and Germany have found that proactive coping is positively correlated with perceived self-efficacy and negatively with job burnout in different professions (Schwarzer and Taubert 1999; Taubert, unpublished thesis 1999; see Chapter 3). In the study by Taubert (unpublished thesis 1999), based on data provided by Greenglass, a Canadian sample and a Polish-Canadian sample were examined with a large battery of psychometric scales, including the PCI. The Proactive Coping subscale correlated with general self-efficacy, $r = 0.70$ and 0.65, respectively. It was negatively associated with depression, $r = -0.49$ and -0.41, and also with self-blame, $r = -0.47$ and -0.47, in these two samples. Moreover, it was positively correlated with some of the Brief Cope (Carver 1997, 1999) subscales, such as Active Coping 0.52 and 0.50, and Planning, 0.42 und 0.45. With Behavioural Disengagement it was negatively correlated -0.42 and -0.54. This attests to the fact that the PCI Proactive Coping subscale yields the desired pattern of associations with other variables (see also Chapter 3, this volume).

A more recent study was conducted with 316 German teachers (Schwarzer, unpublished data). The internal consistency was alpha = 0.86. Correlations with proactive coping were $r = 0.61$ with perceived self-efficacy, $r = 0.50$ with self-regulation, and $r = -0.40$ with procrastination. Job burnout was defined three-dimensionally in terms of emotional exhaustion, depersonalization, and lack of accomplishment (Maslach *et al.* 1996). Burnout is a relevant construct for the validation because it should not be compatible with proactive coping. To illustrate the relationships, the sample was subdivided into low, medium, and high proactive teachers who were plotted against the three dimensions of burnout. Figure 2.2 displays a significant pattern of decreasing burnout with increasing levels of proactive coping. Proactive teachers report less emotional exhaustion, less cynicism, and more personal accomplishments than their reactive counterparts.

The study also included brief scales to assess the three stress appraisal dimensions of challenge, threat, and loss (Jerusalem and Schwarzer 1992). High proactive coping should be associated with high challenge appraisals, whereas low proactive coping should be

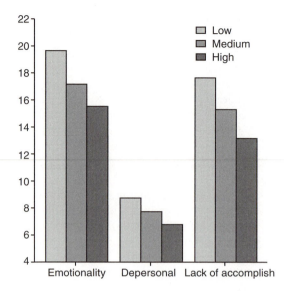

Figure 2.2 Pattern of decreasing burnout with increasing levels of proactive coping.

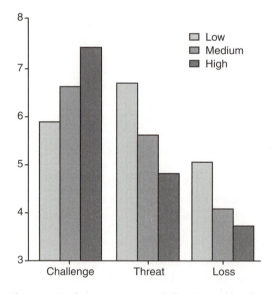

Figure 2.3 Proactive teachers perceive their stress as more challenging, and less threatening and loss-based, than their reactive counterparts.

linked to higher threat and loss appraisals. Figure 2.3 confirms this assumption. Proactive teachers perceive their stress as more challenging, and less threatening and loss-based, than their reactive counterparts.

It is also of note that highly proactive teachers spent an average of about four extra hours per week with their students, whereas the other two groups reported only three

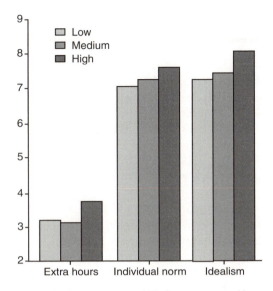

Figure 2.4 Extra hours, individual reference norm, and idealism, as expressed by proactive versus reactive teachers.

unpaid hours. This attests to the professional engagement of proactive teachers. Figure 2.4 shows three dependent variables: extra hours, individual reference norm, and idealism. The latter two were measured by psychometric self-report scales. Individual reference norm pertains to a preference of teachers to judge their students' accomplishments longitudinally with a focus on intraindividual changes, as opposed to social comparison. As can be seen in Fig. 2.4, proactive teachers base their judgments more on intraindividual changes than their reactive counterparts, and they report themselves as being more idealistic. To summarize, proactive teachers in this study experience less job burnout, perceive more challenges and less threat and loss, and display more professional engagement than their reactive counterparts. These and further data (see Chapter 3, this volume) corroborate the usefulness of the construct and the validity of the proactive coping measure.

Conclusions

The field of coping is becoming broader, and now includes positive striving and emotions, goals, benefit finding, and search for meaning. As one example of such a differentiation of concepts, we have chosen Proactive Coping Theory (Schwarzer 2000; Taubert, unpublished thesis, 1999). This theory builds upon Lazarus' (1991) cognitive appraisal approach and adds a temporal and other dimensions to earlier work. Moreover, it bridges the gap between coping theories on the one hand and action and volition theories on the other. Extending coping to tenacious goal pursuit and personal growth offers a more comprehensive picture of humans' struggle with life. Under the assumption that life in itself is necessarily stressful, coping becomes an appropriate label for many human behaviours over and above simple routines and habits. When Selye (1956) coined the term 'eustress' and Lazarus (1966) introduced 'challenge' as one of the major cognitive stress appraisals, the stage was set for a positive understanding of stress and coping. Not until later did Lazarus (1991) add 'benefit' to his appraisal categories, which has now become one of the key arenas in coping research. Proactive coping (Aspinwall and Taylor 1997; Greenglass *et al.* 1999; Schwarzer 2000; Schwarzer and Taubert 1999) is the latest addition to this positive trend and constitutes goal-oriented, long-term behaviours that take place before an actual stress episode occurs. There is not necessarily a concrete 'stressor'. Self-imposed goals and visions may trigger the creation of opportunities and risks, and the struggle for rewards and growth may have its stressful ups and downs, some of them unanticipated. Building a career or a house, writing a book, leading others to success, etc., represent continuous stress situations.

This description of proactive coping is reminiscent of *leadership characteristics*, which will be discussed here in the context of coping. Proactive leadership is a personality characteristic that has implications for motivation and action. It is a belief in the rich potential of changes that can be made to improve oneself and one's environment. This includes various aspects, such as resourcefulness, responsibility, values, and vision.

The proactive leader believes in the existence of sufficient resources, either external or internal. Goods, services, and people can be influenced to support goal attainment. Intelligence, courage, and strength, for example, reside within and allow goal setting and persistence.

The proactive leader takes responsibility for his or her own growth. A life course is not fully determined by external forces, but, rather, it can be chosen. Neither good nor bad events are attributed mindlessly to external causes. Instead, the proactive leader faces reality and adopts a balanced view of self-blame and other-blame in the case of negative events. Two kinds of responsibilities are distinguished: those for past events and those for making things happen. The latter is crucial here. The proactive leader focuses on solutions for problems, no matter who has caused them.

The proactive leader is driven by values. The behaviour of others might be determined by social environment, whereas proactive persons are mindful of their values and choose their path of action accordingly.

A proactive leader has a vision and creates meaning in life by striving for ambitious goals. He or she imagines what could be and sets goals in line with this vision. Total Quality management (TQM), for example, is a principle of continuous improvement within companies. The same idea can be transferred to a leader who constantly strives for self-improvement, accumulates resources, prevents resource depletion, and mobilizes forces with a long-term aim in mind, following a self-imposed mission.

We cannot supply empirical research on proactive leadership. However, the above findings on German teachers point in this direction. Among the teachers who were studied, evidence was found for the beneficial effects of proactive coping, which can be understood as a form of leadership when individuals are in charge of other persons.

In conclusion, a few words on the future of *coping measurement* are in order. The measurement of proactive behaviours, personal growth, positive reappraisals, and positive emotions in the context of stress adaptation should not remain at the level of psychometric scales, but should include dynamic data that account for changes within a particular coping episode. Contrary to the cross-sectional design that characterizes much coping research, theoretical considerations necessitate the examination of coping from a process perspective, where changes can be studied over time. Rather than remaining static, coping responses change in relation to the variations in the situational configuration as well as in response to varying resources. Coping can be understood best when it is regarded as a transactional process (Lazarus 1991), which implies a longitudinal measurement approach. However, it is not sufficient to simply select several points in time because the researcher cannot be certain about the optimal time frame when significant changes take place. Therefore, a more continuous measurement is recommended. The closest to this suggestion is the daily process approach to coping, commonly referred to as experience sampling method (ESM; Tennen *et al.* 2000), where participants respond at least once a day when prompted by an ambulatory device. The main disadvantage of this method, of course, is its reactivity, which means that coping responses are artificially constructed, due to the demands of the particular study design. But the overall approach appears to be promising. Perrez (2001) describes data sources, such as self-report, systematic self-observation, external recording of psychological features with respect to coping behaviour, and the direct recording of psychophysiological and biochemical parameters. In the future, we can expect advances in the computerized simultaneous assessment of such data sources under real-life conditions. In contrast, cross-sectional studies that often rely on hypothetical scenarios or these that require the recall of single or multiple past events will lose their importance.

Acknowledgements

The authors are grateful to Judith Bäßler, Esther Greenglass, and Nina Knoll for valuable comments on an earlier draft of this chapter.

References

Aspinwall, L. G. and Taylor, S. E. (1997). A stitch in time: Self-regulation and proactive coping. *Psychological Bulletin*, **121**, 417–36.

Baltes, P. B. (1997). On the incomplete architecture of human ontogeny: Selection, optimization, and compensation as foundation of developmental theory. *American Psychologist*, **52**, 366–80.

Bandura, A. (1997). *Self-efficacy: The exercise of control*. Freeman, New York.

Baumeister, R. F. (1991). *The meanings of life*. Guilford, New York.

Beehr, T. A. and McGrath, J. E. (1996). The methodology of research on coping: Conceptual, strategic, and operational-level issues, in M. Zeidner and N. S. Endler (eds.), *Handbook of coping-theory, research, applications*, pp. 65–82. New York: Wiley.

Brandtstädter, J. (1992). Personal control over development: Implications of self-efficacy. In R. Schwarzer (ed.), *Self-efficacy: Thought control of action*, pp. 127–45. Washington, DC: Hemisphere.

Carver, C. S. (1997). You want to measure coping but your protocol's too long: Consider the Brief COPE. *International Journal of Behavioral Medicine*, **4**, 92–100.

Carver, C. S. (1999). *Brief COPE* [Online-publication. Available at: *http://www.psy.miami.edu/faculty/CCarver/sclBrCOPE.html*].

Davis, C., Nolen-Hoeksema, S., and Larson, J. (1998). Making sense of loss and benefiting from the experience: Two construals of meaning. *Journal of Personality and Social Psychology*, 75, 561–74.

Dohrenwend, B. S. and Dohrenwend, B. P. (eds.) (1974). *Stressful life events: Their nature and effects*. New York: Wiley.

Folkman, S. and Moskowitz, J. (2000). Positive affect and the other side of coping. *American Psychologist*, 55, 647–54.

Freund, A. M. and Baltes, P. B. (2000). The orchestration of selection, optimization, and compensation: An action-theoretical conceptualization of a theory of developmental regulation, in W. J. Perrig and A. Grob (eds.), *Control of human behavior, mental processes, and consciousness*, pp. 35–58. Mahwah, NJ: Erlbaum.

Greenglass, E. R., Schwarzer, R., and Taubert, S. (1999). *The Proactive Coping Inventory (PCI): A multidimensional research instrument*. [Online publication]: Available at: http://www.psych.yorku.ca/greenglass/.

Hobfoll, S. E. (1988). *The ecology of stress*. Washington, DC: Hemisphere.

—— (1998). *Stress, culture, and community. The psychology and philosophy of stress*. New York: Plenum.

—— Schwarzer, R., and Chon, K. K. (1998). Disentangling the stress labyrinth: Interpreting the meaning of the term stress as it is studied in health context. *Anxiety, Stress, and Coping*, 11, 181–212.

Holmes, T. H. and Rahe, R. H. (1967). The Social Readjustment Rating scale. *Journal of Psychosomatic Research*, 11, 213–18.

Janoff-Bulman, R. (1992). *Shattered assumptions: Towards a new psychology of trauma*. New York: The Free Press.

Jerusalem, M. and Schwarzer, R. (1992). Self-efficacy as a resource factor in stress appraisal processes, in R. Schwarzer (ed.), *Self-efficacy: Thought control of action*, pp. 195–213. Washington, DC: Hemisphere.

Krohne, H. W. (2001). Stress and coping theories, in N. J. Smelser and P. B. Baltes (eds.), *The international encyclopedia of the social and behavioral sciences*, vol. 22, pp. 15163–70. Oxford: England .

Lazarus, R. S. (1966). *Psychological stress and the coping process*. New York: McGraw-Hill.

—— (1991). *Emotion and adaptation*. London: Oxford University Press.

Maslach, C., Jackson, S. E., and Leiter, M. P. (1996). *Maslach Burnout Inventory manual*, 3rd edn. Consulting Psychologists Press, Palo Alto, CA.

Miller, S. M. (1987). Monitoring and blunting: Validation of a questionnaire to assess styles of information seeking under threat. *Journal of Personality and Social Psychology*, 52, 345–53.

Perez, M. (2001). Coping assessment, in N. J. Smelser and P. B. Baltes (eds.), *The international encyclopedia of the social and behavioral sciences*, vol. 4, pp. 2766–70. Oxford: Elsevier, England.

Rothbaum, F., Weisz, J. R., and Snyder, S. (1982). Changing the world and changing the self: A two-process model of perceived control. *Journal of Personality and Social Psychology*, 42, 5–37.

Schwarzer, R. (ed.) (1992). *Self-efficacy: Thought control of action*. Washington, DC: Hemisphere.

—— (1999). Self-regulatory processes in the adoption and maintenance of health behaviors. The role of optimism, goals and threats. *Journal of Health Psychology*, 4, 115–27.

—— (2000). Manage stress at work through preventive and proactive coping, in E. A. Locke (ed.), *The Blackwell handbook of principles of organizational behavior*. Ch. 24, pp. 342–55. Oxford: Blackwell.

—— and **Knoll, N.** Positive coping: Mastering demands and searching for meaning, in S. J. Lopez and C. R. Snyder (eds.), *Handbook of positive psychological assessment*. Ch. 25. Washington, DC: American Psychological Association (in press).

—— and **Renner, B.** (2000). Social-cognitive predictors of health behavior: Action self-efficacy and coping self-efficacy. *Health Psychology*, **19**, 487–95.

—— and **Rieckmann, N.** Social support, cardiovascular disease, and mortality, in G. Weidner, M. Kopp, and M. Kristenson (eds.), *Heart disease: Environment, stress, and gender. NATO science series, series 1: Life and behavioral sciences* Vol. 327. Amsterdam: IOS Press (in press).

—— and **Schwarzer, C.** (1996). A critical survey of coping instruments, in M. Zeidner and N. S. Endler (eds.), *Handbook of coping: Theory, research and applications*, pp. 107–32. New York: Wiley.

—— and **Schulz, U.** The role of stressful life events, in A. M. Nezu, C. M. Nezu, and P. A. Geller (eds.), *Comprehensive handbook of psychology, Vol. 9: Health psychology*, New York: Wiley (in press).

—— and **Taubert, S.** (1999). Radzenie sobie ze stresem: wymiary i procesy [Coping with stress: Dimensions and processes; in Polish]. *Promocja zdrowia nauki spoleczene i medycyna*, **VI, 17**, 72–92.

Selye, H. (1956). *The stress of life*. New York: McGraw-Hill.

Siegrist, J. (1996). Adverse health effects of high-effort/low-reward conditions. *Journal of Occupational Health Psychology*, **1**, 27–41.

Taubert, S. (1999). *Development and validation of a psychometric instrument for the assessment of proactive coping*. Master's thesis. Freie Universität Berlin, Germany (Unpublished).

Taylor, S. E. (1983). Adjustment to threatening events: A theory of cognitive adaptation. *American Psychologist*, **38**, 1161–73.

Tennen, H. and **Affleck, G.** Benefit-finding and benefit-reminding, in C. R. Snyder and S. J. Lopez (eds.), *The handbook of positive psychology*. New York: Oxford University Press (in press).

—— **Affleck, G., Armeli, S.,** and **Carney, M. A.** (2000). A daily process approach to coping. *American Psychologist*, **55**, 626–36.

Wong, P. T. (1998). Implicit theories of meaningful life and the development of the Personal Meaning Profile, in P. T. Wong and P. Fry (eds.), *The human quest for meaning*. pp. 111–40. Mahwah, NJ: Erlbaum.

CHAPTER 3

PROACTIVE COPING AND QUALITY OF LIFE MANAGEMENT

ESTHER R. GREENGLASS

Luck is What Happens When Preparation Meets Opportunity
Elmer Letterman

Coping with stress is the subject of many articles and books. Attention has been focused on coping strategies and the ways in which they can alleviate stress levels and promote higher quality of life. While in the past coping was seen mainly as reactive, a strategy to be used once stress had been experienced, more recently coping is being seen as something one can do *before* stress occurs. Increasingly, coping is seen as having multiple positive functions. The idea that coping can have positive functions parallels recent research highlighting the role of positive beliefs in the promotion of health (Taylor *et al.* 2000). Proactive coping incorporates a confirmatory and positive approach to dealing with stressors. In their introductory article to a *Special Issue on Happiness, Excellence and Optimal Human Functioning* in the premier issue of the *American Psychologist* in the new millennium, Seligman and Csikszentmihalyi (2000) discuss the importance of positive individual traits and positive institutions for improving quality of life and preventing pathology. Proactive coping focuses on improving quality of life and in so doing incorporates elements of positive psychology.

There are several reasons for believing that positive beliefs might contribute to the promotion of well-being. For example, positive beliefs may predict to higher levels of physical health by promoting better health practices. Individuals who have a positive sense of self-worth and believe in their own ability to exert control, may be more likely to practice conscientious health habits. Positive emotional states are related to good social relationships. Self-confident and optimistic individuals may have more social support and/or they may be more effective in mobilizing it when they experience a lot of stress (Taylor and Brown 1994). Also, individuals who have well developed psychosocial resources, including a sense of personal control, high self-esteem and optimism, are more likely to cope proactively with respect to health which may minimize the effects of stress (Aspinwall and Taylor 1997).

This chapter focuses on proactive coping and its function in promoting well-being. Proactive coping is a coping strategy that is multidimensional and forward-looking. Proactive coping integrates processes of personal quality of life management with those of self-regulatory goal attainment. Proactive coping differs from traditional conceptions of coping in three main ways:

1. Traditional coping forms tend to be reactive coping in that they deal with stressful events that have already occurred, with the aim of compensating for loss or harm in the past; proactive coping is more future-oriented. Since the stressful events have already taken place, reactive coping efforts are directed toward either compensating for a loss or alleviating harm. In general, this is the type of coping that has been assessed in much of the research on coping to date. In contrast, proactive coping is oriented more towards the future. It consists of efforts to build up general resources that facilitate promotion of challenging goals and personal growth.

2. The second distinction between reactive coping and proactive coping is that reactive coping has been regarded as *risk* management and proactive coping is *goal* management (Schwarzer 1999a). In proactive coping, people have a vision. They see risks, demands, and opportunities in the future, but they do not appraise these as threats, harm, or loss. Rather, they perceive difficult situations as challenges. Proactive coping becomes goal management instead of risk management.

3. The motivation for proactive coping is more positive than in traditional coping in that it derives from perceiving situations as challenging and stimulating, whereas reactive coping emanates from risk appraisal, that is, environmental demands are appraised negatively, as threats.

A brief history of coping in psychology

Stress and coping have received widespread attention in recent years both in the psychology literature and in the media. This is due to findings that stress is not only widespread, it also has deleterious effects on both physical and mental health. There are large individual differences in the way individuals cope with their stress. It can be said with some certainty that stress and coping are ubiquitous in everyday life and affect everyone. Stress and coping (how individuals manage distressing problems and emotions) have been the focus of a remarkable amount of research over the past few decades. Within psychology, there have been three decades of research on the psychological aspects of stress. Moreover, stress has been documented to occur in virtually all spheres of life including work, school, family, and interpersonal relationships. Considerable research has also implicated stress as in the aetiology of a variety of illnesses including diseases of the heart and circulatory system as well as various cancers. Given the widespread prevalence of stress and the need to reduce it, there has been a proliferation of coping research during the last three decades. Coping strategies play a critical role in an individual's physical and psychological well-being when faced with challenges, negative events, and stress. Coping may also be conceptualized more broadly as part of an approach to life in which an individual's efforts are directed towards goal management and the identification and utilization of social resources to achieve one's goals.

Unlike previous work on coping which emphasized unconscious processes, more recently, research has used self-report measures of coping behaviours. In the face of stressful events, the participant is asked to indicate the kinds of coping behaviour he or she uses

(Lazarus and Folkman 1984). Lazarus (1993) offers the most widely accepted definition of coping: changing cognitive and behavioural efforts to manage psychological stress. In the process-oriented approach to coping put forth by Folkman and Lazarus (1985), coping is seen as a response to demands in stressful situations. Their work has also had a major impact in the way coping has been measured, beginning with the appearance of the *Ways of Coping Checklist* (Folkman and Lazarus 1980), a self-report instrument with 68 items that lists a variety of behavioural and cognitive coping strategies. The checklist is a yes/no format and is answered with regard to a specific event. Two main subscales were developed: a problem-focused coping subscale and an emotion-focused coping subscale. Internal consistency ratings for problem-focused coping were 0.80 and for emotion-focused scale, 0.81 (Folkman and Lazarus 1980).

A revision of the *Ways of Coping Checklist* was reported by Folkman and Lazarus (1985) in which they changed items as well as the response format which now was a four-point Likert scale for the 66 items. A factor analysis of results of questionnaires administered to university students on three occasions resulted in a six-factor solution using the new scale (Folkman and Lazarus 1988; WCQ). On the basis of their findings, eight subscales were developed: planful problem-solving, seeking social support, and six emotion-focused scales. In another study using the WCQ, Folkman *et al.* (1986) performed factor analyses that produced eight coping scales with moderate to high internal consistency ratings and include scales such as 'positive reappraisal' and 'distancing'. This scale continues to be used most in coping research despite weak empirical support for the validity of the coping subscales and modest internal consistency reliabilities (Endler and Parker 1990).

Coping, intentionality, and goal-oriented behaviour

While the objective study of stress and coping has dominated the research sphere for the last three decades, with the *cognitive* revolution came the acknowledgement that intrapsychic processes can, and often do intervene between stressful events and responses. Viewed in this way, coping is part of a psychosocial pattern of reactions—others include social support, self-efficacy, hardiness—posited to mediate the relationship between stress and illness (Somerfield and McCrae 2000). Making life manageable involves a functional consciousness which invokes purposive accessing and deliberating processing of information for selecting, constructing, regulating, and evaluating courses of action. This is achieved through intentional mobilization and productive use of representations of activities, goals, and other future events (Bandura 2001). Coping entails planning, purposiveness, and a cognitive representation of activities, both previous and future. Coping involves the purposive accessing and deliberative processing of information for selecting, constructing, and evaluating action (Bandura 2001). In this way, intentionality is merged with cognitive factors to form coping strategies that develop out of previous behavioural patterns while at the same time being future-oriented.

Functions of coping

These observations suggest that coping may be multifunctional. In the past, the dominant conceptual model used in research focused on coping effectiveness as manifest in the reduction of distress, often to the exclusion of other functions. But, coping may have other functions as well. According to Schwarzer (2000), there are four types of coping.

Reactive coping is defined as an effort to deal with a stressful encounter that has already happened. Since the stressful events have already taken place, coping efforts are directed here to either compensating for a loss or alleviating harm. In general, this is the type of coping that has been assessed in much of the research on coping to date.

Anticipatory coping is defined as an effort to deal with imminent threat; individuals face a critical event that is certain to occur in the near future. In anticipatory coping, there is a risk that a future event may cause harm or loss later on, and the person has to manage this perceived risk. The situation is appraised as an imminent threat. The function of coping may lie in solving the actual problem at hand, such as increasing effort, getting help, or investing other resources. This type of coping also involves investing one's resources to prevent or combat the stressor.

Preventive coping may be defined as an effort to build up general resistance resources that reduce the severity of the consequences of stress, should it occur, and lessen the likelihood of the onset of stressful events in the first place. In preventive coping, individuals face a critical event that may or may not occur in the distant future. Preventive coping involves risk management, but here one has to manage various unknown risks in the distant future.

Proactive coping consists of efforts to build up general resources that facilitate the achievement of challenging goals and promote personal growth. Individuals vary considerably in the resources they bring to stressful situations. Personal resources include coping strategies, personality attributes such as self-efficacy, and social support. Better individual resources empower individuals to cope more effectively with the stress. These ideas owe much to those put forth by Hobfoll in his Conservation of Resources theory (COR). Hobfoll (1988) argued that people work to obtain resources they do not have, retain those resources they possess, protect resources when threatened, and foster resources by positioning themselves so that their resources can be put to best use. According to this theory, stress is predicted to occur as a result of circumstances that represent (1) a threat of resource loss, or (2) actual loss of the resources required to sustain the individual (Hobfoll 1988, 1989).

In proactive coping, people have a vision. They see risks, demands, and opportunities in the far future, but they do not appraise these as threats, harm, or loss. Rather, they perceive difficult situations as challenges. Coping becomes *goal* management instead of *risk* management. Individuals are not reactive, but proactive in the sense that they initiate a constructive path of action and create opportunities for growth. Preventive and proactive coping are partly manifested in the same kinds of overt behaviours as skill development, resource accumulation, and long-term planning. However, the motivation can emanate either from threat appraisal or from challenge appraisal, which makes a difference. Worry levels are high in preventive coping but lower in proactive coping (Schwarzer 2000).

The processes through which people anticipate potential stressors and act in advance to prevent them can be seen as proactive behaviour. To the extent that individuals offset, eliminate, reduce or modify impending stressful events, proactive behaviour can eliminate a great deal of stress before it occurs. The skills associated with this behaviour include planning, goal setting, organization, and mental simulation (i.e. cognitive rehearsal) (Aspinwall and Taylor 1997).

Proactive coping is distinguished by *three* main features (Greenglass *et al.* 1999*a,b*):

(1) it integrates planning and preventive strategies with proactive self-regulatory goal attainment,

(2) it integrates proactive goal attainment with identification and utilization of social resources, and

(3) it utilizes proactive emotional coping for self-regulatory goal attainment.

An important feature of proactive coping is that it often utilizes the resources of others. This includes practical, informational, and emotional resources that can be provided by others.

Social support and stress

Social support is utilized by persons experiencing stress when they draw directly on the resources of their social networks. Social resource factors may serve either as a buffer in the coping process or may directly improve well-being (Cohen and Wills 1985; Greenglass 1993; Hobfoll 1988). In main effects analyses, an inverse relationship has been found between social support and stress with negative correlations being reported between social support and reported stress and strain. The buffer argument suggests that stress may affect some persons adversely, but that those who have social support resources are relatively resistant to the deleterious effects of stressful events. The evidence for the buffering effect of social support on stress is controversial (Himle *et al.* 1991). Cohen and Wills (1985) suggest that the buffering effect of social support may be limited by differences present in various studies including those associated with changing environments as well as particular individual responses to stress.

Since social support is significantly related to health, research is needed to examine the nature of this relationship. According to Bisconti and Bergeman (1999), the study of social support, as well as perceived control over the mobilization of support may provide researchers with understanding of the processes by which social support promotes well-being. These observations highlight the importance of distinguishing conceptually between habitual social resources (social networks) in the coping process, and mobilization of support in a particular stress situation as a unique coping response. Social networks represent the objective basis for social integration. Social integration refers to the structure and quantity of social relationships such as the size and density of networks. Social support refers to the function and quality of social relationships such as perceived availability of help or actual received support. Findings show that social integration is positively associated with health. It may be that individuals who are integrated into their communities are aware that social support is available to them should they need it in a difficult or challenging situation (Schwarzer *et al.* 1994*a,b*).

In the past, research on coping and social support has tended to be separate, conceptually and empirically. However, recently there has been research attention directed towards linking coping and social support in order to evolve an interpersonal theory of coping with stress. For example, DeLongis and O'Brien (1990) in their treatment of how families cope with Alzheimer's disease, discuss how interpersonal factors may be important as predictors of the individual's ability to cope with the situation. They talk about the importance of drawing on the resources of others for coping with difficult situations. Hobfoll *et al.* (1994) also address the interpersonal, interactive nature of coping, and social resource acquisition.

Coping and social support

There are several advantages to linking social support to coping. First, in viewing social support as a form of coping, one can theoretically link areas that have been previously viewed as conceptually distinct. This allows for the elaboration of traditional constructs using theoretical developments in the other area. Second, conceptualization of social support as coping broadens the concept of coping as it has traditionally been defined to include interpersonal and relational skills. Third, this approach recognizes the importance of resources in others which can be incorporated into the behavioural and cognitive coping repertoire of the individual. Moreover, according to the present reformulation, interpersonal strength and relational skills are conceptualized as positive coping strengths, which can be developed.

Research findings suggest that the connection between support and coping is stronger in women. For example, according to Norcross *et al.* (1986), women, compared to men, use more coping forms involving interpersonal relationships. Women, more than men, are expected to be sensitive to others' needs, according to traditional gender-role expectations (Greenglass *et al.* 1982). Additional findings suggest that women may utilize support from others through talking with one another. As Etzion and Pines (1981) explained it, women are more often able to make more effective use of their support networks than men since they tend to talk more with others as a way of coping with stress.

Other research findings suggest that women are able to utilize social support from others to develop instrumental and preventive coping strategies as shown by Greenglass (1993) who examined the role of supervisor and family and friend support in the prediction of various coping strategies in male and female managers. Regression results for women managers showed that supervisor support was linked positively and significantly with preventive and instrumental coping, and that friend and family support also related positively to the development of preventive coping. In contrast, in men managers, only supervisor support predicted positively to preventive coping. Thus, in women, it was more likely that there had been an incorporation of interpersonal support into the construction of cognitive coping forms.

These findings are consistent with the *Functional Support Model*. According to this model (Wills 1990), close relationships help a person cope with stress because in such relationships the person can disclose and discuss problems, share concerns, and receive advice that is keyed to a person's needs. This model suggests that close relationships contribute to well-being through increasing use of more effective coping forms, that is instrumental and internal control, and by decreasing use of negative, emotion-focused coping, with a corresponding decrease in negative affect. For Thoits (1986), social support is seen as coping assistance: coping and social support are seen as having functions in common. These are not only instrumental and emotional, but also perceptual which includes informational support that can alter perceptions of meaningful aspects of stressful situations.

Linking social support and coping, resources from one's network, including information, practical assistance and emotional support, can contribute positively to the construction of individual coping strategies (Greenglass 1993). Proactive coping draws on both internal and external resources. Internal resources include optimism and self-efficacy and refer to the *internal* coping options that are available in a particular stressful encounter. It is vital to feel competent to handle a stressful situation. Perceived competence is crucial, this is often labelled as perceived self-efficacy or optimistic self-beliefs (Bandura 1992). Perceived self-efficacy or optimism is seen as a prerequisite for coping. Social resources refer to *external* coping options available to an individual in a stressful encounter.

Theoretical model for proactive coping: resources and outcome

Figure 3.1 presents a schematic representation of the theoretical relationship between proactive coping, internal and external resources, and various outcomes, both positive and negative.

As can be seen in this diagram, proactive coping mediates between resources and outcomes. Internal resources can include optimism and self-efficacy beliefs and represent affective and cognitive elements, respectively, that define felt competency to handle a stressful situation. External resources are found in the social context within which individual coping develops and includes different types of support such as information, practical help, and/or emotional sustenance. Social support can serve a variety of functions. For example, to the extent that an individual draws on informational support, the perception of the meaningful aspects of a stressful situation can be modified. The sharing of feelings and affect that can occur in an emotionally supportive relationship can also result in a

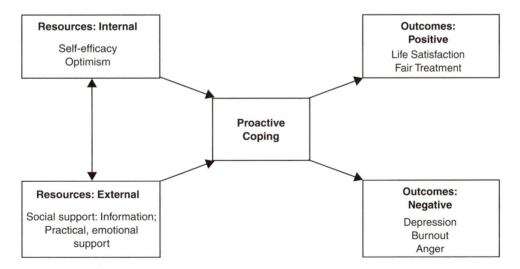

Figure 3.1 Theoretical model: resources, proactive coping, and outcomes.

change in the meaning of a stressful situation for an individual. Thus, cognitive changes can occur in one's perception of a stressful situation as a result of affective support.

At the same time, self-efficacy and social support are positively related to each other; to the extent that individuals possess self-efficacy, they also tend to report significantly more support from those around them. People with a high sense of social efficacy create social support for themselves. Perceived self-efficacy reduces vulnerability to depression through the cultivation of socially supportive networks (Holahan and Holahan 1987a,b). Social support enhances perceived self-efficacy. This, in turn, fosters successful adaptation and reduces stress and depression. Thus, a strong sense of social efficacy facilitates development of socially supportive relationships and reciprocally, social support enhances perceived self-efficacy (Bandura 1992). Proactive coping is seen as directly reducing negative outcomes including depression and burnout, especially emotional exhaustion and cynicism as well as anger feelings. Because proactive coping is a positive strategy that is seen as promoting self-growth, professional efficacy, and life satisfaction may be seen to increase with this kind of coping.

Development of the proactive coping inventory

We developed the Proactive Coping Inventory (PCI) in order to have a multidimensional coping inventory that would allow assessment of the different aspects of coping used by individuals during stressful times as well as in anticipation of stress and difficult situations ahead (Greenglass et al. 1999a). The PCI incorporates planning and preventive strategies with proactive self-regulatory goal attainment. It integrates proactive goal attainment with identification and utilization of social resources, and it utilizes proactive emotional coping for self-regulatory goal attainment.

In the first stage of the development of the PCI, students and psychologists assisted in generating 137 items which represented a wide range of coping behaviours. These items were derived from responses to the following questions: (1) Think back to problems you have had in the last six months, what specifically did you do to try to solve them? It may help to think specifically of one problem. (2) Did your efforts help? (3) Describe how you felt at the time.

Using precepts from Schwarzer's Proactive Coping Theory (Schwarzer 1999a), these items were then divided into 18 subscales and five dimensions, describing various dimensions of behaviour and cognition that are important for proactive coping. These included three dimensions of stress appraisal, two forms of proactive reflective coping, four dimensions of proactive resource management, three of proactive emotional coping and five forms of proactive goal-oriented coping action. Some of the dimensions were: Proactive stress appraisal, proactive reflective coping, proactive resource management, proactive emotional coping, and proactive goal-oriented coping action.

The item pool was then analysed and reduced in order to develop a set of proactive coping scales with good psychometric properties. At this stage a three-item scale measuring Avoidance Coping was included. As this concerned delay of coping rather than coping itself, this scale has been omitted from the present discussion. What is presented here is an analysis of the other items carried out separately for each of three samples: a Canadian Student sample, a Polish-Canadian sample, and a Canadian Adult sample as described below. There were six new scales consisting of a total of 52 items developed from the original 137 PCI item set using statistical techniques such as Pearson product–moment correlation, factor analysis, principal component analysis, and reliability procedures.

Theoretically, proactive coping is driven by a Proactive Attitude, which is a relatively persistent personal belief in the rich potential of changes that can be made to improve oneself and one's environment. This includes various facets such as resourcefulness, responsibility, values, and vision. A primary draft of the scales was developed using the Canadian Student sample and then tested with the Polish-Canadian sample and further validated with the Canadian Adult sample. The six scales of the PCI are, the Proactive Coping Scale, the Reflective Coping Scale, Strategic Planning, Preventive Coping, Instrumental Support Seeking, and Emotional Support Seeking.

In the Canadian Student sample, the respondents were college students recruited for the survey during class. The sample consisted of 252 individuals, 66 males and 179 females (seven did not indicate their gender). Age ranged from 17 to 60 years, mean age was 21.74 years. All were undergraduate students. The Polish-Canadian sample consisted of 144 Polish immigrants living in Canada. There were 46 males and 98 females. They were recruited in the Polish-Canadian community in Toronto. Age ranged from 16 to 60 years, mean age was 38.93 years. Only 18 were students and the remaining respondents, 126, were adults. Of the 144 respondents, 68 held white-collar positions and 48 were in blue-collar occupations.

A further validation study is described below which illustrates how the use of proactive coping can lead not only to lower burnout and anger, but also to positive outcomes including greater professional efficacy, fairer treatment at work, and greater life satisfaction (Greenglass 2000). In this study, we included 178 men and women who were employed in a variety of mainly white-collar occupations in a large Canadian city. Approximately two-thirds were non-university educated and 57 per cent were married and living with their spouse/partner. Respondents filled out anonymous and confidential questionnaires. This third group is referred to as the Canadian Adult sample.

The PCI subscales

The Proactive Attitude Scale (Schwarzer 1999b) and the General Perceived Self-Efficacy Scale (Schwarzer 1998) were used as external criteria during construction of the Proactive Coping Scale. Proactive coping integrates motivational and intentional aspects with volitional maintenance processes. The Proactive Coping Scale ($\alpha = 0.85$) consists of 14 items and combines autonomous goal setting with self-regulatory goal attainment cognitions and behaviour. The Reflective Coping Scale ($\alpha = 0.79$), with 11 items, describes simulation and contemplation about a variety of possible behavioural alternatives by comparing their imagined effectiveness, and includes brainstorming, analysing problems and resources, and generating hypothetical plans of action. Strategic Planning ($\alpha = 0.71$) is a four-item scale that focuses on the process of generating a goal-oriented schedule of action in which extensive tasks are broken down into manageable components. Preventive Coping ($\alpha = 0.83$) (10 items) deals with anticipation of potential stressors and the initiation of preparation before these stressors develop fully. Preventive Coping is distinct from proactive coping. Preventive Coping effort is directed toward a potential threat in the future by considering experience, anticipation, or knowledge. In comparison, Proactive Coping is not based on threat but is driven by goal striving. Instrumental Support Seeking ($\alpha = 0.85$) (eight items) focuses on obtaining advice, information, and feedback from people in one's social network when dealing with stressors. Emotional Support Seeking ($\alpha = 0.73$), a five-item scale, is aimed at regulating temporary emotional distress by disclosing feelings to others, evoking empathy, and seeking companionship from one's social network. It is emotional self-regulation with the assistance of significant others. Internal consistencies reported here are for the Canadian Student sample and range from 0.71 to 0.85. The Cronbach alphas for the PCI subscales in the Polish-Canadian sample are similar to those in the Canadian Student sample, ranging from 0.64 to 0.84. In general, each of the scales showed good item–total correlations and acceptable skewnes as an indicator of symmetry around the mean. Principal component analyses confirmed their factorial validity and homogeneity. The complete PCI can be found in Table 3.1.

Table 3.1 Proactive Coping Inventory—items for the six subscales, instructions, and scoring

---

Instructions to Subjects:

 Title of Scale Given to Respondents: Reactions to Daily Events Questionnaire
 '*The following statements deal with reactions you may have to various situations. Indicate how true each of these statements is depending on how you feel about the situation. Do this by checking the most appropriate box.*'
 Respondents are presented with four alternatives: 'not at all true', 'barely true', 'somewhat true', 'completely true.'
Scoring: 1 is assigned to 'not at all true, 2 to 'barely true', 3 to 'somewhat true', and 4 to 'completely true'.

Proactive Coping Inventory Items by Sub-scale

The Proactive Coping Scale
 1. I am a 'take charge' person.
 2. I try to let things work out on their own (reverse items).
 3. After attaining a goal, I look for another, more challenging one.
 4. I like challenges and beating the odds.
 5. I visualize my dreams and try to achieve them.
 6. Despite numerous setbacks, I usually succeed in getting what I want.
 7. I try to pinpoint what I need to succeed.
 8. I always try to find a way to work around obstacles; nothing really stops me.
 9. I often see myself failing so I do not get my hopes up too high (reverse items).
 10. When I apply for a position, I imagine myself filling it.
 11. I turn obstacles into positive experiences.
 12. If someone tells me I can't do something, you can be sure I will do it.
 13. When I experience a problem, I take the initiative in resolving it.
 14. When I have a problem, I usually see myself in a no-win situation (reverse items).

Reflective Coping Scale
 1. I imagine myself solving difficult problems.
 2. Rather than acting impulsively, I usually think of various ways to solve a problem.
 3. In my mind I go through many different scenarios in order to prepare myself for different outcomes.
 4. I tackle a problem by thinking about realistic alternatives.
 5. When I have a problem with my co-workers, friends, or family, I imagine beforehand how I will deal with them successfully.
 6. Before tackling a difficult task I imagine success scenarios.
 7. I take action only after thinking carefully about a problem.
 8. I imagine myself solving a difficult problem before I actually have to face it.

Table 3.1 (*Contd*)

Proactive Coping Inventory Items by Sub-scale

9. I address a problem from various angles until I find the appropriate action.
10. When there are serious misunderstandings with co-workers, family members or friends, I practice before how I will deal with them.
11. I think about every possible outcome to a problem before tackling it.

Strategic Planning Scale
1. I often find ways to break down difficult problems into manageable components.
2. I make a plan and follow it.
3. I break down a problem into smaller parts and do one part at a time.
4. I make lists and try to focus on the most important things first.

Preventive Coping Scale
1. I plan for future eventualities.
2. Rather than spending every cent I make, I like to save for a rainy day.
3. I prepare for adverse events.
4. Before disaster strikes I am well-prepared for its consequences.
5. I plan my strategies to change a situation before I act.
6. I develop my job skills to protect myself against unemployment.
7. I make sure my family is well taken care of to protect them from adversity in the future.
8. I think ahead to avoid dangerous situations.
9. I plan strategies for what I hope will be the best possible outcome.
10. I try to manage my money well in order to avoid being destitute in old age.

Instrumental Support Seeking Scale
1. When solving my own problems other people's advice can be helpful.
2. I try to talk and explain my stress in order to get feedback from my friends.
3. Information I get from others has often helped me deal with my problems.
4. I can usually identify people who can help me develop my own solutions to problems.
5. I ask others what they would do in my situation.
6. Talking to others can be really useful because it provides another perspective on the problem.
7. Before getting messed up with a problem I'll cal a friend to talk about it.
8. When I am in trouble I can usually work out something with the help of others.

Emotional Support Seeking Scale
1. If I am depressed I know who I can call to help me feel better.
2. Others help me feel cared for.
3. I know who can be counted on when the chips are down.
4. When I'm depressed I get out and talk to others.
5. I confide my feelings in others to build up and maintain close relationships.

Interrelationships among the PCI scales

According to theory, when faced with stress, the proactive coper invokes several cognitive and psychosocial processes. Since proactive coping involves purposive accessing of information for selecting, and constructing courses of action, reflective coping should be associated positively with proactive coping. At the same time, the proactive coper integrates planning, preventive strategies, and social resources with self-regulatory goal setting. This means that proactive coping should be associated as well with planning, prevention strategies, and identifying and seeking support resources. The interrelationships among the

PCI scales were examined in all three samples using Pearson's product–moment correlations with remarkably consistent results as may be seen in Table 3.2.

As expected, proactive coping scores correlated positively with some of the other PCI scales including preventive and reflective coping, strategic planning, and support seeking. It was originally stated that proactive coping was multidimensional. These findings support this notion by indicating in all three samples positive correlations between the proactive coping subscale and the other PCI subscales, but with clear evidence of clusters marking several distinct dimensions.

Instrumental and emotional support seeking were highly correlated with each other in all samples; however, results of factor analyses confirmed they were in fact separate factors (Taubert 1999). Further findings indicate that reflection is strongly related to preventive coping and planning in all three samples, as seen in relatively high correlations between reflective coping, preventive coping, and strategic planning. Reflection is clearly part of preventive coping and strategic planning. Planning and prevention were moderately correlated with each other in all three samples, an expected finding given they both involve a cognitive orientation towards anticipatory preparation for future eventualities.

Do men and women differ in how they cope?

The men and women in the Canadian Student and the Polish-Canadian samples were contrasted on each of the six subscales. There were only two subscales on which gender differences were observed. In each of the Canadian Student and Polish-Canadian samples, women were significantly higher than men on both the Instrumental Support Seeking and

Table 3.2 Intercorrelations between subscales of the PCI in Canadian student, Polish-Canadian, and Canadian adult samples

PCI subscale	Proactive coping	Reflective coping	Strategic planning	Preventive coping	Instrum. sup. seek	Emotional sup. seek
Proactive		0.37	0.38	0.43	0.24	0.30
coping	1.00	0.42	0.29	0.43	0.14	0.29
		0.46	0.43	0.53	0.18	0.25
Reflective			0.53	0.66	0.10	0.08
coping		1.00	0.55	0.62	0.18	0.21
			0.59	0.64	0.31	0.26
Strategic				0.46	0.16	0.10
planning			1.00	0.51	0.13	0.07
				0.56	0.30	0.20
Preventive					0.10	0.09
coping				1.00	0.06	0.11
					0.25	0.27
Instrum.						0.76
sup. seek.					1.00	0.77
						0.70

Line 1 in each data cell from Canadian Student sample, ($N = 248$).
Line 2 in each data cell from Polish-Canadian sample, ($N = 144$).
Line 3 in each data cell from Canadian Adult sample, ($N = 178$).
$p < 0.05 = 0.18$ to 0.19; $p < 0.01 = 0.20$ to 0.26; $p < 0.001 = 0.27$ to 0.77.

the Emotional Support Seeking Scales, using two-tailed T-tests. (The details of the significant contrasts only are shown in Table 3.3).

What this suggests, is that women are more likely than men to turn to others in their social networks for help when they have a problem. They may be seeking advice, information, practical assistance, and/or emotional support from others with whom they have relationships. Such observations are consistent with previous work examining gender differences, particularly the findings indicating that women, more than men, utilize social support in coping with stress. Close relationships can help a person cope with stress. In such relationships people can disclose and discuss problems, share concerns, and receive advice that is keyed to their needs (Solomon and Rothblum 1986). These relationships can also provide useful information, practical advice, and morale boosting, all of which can assist an individual in dealing with their stressors (Greenglass *et al.* 1996).

Previous research also suggests that the connection between social support seeking and coping is stronger in women. For example, according to Norcross *et al.* (1986), women, compared to men, use more coping forms involving interpersonal relationships. Women, more than men, are expected to be sensitive to others' needs, according to traditional gender-role expectations (Greenglass *et al.* 1982). Additional findings suggest that women may utilize support from others through talking with one another. According to Etzion and Pines (1981), women are more often able to make more effective use of their support networks than men since they tend to talk more with others as a way of coping with stress.

Other research findings suggest that women are able to utilize social support from others to develop instrumental and preventive coping strategies as shown by Greenglass (1993) who examined the role of supervisor and family and friend support in the prediction of various coping strategies in male and female managers. Multiple regression results in women managers were that supervisor support predicted positively and significantly to preventive and instrumental coping, and that friend and family support predicted positively to the development of preventive coping. In contrast, in men, only supervisor support predicted positively to preventive coping. Thus, in women, there is more likely to

Table 3.3 Significant gender differences on PCI scales: Canadian student and Polish-Canadian samples

Scale	Men		Women			
	Mean	SD	Mean	SD	df	*T*
Canadian student sample						
Emotional support seeking	14.65	3.26	15.88	2.96	242	−2.81**
Instrumental support seeking	28.96	5.47	31.43	5.76	242	−3.01**
Polish-Canadian sample						
Emotional support seeking	12.27	2.43	13.60	2.40	142	−3.08**
Instrumental support seeking	24.95	4.97	26.78	5.11	142	−2.02**

**$p<0.01$.

be an incorporation of interpersonal support into the construction of cognitive coping forms. Similar findings were reported in another study of government workers in which the relationship between co-worker support and various kinds of coping strategies were examined (Fiksenbaum and Greenglass, under review). In women and not men, co-worker support was the main predictor of coping, particularly instrumental and preventive types of coping. Women are socialized to be more communally oriented and women's coping emphasizes collaborative relationships, thus expressing itself in their report of greater co-worker support. The present data extend previous findings by showing that women utilize co-worker support to cope more effectively with their job stress. Thus, women are more likely than men to seek social resources from others and to use other people's advice in solving their own problems.

The validity of the PCI: or, does proactive coping really measure coping

In developing a new scale, it is important to demonstrate that the concept assessed in the scale is in fact a valid measure. To the extent that the proactive coping scale, for example, is consistent with other coping scales that measure activity and initiation in coping and is inconsistent with those assessing passivity and self-blame, it can be argued that the proactive coping scale possesses validity.

The construct validity of the PCI subscales was explored by having participants in the Canadian Student and Polish-Canadian samples complete measures of other coping styles and then examining the relationship between the PCI subscales and these additional measures as shown in Table 3.4. In particular, the other measures we used were Active Coping, Denial, Use of Instrumental Support and Use of Emotional Support, all from The Brief COPE, a coping inventory composed of 14 subscales (Carver 1997). Coping subscales from the *Coping inventory* of Peacock and Wong (1990) were also administered to participants in both samples. These included, Internal Control, a measure of the extent to which the individual takes the initiative in coping efforts, and Self-Blame.

Proactive coping scores correlated moderately highly with active coping and internal control, ranging from 0.46 to 0.62 in both samples, as expected. Moderately high negative correlations were observed between proactive coping, denial, and self-blame. Since proactive coping involves the perception of risks as challenges rather than threats and includes behavioural initiation, this type of coping is inconsistent with approaches that are less active, defeatist, and involve self-blame and denial. Reflective coping correlated moderately highly with internal control and active coping, thus highlighting the purposive accessing and deliberative processing of information for selecting, constructing, and evaluating action.

Strategic planning and preventive coping were both highly correlated with internal control and moderately with active coping. Correlations between instrumental and emotional support seeking scales, active coping, and internal control, were low in both samples. However, when scores on the two PCI support seeking scales were correlated with two of the COPE scales assessing use of instrumental and emotional support, correlations were higher, ranging from 0.50 to 0.65. As expected, there were non-significant correlations

Table 3.4 Correlations between the PCI and External Coping Scales by Carver and Peacock and Wong

External coping scale	PCS	PREV	RFFL	EMOS	INST	STRAT
Canadian student sample						
Carver (1997)						
Act. cop	0.52***	0.30***	0.33***	0.15*	0.17**	0.25***
Denial	−0.31***	−0.11	−0.02	−0.12	−0.04	−0.13*
Inst. sup.	0.07	−0.03	0.04	0.60***	0.65***	0.03
Emot. sup.	0.07	−0.02	0.07	0.60***	0.54***	0.04
Peacock & Wong (1990)						
Internal control	0.62***	0.56***	0.60***	0.13*	0.14*	0.57***
Self-Blame	−0.47***	−0.12	−0.04	−0.18**	−0.05	−0.12
Polish-Canadian sample						
Carver (1997)						
Act. cop	0.50***	0.30***	0.33***	0.11	0.10	0.37***
Denial	−0.14	−0.10	−0.10	−0.07	−0.04	−0.14
Inst. sup.	0.00	−0.06	0.08	0.59***	0.64***	0.08
Emot. sup.	0.05	−0.03	0.04	0.56***	0.50***	−0.01
Peacock & Wong (1990)						
Internal control	0.46***	0.56***	0.46***	0.06	0.03	0.51***
Self-Blame	−0.47***	−0.09	−0.12	−0.05	−0.00	−0.08

$*p < 0.05$; $**p < 0.01$; $***p < 0.001$.

between Carver's two support scales, proactive coping, strategic planning, preventive coping, and reflective coping (see Table 3.4).

To summarize, proactive coping is an active coping style, with strong elements of internal control, strategies that are based on individual initiation and self-determination. Thus, the proactive coper takes initiative, is active when faced with stressors, and mobilizes resources. At the same time, proactive coping is inconsistent with denial and self-blame since the individual who employs proactive coping takes responsibility for his or her actions but does not engage in self-blame when faced with the possibility of failure. The findings provided here suggest that proactive coping is not self-defeating but self-initiating. To the extent that preventive coping and strategic planning were highly correlated with active coping and internal control, they too reflect the initiation and preparation that characterize these coping styles. Since the PCI instrumental and emotional support seeking subscales correlated highly with the additional social support scales (Carver 1997), this increases our confidence that the PCI support subscales are in fact measuring support seeking.

Application of the PCI to the study of work stress and burnout

An important application of coping theory and research is in the area of occupational stress which has received considerable research attention in recent years. This is to be expected given the amount of time people spend on work-related activities. Burnout may be defined as a state of physical, emotional, and mental exhaustion that results from long-term involvement in work situations that are emotionally demanding (Maslach and Jackson 1986). Stress and burnout are major factors in the development of both physical and psychological illness (McGrath *et al.* 1989). Burnout is also related to self-reported measures of personal distress (Belcastro and Gold 1983; Greenglass 1991; Greenglass *et al.* 1990; Schaufeli and Enzmann 1998). Burnout in teachers correlates positively with depression, anxiety and somatization (Greenglass *et al.* 1990; Bakker *et al.* 2000).

Personal resources, coping, and work stress

Individuals vary in their reactions to workplace distress. Research supports the idea that personal resources can affect individuals' reactions to stress and burnout. Individuals who are affluent, healthy, capable, and optimistic are resourceful and thus are less vulnerable to work stress. When confronting stress, perceived competence is crucial, labelled as perceived self-efficacy or optimistic self-beliefs. Perceived self-efficacy and optimism are seen as prerequisites for coping with stresses including job loss, and work overload. Perceived self-efficacy, as a personal resource, reflects the person's optimistic self-beliefs about being able to deal with critical demands by means of adaptive actions. It can also be regarded as an optimistic view of one's capacity to deal with stress. Low self-efficacy is a central factor in the aetiology of burnout (Cherniss 1990). For Leiter (1991), burnout is inconsistent with a sense of self-determination or self-efficacy; burnout diminishes the potential for subsequent effectiveness.

Coping strategies and behaviours at work involving mastery or problem-solving are associated with more positive outcomes and decreased distress than are escape or more passive forms of coping (Leiter 1991; Armstrong-Stassen 1994). Research with nurses experiencing hospital downsizing showed that individual skills, particularly coping ability, predict their feelings about professional accomplishments as well as their depression and anxiety. At the same time, nurses with higher professional efficacy may be more likely to engage in control-oriented coping than those who are lower on professional efficacy (Greenglass and Burke 2000).

Discussion of factors that increase professional efficacy and decrease burnout, and the demonstration that control coping and self-efficacy contribute to higher feelings of professional competence, coincide with notions emphasizing positive psychology and the need to study their determinants and effects (Seligman and Csikszentmihalyi 2000). Moreover, these observations have theoretical and applied implications for the alleviation of stress and burnout. In focusing on positive skills, including coping and self-determination, as opposed to the negative emphasis that has characterized much of the psychological research, it is possible to develop individual and social programmes to prevent the development of burnout in individuals and enhance their quality of life. These programmes would focus more on self and professional enhancements and may be just as significant for burnout prevention as strategies to reduce the risk of burnout.

Individual resources can also reduce an individual's anger. Ausbrooks *et al.* (1995) explored the relationship between trait anger, modes of anger expression, dispositional optimism, and self-efficacy in college students. Dispositional optimism and self-efficacy were positively correlated with a tendency to express anger through discussion, and negatively correlated with a tendency to suppress anger.

Proactive coping, burnout, and anger at work

While work stress is ubiquitous, individuals vary in their skills and ability to cope with stress and their efforts vary considerably in the degree of success in reducing levels of work stress. To date, research examining the role of coping in reducing burnout has predomin-antly employed a bipolar definition of coping: control versus escape, active versus passive, problem-focused versus emotion-focused. Restricting coping to a bipolar definition has resulted in the exclusion of psychosocial and cognitive factors which play a major role in the construction of coping strategies. For example, this conceptualization of coping dis-regards social support seeking and the role that social support plays in alleviating stress and burnout. It also ignores the role of reflection and planning in coping with the anticipation of stress in the future.

Considerable research demonstrates the role of social support in alleviating burnout and stress (Greenglass *et al.* 1998; Greenglass 1998; Himle *et al.* 1991). At the same time, reliance on the active versus passive, emotion versus problem type, control versus escape typologies of coping, assumes that the only goal a person has when faced with stress, is to minimize it. However, people approach difficult situations with multiple goals. For example, rather than minimizing distress, one might value maintaining social relationships, completing a task, or beating a competitor (Coyne and Racioppo 2000). These observations point to the import-ance of re-evaluating the concept of coping, particularly the need to question the assump-tions regarding the goals of coping. It is suggested here, that coping can have multiple functions, only one of which may be to minimize stress, once it has occurred. For example, proactive coping can promote the setting of challenging goals and acceptance of experiences promising personal growth. Thus proactive coping can initiate constructive paths of action that create opportunities for self-development.

There are three ways in which conceptualizations regarding coping need to be modified. First, contrary to common usage, coping can be treated as a multidimensional construct (Endler and Parker 1994), not unidimensional. Coping entails behaviour, intentions, and cognitions that can vary simultaneously on several dimensions. Second, coping does not occur in a social vacuum. The assumption that the individual is autonomous and copes independently of others, has been challenged (Hobfoll 1998). Thus, considerations of coping need to take account of the social context in which the individual faces stresses. To the extent individuals can identify and mobilize social resources, they can increase the effectiveness of their coping strategies. Third, the function of coping may not be only to alleviate distress, but also to increase potential for growth, satisfaction, and quality of life. Normal human perceptions, marked by a positive sense of self, a sense of personal control and an optimistic view of the future may represent reserve resources that help people man-age the ebb and flow of everyday life (Taylor 1983; Taylor and Brown 1988). Coping, then, need not be restricted to being reactive in that it is directed to either compensating for a loss or alleviating harm after a stressful event has occurred (see p. 37). To the extent that coping efforts are directed toward prevention, building up resources, and setting goals for improving one's quality of life, coping is *proactive*.

Proactive coping and work stress

Proactive coping can be particularly valuable in alleviating work stress. When work demands are excessive and/or incompatible with one another, continued attempts to meet these demands will be emotionally distressful. The workplace can be a source of frustration and anxiety. Spector (1987) reported significant positive correlations of excessive work-loads, anxiety, frustration, and health symptoms. Work stress can also trigger anger feelings which can result in higher levels of anxiety. Burnout is considered a special type of prolonged exposure to occupational stress and results from interpersonal demands at work (Maslach and Jackson 1986). Burnout consists of three different dimensions: Emotional exhaustion, cynicism, and reduced professional efficacy (Schaufeli *et al.* 1996). Emotional exhaustion is defined as the depletion of energy; those who are exhausted feel over-extended, drained, and unable to recover. Cynicism refers to distancing oneself from work itself and, to the development of negative attitudes toward work in general. Professional efficacy is a sense of professional accomplishment and competence. This sense of accomplishment diminishes during burnout.

External stressors contribute to emotional exhaustion (Greenglass *et al.* 1997, 1998) and it has been suggested that emotional exhaustion is associated with somatization (Schaufeli and Van Dierendonck 1993; Greenglass *et al.* 1997). Cynicism is often a response to exhaustion (Greenglass *et al.* in press), and low professional efficacy is a function of higher cynicism. Work stress can also trigger anger feelings which can result in higher levels of anxiety. In particular, perceived unfair treatment at work has been cited as a precipitant of anger and distress (Thomas 1993; Schaufeli and Enzmann 1998). According to Equity Theory, people pursue reciprocity in their interpersonal and organizational relationships. What they invest and gain from a relationship should be proportional to the investments and gains of the other party in the relationship. When they perceive relationships are inequitable, they feel distressed and are motivated to restore equity (Schaufeli and Enzmann 1998). Unfair treatment at work involves lack of equity and therefore, may well lead to anger.

Use of disclosure and active coping techniques, including access to and use of social support resources, should lead to communicative non-threatening expression of anger and hostility (Stoney and Engebretson 1994). This suggests that anger-provoking situations may be redefined or restructured cognitively so as to be less threatening, thereby leading to lower levels of anger. People who display health benefits following disclosure also show increased insight and cognitive restructuring over time, compared with those who do not experience improved health (Pennebaker 1993). Social sharing or talking about feelings, including anger, can be aimed at solving problems or lessening emotional distress.

Proactive coping and stress

A study is described here that illustrates how use of proactive coping can lead not only to lower burnout and anger but also to positive outcomes including greater professional efficacy, fairer treatment at work and greater life satisfaction (Greenglass 2000). In this study, it was expected that individuals who used higher levels of proactive coping would experience lower burnout and anger, a greater sense of professional efficacy, perceive more fair treatment at work and experience greater life satisfaction. The sample for this study is the Canadian Adult Sample consisting of 178 adults (see p. 45 for a description of the demographics of this sample).

The outcome measures: Burnout, anger, fair treatment, and life satisfaction

In order to assess job burnout, the general burnout questionnaire (Schaufeli *et al.* 1996) was employed. This measure yields scores on three different scales: emotional exhaustion, cynicism, and professional efficacy. Emotional exhaustion, usually considered the prototype of stress, consists of five items. Being emotionally exhausted is similar to being emotionally overextended and often results from having too much to do at work with not enough support. A sample item from the emotional exhaustion scale is, 'I feel emotionally drained from my work'. Cynicism at work refers to an indifferent or distant attitude towards work. An example of an item in this scale is, 'I just want to do my job and not be bothered'. Professional efficacy, a six-item scale, is the positive dimension assessed in this burnout measure and refers to a person's satisfaction with past and present accomplishments and expectations of continued effectiveness at work. A sample item is, 'In my opinion, I am good at my job'. When people experience burnout at work, they will have lower scores on this latter scale and higher scores on cynicism and exhaustion.

Since anger can accompany job stress, the experience of anger was also measured in this study. The experience of anger at work was assessed using one scale from the *State-trait anger expression inventory (STAXI)* developed by Spielberger (1988). The STAXI is a self-report measure consisting of six scales. State anger (S-Anger), one of these scales, is a 10-item measure that indicates the intensity of one's angry feelings at a particular time. In the present study, the instructions for this scale were modified to ask respondents to indicate how they felt at the present time about working in their jobs. An item from this scale is, 'I am furious'. Depression was also assessed in an 11-item measure using a subscale from the Hopkins symptom checklist (HSCL) (Derogatis *et al.* 1979). A sample item of depression is, 'Indicate how often you have "felt blue" during the last three months'?

In order to assess perceptions of fair treatment at work, we asked respondents to indicate how fairly they were treated at work in a variety of areas including their pay. An example of an item is, 'I am paid fairly in my job'. Respondents were asked to check one number that best described their feelings on a scale that went from 1, strongly agree to 5, strongly disagree. *Life satisfaction* was measured by a three-item measure ($\alpha = 0.90$) (Bachman *et al.* 1967). Respondents answered on a seven-point response scale. An example of an item from this scale is, 'I am very satisfied with life'.

PCI scales and outcomes

In order to shed further light on the content of the PCI subscales, relationships between the various outcome measures and PCI subscales were examined. The results are set out in Table 3.5. The outcomes that were included are, state anger, depression, emotional exhaustion, and cynicism, as well as professional accomplishment, perception of fair treatment at work and life satisfaction. It was expected that people would experience less distress including lower anger, depression, emotional exhaustion, and cynicism when they used higher proactive coping. Thus, to the extent that individuals employ planning, goal setting, organization, and mental simulation in their coping strategies, they would be less likely to report distress symptoms of various kinds.

It was also expected that proactive coping would lead to greater perception of fair treatment at work, higher levels of professional efficacy, and greater life satisfaction. Individuals who employ coping strategies based on proactivity are more likely to perceive that they are fairly treated at work. This is because individuals who use proactive coping believe in their ability to successfully tackle challenges, to envision success, and to effectively use the

Table 3.5 Correlations between PCI scales and outcome measures: Employed adult Canadian sample ($n = 178$)

Outcome measure	PCI scale					
	Proactive coping	Reflect coping	Strategic planning	Preventive coping	Instrumental sup. seek	Emotional sup. seek
Emotional exhaustion	−0.25**	−0.08	−0.13	−0.23**	−0.15*	−0.16*
Cynicism	−0.32***	−0.11	−0.24**	−0.21**	−0.08	−0.14
Professional efficacy	0.29***	0.18*	0.15*	0.17*	0.05	0.02
Depression	−0.35***	−0.13	−0.20**	−0.26***	−0.11	−0.13
State anger	−0.24**	−0.04	−0.22**	−0.14	−0.13	−0.14
Life satisfaction	0.29***	0.24**	0.21**	0.28***	0.22**	0.18*
Fair treatment	0.32***	0.15*	0.16*	0.30***	0.17*	0.28***

*$p < 0.05$; **$p < 0.01$; ***$p < 0.001$.

resources at hand to solve problems. Thus, they are less likely to perceive unfair treatment by others as undermining their efforts at work. In effect, since they feel prepared to deal with stress, they may be less likely to blame others when things do not go their way. Professional efficacy should also increase with greater proactive coping since individuals who believe in their ability to deal effectively with challenges would also have expectations of continued effectiveness at their job.

Results for the proactive coping scale were as follows: Moderate negative correlations were found between proactive coping and state anger, depression, emotional exhaustion, and cynicism, and moderate positive correlations were found between proactive coping, life satisfaction, and fair treatment. These findings provide additional evidence for the construct validity of the proactive coping scale. As expected, higher coping scores were related to lower scores on scales measuring distress.

In addition, higher proactive coping scores were related to higher scores on positive outcome measures including, professional efficacy, life satisfaction, and fair treatment. Few significant correlations were observed between reflective coping and either negative or positive outcome measures. Rather than relating directly to outcome measures, as did the proactive coping scale, reflective coping appears to play a role in facilitating and promoting the other coping strategies. The moderate-to-high correlations observed between reflective coping, and proactive coping, strategic planning, and preventive coping in all three samples (see Table 3.2) point to the importance of reflection in the development of coping strategies that are cognitively oriented towards anticipatory preparation for future eventualities. These findings suggest that temporally, reflective coping may precede proactive coping, strategic planning, and preventive coping.

In Table 3.5, moderate-to-low negative correlations were observed between strategic planning, anger, depression, and cynicism. Thus, to the extent that individuals confront stressors not by tackling the 'whole' problem but rather by breaking it down into smaller parts and focusing on one part at a time, they are less likely to experience anger and cynicism towards others and their jobs. As a result, they feel less depressed. Frustration is often a precursor of anger and cynicism. It may be that use of strategic planning gives the individual a sense of control over stressors, thus resulting in less frustration, anger, and cynicism. Preventive coping was associated with lower burnout—lower emotional exhaustion, lower cynicism, and higher professional efficacy, as well as lower depression. Items on the preventive coping subscale involve cognitions that take preventive measures before the stressful event occurs, in order to prevent harm.

Burnout is a state of emotional exhaustion that results from long-term involvement in work situations that are emotionally demanding. Thus, to the extent that individuals use preventive coping, they may be able to curtail an emotionally demanding situation, thus preventing burnout from setting in. Low or non-significant correlations were found between negative outcome measures and both support seeking scales. Thus, seeking social support may not have a direct impact on outcomes *per se*. Rather, since social support seeking was significantly related to all of the proactive coping subscales, it is possible that the role of support seeking on outcomes is mediated by coping (see Table 3.2).

In examining relationships between PCI subscales, life satisfaction, and fair treatment (see Table 3.5), results of correlational analyses showed that, in general, scores on these positive measures increased with coping scores. Thus, to the extent that individuals employ strategies that include planning, goal setting, mental simulation, and seeking social resources, they are more likely to perceive that they are treated fairly at work and they experience more satisfaction with life.

Summary

A new coping instrument, the PCI, is described here. The subscales of the PCI have good reliability and construct validity, as demonstrated in three different samples of respondents. In this chapter, we have demonstrated the validity of the PCI in the following ways: (a) there are moderate-to-high positive correlations between PCI subscale scores and scores on external coping instruments that measure internal control and active coping, (b) there are moderately negative correlations between PCI subscale scores and self-blame and denial, indicating that proactive coping is inconsistent with self-defeat, (c) the emotional support seeking and instrumental support seeking scales are highly correlated with two external coping scales measuring use of social support, thus confirming the construct validity of the support seeking scales, and (d) proactive coping styles are associated with higher life satisfaction, higher professional efficacy and perceptions of fair treatment at work.

The PCI appears to be a promising coping inventory to assess skills in coping with distress as well as those that promote greater well-being and greater satisfaction with life. Since coping is a process over time, which changes, ebbs, and flows, depending on situational factors, longitudinal designs are needed to assess how the PCI contributes to this process. The findings reported here are rich with hypotheses for future research into the processes that simultaneously operate to reduce distress and promote well-being. For example, reflection, particularly envisioning successful outcomes, should be a contributing factor to proactive coping, planning, and prevention. This notion can be tested empirically by measuring reflective coping at one point in time, later measuring proactive coping, planning, and preventive coping, and assessing the extent to which reflection contributes to these other coping strategies later in time, using structural equation modelling. In this way, the role of reflection can be directly assessed in so far as it contributes to coping strategies. The use of social resources, both instrumental and emotional, and their role in promoting proactive coping, reflective coping, planning, and prevention, can also be tested over time, using similar designs and statistical analyses. To the extent that social support varies, one may expect different results when examining its contribution to proactive coping, for example.

The PCI, with its six subscales, offers many possibilities for testing hypotheses relevant to increasing our understanding of the process of coping. The PCI envisions coping within a social context rich in resources for the proactive individual. At the same time, the PCI integrates affective, cognitive, intentional, and social factors into a set of coping strategies that will enable individuals to deal with challenges by constructing paths of action for personal growth and the promotion of goals. Taken together, our research indicates that proactive coping is a useful coping strategy to both prevent and contend with work-related burnout. As expected, proactive coping contributed positively to professional efficacy. This is because proactive coping focuses on accumulating resources and setting goals for improvement, efforts which contribute positively to a sense of professional accomplishment and competence, that is, professional efficacy. Thus, to the extent that individuals employ coping strategies at work based on proactivity, they are more likely to experience a higher sense of professional efficacy in their jobs. Thus, proactive coping would appear to be a useful tool in managing work-related stress and burnout and in promoting a higher level of professional competence at work. Implications for practice are that by teaching individuals to employ proactive coping strategies at work, distress can be significantly reduced and feelings of professional competence can be increased.

References

Armstrong-Stassen, M. (1994). Coping with transition: A study of layoff survivors. *Journal of Organizational Behaviour*, 15, 597–621.

Aspinwall, L. G. and Taylor, S. E. (1997). A stitch in time: Self-regulation and proactive coping. *Psychological Bulletin*, 121, 417–36.

Ausbrooks, E. P., Thomas, S. P., and Williams, R. L. (1995). Relationships among self-efficacy, optimism, trait anger, and anger expression. *Health Values: The Journal of Health Behaviour Education and Promotion*, 19, 46–54.

Bachman, J., Kahn, R. L., Davidson, T., and Johnston, L. (1967). *Youth in transition*, Vol. 1, Ann Arbor, MI: Institute for Social Research.

Bakker, A. B., Schaufeli, W. B., Demerouti, E., Janssen, P. M. P., Van der Hulst, R., and Brouwer, J. (2000). Using equity theory to examine the difference between burnout and depression. *Anxiety, Stress, and Coping*, 13, 247–68.

Bandura, A. (1992). Exercise of personal agency through the self-efficacy mechanism, in R. Schwarzer (ed.), *Self-efficacy: Thought control of action*, (pp. 3–38). Washington: Hemisphere.

—— (2001). Social cognitive theory: An agentic perspective. *Annual Review of Psychology*, 52, 1–26.

Belcastro, P. A. and Gold, R. S. (1983). Teacher stress and burnout: Implications for school health personnel. *Journal of School Health*, 53, 404–7.

Bisconti, T. L. and Bergeman, C. S. (1999). Perceived social control as a mediator of the relationships among social support, psychological well-being, and perceived health. *The Gerontologist*, **39**, 94–103.

Carver, C. S. (1997). You want to measure coping but your protocol's too long: Consider the Brief COPE. *International Journal of Behavioural Medicine*, **4**, 92–100.

Cherniss, C. (1990). The human side of corporate competitiveness, in D. B. Fishman and C. Cherniss (eds.), *The human side of corporate competitiveness*. Newbury Park, CA: Sage Publications.

Cohen, S. and Wills, T. (1985). Stress, social support and the buffering hypothesis. *Psychological Bulletin*, **98**, 310–57.

Coyne, J. C. and Racioppo, M. W. (2000). Never the twain shall meet? Closing the gap between coping research and clinical intervention research. *American Psychologist*, **55**, 655–64.

De Longis, A. and O'Brien, T. (1990). An interpersonal framework for stress and coping: An application to the families of Alzheimer's patients, in M. A. P. Stephens, J. H. Crowther, S. E. Hobfoll, and D. L. Tennenbaum (eds.), *Stress and coping in later life families*, pp. 221–39. New York: Hemisphere.

Derogatis, L. R., Lipman, R. S., Rickels, K., Uhlenhuth, E. H., and Cori, L. (1979). The Hopkins Symptom Checklist (HSCL): A self report symptom inventory. *Behavioural Science*, **19**, 1–15.

Endler, N. S. and Parker, J. D. A. (1990). *The coping inventory for stressful situations (CISS): Manual.* Toronto: Multi-Health Systems, Inc.

—— (1994). Assessment of multidimensional coping: Task emotion, and avoidance strategies. *Psychological Assessment*, **6**, 50–60.

Etzion, D. and Pines, A. (1981). *Sex and culture as factors explaining reported coping behaviour and burnout of human service professionals: A social psychological perspective.* Tel Aviv: Tel Aviv University. The Israel Institute of Business Research.

Fiksenbaum, L. and Greenglass, E. R. Interpersonal predictors of coping (under review).

Folkman, S. and Lazarus, R. S. (1980). An analysis of coping in a middle-aged community sample. *Journal of Health and Social Behaviour*, **21**, 219–39.

—— (1985). If it changes it must be a process: A study of emotion and coping during three stages of a college examination. *Journal of Personality and Social Psychology*, **48**, 150–70.

—— (1988). The relationship between coping and emotion: Implications for theory and research. *Social Science Medicine*, **26**, 309–17.

—— Dunkel-Schetter, C., De Longis, A., and Gruen, R. J. (1986). The dynamics of a stressful encounter: Cognitive appraisal, coping, and encounter outcomes. *Journal of Personality and Social Psychology*, **50**, 992–1003.

Greenglass, E. R. (2000). Work rage and its psychological implications. *Invited paper presented at the 21st International STAR Conference*, Bratislava, July 20–22, Slovakia.

Greenglass, E., Fiksenbaum, L., and Burke, R. J. (1996). Components of social support, buffering effects and burnout: Implications for psychological functioning. *Anxiety, Stress, and Coping*, **9**, 185–97.

—— Schwarzer, R., Jakubiec, D., Fiksenbaum, L., and Taubert, S. (1999a). The Proactive Coping Inventory (PCI): A Multidimensional Research Instrument. *Paper presented at the 20th International Conference of the Stress and Anxiety Research Society (STAR)*, Cracow, July 12–14, Poland.

Greenglass, E. R., Schwarzer, R., and Taubert, S. (1999b). *The Proactive Coping Inventory (PCI): A multidimensional research instrument.* [Online publication]. Available at: *http:// www.psych.yorku.ca/greenglass/*.

Greenglass, E. R. (1982). *A world of difference: gender roles in perspective*. Toronto: Wiley.

—— (1991). Burnout and gender: Theoretical and organizational implications. *Canadian Psychology*, **32**, 562–72.

—— (1993). The contribution of social support to coping strategies. *Applied Psychology: An International Review*, **42**, 323–40.

—— (1998). The Proactive Coping Inventory (PCI), R. Schwarzer (ed.), *Advances in health psychology research*, Vols. CD-ROM. Berlin: Free University of Berlin.

Greenglass, E. and Burke, R. J. (2000). Hospital downsizing, individual resources and occupational stressors in nurses. *Anxiety, Stress, and Coping: An International Journal*, **13**, 371–90.

Greenglass, E. R., Burke, R. J., and Fiksenbaum, L. (2001). Workload and burnout in nurses. *Journal of Community and Applied Social Psychology*, **11**, 211–15.

—— and Konarski, R. (1997). The impact of social support on development of burnout in teachers: Examination of a model. *Work and Stress*, **11**(3), 267–78.

Greenglass, E., Burke, R. J., and Konarski, R. (1998). Components of burnout, resource and gender-related differences. *Journal of Applied Social Psychology*, **28**, 1088–106.

Greenglass, E. R., Burke, R. J., and Ondrack, M. (1990). A gender-role perspective of coping and burnout. *Applied Psychology: An International Review*, **39**, 5–27.

Himle, D. P., Jayaratne, S., and Thyness, P. (1991). Buffering effects of four social support types on burnout among social workers. *Social Work Research and Abstracts*, **27**, 22–7.

Hobfoll, S. E. (1988). *The ecology of stress*. Washington, DC: Hemisphere.

—— (1989). Conservation of resources: A new attempt at conceptualizing stress. *American Psychologist*, **44**, 513–24.

—— (1998). *Stress, culture and community: The psychology and philosophy of stress*. New York: Plenum.

—— and Dunahoo, C. L., Ben-Porth, Y., and Monnier, J. (1994). Gender and coping: The dual-axis model of coping. *American Journal of Community Psychology*, **22**, 49–82.

Holahan, C. K. and Holahan, C. J. (1987*a*). Self-efficacy, social support, and depression in aging: A longitudinal analysis. *Journal of Gerontology*, **42**, 65–68.

—— (1987*b*). Life stress, hassles and self-efficacy in aging: A replication and extension. *Journal of Applied Social Psychology*, **17**, 574–92.

Lazarus, R. S. (1993). Coping theory and research: Past, present and future. *Psychosomatic Medicine*, **55**, 234–47.

—— and Folkman, S. (1984). *Stress, appraisal and coping*. New York: Springer.

Leiter, M. P. (1991). Coping patterns as predictors of burnout: The function of control and escapist coping patterns. *Journal of Organizational Behaviour*, **12**, 123–44.

Maslach, C. and Jackson, S. E. (1986). *Maslach Burnout Inventory Manual*, 2nd edn. Palo Alto, CA: Consulting Psychologists Press.

McGrath, A., Houghton, D., and Reid, N. (1989). Occupational stress, and teachers in Northern Ireland. *Work and Stress*, **3**, 359–68.

Norcross, J. C., DiClemente, C. C., and Prochaska, J. O. (1986). Self-change of psychological distress: Laypersons' versus. psychologists' coping strategies. *Journal of Clinical Psychology*, **42**, 834–40.

Peacock, E. J. and Wong, P. T. (1990). The Stress Appraisal Measure (SAM): A multidimensional approach to cognitive appraisal. *Stress Medicine*, **6**, 227–36.

Pennebaker, J. W. (1993). Putting stress into words: Health, linguistic, and therapeutic implications. *Behaviour Research and Therapy*, 31, 539–48.

Schaufeli, W. B. and Van Dierendonck, D. (1993). The construct validity of two burnout measures. *Journal of Organizational Behaviour*, 14, 631–47.

—— and Enzmann, D. (1998). *The burnout companion to study and practice: A critical analysis*. London: Taylor & Francis.

—— Leiter, M. P., Maslach, C., and Jackson, S. E. (1996). *MBI general survey*. Palo Alto, CA: Consulting Psychologists Press, Inc.

Schwarzer, R. (1998). *General Perceived Self-Efficacy in 14 Cultures*. On-line. Available: http://user-page.fu-berlin.de/~health/lingua5.htm.

—— (1999a). Proactive Coping Theory. Paper presented at the 20th International Conference of the Stress and Anxiety Research Society (STAR), Cracow, July 12–14, Poland.

—— (1999b). The Proactive Attitude Scale (PA Scale). [Online]. Available: http://userpage. fu-berlin.de/~health/proactive.htm.

—— Dunkel-Schetter, C., and Kemeny, M. (1994). The multidimensional nature of received social support in gay men at risk of HIV infection and AIDS. *American Journal of Community Psychology*, 22, 319–39.

—— Hahn, A., and Schröder, H. (1994). Social integration and social support in a life crisis: Effects of macrosocial change in East Germany. *American Journal of Community Psychology*, 22(5), 685–706.

—— (2000). Manage stress at work through preventive and proactive coping. In E. A. Locke (ed.), *The Blackwell handbook of principles of organizational behaviour*, Ch. 24, pp. 342–55. Oxford, UK: Blackwell.

Seligman, M. E. P. and Csikszentmihalyi, M. (2000). Positive psychology: An Introduction. In Special issue on happiness, excellence and optimal human functioning. *American Psychologist*, 55, 5–14.

Solomon, L. J. and Rothblum, E. D. (1986). Stress, coping, and social support in women. *The Behaviour Therapist*, 9, 199–204.

Sommerfield, M. R. and McCrae (2000). Stress and coping research: Methodological challenges, theoretical advances and clinical applications. *American Psychologist*, 55, 620–25.

Spector, P. E. (1987). Interactive effects of perceived control and job stressors on affective reactions and health outcomes for clerical workers. *Work and Stress*, 1, 155–62.

Spielberger, C. D. (1988). *State-Trait Anger Expression Inventory*. Tampa, Florida: Psychological Assessment Resources.

Stoney, C. M. and Engebretson, T. O. (1994). Anger and hostility: Potential mediators of the gender difference in coronary heart disease, in A. W. Siegman and T. W. Smith (eds.), *Anger, hostility, and the heart*, pp. 215–37. Hillsdale, NJ: Lawrence Erlbaum Associates, Publishers.

Taubert, S. (1999). *Development and validation of a psychometric instrument for the assessment of proactive coping*. Diploma Thesis, Free University of Berlin, Berlin, Germany.

Taylor, S. E. (1983). Adjustment to threatening events: A theory of cognitive adaptation. *American Psychologist*, 38, 1161–73.

—— and Brown J. D. (1988). Illusion and well-being: A social psychological perspective on mental health. *Psychological Bulletin*, 103, 193–210.

—— (1994). Positive illusions and well being revisited: Separating fact from fiction. *Psychological Bulletin*, 116, 21–7.

Taylor, S. E. Kemeny, M. E., Reed, G. M., Bower, J. E., and Gruenewald, T. L. (2000). Psychological resources, positive illusions, and health. *American Psychologist*, 55, 99–109.

Thoits, P. A. (1986). Social support as a coping assistance. *Journal of Consulting and Clinical Psychology*, 54, 416–23.

Thomas, S. P. (1993). *Women and anger*. New York: Springer Publication Company.

Wills, T. A. (1990). Social support and interpersonal relationships, in M. S. Clark (ed.), *Review of personality and social psychology*, Vol. 12, pp. 265–89. Newbury Park, CA: Sage.

CHAPTER 4

ALONE TOGETHER: COMPARING COMMUNAL VERSUS INDIVIDUALISTIC RESILIENCY

STEVAN E. HOBFOLL

The study of stress has emphasized people's resiliency. Given the vicissitudes of the human drama, it is a wonder that anyone is left physically or psychologically healthy. However, since the early report by Jahoda (1958) from the Commission on Mental Health, there has been a recognition that people are to a large extent able to adjust to the multitude of stressors they confront. This does not mean that they necessarily thrive in all instances, although many do thrive. However, it does mean that through it all people survive and that most people continue to function in their roles.

The most carefully studied domain of research on resiliency relates to the contribution of individual effort and control. Indeed, if any concept has been exported abroad from the US it is the concept that people can obtain their goals and face adversity through individual effort. Psychology, likewise, has championed this dominance with the self-focused concepts of self-efficacy, sense of personal mastery, and sense of personal control. In a review of the literature, Skinner (1996) notes over 100 concepts related to personal control that have been studied in psychology. Despite this plethora of research and theory, it is my thesis that the idea of the crystalized self that is in control of the environment and of effort is largely a myth related to the vision of middle class America and the Protestant Ethic. I will argue in this paper that self-efficacy is interwoven with collective efficacy and that even when individuals largely deny the role of others in assisting them in meeting their goals, that the social context moves the individual forward to a much greater extent than individuals can ever move the collective forward.

This is not to say that people do not have a sense of self-efficacy, but that it is a viewpoint, rather than a reflection of the actual nature of how stress resiliency and goal achievement takes place. This is poignantly portrayed in the novel by Tom Wolff (1987), *The bonfire of the vanities* in which the leaders of Wall Street are depicted as seeing themselves as 'Masters of the Universe'. Following a car accident in a moment's error of taking the wrong road into the wrong neighbourhood, the protagonist's power is diminished directly and entirely as the crime dissolves his social status. We have come to imagine that self-reliance is the central characteristic of those at the top of the economic pyramid. That these individuals cannot fix their own cars, care for their own homes or lawns, or work any of the machines that power their industry is ignored. It is the man, or more aptly put, woman, on the shop floor who has actual self-reliance, but our social constructions have allowed us, like characters in Lewis Caroll's *Through the looking-glass* to construe a world of opposites.

Historical context

Individualism and collectivism actually lie on a continuum. When we attempt to separate the concepts we lose much of the fabric of self-in-social context. However, the study of stress and coping has come at a certain historical time and researchers have failed to consider that they were capturing this socio-historical context when they conducted their work. For this reason, it is important to step back and examine the historical under-pinnings of the concept of self and of individual control of effort and goal achievement.

It has been noted historically that as the concept of self emerged during the late Middle Ages in Europe (Baumeister 1987; Sampson 1988) it increasingly modified the more omnipresent collectivist model. Still, it is clear that individualism and collectivism coex-isted, even where individualism has predominated as Protestant culture gained currency. Nor should we infer that the ages that preceded the emergence of a strong sense of self in literature, the arts, and philosophy were entirely collectivist. Baumeister (1987) argues that from about the eleventh through the fifteenth century that the concept of a single, separable self crystallized in Europe. This was personified by notions of individual salvation, self-related concepts of honor, glory, and virtue, and identification other than in set roles proscribed by God or destiny.

Based largely on a philosophy of self that was derived from religious philosophy, neither Jewish nor Christian Europe envisioned a demarcation between the self and the com-munity in the process of facing adversity. This split between self and collective actually emerged during fairly recent times and may have been responsible, in part, for the schism between the individualistic and communal perspective in Western thought within psychology. Even Puritanism, which placed a greater emphasis on individual action than had earlier Christian or Jewish ideals, had a central, paramount collective element. Hence, although it has been ascribed to the Protestant movement, the underlying philosophy of early Protestant teachings greatly valued community relations and people's ties with each other (Weintraub 1978; Whyte 1960).

This raises the thesis that the self as inconsistent with the collective is actually a more secular notion that evolved during the Romantic period in the late eighteenth to early nine-teenth century. Romanticism argued that the self and personal motivation existed outside of religious salvation alone. Romanticism in particular idealized individual effort in terms of love for creative work. In this way, human potential emerged in terms of personal ful-fillment. Romanticism also placed an ideal on individual isolation. This is epitomized in Thoreau's image of the individual living in the woods, separated from society at Walden Pond. Thoreau was said to have no profession, he never married, he lived alone, he never attended Church, he abstained from both the privileges and duties of citizenship, and refused to pay taxes (Eliot 1989).

Romanticism began to reveal an hostility toward society. Wrote Emerson in his famous essay *Self reliance* (1841),

Society never advances. It recedes as fast on one side as it gains on the other. Its progress is only apparent like the workers of a treadmill. It undergoes continual changes; it is barbarous, it is civilized, it is christianized, it is rich, it is scientific; but this change is not an amelioration.   (p. 80)

Moreover, Emerson associated creativity, and non-conformity with isolationism.

We must go alone. Isolation must precede true society. I like the silent church before the service begins . . . How far off, how cool, how chaste the persons look, begirt each one with a precinct or sanctuary. So let us always sit. Why should we assume the faults of our friend, or wife, or father, or child, because they sit around our hearth, or are said to have the same blood? . . . the whole world seems to be in conspiracy to importune you with emphatic trifles. Friend, client, child, sickness, fear, want , charity, all knock at once at thy closet door and say, 'Come out unto us.'—Do not spill thy soul; do not all descend; keep thy state; stay at home in thine own heaven; come not for a moment into their facts . . . .   (p. 73)

Romanticism nevertheless remained linked to the importance of the commons. However, the late nineteenth and early twentieth century saw the real emergence of viewing society as an outright evil. This theme emerged in the sociological treatise on alienation of Durkheim (1995/1897), in literary themes of society (e.g. Kafka), and in the muckraker journalism of Sinclair (see Klein 1964). Urbanization and industrialization acted to disengage individuals from communal access to resources, as they became increasingly treated as cannon fodder for society's advancement. Taylor (1911), the father of American industrial philosophy, argued that maximum efficiency could be achieved by treating individuals as replaceable cogs and divorcing them from attachment to the whole product. He felt it was unnecessary for them to demonstrate initiative, judgment, or skill. Given the driving force of industrialization, the advancement of this philosophy meant the dissolution of social contract between the self and society.

The belief in the value of the collective was further shattered in the West by the death and destruction wrought by the First World War. The 'war to end all wars' imbued an image of the state as disregarding of individuals' welfare and disinterested in their very lives. The trench warfare of the Western front had millions go to their death until the French soldiers mutinied *en masse* and refused to attack further. They would only defend French soil. The Russian army in the East became so despondent that they dropped their weapons and began walking home to aid the revolution (Golovine 1931). In the US the anarchist movement gained momentum at this time, with their theme that no government collective can represent individual need (DeLeon 1978).

The relevance of this for psychology is that the individualism of psychology may stem in large part from this Zeitgeist, as it was during this period that American Psychology began to define itself. This rejection of the collective and championing of individualism was further catalysed by the Second World War in which American individualism was seen as conquering two of the three evils of the collective, Japanese Imperialism, and German Naziism. The remaining collective evil in the American psyche, was communism, and the Cold War which followed the Second World War only ended with the collapse of the Berlin Wall, some 50 years later. Indeed, it is likely that had psychologists raised issues of collectivism in any positive tone in the 1950s, they would have been black-listed. Hence we have the Asch experiments (1955), the Milgram studies (1963), and the Rokeach (1960) traditions with their attacks on the evil of group think, dogmatism, and blind allegiance to authority. Perhaps what was most upsetting about Milgram's findings was that this same blind allegiance to authority could be demonstrated in those raised on individualism and democracy. What Asch, Milgram, and Rokeach were trying to communicate was that people bred on individualism and independence from social conformity were quite conforming and influenced by group pressure.

Although we seldom raise these socio-historical questions, they are clearly linked to the emergent image of the isolated, self-contained individual 'a sense of self with a sharp boundary that stops at one's skin and clearly demarcates self from nonself' (Spence 1985, p. 1288). Being psychology's predominant model, it becomes clear how the study of coping was framed in terms of individual action, with only secondary emphasis placed on social context. Even where social support is raised, it is framed in terms of its aid to the individuals' effort. Indeed, much has been made of the fact that the individual does well not to actually use the support, but to know that it is there (Sarason *et al.* 1990). Bowlby's (1969) very concept of attachment is seen as the secure base from which the individual must *individuate* in order to be healthy.

These individualistic notions stand in contrast to the ensembled individualism that could be derived from other cultural models. Sampson (1988) contrasts the predominant model in American psychology to that of ensembled individualism. Ensembled individualism is personified by fluid interaction with others, lack of clear self–other boundaries and sharing of control between the self, others, and the environment. In contrast, within the concept of the crystalized self, acts of coping between the self and others are identified by exchange characteristics, give and take, in a rational–legal approach to coping (Gerth and Mills 1946). In this way, self-reliance demands a clearly defined self that demarcates the individual from his or her social ties (Perloff 1987). In contrast, communal notions put weight on the bonds between people. The unit of 'self' is shared, rather than individuated (Mills and Clark 1982). The self become the 'us' or 'we', rather than the 'I'. Seeing social support within the boundaries of the crystalized self means there is a tabulating of effort-out and effort-in on a tit-for-tat basis. The central question is 'what did I get?' in relation to 'what did I give?' In comparison, when the self is based on the 'we', the question becomes 'how did the social unit to which I belong benefit?' This does not mean that self-reliance does not allow for the inclusion and involvement with others. Nevertheless, self-reliance views relationships in terms of exchange principles, rather than obligations and mutuality (Clark *et al.* 1986).

Interestingly, there is actually much collectivism within American Society, even if it is not well-represented in Western ideology or American psychology. Sampson (1988) and Baumeister (1987) conclude that individualistic models overstate European and American culture's personification of individual ideals. This is even more true where subcultures of immigrants have entered American society and transported their communal ideologies. This not only impacts their lives, but leaks into the greater culture through their social involvement and through their cultural contributions as owners and managers of businesses, in the arts, and in politics. Thus, collectivist principles have entered American culture with the arrival of Italian-Americans, American Jews, African Americans, Hispanic Americans, and Asian Americans (Riger 1993; Sampson 1988).

This means that we should look for a balance between individual and collectivist notions when considering coping, as cultural roots have probably instilled both individual-based and collectively-oriented models for our thinking, behaviour, and emotional responding. A collectivist approach may be more true of women than men (Riger 1993) and of African Americans than WASPS, but these modes are in fact often blended and encompass aspects of each source. It is in this vein and towards these ends that we have embarked on a research programme to look at individualistic and communal coping and individualistic versus communal sense of mastery.

Individual versus communal-mastery

In a series of studies we examined whether we could construe the ensembled self as the base for action and effectance (Guisinger and Blatt 1994; Markus and Kitayama 1991, 1994) and apply it to Western samples. To do so, we developed a measure of communal-mastery and tested whether individuals see themselves as able to be effective in achieving their goals and coping with life challenges by virtue of their being attached to significant others.

As I have already discussed, effectance has almost entirely been studied from a view of the self as the operating agent and the progenitor of successful stress resistance. Thus, key stress resistance resources that have been examined look at individuals as independent actors who ascribe their goal attainment to personal initiative. This includes self-efficacy (Bandura 1982; 1997), mastery (Pearlin *et al.* 1981), hardiness (Kobasa 1979), and internal locus of control (Rotter 1966; Levenson 1981). This point is made clear in a research experience that we had studying men with severely debilitating chronic pulmonary disorder. The man being interviewed was wheel-chair bound, helped at every step by his devoted wife of 40 years. She plumped his pillows, made his meals, did the shopping, repaired minor household problems, and washed and bathed him. When asked by our interviewer who offered him support he answered 'I am totally independent. That's what's wrong with America. Everyone is dependent on others. I was raised to believe that you got it done yourself or it didn't get done'. And here lies the point. This is what he was *raised to believe*, and his current dependent circumstances were not going to alter that belief, however overwhelming the evidence.

The reliance of the self, in turn, has led to a negative valence being placed on dependence, which is often interpreted as a sign of weakness and unmanliness (Guisinger and Blatt 1994; Kitayama *et al.* 1997; Riger 1993; Sampson 1988; Triandis 1989). Collective action is viewed in the Western context of stress research as somehow lower than independent action and the use of supportive social ties is seen as a secondary, even inferior, coping mechanism. In this regard, it has been noted in a number of investigations that even when reaching out for social support from intimate others, people feel very uncomfortable (Hobfoll and Lerman 1989; Kaniasty and Norris, 2000).

This does not mean that ascribing a sense of personal agency in meeting life challenges is negative. In fact, given its cultural consistency and saliency as a valued self-belief, we would expect that those who have a sense of personal mastery or self-efficacy will be more effective at meeting life challenges. The research clearly bares this out, such that those who are higher in self-efficacy, hardiness, and personal mastery have been found to be more likely to take action when coping, rather than being passive or avoidant and are less likely to experience psychological distress when faced with even severely stressful circumstances. It can even be argued that this sense of self-effectance is a central organizing resource, and those who possess it are also more capable of rallying other resources when they need them (Bandura 1997; Holahan and Moos 1991; Kobasa and Puccetti 1983; Schwarzer 1992; Thoits 1994).

Communal-mastery

People's collective sense of agency may be a view of the self, even if less culturally manifest in the West. Lyons *et al.* (1998) suggest that understanding communal aspects of coping may be a key to further advances in examining the stress process. Those high in communal mastery might approach challenges by problem-solving in relation to others, rather than alone or in competition with others (Dunahoo *et al.* 1998). This would entail not only their use of social support, but their seeing their effectance as based on their being integrated in the social group. Even the nature of the challenge might not be seen so much as a personal threat, as much as a threat to the group's integrity or attachment to the group. Thus, they would not only use social support more, but might also be willing to make more self-sacrifice if relying on the group would be deleterious to others (Riley and Eckenrode 1986).

This raises the issue of the costs of social connectedness. Relying on others means that one is more socially attached, likely to incur more social obligations, and more likely to be exposed to the stress of others. Social attachments expose individuals to others' stress through the processes of stress contagion (Almeida and Kessler 1998; Kessler *et al.* 1985; Riley and Eckenrode 1986) and the pressure-cooker effect (Hobfoll and London 1986). More socially embedded individuals are likely to find themselves involved with others' lives in a way that increases their emotional and task burden. This translates to the fact that a more independent style may be more efficient for the self, but less effective for the group (Fukuyama 1995; Yamaguchi 1994). Thus, whereas a positive caring attitude toward others leads to well-being, a focus on others to exclusion of the self has been found to be related to greater psychological distress (Fritz and Helgeson 1998). A more socially interwoven style would more efficiently protect the group, but in some sense sacrifice the individual (Clark *et al.* 1986; Yamaguchi 1994).

Examining the correlates and impact of communal- versus self-mastery

In a first series of studies we compared the correlates and impact of personal agency and communal-mastery (Hobfoll *et al.* in press). A series of three studies were conducted to test our theoretical arguments and to develop a new measure of communal-mastery (see Appendix 4A). This first series of studies focused on university populations. To avoid repeating the mistaking of basing concepts on the 19-year-old college sophomore, we went to 2-year community colleges attended by older individuals who are largely coming to study part-time and either working full-time or homemakers. These studies were intended to explore the correlates of personal agency and communal-mastery with variables identified with the stress process (e.g. personal resources, coping, social support, and psychological distress) in order to judge their distinctiveness and overlap.

We hypothesized that personal agency would be more closely related than communal mastery to individualized modes of coping such as aggressive action and a more decisive–individualized action orientation, but less strongly related to indicators of social coping such as use of social joining to meet goals (i.e. coalition building), and levels of social support.

Communal-mastery, in contrast, is hypothesized as being more closely related to coping through greater use of social support and forming coalitions, less aggressive/antisocial action, and a communal leadership style, such that the individual leads by example rather than through use of authority. Compared to self-mastery, communal-mastery will be more strongly related to worries about the needs and views of others.

Our 10-item measure of communal-mastery had sound psychometric properties. Internal reliability was at a level usually considered acceptable for self-constructs (Pearlin *et al.* 1981; Scheier and Carver 1985; Schwarzer *et al.* 1997). As predicted, communal-mastery was a better predictor than self-mastery of prosocial coping and social support. Interestingly, communal-mastery was an equally good predictor as self-mastery of active-asocial kinds of coping.

Also as predicted, self-mastery was more strongly associated with lower levels of anger and depressive mood, as would be suggested by our thinking on the cost of connectiveness (Kessler *et al.* 1985). Those high in communal mastery were significantly lower in psychological distress than those low in communal mastery, but the influence of communal mastery was nevertheless not as strong as that of self-mastery. Hence although communal-mastery was related to lower psychological distress, it seems to come at a cost compared to self-mastery.

We had also predicted that self-mastery would be more strongly associated with aggressive/individualistic coping, but our findings did not bear this out. Two weak-significant correlations did support this hypothesis, those high in self-mastery using significantly more aggressive coping and those high in communal-mastery using significantly less antisocial coping. However, these correlations were not independent of age and gender. Women were more likely to report higher communal coping, consistent with the view of women's behaviour being more socially involved (Eagly 1987). Bandura *et al.* (2001) also found self-regulatory efficacy to be negatively related to transgressive behaviour, further suggesting that self-mastery is not related to aggressive action.

The superior predictive power of self-mastery over communal-mastery in some instances and of communal-mastery over self-mastery in other comparisons was generally consistent with predictions. Moreover, the pattern speaks to the discriminant validity of the two concepts as we have interpreted them (Kazdin 1992). It is notable that although communal mastery was derived, in part, from restructured self-mastery items, the two constructs are clearly distinguishable and their areas of non-overlap support each's construct validity.

Study 2 extended Study 1 using a larger sample, somewhat older and more representative of the community. We also investigated the association of communal-mastery and self-mastery with physical symptoms. As in the first study, we expected that communal-mastery should be positively related to active-asocial coping, in a similar manner to self-mastery. Communal-mastery should once again be more closely associated with social processes emblematic of prosocial coping and social support. Self-mastery should, in turn, be more strongly related to lower psychological distress, and less physical symptoms.

Communal-mastery was a consistently better predictor of prosocial coping and social support, as we had predicted. Also, as in Study 1, self-mastery was a stronger predictor of lower anger, depression, and physical symptoms. This suggests the greater 'efficiency' of personal agency compared with shared agency in meeting the goals of the individuated self. Communal-mastery was also effective, in that those high in communal-mastery had lower psychological distress and less symptoms than those low in communal-mastery. However, individuals can more directly attend to their personal agenda than they can when they interweave their goal-directed efforts with the needs of others whom they include as part of their collective (Kitayama *et al.* 1997; Markus and Kitayama 1991; Triandis 1989).

As in Study 1, neither self-mastery nor communal-mastery were related to individualistic–aggressive coping strategies. This suggests that individualism should not be impugned by presuming that it is alligned with the more aggressive, antisocial aspects of some individualistic societies as suggested by Rollo May (1953) or more recently by Hall and Barongan (1997). We have shown that antisocial copers are more individualistic, but the reverse does not hold (Dunahoo *et al.* 1998).

Study 3 results pointed to the cognitive underpinnings of these differences between communal-and self-mastery. In Study 3 we substituted a widely used generalized measure of self-efficacy (Schwarzer *et al.* 1997) as our indicator of personal agency. This allowed for a comparison of communal-mastery with a measure similar to self-mastery conceptually, but which has a different item pool. By so doing, we could examine the more conceptual distinctiveness between individualistic versus communal goal-directed orientations.

In Study 3 we again predicted that self-efficacy and communal-mastery would both be related to active-asocial coping. We further hypothesized that communal-mastery would be more closely related to prosocial coping and receipt of social support than self-efficacy. Similarly, we introduced a measure of social alienation. This permitted an examination of whether communal-mastery would be more closely related to social alienation (in the negative direction because of the way the alienation instrument is keyed to indicate less positive social relations) than self-efficacy.

We also added a set of more cognitive outcome variables in order to focus on how people construe their cognitions that might underlie their actions. We predicted that self-efficacy would be more strongly related to greater goal-directedness in the form of decision-related action (or 'initiative', Kuhl 1994). This follows because people high in communal orientation tend to be more cautious because they must carefully consider the well-being of others who share their setting (Fukuyama 1995; Triandis 1989). Those with a more individualistic orientation toward goal directedness tend to be quicker to decide and quicker to act. This also led us to predict that that self-efficacy would be more closely, negatively, related to individuals' concern about the role of powerful others, worry about social relationships, and fear of negative evaluation. Said another way, we expected that self-mastery would be more strongly related to not considering relationship factors.

Our findings indicated that self-efficacy was related to less concern with social relationships, less fear of negative censure of others, and less feeling that powerful others are in control than was communal-mastery. Communal-mastery appears to be related to greater concern for others, less alienation from social relationships, and more close attachments to a supportive social network from which satisfaction can be derived. These findings suggest that the cognitions that underlie people's behaviour fall in line with the cultural affordances that we have outlined for those whose sense of mastery rests in more individual versus ensembled spheres.

Examining the role of self- and communal-mastery among inner-city women

Having a validated measure that fit the basic theoretical cast that we had envisioned we turned to two more 'real-world' samples of adults who were challenged by considerable, chronic stressful life conditions. In the first of these studies, we examined inner-city women because they are a group that are subjected to multiple stressors due to poverty, violence, and gender-power disadvantages (Belle 1990; Seguin *et al.* 1995). If African American, they are likely to undergo additional stress associated with racism (Belle 1990; McLoyd 1990). Nevertheless, many inner-city women are able to rely on personal and social resources to aid their stress-resistance as well. Killingsworth-Rini *et al.* (1999) found that pregnant, inner-city women who possessed greater sense of mastery had healthier birth outcomes including greater gestational age and infant birth weight, controlling for the impact of stressful events in their lives. Ennis *et al.* (2000) also found that inner-city women with greater self-mastery had less depressive moods and that this partially offset the negative impact of economic stress.

There is reason to believe that both self-mastery and communal-mastery might contribute to inner-city women's well-being in the face of ongoing stress. Those high in self-mastery are likely to feel that they can rely on their inner strengths to overcome challenges (Pearlin *et al.* 1981). Communal-mastery may, in turn, act as a resources because it enables women to see that they can succeed by virtue of their close connections to others (see Taylor and Roberts 1995). The origins of communal-mastery suggest that it would be related to women maintaining a strong social network which they can rely upon not only for aid, but for the positive sense that these connections provide.

As outcome variables, we examined both depressive mood and anger. Depressive mood is important because it is related to poor functioning and emotional pain (Gotlib *et al.* 1995). We were also interested in anger because it is related to interpersonal difficulties and health difficulties (Johnson 1990). Anger tends to alienate potential support (Lane and Hobfoll 1992) and although there is less work on women's anger, women most certainly experience feelings of anger and are affected by it (Thomas 1993).

We also considered social support as an important outcome variable. Stressful conditions tend to deteriorate support, just when people most need it (Kaniasty and Norris 1993). In their support deterioration model, Kaniasty and Norris (1993) suggest that the loss of support heightens people's vulnerability to the ongoing stress process. Given inner-city women's chronic stress exposure, this makes the study of sustaining social support particularly poignant in such circumstances.

We examined a group of 61 inner-city women over a nine-month period. Women were interviewed at one of two community health clinics and three months and nine months later. Women were low income (82 per cent with incomes below $15,000 per year), averaged about 21 years of age, and 63 per cent had finished high school, with 33 per cent not having completed high school. The majority were African American ($n = 41$), with the remainder ($n = 20$) being European American.

They were administered a broad battery of questionnaires during the three interviews. These included measures of stress, depressive mood, anger, social support satisfaction, number of intimate supporters, self-mastery, and communal-mastery. As a measure of stress we used the material stress subscale of the Conservation of Resources Evaluation (the COR-E) that measures people's report of losses in the material domain over the prior three months (Hobfoll and Lilly 1993). These include loss of transportation, necessary appliances (e.g. washing machine, stove), loss of ability to purchase proper clothing, etc. Prior studies have found resource loss to be a strong predictor of stress outcomes (Freedy *et al.* 1992, 1994; Ironson *et al.* 1997). We added material loss scores at Time-1 and Time-2 ($á = 0.89$) to assess women's stress experience over this six-month period.

The findings generally supported our predictions. Predicting depressive mood at the final follow-up, stress was related to increased depressive mood over and above the impact of initial depressive mood. Both self-mastery and communal-mastery were related to lower depressive mood. However, neither mastery indicator made an independent increase in the explained variance over the other. Similarly for anger, stress was related to greater anger at follow-up controlling for initial and self-mastery and communal-mastery were related to lower anger at follow-up. In this case, each made a borderline ($p < 0.10$) independent contribution to the explained variance after the other was entered. Hence, both self-mastery and communal-mastery were related to lower psychological distress over this nine-month period. The results indicated that neither self-nor communal-mastery had a stronger influence on emotional outcomes than the other. This suggests that the active ingredient within mastery may not be the self-dominant aspect (Bandura 1997). Rather, it would appear that routes to success may be exerted via self or communal processes.

Turning to social support, communal-mastery was more closely related to preserving social support than self-mastery. Stress was not related to support satisfaction at follow-up, controlling for initial support satisfaction. However, both self-mastery and communal-mastery were related to increased support satisfaction. In addition, inclusion of communal-mastery in the final model step had a borderline independent effect, but self-mastery did not. Looking at number of intimate supporters, stress was found to be related to decreased support. More pointedly, communal-mastery, but not self-mastery, was related to increased number of intimate supporters. Further, communal-mastery had an independent influence on increasing number of supporters, over and above the influence of self-mastery.

We cannot conclude from this investigation whether support maintenance is a matter of perceived support or taps the actual supportive transactions that women received. Just as the self-focused view may lead to self illusions, a communally focused view may lead women to pay closer attention to their social connections. Still, because, research has found that perceptions of social support are paramount (Sarason *et al.* 1990), communal-mastery may be more closely linked with such perceptions.

Native American culture and life circumstances

In a final study of how communal-versus self-mastery acted as resistance resources for people undergoing high levels of chronic life stress, we investigated these resources among

Native American women living on Indian Reservations in the Pacific Northwest. Native American culture is traditionally based on collectivist principles. It emphasizes fitting in, reliance on the social group, and being intertwined with others on the family and tribal levels (LaFromboise 1992; Sutton and Nose 1996). The cultural ideal is to succeed as part of the group and family. If individuals in the West tend to be individuated (Baumeister 1987; Sampson 1988), Native Americans perceive less distinct boundaries between the self and others (Smith 1981). This makes Native Americans an excellent group for comparing the influence of self- versus communal-mastery).

Native Americans are among the poorest ethnic groups in the US and those living on reservations have little economic opportunity (Mihesuah 1996). The poverty experienced by reservation-based Indians has been called a state of mental health crisis (Grossman *et al.* 1994; Fujiura *et al.* 1998). Those few studies that have been conducted on Native Americans have mainly addressed their disability, alcoholism, drug use, and alienation (Blum *et al.* 1992; Debruyn *et al.* 1992; Nelson *et al.* 1992; Robin *et al.* 1997). There have been almost no studies of factors linked to their resilience, nor that have addressed Native Americans' coping from a culturally consonant perspective. By examining Native Americans' stress resistance as a product of their communal-mastery it may be possible to provide insight into culturally based resources that serve Native Americans confronting the considerable stressors they encounter. By studying the resilience of Native Americans, we may also illuminate the culturally nested nature of stress resistance.

Native Americans responded to questionnaires that assessed their self-mastery and communal-mastery (Hobfoll *et al.* in press). Because of the nature of their collectivist culture and worldview, we hypothesized that communal-mastery would be a more central resistance resource for these women than their sense of self-mastery. We also assessed their depressive mood and anger as indications of their psychological distress (Gotlib *et al.* 1995; Johnson 1990; Spielberger 1985; Thomas 1993). In order to examine stress in their lives, we assessed their resource loss during the prior three months. We looked at a broad spectrum of resource loss, including object resources (e.g. car, washing machine), personal resources (e.g. self-esteem, job skills), condition resources (e.g. stable employment), and energy resources (e.g. credit, health insurance) (Hobfoll 1988, 1998).

We predicted that women who were high in communal-mastery would be less negatively impacted by high stress circumstances than women who were low in communal-mastery. In contrast, we did not think the two groups would differ greatly when not experiencing high stress conditions. This has been called a stress-buffering effect. Due to their communal heritage, we also hypothesized that women would be more strongly impacted by their sense of communal-mastery than their sense of self-mastery. We further reasoned that the beneficial impact of communal-mastery would be independent of the impact of social support. This is important because communal-mastery and social support are potentially overlapping as both relate to an attachment with a strong social network. This follows because within communal cultures people do not necessarily rely more on social support. Rather, they view their success as interwoven with beliefs surrounding the social group as the primary operative in their sense of how they see themselves and how they construct and approach goals.

We recruited 160 women at community centers that foster educational and social activities at Little Big Horn, Dull Knife, Blackfoot, and Fort Bellnap reservations in rural Montana. These centers are major interaction points within the community and include women with wide levels of educational attainment. The reservations are extremely rural and sparsely populated. To participate in the study women needed to be: (1) Native American, (2) unmarried, and (3) between the ages of 16 and 29. These criteria were set in order to target single women because of their higher risk for economic difficulties and special health needs due to their being in their sexually active years. Of the original 160 women, 64 per cent completed questionnaires three months later. They were on an average 20 years of age, had incomes almost uniformly well below the poverty level, and 67 per cent were unemployed (although some of these were in school). Tribal affiliations was as follows: Assininboine (3.8 per cent); Blackfeet (25.5 per cent), Crow (22.9 per cent); Gros Ventre (1.3 per cent), Northern Cheyenne (26.8 per cent); Sioux (4.5 per cent), other/mixed (15 per cent). The largest percentage were Catholic (41.9 per cent), Native American Church (14.6 per cent), and Protestant (8.9 per cent).

Our results consistently supported our hypotheses. Native American women who were higher in communal-mastery were less negatively affected by increasing stressful conditions than women who were lower on communal-mastery. Self-mastery was also related to lower anger and depressive mood. However, as we predicted based on cultural considerations, the impact of self-mastery on stress resistance was not found to be independent of the impact of communal-mastery. Thus, women who were high in communal-mastery were less likely to increase in anger or depressive mood, even when confronted with stressful life conditions. Finally, the impact of communal-mastery was independent of the influence of social support. Thus although social support and communal-mastery were strongly correlated, communal-mastery's contribution was almost entirely independent of social support. It is important to underscore that these findings were noted prospectively, controlling for initial anger and depression levels.

Markus and Kitayama (1991) theorized that individuals from collectivist cultures organize their sense of self according to meanings and practices that promote the fundamental nature of connectedness with others. The current study extends this notion to people's action-orientation, whereas prior studies have focused on the formation and preservation of self-esteem versus self-criticism (Kityama et al. 1997). It is important to note that if we had only studied self-mastery or self-efficacy, as prior studies have done, we would have found support for these self-oriented concepts. But the cultural dominance of people's communal construction of the self would have been lost. Kitayama et al. (1997) highlight that 'psychological processes and a cultural system are mutually constitutive'. Psychological tendencies and processes both support individuals actions within their cultural context and how they cognitively construe these situations. For Native American women, the way they construed their actions were culturally consistent with a collectivist more than an individualistic viewpoint.

The findings also have implications for extending efficacy and self-regulation theories across East–West boundaries. Across these cultures, people have an advantage in withstanding stress if they are active in engaging their environment successfully. They need positive expectations about their ability to problem solve and meet challenges. Berry (1969) termed this the *etic* (culture-common) element. However, the expression of that efficacy would appear also to be characterized by an *emic* (culture-specific) element. This emic element hinges on whether the active agent is the crystalized self or the socially embedded self (Guisinger and Blatt 1994).

Examining resiliency in cultural context

Our findings suggest that the almost sole reliance on personal agency in the stress literature limits our understanding about the possible role that attachments to others has for the self. From an individualistic viewpoint, others are seen as supporting the self, providing love and instrumental help, and creating a sense of belonging. In the collectivist schema, the self–other boundary is less clear. The self and other are interconnected from an action and decision viewpoint. In an extreme case, there may exist no self that is separated from the collective. What I have tried to illustrate in this chapter and through these studies is that these different selves relate to different meanings and actions that are taken in the service of coping with difficult life circumstances.

Personal agency is linked to acting more assertively, being more independent from others, and worrying less about social relationships. Communal-mastery, in contrast, is linked closely to social means of coping, looking to social support, and greater inter-dependence. This distinction, however, should not be exaggerated as indicating that individualistic views of agency are linked to antisocial processes as Hall and Barongan (1997) suggested. Personal agency is less communal, and in some ways more asocial, but it is not linked to antisocial coping. We found those with higher sense of self agency to also be more socially involved than those low in self agency. This is a key theoretical point because even in individualistic cultures people have deep social bonds, exist as colleagues, friends, lovers, partners, and group members. They construct social goals and become debilitated if socially isolated. The independent self is not a social hermit and the ensembled self is not inextricably enmeshed with others and entirely dependent (Guisenger and Blatt 1994). Instead, these concepts exist on a continuum in which, 'Within a given culture . . . individuals will vary in the extent to which they are good cultural representatives and construe the self in the mandated way' (Markus and Kitayama 1991, p. 226).

Until this point, our research has examined generalized mastery tendencies that are decon-textualized. Bandura (1997) instead has emphasized study of self-efficacy *vis a vis* target goals. Our work falls more in line with seeing self-efficacy and self-mastery as general personality traits or styles, as has most research to date on mastery, hardiness, and locus of control (Pearlin *et al.* 1981; Thoits 1994). Schwarzer (1992) has re-conceptualized self-efficacy as a generalized personality trait or style as well. Using his scale, as we did in one of our studies, this alternative view of self-efficacy is being investigated in Eastern and Western cultures. It is our intent to examine context-specific communal-mastery in future studies in order to bet-ter understand in which contexts self-mastery versus communal-mastery are more strongly related to how people cope and their resiliency in the face of different kinds of stressors.

In conclusion, we see communal-mastery as a viable construct that has the potential for widening our multicultural view of stress resistance and resiliency. It is not a better way of doing things; it is another way. Nor is it more humane, or in all instances even more socially involved. Communal processes often demand isolation in order to sacrifice for the group and preservation of privacy and borders between people in their social worlds in order to preserve honor. Moreover, given the Western emphasis on self-esteem, many aspects of communal-mastery may be experienced by Westerners as demeaning of the self. For example, women have experienced greater work advancement and equality in individual-istic cultures than in communal cultures.

Future research might also examine other foci of mastery other than on the dimension of independent self versus communal self. For example, in familial cultures the family group is seen as the central domain of agency, not the individual or the broader social collective (Fukuyama 1995). Hence a culture could be individual-familial, collective-familial, individual-non-familial, or collective non-familial. Furthering our understanding of these levels of cultural affordances and self-construels will aid our general understanding of both stress resistance and how the self operates within cultures. Clearly our work is preliminary and only represents first steps, but it will hopefully lead to knew insights into the process of resiliency on that is not defined within a single culture.

Acknowledgements

This research was made possible through the support of the NIMH Office of AIDS Research, Grant #RO1 MH45669 and the Applied Psychology Center which was founded through the support of the Ohio Board of Regents. I would also like to thank Kristen Mickelson for her helpful comments. I am grateful to the study participants and to the Tribal Councils of the Little Big Horn, Dull Knife, Blackfoot, and Fort Bellnap Reservations for their support.

Appendix 4A. Communal-mastery scale items

1. By joining with friends and family, I have a great deal of control over the things that happen to me.
2. Working together with friends and family I can solve many of the problems I have.
3. There is little I can do to change many of the important things in my life, even with the help of my family and friends (reverse coded).
4. Working together with people close to me I can overcome most of the problems I have.
5. What happens to me in the future mostly depends on my ability to work well with others.
6. I can do just about anything I set my mind to do because I have the support of those close to me.
7. With the help of those close to me I have more control over my life.
8. What happen to me in the future mostly depends on my being supported by friends, family, or colleagues.
9. I can meet my goals by helping others meet their goals.
10. Friends, family, and colleagues mainly get in the way of my accomplishing goals (reverse coded).

References

Aldwin, C. M. (1994). *Stress, coping, and development: An integrative perspective*. New York: Guilford Press.

Almeida, D. M. and Kessler, R. C. (1998). Everyday stressors and gender differences in daily distress. *Journal of Personality and Social Psychology*, **75**, 670–80.

Asch, S. E. (1955). Opinions and social pressure. *Scientific American*, 31–5.

Bandura, A. (1982). Self-efficacy mechanism in human agency. *American Psychologist*, **37**, 122–47.

—— (1997). *Self efficacy: The exercise of control*. New York: W. H. Freemann & Company.

Bandura, A., Caprara, C., Barbaranelli, C., Pastorelli, and Regalia, G. V. (2001). Sociocognitive self-regulatory mechanisms governing transgressive behavior. *Journal of Personality and Social Psychology*, **80**, 125–35.

Baumeister, R. F. (1987). How the self became a problem: A psychological review of historical research. *Journal of Personality and Social Psychology*, **52**, 163–76.

Belle, D. (1990). Poverty and women's mental health. *American Psychologist*, **45**, 385–9.

Berry, J. W. (1969). On cross-cultural comparability. *International Journal of Psychology*, **4**, 119–28.

Blum, R. W., Harmon, B., Harris, L., Bergeisen, L., and Resnick, M. D. (1992). American-Indian Alaska native youth health. *Journal of the American Medical Association*, **267**, 1637–44.

Bowlby, J. (1969). *Attachment and loss*. N. Y., New York: Basic Books.

Carroll, L. (1987). Through the looking-glass. Topsfield, MA: Salem House.

Clark, M. S., Mills, J., and Powell, M. C. (1986). Keeping track of needs in communal and exchange relationships. *Journal of Personality and Social Psychology*, **51**, 333–8.

Debruyn, L. M., Lujan, C. C., and May, P. A. (1992). A comparative study of abused and neglected American-Indian children in the Southwest. *Social Science and Medicine*, **35**, 305–15.

DeLeon, D. (1978). *The American as anarchist: Reflections on indigenous radicalism*. Baltimore: John Hopkins University Press.

Dunahoo, C. L., Hobfoll, S. E., Monnier, J., Hulsizer, M. R, and Johnson, R. (1998). There's more than rugged individualism in coping. Part 1: Even the Lone Ranger had Tonto. *Anxiety, Stress, and Coping*, **11**, 137–65.

Durkheim, E. (1995/1897). Forms of social solidarity and the division of labour and social differentiation, in F. Anthias and M. P. Kelly (eds.), *Sociological debates: Thinking about the 'social'*, pp. 171–86. Dartford, UK: Greenwich University Press.

Eagly, A. H. (1987). *Sex differences in social behavior: A social-role interpretation*. Hillsdale, NJ: Erlbaum.

Eliot, T. S. (1989). *Homage to John Dryer: Three essays on poetry of the seventeenth century*. Times Literary Supplement [reprint].

Emerson, R. W. (1841). *Self reliance*. New York: Thomas Crowell.

Ennis, N., Hobfoll, S. E., and Schroder, K. E. E. (2000). Money doesn't talk, it swears: How economic stress and resistance resources impact inner-city women's depressive mood. *American Journal of Community Psychology*, **28**, 149–73.

Freedy, J. R., Saladin, M. E., Kilpatrick, D. G., Resnick, H. S., and Saunders, B. E. (1994). Understanding acute psychological distress following natural disaster. *Journal of Traumatic Stress*, **7**, 257–73.

——Shaw, D. L., Jarrell, M. P., and Masters, C. R. (1992). Towards an understanding of the psychological impact of natural disasters: An application of the conservation of resources stress model. *Journal of Traumatic Stress*, **5**, 441–54.

Fritz, H. L. and Helgeson, V. S. (1998). Distinctions of unmitigated communion from communion: Self-neglect and over involvement with others. *Journal of Personality and Social Psychology*, **75**, 121–40.

Fujiura, G. T., Yamaki, K., and Czechowicz, S. (1998). Disability among ethnic and racial minorities in the United States. *Journal of Disability and Human Development*, **9**, 111–27.

Fukuyama, F. (1995). *Trust: The social virtues and the creation of prosperity*. New York: Free Press.

Gerth, H. H. and Mills, C. W. (1946). *From Max Weber: Essays in sociology*. New York: Oxford University Press.

Golovine, N. N. (1931). *The Russian army in the World War*. New Haven, CT: Yale University Press.

Gotlib, I., Lewinsohn, P. M., and Seeley, J. R. (1995). Symptoms versus a diagnosis of depression: Differences in psychosocial functioning. *Journal of Consulting and Clinical Psychology*, **63**, 90–100.

Grossman, D. C., Krieger, J. W., Sugarman, J. R., and Forquera, R. A. (1994). Health status of urban American Indians and Alaska natives: A population-based study. *Journal of the American Medical Association*, **271**, 845–50.

Guisinger, S. and Blatt, S. J. (1994). Individuality and relatedness: Evolution of a fundamental dialectic. *American Psychologist*, **49**, 104–11.

Hall, G. C. and Barongan, C. (1997). Prevention of sexual aggression: Sociocultural risk and protective factors. *American Psychologist*, **52**, 5–14.

Hobfoll, S. E. (1988). *The ecology of stress*. New York: Hemisphere Publishing Corporation.

—— (1998). *Stress, culture, and community: The psychology and philosophy of stress*. New York: Plenum.

—— Jackson, A., Young, S., Pierce, C. A., and Hobfoll, I. H. The impact of communal-mastery versus self-mastery on emotional outcomes during stressful conditions: A prospective study of Native American women. *American Journal of Community Psychology* (in press).

—— and Lerman, M. (1989). Predicting receipt of social support: A longitudinal study of parents' reactions to their child's illness. *Health Psychology*, **8**, 61–77.

—— and Lilly, R. S. (1993). Resource conservation as a strategy for community psychology. *Journal of Community Psychology*, **21**, 128–48.

—— and London, P. (1986). The relationship of self-concept and social support to emotional distress among women during war. *Journal of Social and Clinical Psychology*, **4**, 189–203.

Hobfoll, S. E., Schröder, K. E. E., Wells, M., and Malek, M. Communal versus individualistic construction of sense of mastery in the facing life challenges. *Journal of Social and Clinical Psychology* (in press).

Holahan, C. J. and Moos, R. H. (1991). Life stressors, personal and social resources and depression: A four-year structural model. *Journal of Abnormal Psychology*, **100**, 31–8.

Ironson, G., Wynings, C., Schneiderman, N., Baum, A., Rodriguez, M., Greenwood, D. *et al.* (1997). Posttraumatic stress symptoms, intrusive thoughts, loss, and immune function after Hurricane Andrew. *Psychosomatic Medicine*, **59**, 128–41.

Jahoda, M. (1958). *Current concepts on positive mental health; a report to the staff director, Jack R. Ewalt, 1958*. New York: Basic Books.

Johnson, E. H. (1990). *The deadly emotions: The role of anger, hostility, and aggression in health and emotional well-being*. New York: Praeger.

Kaniasty, K. and Norris, F. (1993). A test of the social support deterioration model in the context of natural disaster. *Journal of Personality and Social Psychology*, **64**, 395–408.

—— —— (2000). Help-seeking comfort and receiving social support: The role of ethnicity and context of need. *American Journal of Community Psychology*, **28**(4), 545–81.

Kazdin, A. (1992). *Research design in clinical psychology*. New York: Oxford.

Kessler, R. C., McLeod, J. D., and **Wethington, E.** (1985). The costs of caring: A perspective on the relationship between sex and psychological distress, in I. G. Sarason and C. R. Sarason (eds.), *Social support: Theory, research and application*. The Hague: Martinus.

Killingsworth Rini, C., Dunkel-Schetter, C., Wadhwa, P. D., and Sandman, C. A. (1999). Psychological adaptation and birth outcomes: The role of personal resources, stress, and sociocultural context in pregnancy. *Health Psychology*, **18**, 333–45.

Kitayama, S., Markus, H. R., Matsumoto, H., and Norasakkunkit, V. (1997). Individual and collective processes in the construction of the self: Self-enhancement in the United States and self-criticism in Japan. *Journal of Personality and Social Psychology*, **72**, 1245–67.

Klein, M. (1964). *After alienation: American novels in mid-century*. Cleveland: World Publishing.

Kobasa, S. C. (1979). Stressful life events, personality, and health: An inquiry into hardiness. *Journal of Personality and Social Psychology*, **37**, 1–11.

—— and **Puccetti, M. C.** (1983). Personality and social resources in stress resistance. *Journal of Personality and Social Psychology*, **45**, 839–50.

Kuhl, J. (1994). Action versus state orientation: Psychometric properties of the Action Control Scale (ACS-90), in J. Kuhl and J. Beckmann (eds.), *Volition and personality: Action versus state orientation*, pp. 47–59. Seattle: Hogrefe and Huber Publishers.

LaFromboise, T. D. (1992). An interpersonal analysis of affinity, clarification, and helpful responses with American Indians. *Professional Psychology: Research and Practice*, **23**, 281–6.

Lane, C. and **Hobfoll, S. E.** (1992). How loss affects anger and alienates potential supporters. *Journal of Consulting and Clinical Psychology*, **60**, 935–42.

Levenson, H. (1981). Differentiating among internality, powerful others, and chance, in H. M. Lefcourt (ed.), *Research with the locus of control construct, Vol. 1: Assessment methods*, pp. 15–63. New York: Academic Press.

Lyons, R. F., Mickelson, K. D., Sullivan, M. J., and **Coyne, J. C.** (1998). Coping as a communal process. *Journal of Social and Personal Relationships*, **15**, 579–605.

Markus, H. R. and **Kitayama, S.** (1991). Culture and the self: Implications for cognition, emotion, and motivation. *Psychological Review*, **98**, 224–53.

—— —— (1994). A collective fear of the collective: Implications for selves and theories of selves. *Personality and Social Psychology Bulletin*, **20**, 568–79.

May, R. (1953). *Man's search for himself*. New York: Norton.

McLoyd, V. C. (1990). The impact of economic hardship on black families and children: Psychological distress, parenting, and socioemotional development. *Child Development*, **61**, 311–46.

Mihesuah, D. A. (1996). *American Indians: Stereotypes and realities*. Atlanta, GA: Clarity Press.

Milgram, S. (1963). Behavioral study of obedience. *Journal of Abnormal and Social Psychology*, **67**, 371–78.

Mills, K. and **Clark, M. S.** (1982). Communal and exchange relationships, in L. Wheeler (ed.), *Review of personality and social psychology*, Vol. 3. Beverly Hills, CA: Sage.

Nelson, S. H., McCoy, G. F., Stetter, M., and **Vanderwagen, W. C.** (1992). An overview of mental health services for American-Indians and Alaska natives in the 1990s. *Hospital and Community Psychiatry*, **43**, 257–61.

Pearlin, L. I., Lieberman, M. A., Menaghan, E. G., and **Mullan, J. T.** (1981). The stress process. *Journal of Health and Social Behaviour*, **22**, 337–56.

Perloff, R. (1987). Self-interest and personal responsibility redux. *American Psychologist*, **42**(1), 3–11.

Riley, D. and Eckenrode, J. (1986). Social ties: Subgroup differences in costs and benefits. *Journal of Personality and Social Psychology*, **51**, 770–8.

Riger, S. (1993). What's wrong with empowerment. *American Journal of Community Psychology*, **21**, 279–92.

Robin, R. W., Chester, B., Rasmussen, J. K., Jaranson, J. M., and Goldman, D. (1997). Prevalence, characteristics, and impact of childhood sexual abuse in a Southwestern American Indian tribe. *Child Abuse and Neglect*, **21**, 769–87.

Rokeach, M. (1960). *The open and closed mind; investigations into the nature of belief systems and personality systems*. New York, NY: Basic Books.

Rotter, J. B. (1966). Generalized expectancies for internal versus external control of reinforcement. Psychological *Monographs*, **80**, (Whole No. 609).

Sampson, E. E. (1988). The debate on individualism: Indigenous psychologies of the individual and their role in personal and societal functioning. *American Psychologist*, **43**, 15–22.

Sarason, B. R., Pierce, G. R., and Sarason, I. G. (1990). Social support: The sense of acceptance and the role of relationships, in B. R. Sarason, I. G. Sarason, and G. R. Pierce (eds.), *Social support: An interactional view*, pp. 97–128. New York: Wiley.

Scheier, M. F. and Carver, C. S. (1985). Optimism, coping, and health: Assessment and implications of generalized outcome expectancies. *Health Psychology*, **4**, 219–47.

Schwarzer, R. (1992). Self-efficacy in the adoption and maintenance of health behaviors: Theoretical approaches and a new model, in R. Schwarzer (ed.), *Self-efficacy: Thought control of action*, pp. 217–43. Washington, DC: Hemisphere Publishing Corporation.

Schwarzer, R., Bäßler, J., Kwiatek, P., Schröder, K., and Zhang, J. X. (1997). The assessment of optimistic self-beliefs: Comparison of the German, Spanish, and Chinese versions of the general self-efficacy scale. *Applied Psychology: An International Review*, **46**, 69–88.

Seguin, L., Potvin., L., St. Denis, M., and Loiselle, J. (1995). Chronic stressors, social support, and depression during pregnancy. *Obstetrics and Gynaecology*, **85**, 583–9.

Skinner, E. A. (1996). A guide to the construct of control. *Journal of Personality and Social Psychology*, **71**, 549–70.

Smith, J. (1981). Self and experience in Maori culture, in P. Heelas and A. Lock (eds.), *Indigeneous psychologies: The anthropology of the self*, pp. 145–59. London: Academic Press.

Spence, J. T. (1985). Achievement American style: The rewards and costs of individualism. *American Psychologist*, **40**(12), 1285–95.

Spielberger, C. D., Johnson, E. H., Russell, S. F., Crane, R. J., Jacobs, G. A., and Worden, T. J. (1985). The experience and expression of anger. Construction and validation of an anger expression scale, in M. A. Chesney and R. H. Rosenman (eds.), *Anger and hostility in cardiovascular and behavioral disorders*, pp. 5–30. Washington, DC: Hemisphere.

Sutton, C. T. and Nose, M. (1996). American Indian families: An overview, in M. McGoldrick, J. Giordano, and J. K. Pears (eds.), *Ethnicity and family therapy*, pp. 31–44. New York: Guilford.

Taylor, F. W. (1911). *The principles of scientific management*. New York: Harper & Brothers.

Taylor, R. D. and Roberts, D. (1995). Kinship support and maternal adolescent well-being in economically disadvantaged African American Families. *Child Development*, **66**, 1585–97.

Thoits, P. (1994). Stressors and problem-solving: the individual as psychological activist. *Journal of Health and Social Behaviour*, **35**, 143–60.

Thomas, S. P. (1993). *Women and anger*. New York: Springer.

Triandis, H. C. (1989). Self and social behavior in differing cultural contexts. *Psychological Review*, **96**, 269–89.

Weitraub, K. J. (1978). *The value of the individual: Self and circumstance in autobiography.* Chicago: University of Chicago Press.

Whyte, W. H. (1960). *The uncoscious before Freud.* New York: Basic Books.

Wolff, T. (1987). *The bonfire of the vanities.* New York: Farrer.

Yamaguchi, S. (1994). Collectivism among the Japanese: A perspective from the self. In Kim, U., Triandis, H., Kâ_itçiba_i, Ç., Choi, S., and Yoon G., (eds.), *Individualism and collectivism: Theory, method and applications. Cross-cultural research and methodology series*, Vol. 18. Thousand Oaks, CA: Sage.

CHAPTER 5

WORK STRESS AND COPING IN ORGANIZATIONS: PROGRESS AND PROSPECTS

RONALD J. BURKE

In 1979 I undertook a review of the published literature examining coping with work stress in organizational settings (Burke and Weir 1980). The literature was just beginning to accumulate and was varied. I concluded my review with a suggested research framework which built heavily on the then recent writing and research of Richard Lazarus and his colleagues (Lazarus and Folkman 1984). This group proposed a transactional model of stress and coping that included both cognitive and emotional dimensions, building heavily on the concept of appraisal. They also advocated an approach to research using their model that was intrapersonal and processual as well as contributing a multi-item measure of coping behaviours, the *Ways of Coping Checklist* (Folkman and Lazarus 1988). We appeared to be on the threshold of ground-breaking research and writing on stress and coping in 1980.

Unfortunately, anticipated progress in our understanding of coping processes in organizations has been hard to come by. I did not test the integrative research model I proposed in 1980, and few others did either. There has been a tremendous amount of attention devoted to coping processes since that time, but the quality and value of much of this work has come into question. Coping is a complex process; perhaps our expectations were too high.

This chapter selectively reviews the coping literature, focusing on the workplace, that has appeared since 1980. It summarizes some firm conclusions about coping with work stress supported by research findings. The question of why so little understanding of stress and coping at work has been achieved is also addressed. Future research issues are identified as well. A discussion of group-level and organizational-level interventions is provided since some writers (Pearlin 1991) have suggested that individual-level coping with stresses in the workplace is likely to have limited value.

This chapter is structured as follows:

- a 1980 perspective
- why we fell short
- manager's well-being and health
- organizational change, individual coping strategies and psychological effects
- improving coping in organizations
- where do we go from here.

A 1980 perspective

Occupational stress or job stress has been studied extensively in organizational behaviour for about 20 years, about as long as researchers have studied coping processes. Research in this field, stress is best viewed as a field rather than as a single variable, deals with the negative effects of the workplace environment on an employee's health and well-being (Burke 1988). It is a field of study and practice emphasizing the relationship of stimuli or events in the workplace and unhealthy responses of the people working there.

The level of stress a person experiences, and the negative effects that may occur, depends on how, and how well, the person copes in stressful situations. Coping refers to efforts to master conditions that tax or exceed one's adaptive resources (Lazarus and Folkman 1984). These stress-incurring conditions may be harm, threat, or challenge. Stress and coping are seen as a dynamic process having four major components: (a) environmental stressors (demands, constraints, opportunities), (b) a cognitive appraisal of these stressors as representing situations in which the person is not sure how to respond and the stakes are high, (c) the experience of strain (physiologically or behaviourally), and (d) coping behaviours or coping strategies.

A framework for the study of coping in organizations

The vast majority of studies on coping with stress in organizations prior to 1980 had been carried out without reference to a theoretical model of coping behaviour. Instead, most of this literature either described coping behaviours, related these behaviours to some antecedents or consequences, or offered a taxonomy of coping responses.

I concluded my 1979 chapter with a model of coping behaviour in organizations (see Fig. 5.1) built on earlier frameworks for the study and understanding of stress in the organizational environment. The purpose of creating a model was to integrate elements of

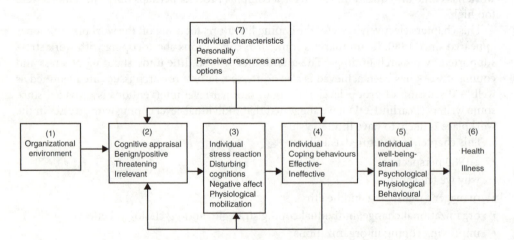

Figure 5.1 Model of coping with the stresses of managerial occupations.

the coping process into the more general stress paradigms so that greater emphasis would be given to individual coping responses in the research on organizational stress.

Organizational environment

Taking one component of the model at a time, the model begins with the panel *organizational environment*. This refers to a wide range of stimulus conditions in work environments which may become sources of stress for individuals. In a review article, Cooper and Marshall (1978) listed the following: sources intrinsic to the job (poor physical work conditions, time pressures); sources related to roles in the organization (role ambiguity, role conflict, responsibility for people); sources related to career development (underpromotion, lack of job security); sources connected with relationships at work (poor relations with boss, subordinates, colleagues); and sources related to organizational structure and climate (level of participation in decision-making, office politics).

Cognitive appraisal

The next panel refers to the mental process of placing a past, present, or future event into one of a series of evaluative categories depending on an individual's interpretation of that event for his well-being. Thus, an individual may consider an event to be irrelevant, benign/positive, or threatening (Lazarus 1999). The latter are events where individuals anticipate or experience some loss (self-esteem, a loved one), some personal injury, some barriers or obstacles to need fulfilment and some challenge where the outcome is uncertain. Such events motivate the individual to search for ways to cope.

Individual stress reactions

The next component in the model consists of individual reactions to the perception of threat. These reactions can have a number of manifestations such as the arousal of disturbing thoughts and images, negative feelings (anxiety, fear, depression), and physiological responses described as the 'fight-or-flight' response or as the body's general alarm response. The degree of the threat will influence the intensity of response and the motivation of the individual to seek a coping response.

Individual coping behaviours

The next panel in the sequence consists of the individual's conscious or sub-conscious selection of a response or set of responses to mitigate and overcome the stressful person–environment interaction. Different authors have made efforts to loosely classify coping behaviours according to their function, their form, and their quality. Coping responses had been distinguished in terms of whether the coping is directed at the environmental stressor or the resultant affect it elicits in the individual. A similar distinction was drawn between instrumental coping which is directed at altering the troubled transaction between the person and his environment and palliative coping which is directed at the regulation of emotional responses and reactions. Four coping modes are often included under the two main functions described above (the instrumental and the palliative regulation of emotions): (1) information seeking, (2) direct action, (3) inhibition of action, and (4) intrapsychic. These forms of coping may appear in anticipatory and corrective coping experiences and can be aimed at the environment or the self.

Coping behaviours may be effective or ineffective to varying degrees in improving the troubled person–environment relationship. Among the ineffective coping behaviours are those that might work in the short run but not in the long run, and those that appear to work but at the cost of the individual's morale, health, and life goals. This is most apparent in the case where an individual chronically uses certain palliative measures (such as alcohol, overeating, smoking, repression) to deal with stress in his or her life, and never confronts the actual problem. The outcome of the individual's coping behaviour, whether effective or ineffective (and to what degree) will be input to the ongoing cognitive appraisal process (the feedback loop shown in Fig. 5.1) and will influence the extent to the work-related strain experienced by the job incumbent. There are also certain coping methods referred to as self-management techniques (e.g. meditation) which can directly alter the individual stress reactions.

Individual strain/well-being

This panel refers to signs and symptoms of mental and physical strain which may become evident if the individual–work environment problems are not mitigated or resolved. These may be manifested as chronic disturbances of mood or cognitive processes, low morale, loss of energy, job dissatisfaction, psychosomatic symptoms, high blood pressure, high serum cholesterol, frequent dispensary visits, absenteeism, heavy drinking, disturbance in work and family relationships, and erratic behaviour, among others.

Health/illness

The end panel in the schema indicates that work-related strain, if prolonged and uncorrected, can eventually result in mental and physical breakdown (mental illness, coronary heart disease (CHD), hypertension, ulcer, etc.). This view was supported by the accumulating evidence which links work environment factors to illness in management populations.

Individual characteristics

There are a large number of individual characteristics which form an important group of variables mediating both cognitive appraisal processes (panel 2) and coping behaviours (panel 4) of individuals. These include personality traits, and perceived resources and options in the organizational and extraorganizational environment (home, community) as well as within oneself. Some of the individual characteristic factors which have been identified are the following:

(1) extent of individual's behavioural skill repertoire (assertiveness, problem-solving, conflict resolution);
(2) the extent and outcome of one's past experiences with similar stress;
(3) the individual's physical condition and mental state;
(4) the extent, availability, and quality of one's social support both at work and outside work;
(5) personality factors (self-esteem, flexibility-rigidity, Type A);
(6) how much advance warning one has of an approaching stressful event;

(7) how constrained the individual typically is by social, cultural, or organizational norms;

(8) the intensity and extent of other chronic and/or discrete stressful life events (financial problems, alcoholic spouse);

(9) the extent and quality of organizational processes and programmes which aid or facilitate an individual's instrumental or palliative coping efforts (e.g. training); and

(10) the extent to which the individual feels locked-in.

The model easily expands to include variables such as environmental turbulence at the organizational level, and performance in work and non-work roles, at the individual level.

Why we fell short

We optimistically believed we were on the threshold of significant breakthroughs in our understanding of work stress and coping in organizations in 1980. As I write this chapter, those feelings of optimism have been tempered or replaced by a less sanguine view of our understanding of individual coping processes in organizations.

Coping is a complex and dynamic process. One can debate whether questionnaires can even tap this reality (Coyne and Gottlieb 1996; Dewe 2000; Dewe and Guest 1990; Ptacek et al. 1994). How does one assess the adequacy/usefulness of resources from external sources? How can one measure the effectiveness of a particular coping strategy as opposed to whether or not the respondent used it (Stone et al. 1988, 1991)? How does one tap the transactional nature of coping? Coping strategies are often revised in real-time as new data emerges. There is also a span of time between use of a coping strategy and its success. In addition, one's coping efforts often create additional problems (Schoenpflug and Battman 1988). Coping may include periods of trial and error. An action can be effective in the short run but become less effective over time. Coping activities inevitably involve feedback loops (Edwards 1988).

Carver (1996) lists some provocative, central, and still unanswered questions about coping.

1. What is the ordinary balance of helpful coping to harmful coping? Do the ways people cope more typically facilitate positive outcomes or do they more typically interfere? (Or is coping really irrelevant—just whatever happens to go on while time passes and adaptation eventually takes place?)

2. Are some coping responses helpful in some circumstances but harmful in others? Is it critical that the coping responses selected by the person match the class of situation being confronted?

3. What outcome measure (or measures) should serve to validate coping as being successful or unsuccessful? Distress? Health? Task performance while under stress? Extent of rigidity of personality over time?

4. How long a time lag should there be between assessment of coping and assessment of the consequences of coping? Are there critical periods within which coping is most important, and after which it matters less?

5. Should coping be thought of as a volitional strategy or tactic, or should it be thought of as a *reaction?*

6. Does coping differ in fundamental ways from 'behaviour in general', or is coping simply behaviour that occurs under conditions of adversity?

7. Do the people's reports about the ways they coped tell us how they really coped, or only how they *think* they coped?

8. Does it make any sense to use the word cope when people are responding to challenges (opportunities), as opposed to threats (situations with potential for harm)?

He also notes that some coping responses are more harmful than helpful. The coping literature has become so diverse, so voluminous, to be 'unmanageable' (p. xii).

Sommerfield and McCrae (2000) write 'the explosion of interest in coping has yielded little and the field is in crisis' (p. 620). Hobfoll *et al.* (1998) observe that coping is probably the most widely studied topic in contemporary psychology. Lazarus (1999) concluded that the quality of research on stress and coping is not matched by its quantity.

Hobfoll *et al.* (1998) using the key words stress and coping found over 29,000 research articles published between 1984 and 1998. Sommerfield and McCrae (2000) used the term coping behaviour and found almost 14,000 articles published from 1962 to 1994. We have, during this time learned little about how coping processes operate and whether coping helps. This work has had no meaningful influence on interventions for managing stress. Critics of this research use words such as 'disappointing', 'tentative', 'modest', 'sterile', 'stagnated', and 'trivial' to characterize the coping literature (Sommerfield and McCrae 2000).

There is a huge gap between the transactional process theories of stress and adaptation and the methodology of most coping research. Process theories of stress and adaptation call for a longitudinal, process-oriented, ipsative–normative research design. Most research to date is between-person, cross-sectional, using paper and pencil measures that cannot capture the complex and dynamic nature of coping (Tennen *et al.* 2000).

Coping strategies are likely to be effective if they address or match demands of the stressor. Begley (1998) lists five reasons why it will be difficult to determine proper matches between a stressor and coping strategies chosen to respond to it. Coping strategies may reduce distress in short run and increase distress in the long run, or they may increase distress in the short run but decrease it in the long run. Coping strategies may reduce some forms of distress while increasing other forms of distress. Some coping strategies that may be effective may have large costs associated with them. Use of some resources to deal effectively with a particular stressor may increase risks or difficulties in other areas. The person may lack the means, skill, or motivation to effectively use a particular coping strategy.

It may also be important to be more realistic about what one might expect to be the contributions of coping. Coping may have only modest benefits (Menaghen and Merves 1984). First, individuals have already spent years coping and may have learned all that they can about it. In addition, as Pearlin (1991) writes, coping may be relatively ineffective in the workplace, a setting where group or organizational level strategies may be the only way to reduce strains caused by job stress. Finally, coping behaviours are influenced by characteristics of the person, particularly personality traits, and personality traits are very difficult to change.

Over the past decade, the models used to describe the experience of work stress have become more comprehensive with the role of coping occupying a central role in them. Yet coping remains poorly defined and inadequately measured (Dewe and Guest 1990).

Individual differences not only influence the perceptions of stress in the work environment and how demanding these stressors are, they also moderate the stress–strain relationship and the ways individuals cope with stress (Bolger 1990; Scheier *et al.* 1986; Schwartz and Stone 1993). Personality is one such variable (e.g. Type A, hardiness, locus of control, self-esteem, sense of coherence (SOC), negative affectivity).

Manager's well-being and health

Although the managerial job has been considered to be a demanding one (Burke 1988), there is considerable evidence that manager's and professional's psychological well-being and physical health are generally positive (the famous Whitehall studies). In this well known investigation, a large sample of British civil servants completed lengthy interviews and questionnaires as well as undertaking physical examinations over a number of years. The sample was divided into five levels based on occupational categories. Individuals in the highest level (e.g. directors, senior managers) were generally healthier than individuals in the lower categories (Marmot *et al.* 1991; Hemingway *et al.* 1997; Stansfeld *et al.* 1997). Explanations for these findings included both the nature of the jobs, with job control (greater at higher levels) being a significant factor, as well as type and amount of social support (Marmot *et al.* 1997, 1987, 2000; Marmot 1997; Stansfeld *et al.* 1998). These findings are consistent with studies examining the relationship of social class or socio-economic status and health. There are a number of factors under the umbrella of social class or socio-economic status that could account for these conclusions. These factors include education, income, health behaviours, help-seeking behaviours, the nature of the jobs and work experiences, aspects of coping behaviour, and attitudes and skills required to acquire and perform managerial and professional work. Other individual characteristics have also been shown to facilitate coping with stress.

Resources

Men and women in managerial jobs have many resources likely to be relevant to coping and health. These individuals are typically highly educated, come from family backgrounds likely to be middle or upper social classes, to have been exposed to family values supporting responsibility, discipline, achievement, and success, and to have developed a sense of confidence.

This educational experience, coupled with experiences in the work place, likely contribute to self-confidence, feelings of mastery and control, processes of goal-setting, and working towards the achievement of goals, some sense of empowerment, cognitive problem-solving skills, interpersonal problem-solving skills, and experiences in the use of all these resources.

Hardiness

Maddi and Kobassa (1984) undertook a large-scale study of senior managers looking at factors that buffer the harmful effects of stress. They collected data from 259 executives, over a period of several years, a longitudinal study, using both questionnaires and semi-structured interviews, as well as objective health indicators (e.g. blood pressure readings taken by physicians). They were most interested in high stress/low illness managers, believing that this group would have a distinctive personality and behavioural style. This constellation, which they termed hardiness, would help these managers cope with stresses so that resulting strains do not lead to illness. They found that hardiness, a personality and behaviour constellation, emerged as a key coping resource. They found that executives high on hardiness had low blood pressure as well as being low on psychological well-being indicators (anxiety, depression, suspiciousness).

Hardiness had three components; commitment, control, and challenge. Commitment refers to the state of being interested and involved completely in whatever the individual is doing. The opposite state is one of alienation. The individual is bored, uninvolved with activities they see as meaningless. Control refers to a belief that the individual can act and influence events that affect them. The opposite state, powerlessness, views individuals as passive victims of forces beyond their control. A sense of challenge refers to individual perceptions that though difficult at times, life is exciting. The opposite condition, a sense of threat, view life events in fearful and disruptive ways.

These three features, comprising hardiness, influence coping in significant ways. Individuals with a high sense of commitment, control, and challenge are more likely to respond to stressors with transformational than with regressive coping. Transformational coping involves interacting with and changing external demands in an optimistic and decisive way. Regressive coping involves thinking about external demands in a pessimistic way and avoiding contact with them.

They report (Kobassa et al. 1983) that Type A behaviour was unrelated to hardiness. They found that managers high in Type A behaviour and low in hardiness were in poorest health.

Hardiness was also found to be independent of health practices (diet, smoking, alchohol intake, drug use, relaxation, and meditation, physical exercise), independent of consititutional health (number of illnesses having a presumed hereditary basis that managers' natural parents may have suffered), and a very small relationship between hardiness and social support (Kobassa et al. 1981).

Maddi and Kobassa (1984), based on interview findings, propose that hardiness develops through experiences children have with their parents and others fairly early in life. Interestingly, they report no relationship between hardiness and demographic factors such as age, level of education, religious practice, ethnicity, and level of parents education (Kobassa et al. 1982a,b).

Sense of coherence

Antonovsky (1987) was also interested in the question of why some individuals with high stress loads not only survive but even thrive. He proposed the concept of SOC as one explanation. He defined SOC as 'a global orientation that expresses the extent to which one has a persuasive, enduring though dynamic feeling of confidence that (1) the stimuli deriving from one's internal and external environments in the course of living are structured, predictable, and explicable; (2) the resources are available to one to meet the demands posed by these stimuli; and (3) these demands are challenges, worthy of investment and engagement' (Antonovsky 1987, p. 19).

SOC is a way of making sense of the world around one, a way of making sense of the numerous stressors with which one is faced. SOC is a cognitive concept. Antonovsky identifies three components of SOC: comprehensibility, manageability, and meaningfulness. *Comprehensibility* refers to the extent to which one perceives the events that one faces as making sense are explainable, predictable, and orderly. *Manageability* refers to the perceived predictability that things will work out as well as can be expected, the perception that resources (one's own or others) are available, adequate to meet the demands of these events. *Meaningfulness* refers to the extent to which one believes that life makes sense emotionally and that the demands in the events one is facing pose welcome challenges and are worth investing energy in dealing with.

Antonovsky reports that Israeli army officer trainees scored higher on SOC than did an Israeli national sample. These young men are an extremely select group, in great physical health, and highly motivated to succeed in a challenging situation.

The three components of the SOC were found to be highly intercorrelated. SOC scores correlated significantly with locus of control (internal), negatively with anxiety. Antonovsky believes that life experiences and their context leads to the development of SOC. A strong SOC is not a coping style. What the SOC does is to select a particular coping strategy that seems to be well suited to deal with the stressors being addressed. This idea appears to be related to the Lazarus concepts of primary and secondary appraised. SOC would be related to the use of more constructive behaviours (talk to others, adaptive health behaviours).

Flow

Csikszentmihalyi (1990) uses the term optimal experience to refer to times when individuals feel in control of their actions, masters of their own destinies. Optimal experiences commonly result from hard work and meeting challenges head on. Individuals make optimal experiences happen. Optimal experiences contribute to a sense of mastery, of participating in the events of one's life. Csikszentmihalyi developed a theory of optimal experience based on the concept of flow, a state in which individual's become so involved in an activity that nothing else matters.

Csikszentmihalyi believes that since so much time is invested and spent in working, the experience of flow at work is likely to have significant effects on one's quality of life. Flow also plays a major role in how people respond to stress. Csikszentmihalyi reports data showing that women and men experience more flow at work than in leisure. He also reports that managers and supervisors were more often in flow at work (64 per cent) than were clerical workers (51 per cent) and blue collar workers (49 per cent). Apathy was reported at work more often by blue collar workers than managers (23-versus 11 per cent), and in leisure more often by managers than by blue collar workers (61-versus 46 per cent). Certain activities are more conducive to flow as they make optimal experience easier to achieve (e.g. learning skills, goals, feedback, control).

Effective coping involves transforming a negative situation into a flow activity. This is likely to be realized if particular conditions exist. These include self-assurance, belief in one's own resources; attention is focused outward on one's environment; and the discovery of new goals and new solutions (Seligman and Czikszentmihaly, 2000).

Resonance

Clawson (1999) identifies resonance as the key underlying superior performance, even world class performance, in any field of endeavour. Resonance is a special type of experience that high level performance in a chosen valued field brings to an individual. People who perform at their best report a common experience. Professional athletes refer to it as 'being in the zone'; jazz musicians refer to it as 'being in the groove', managers use the term 'resonance' to capture these experiences.

What does resonance look like? Managers experiencing resonance are performing at the peak of their profession and likely at the peak of their abilities. These individuals have goals and dreams. They spend vast amounts of time preparing for their efforts. They encounter and have to overcome setbacks, obstacles and minor successes in achieving their dreams. Setbacks and obstacles, often demand more intensive efforts. This is a state similar to what Csikszentmihalyi (1990) has termed 'flow' and likely to include self-efficacy (Bandura 2001) as well.

Optimism

Seligman and Czikszentmihalyi (2000) advocate moving away from an emphasis on treatment built on the disease model to a focus on prevention. Prevention researchers have found that there are 'human strengths that act as buffers against psychological distress and illness: courage, optimism, interpersonal skills, hope, honesty, perseverance, a work ethic, and the capacity for flow and insight' (Seligman and Czikszentmihalyi 2000, p. 7). There is a need for a new science of strength, virtues, and resilience. Individuals are not passive beings responding to external events or stimuli. Instead they make decisions, have choices, show preferences, and can be successful and agenetic.

Peterson (2000) sees optimism at having cognitive, emotional, and motivational components. People high in optimism tend to have better moods, to be more persevering and successful, and to be in better health (Fredrickson 1998; Fredrickson and Levenson 1998; Segerstrom et al. 1998; Taylor and Brown 1998; Taylor et al. 2000). Optimism is obviously an individual difference variable. It has been proposed that optimism can be dispositional in the form of a global belief expectation that good things will be plentiful in the future, as well as an explanatory style, how a person explains good or bad events. Emotional states may also be associated with psychological resilience. These states likely influence the availability of psychological resources (humor, optimism).

Salovey et al. (2000) review literature supporting a positive association between positive emotional states and physical health. Negative emotional states are proposed to be associated with unhealthy patterns of physiological functioning whereas positive emotions are associated with healthier patterns of responding (Friedman 1992).

Folkman and Moskowitz (2000) contend that positive affect can co-occur with distress during the experience of stress and coping, that positive affect in the context of stress has important adaptational significance of its own, and coping processes that generate and sustain positive affect in the context of stress involve meaning.

Positive affect can provide a psychological break or respite, can support continued coping efforts, and can replenish resources that have been depleted by the stress. Positive affect can promote better problem-solving, creativity, and flexibility in thinking (Folkman 1997). Positive affect can serve as a buffer against adverse physiological consequences of stress (Peterson 1988; Peterson and Bossio 1991; Peterson *et al.* 1988; Scheier and Carver 1985, 1992). Positive affect may also counter depression (Peterson and Seligman 1984). Positive affect may be generated in the coping process itself. Positive reappraisal can increase positive affect (cup half-full). The use (successful) of problem-focused coping, increasing one's sense of mastery and control, can create positive affect.

Organizational change, individual coping strategies, and psychological effects

Although a wide variety of work stressors have been considered in studies of individual coping in organizations, this selective review will give priority to individual efforts to cope with organizational change. Organizational change has been identified as an increasingly common experience at work (Burke 2001).

The pervasiveness of occupational stress has highlighted the central role played by coping responses on the stress well-being relationship (Zeidner and Endler 1996). A number of conceptualizations and measures have been proposed (Schwarzer and Schwarzer 1996). Two underlying dimensions have fairly consistently been suggested to encompass more specific coping behaviours and emotions. One dimension consists of terms such as control, proactive, take charge, instrumental, attentive, vigilant, and confrontation; the other dimension consists of terms such as escapist, avoidance, palliative, and emotional (Latack and Havlovic 1992; Leiter 1991; Lazarus and Folkman 1984; Schwarzer and Schwarzer 1996).

Ashford (1988) studied coping mechanisms used by employees of the Bell Telephone system during a major organizational divestiture. Ashford (1988) collected data from 180 managers and professionals in the marketing department of a regional Bell Telephone company. Data where collected at two points of time about six months apart. Ashford considered the relationship of transition stressors (e.g. greater uncertainty) with levels of employee stress as well as the role of coping resources and coping responses (strategies, behaviours) in minimizing the potentially adverse effects of transition stressors. Coping resources embody what is available to individuals in developing their coping repertoires, not what they do. Coping resources include feelings of control or mastery, feelings of self-efficacy, one's beliefs about their ability to master a situation, lack of self-denigration, and tolerance for ambiguity.

Ashford found that coping resources and coping responses were only somewhat useful in buffering the efforts of the transition stressors, having only small effects. Feelings of personal control and tolerance of ambiguity seemed to be the most useful buffers of transition stress. Among the coping responses, sharing worries and concerns emerged as the most effective buffering response, related perhaps to social support. Asking others for feedback was found to increase stress levels of the transition.

Terry and Callan (2000) use features of the Lazarus and Folkman model (1984) to understand individual's adjustment to a major organizational change. The model proposes that an understanding of how individuals adjust to organizational change involves knowledge of the event (change) characteristics, employee appraisals of the change, their coping resources, and access to personal and social resources. Event characteristics include stressors associated with the change and how the change processes were managed (e.g. communication, participation). Appraisal would include perceptions of controllability and ability to deal with the event (the change). Coping strategies involve both problem-focused and emotion-focused approaches. Coping resources include stable characteristics of the individual (e.g. negative affectivity, neuroticism, self-esteem, locus of control) and resources in one's social environment (e.g. social support).

This model was to tested in a study of the merger of two airlines. Respondents were 463 fleet staff (mostly pilots) and in a study of the merger of two government departments ($N = 140$ middle managers and supervisors).

In the airline merger study, there was evidence of a link between employee's perceptions of the merger event characteristics and levels of adjustment (psychological distress, job satisfaction). Respondents who perceived that the merger had been implemented in a positive manner (consulted, informed) felt less threat than those who perceived that the merger was implemented badly. Respondents perceiving a positive-implementation were more likely use more problem-focused coping responses. Perceptions of event controllability and self-efficacy were related to greater use of problem-focused coping strategies. Use of problem-focused coping was related to better adjustment while use of emotion-focused coping was related to poorer adjustment. Personal resources (e.g. neuroticism) also played a role. Persons high on neuroticism appraised the merger as more threatening, used more emotion-focused coping strategies, and reported poorer adjustment. Supervisor support was found to influence perceptions of the way the merger was implemented (positively), be associated with lower threat of the event (more controllability), more use of problem-focused coping strategies and better adjustment.

In the study of the public sector merger, a similar research model was used, with some changes in the measures included. In this research, self-esteem and generalized control beliefs were related to appraisals of the merger event and coping strategies but not to adjustment. Uncertainty associated with the merger event, as well as merger stress, were related to psychological adjustment (distress). Use of emotion-focused coping was related to poorer adjustment while greater use of problem-focused coping was related (modestly) to better adjustment.

We tested a research model incorporating work and non-work stressors, work–family conflict, active and escapist coping, and individual well-being in a large sample of police officers (Burke 1998). About 400 police officers participated by completing anonymous questionnaires. Concepts in the model were assessed using multiple item scales having satisfactory psychosometric properties. Two well-being outcomes, job satisfaction, and psychosomatic symptoms were considered. LISREL analyses were undertaken in which relationships among all variables in the model were considered simultaneously. Use of active coping was negatively related to use of escapist coping; escapist coping was positively related to work–family conflict and psychosomatic symptoms while active coping was positively related to job satisfaction.

The role of coping in this study, while consistent with previous research conclusions, offered some new findings as well. Respondents making greater use of escapist coping reported greater work–family conflict and more psychosomatic symptoms. Use of active coping, while positively related to levels of job satisfaction, had no direct relationship with either work–family conflict or psychosomatic symptoms. Thus the relationships between use of active coping, use of escapist coping, and work–family conflict was the same in both analyses, but active and escapist coping had different direct effects on the two well-being measures (job satisfaction and psychosomatic symptoms). This suggests the need to include a number of outcome measures of coping in future research (Latack 1986; Latack and Havlovic 1992). In addition, use of active coping was found to be associated with less use of escapist coping.

Consistent with other findings, individuals having stronger Type A behaviour predispositions made greater use of active than escapist (passive) coping responses. Interestingly, this behaviour predisposition was also associated with greater work–family conflict and more psychosomatic symptoms. The potential benefits of active coping did not appear in this analysis.

Police officers reporting more work stressors also made greater use of escapist coping. There are several possible explanations for this finding. It has been observed by others that the macho police culture supports the use of alcohol as a stress reduction response. In addition, the work stressors examined in this study may not be readily addressed by individual initiative and actions (Burke 1993).

In a second study, a research model incorporating hospital restructuring stressors, job satisfaction, psychosomatic symptoms, and active and escapist coping was tested in a large sample of nursing staff (Burke and Greenglass 2000). Almost 1400 staff nurses participated by completing anonymous questionnaires. Concepts in the model were assessed using multiple-item scales having satisfactory psychometric properties. A LISREL analysis was undertaken in which relationships among all variables in the model were considered simultaneously. Use of active coping was negatively related to the use of escapist coping; use of escapist coping was positively related to future threats to security and psychosomatic symptoms and negatively related to self-reported job satisfaction; use of active coping was related to perceptions of less extensive hospital restructuring, greater job satisfaction, and fewer psychosomatic symptoms.

The role of coping in this study, while consistent with previous research conclusions, also offered some new findings. Respondents making grater use of control coping indicated higher levels of work satisfaction and fewer psychosomatic symptoms; respondents making greater use of escape coping reported lower levels of work satisfaction and more psychosomatic symptoms. Others (Burke 1998; Leiter 1991) have reported similar findings. The negative relationship between control and escapist coping has also been observed in other samples (Burke 1998).

The positive relationships between use of control coping and extent of hospital restructuring initiatives, and between use of escape coping and future workplace threats, also extends research on coping responses to new areas. The research model hypothesized a negative relationship between use of control coping and extent of restructuring, as well as between use of escape coping and future workplace threats. The findings obtained here were contrary to the former but did support the latter.

Use of control coping, more specifically, appeared to have positive consequences on a number of fronts. Nursing staff making greater use of control coping made less use of escapist coping, and experienced more extensive hospital restructuring, fewer psychosomatic symptoms, and greater job satisfaction. These results suggest that educational interventions designed to improve coping resources may have tangible value despite suggestions to the contrary (Burke 1993).

Koeske *et al.* (1993), in a four-wave panel study, examined use of control and avoidance coping and measures of stress, strain, and negative consequences (burnout, job dissatisfaction, intention to quit, physical symptoms, and life satisfaction). Data were collected from 57 case managers (mostly social workers) working with mentally ill clients using questionnaires at four points in time (entry, 3 months, 1 year, 18 months). Case managers using more control coping reported lower levels of negative consequence while those making greater use of avoidance coping reported higher levels of negative consequences.

Bowman and Stern (1995) studied whether the effectiveness of occupational coping strategies was related to their fit with the controllability of the work stressor. Lazarus and Folkman (1984) suggest that problem-focused coping would be more effective with stressors perceived as controllable (could be changed by one's actions) while emotion-focused coping would be more effective in situations that must be accepted (cannot be changed). Bowman and Stern (1995) asked 187 medical centre nurses to first describe two stressful occupational episodes varying in perceived controllability and indicate their coping strategies used. Outcome measures included perceived coping effectiveness, job affect, and psychological adjustment. Using problem-solving strategies was related to perceived coping effectiveness only for high control episodes. Differential use of coping across the two levels of controllability was unrelated to job affect and psychological adjustment. Use of avoidance coping was strongly related to negative work affect. Both problem reappraisal and problem-solving strategies were related to positive effect at work.

Bowman and Stern (1995) note that emotion-focused coping strategies can be of two types: problem reappraisal-efforts to manage the appraisal of the stressfulness of an event, and avoidance (emotional management)—efforts to reduce tension by avoiding dealing with the problem. Problem reappraisal has been found to be associated with fewer psychological symptoms (Parkes 1990) whereas escape/avoidance types of emotion-focused coping has been found to be associated with negative psychological outcomes (Aldwin and Revenson 1987).

Begley (1998) studied six coping strategies along with restructuring stressors as predictors of psychological health (depression, irritation, somatic complaints) and turnover among nurses and clinicians in the psychiatric division of a medium-sized US hospital. Data was collected at three points in time: three months prior to consolidation, shortly after, and six months following the consolidation. The two stressors included: researcher rankings of extent to which units were affected by the consolidation and rankings by their senior managers of how stressful the consolidation process was for employees in each unit. The six coping strategies were a measure of behavioural disengagement (intention to quit) and five coping strategies from the COPE Inventory (Carver *et al.* 1989). These were: action planning, seeking emotional support, use of alcohol and drugs, positive reinterpretation, and acceptance.

A distinction can be made between dispositional and situational coping strategies. Begley (1998) found that use of intent to quit and acceptance increased between the first and second data collections while use of action planning and seeking social support decreased. Intent to quit was found to predict mental distress at a later point. Intention to quit and consolidation stress predicted mental distress while positive reinterpretation, use of alcohol and drugs, and lower unit impact predicted somatic complaints shortly after the consolidation. Use of alcohol and drugs was the strongest predictor of mental stress six months following the consolidation.

Armstrong-Stassen (1998) considered four coping strategies (positive thinking, direct action, help seeking, avoidance–resignation) in a study of gender and organizational level on how survivors appraise and cope with organizational downsizing. The first three represent control-oriented strategies; the last, escape coping. Survivors were found to use all four coping responses, with help-seeking being most common. Survivors perceiving the workforce reduction as more stressful (more injustice, more perceived job insecurity) were less likely to use direct action coping and more likely to use help-seeking. Survivors making greater use of help-seeking also reported more negative emotional reactions. Gender effects on coping were few. Organizational levels effects were more common and consistent. Survivors at lower organizational levels reported more powerlessness, more downsizing stress, less use of positive thinking and direct action coping, and more use of help-seeking. There were no differences in use of avoidance/resignation coping or, surprisingly, on negative emotional reactions.

There are some common conclusions one can draw from these studies of organizational change, individual coping strategies, and psychological effects. First, all employ fairly comprehensive research frameworks to more fully understand a complex area of study. Second, most find the simple distinction between active and passive individual coping strategies to be useful. It is commonly reported that greater use of active strategies is associated with better psychological health while greater use of passive strategies is associated with poorer psychological health. Third, there is a suggestion in some of the studies that individual coping strategies may be of limited value.

Improving coping in organizations

Most occupational stress researchers advocate a person–environment fit model for understanding work stress (Edwards 1988). According to this view, to understand the experience of work stress one must consider the environment, both subjective and objective, that the individual is encountering (i.e. potential sources of occupational stress and their magnitude). One must also consider stable individual difference characteristics and predispositions which influence both the nature and strength of occupational stressors that are perceived, coping resources and responses that are available and utilized, and emotional and physical well-being. The experiencing of occupational stress results from a person–environment interaction or transaction, particularly instances of person–environment misfit.

The person–environment fit model also has implications for reducing the incidence of occupational stress. It follows that there are two broad approaches for minimizing the experience of work stress. One approach involves enhancing or augmenting the strengths of individuals. If individuals at work had more competence, resources, and resilience, they would experience fewer adverse consequences form occupational stress. There is a considerable literature on this approach (Ivancevich and Matteson 1987, 1988; Ivancevich *et al.* 1990), and evidence that some individual-level interventions can make a difference in temporarily reducing adverse responses to perceived stressors (Murphy 1988).

Organizational- versus individual-level interventions

Cartwright and Cooper (1996) write that organizational constraints place limits on the range of coping responses available to the individual at work. As a result, stressors can be successfully reduced only if the organization shares responsibility for coping. In their view, many of the stressors in the work environment are not within the direct control of the individual.

The importance of organizational-level interventions aimed at environmental sources of professional and managerial stress, rather than individual-level interventions, emerges from a field experiment conducted by Ganster et al. (1982). They evaluated a stress management training programme in a field experiment involving 99 public agency employees randomly assigned to treatment ($n = 60$) and control ($n = 39$) groups. The training programme consisted of 16 h of training spread over eight weeks. Participants were taught progressive relaxation and cognitive restructuring techniques. Dependent variables were epinephrine and norepinephrine excretion at work, anxiety, depression, irritation, and somatic complaints, all measured at three times (pre-test, post-test and four months after treatment). Those participants who received treatment exhibited significantly lower epinephrine and depression levels than did controls at the post-test, and four-month follow-up levels did not regress to initial pre-test levels. However, the effects of treatment were not found in a subsequent intervention on the original control group.

Research conducted by Shinn et al. (1984) comes to the same conclusion. They collected data from 141 human service workers using questionnaires to assess job stressors, coping strategies, and various aspects of strain (alienation, satisfaction, symptomology). Coping (efforts to reduce stressors and strain) was assessed at three levels: by individual workers, by groups of workers helping one another (social support), and by the human service agencies which employed them. Although many more individual coping responses were mentioned than group or agency-initiated responses, only the group responses were associated with low levels of strain. Unfortunately, not enough agency-initiated responses were identified to undertake a meaningful analysis. Thus it appears that, in the work setting, individual coping responses may be less useful than higher-level strategies involving groups of workers or entire units or organizations. Pearlin (1991) also concludes that chronic, organizationally generated stressors may be resistant to reduction through individual coping efforts.

Burke (1993) reviewed 10 organizational-level interventions to reduce stress at work which have been examined in various field studies. These interventions were generally found to have positive effects, and given the limited success of individual-level, intervention in addressing occupational sources of stress should be encouraged.

Heaney et al. (1995) report the results of a field experiment of the role of worksite coping resources in improving mental health. A large number of direct care staff and managers from group homes that provided residential care for developmentally disabled or mentally ill adults ($n = 1375$) took part. A training programme designed to increase individual and group psychosocial coping resources and individual's abilities to use these resources when coping with job demands was provided to experimental homes but not to control homes. Social support and perceived control were emphasized in the training programme.

Social support can directly enhance psychological well-being through increasing self-esteem, raising morale, and providing a sense of connection, community, and being cared for. Social support can also influence psychological well-being by affecting coping behaviours. Social support can increase control through aid or advice on how to deal with a stressful situation. Social support can make a stressful situation seem less threatening. Social support can also shift one's focus away from a stressful situation. Finally social support, through understanding and validation, can reduce psychological distress.

Employee perceptions of control can be heightened by providing a structure and climate that increases employee participation in decision making. To the degree that employees can influence decisions at work, their perceptions of control over work stressors is likely to be increased. Access to information, being heard by others, and developing greater understanding of experiences and events at work are also likely to influence one's feelings of control at work (Sutton and Kahn 1987).

The training programme taught employees about the helping potential of support and built skills in accessing support from others at work and the concept of group problem-solving meetings and skills needed to use group decision making approaches in team meetings.

The results indicated that the training programme enhanced the work team climate and reduced depressive symptoms and somatization in those most at risk of leaving their jobs. The training programme was also shown to increase supervisor support on the job and to strengthen perceptions of coping abilities among care givers most likely to take part in the programme.

Where do we go from here?

Research on managerial coping is still in its infancy. Giant steps will have to be taken before we can develop a good understanding of what kinds of coping strategies work effectively for which people in which situations; what properties of the person or environment increase or diminish an individual's coping effectiveness; what are the outcomes of using certain strategies versus others for the individual, his or her team and the organization as a whole (Coyne 1997; Coyne and Racioppo 2000; Lazarus 1993).

What appears to be needed are basic observations, surveys, interviews, and descriptions of phenomena which are perceived as stressful, and of individuals' reactions, and coping approaches (Lazarus 1993, 2000). Here we can examine how individuals cope in their day-to-day lives with real life person–environment problems using their full range of coping techniques. We also advocate studies where one person is followed in different situations over time so that a researcher can assess:

(1) how the individual copes with a specific stressful encounter over time, thus defining the process involved,

(2) the individual's coping over a series of encounters, thus determining what variation in emotional, physiological, cognitive, and behavioural responses appear in different situations, and

(3) the presence of stable factors that are carried over from one context to another.

This suggests following individuals over a period time, seeing them frequently to identify the stressful person–environment transactions, what individuals thought, felt, did, and in what sequence in response to these situations. This approach provides a concurrent examination of the problem event, the environment-social context, the emotional, physiological, cognitive, and behavioural responses to provide a comprehensive data base for studying coping.

Identification and assessment of potential stressors

An important part of furthering information about coping is knowing specifically what it is people are coping with, how frequently they experience stressful situations in their daily lives, how intense the stress experience is in each situation (Dewe 1989, 1991; Folkman *et al.* 1986). It is necessary, therefore, to continue the work of identifying the range of person–environment problems that arise out of work-related events, to differentiate them from those problems that are manifested in work settings but arise out of personal life events, and to study the interaction between the two life domains.

Identification and measurement of coping strategies

A study of coping activities requires a method of valid and reliable measurement and a framework for analysing responses to stressful encounters. We know that individuals engage in an array of cognitive, interpersonal, and physical behaviours to manage a stressful encounter. A first-order priority should be a cataloguing of these activities in a descriptive form readily understandable and requiring the least amount of inference on the part of the researcher. To manufacture such a list necessitates real-life observations, surveys, and interviews of people in organizations as they transact difficult day-to-day situations.

Mediating variables

There a number of mediators (characteristics and resources of the environment or the individual) which serve to diminish or intensify the impact of a given stress on an individual's perceptions and assessment of his environment and his coping responses to it (Israel *et al.* 1989). We have described a number of these factors earlier in the section on the coping model. Again, the problem becomes one of clearly identifying, operationalizing, and measuring these variables and their relative positive or negative influence.

Coping outcomes

The assessment of the relative effectiveness of a coping activity or process presents a number of problems. How does one determine which outcome criteria he should use to make this evaluation? Clearly this depends on the system of values we carry into the research situation. Do we settle for a reduction of stress, the absence of distress, and pathology or are we aiming for positive affect, good health, and effective performance? The possible outcome criteria are numerous as indicated earlier in the chapter. What complicates the selection of outcome criteria is that what maybe 'good' for individuals and what may be 'good' for the organization may be mutually exclusive or conflicting in some situations. Do we choose one over the other in determining effectiveness, do we seek a compromise between the two, or will choice of criteria vary in response to factors deemed more significant at a particular point in time? The use of multiple outcome criteria is also necessary to avoid assessing a coping mœuver positively when, in fact, it is a palliative measure providing psychological relief but obfuscating some destructive physiological process (such as denial of real needs and feelings and developing ulcers).

Another parameter to be considered is the time-period in which the measures are taken. To attain a better understanding of the time patterning of effective coping and positive outcomes many more studies of a longitudinal nature will need to be undertaken.

Conclusions

The complex and changing environment of modern organizations present a never-ending array of stimuli, pressures, and demands which can become sources of stress for executives. Individuals in these positions will continue to be faced with the struggle of mastering or overcoming the threats they encounter in whatever unique, stereotypic, and diverse methods they can muster.

But, it is clear that some individuals will cope more effectively than others. The failure of some will be plainly revealed in such forms as absenteeism alcohol and drug abuse, deficient performance, reduced productivity, barren personal relationships, and illness. The cost of this failure to organizations is serious; to the individual it can be devastating.

Effective coping in organizational life depends on individuals having skills relevant to the types of stressful transactions they face in their day-to-day work activities and having helpful resources in their organizational and extra-organizational environments to draw on. At the most fundamental level, managers need to acquire skills in such areas as gathering and utilizing information, task organization and delegation, contingency planning, establishing priorities, timing and pacing of activities, identification of alternative strategies, effective utilization of available resources, sensitivity to environmental cues of impending threat, awareness of subjective cues indicating a stressed state; consciousness of specific personal vulnerabilities in the work setting, and individual stress management techniques. Organizations, whether out of self-interest or humanistic inclinations can contribute enormously to the support and development of their managers' coping capacities in these and other consequential areas (Dewe *et al.* 2000; Murphy 1996; Murphy *et al.* 1995). The effect of research can be to illuminate the directions which are most profitable for organizations and individuals to take to advance the coping skills of managers.

The ultimate objective, as we see it, is a vigorous and high-performing employee. This can be best accomplished through the management of executive stress and its containment at a level congruent with the perception of challenge versus threat, with effective functioning versus dysfunction, and with personal growth versus personal constriction.

Acknowledgements

Preparation of this chapter was supported in part by the School of Business, York University and the Social Sciences and Humanities Research Council. Sandra Osti prepared the manuscript. Tijen Harcar assisted with the literature review. My friend and colleague Esther Greenglass provided helpful comments on the manuscript.

References

Aldwin, C. M. and Revenson, T. A. (1987). Does coping help? A re-examination of the relation between coping and mental health. *Journal of Personality and Social Psychology*, **53**, 337–48.

Antonovsky, A. (1987). *Unraveling the mystery of health: How people manage stress and stay well*. San Francisco, CA: Jossey-Bass.

Armstrong-Stassen, M. (1998). The effect of gender and organizational level on how survivors appraise and cope with organizational downsizing. *Journal of Applied Behavioral Science*, **34**, 125–42.

Ashford, S. J. (1988). Individual strategies for coping with stress during organizational transitions. *Journal of Applied Behavioral Science*, **24**, 19–36.

Bandura, A. (2001). Social cognitive theory: An agentic perspective. *Annual Review of Psychology*, **52**, 1–26.

Begley, T. M. (1998). Coping responses as predictors of employee distress and turnover after on organizational consolidation: A longitudinal analysis. *Journal of Occupational and Organizational Psychology*, **71**, 305–29.

Bolger, N. (1990). Coping as a personality process: A prospective study. *Journal of Personality and Social Psychology*, **59**, 525–32.

Bowman, G. D. and Stern, M. (1995) Adjustment to occupational stress: The relationship of perceived control to effectiveness of coping strategies. *Journal of Counseling Psychology*, **42**, 294–303.

Burke, R. J. (2001). Organizational Transition, in C. L. Cooper and R. J. Burke (eds.), *The new world of work*, pp. 3–28. London: Blackwell.

—— (1998). Work and non-work stressors and well-being among police officers: The role of coping. *Anxiety, Stress, and Coping*, **14**, 1–18.

—— (1993). Organizational level interventions to reduce occupational stress. *Work and Stress*, **7**, 77–87.

—— (1988). Sources of managerial and professional stress in large organizations, in C. L. Cooper and R. Payne (eds.), *Causes coping and consequences of stress at work*, pp. 77–114. New York: John Wiley.

—— and Greenglass, E. R. (2000). Hospital restructuring and nursing staff well-being: The role of coping. *International Journal of Stress Management*, **7**, 49–59.

—— and Weir, T. (1980). Coping with the stress of managerial occupations, in C. L. Cooper and R. Payne (eds.), *Current concerns in occupational stress*, pp. 299–335. New York: John Wiley.

Cartwright, S. and Cooper, C. L. (1996). Coping in occupational settings, in M. Zeidner and N. S. Endler (eds.), *Handbook of coping: Theory, research, applications*, pp. 202–20. New York: John Wiley.

Carver, C. S. (1996). Forward, in M. Zeidner and N. S. Endler (eds.), *Handbook of coping: Theory, research, applications*, pp. xi–xiii. New York: John Wiley.

—— and Scheier, M. F. (1994). Situational coping and coping dispositions in a stressful transaction. *Journal of Personality and Social Psychology*, **66**, 184–95.

Carver, C., Scheier, M. and Weintraub, J. (1989). Assessing coping strategies: A theoretically based approach. *Journal of Personality and Social Psychology*, **56**, 267–83.

Clawson, J. C. (1999). *Level three leadership: Getting below the surface*. Upper Saddle River, NJ: Prentice Hall.

Cooper, C. L. and Marshall, J. (1978). Sources of managerial and white collar stressm, in C. L. Cooper and R. Payne (eds.), *Stress at work*, pp. 81–105. New York: John Wiley.

Coyne, J. C. (1997). Improving coping research: Raze the slum before any more building. *Journal of Health Psychology*, **2**, 153–5.

—— and **Gottlieb, B. H.** (1996). The mismeasure of coping by checklist. *Journal of Personality*, **64**, 959–91.

—— and **Racioppo, M. W.** (2000). Never the twain shall meet? Closing the gap between coping research and clinical intervention research. *American Psychologist*, **55**, 655–64.

Csikszentmihalyi, M. (1990). *Flow: The psychology of optimal experience.* New York: Harper & Row.

Dewe, P. (2000). Measures of coping with stress at work: A review and critique, in P. Dewe, M. Leiter and T. Cox (eds.), *Coping, health and organizations*, pp. 3–28. London: Taylor & Francis.

—— (1991). Primary appraisal, secondary appraisal and coping: Their role in stressful work encounters. *Journal of Occupational Psychology*, **64**, 331–51.

—— (1989). Examining the nature of work stress: Individual evaluations of stressful experiences and coping. *Human Relations*, **42**, 993–1013.

—— **Leiter, M. P.,** and **Cox, T.** (2000). *Coping, health and organizations.* London: Taylor & Francis.

—— and **Guest, D. E.** (1990). Methods of coping with stress at work: A conceptual analysis and empirical study of measurement issues. *Journal of Organizational Behaviour*, **11**, 135–50.

Edwards, J. R. (1988). The determinants and consequences of coping with stress, in C. L. Cooper and R. L. Payne (eds.), *Causes, coping and consequences of stress at work*, pp. 233–63. New York: John Wiley.

Folkman, S. (1997). Positive psychological states and coping with severe stress. *Social Science and Medicine*, **45**, 1207–21.

—— and **Moskowitz, J. T.** (2000). Positive affect and the other side of coping. *American Psychologist*, **55**, 647–54.

—— and **Lazarus, R. S.** (1988). *Manual for the ways of coping checklist.* Palo Alto, CA: Consulting Psychologists Press.

—— —— **Dunkel-Schetter, C., DeLongis, A.,** and **Gruen, R.** (1986). The dynamics of a stressful encounter: Cognitive appraisal, coping and encounter outcomes. *Journal of Personality and Social Psychology*, **50**, 992–1003.

Fredrickson, B. L. (1998). What good are positive emotions? *Review of General Psychology*, **2**, 300–19.

—— and **Levenson, R. W.** (1998). Positive emotions speed recovery from the cardiovascular sequelae of negative emotions. *Cognition and Emotion*, **12**, 191–220.

Friedman, H. S. (1992). *Hostility, coping, and health.* Washington, DC: American Psychological Association.

Ganster, D. C., Mayes, B. T., Sime, W. E., and **Tharp, G. D.** (1982). Managing occupational stress: A field experiment. *Journals of Applied Psychology*, **67**, 533–42.

Heaney, C. A., Price, R. H., and **Rafferty, J.** (1995). Increasing coping resources at work: A field experiment to increase social support, improve work team functioning, and enhance employee mental health. *Journal of Organizational Behavior*, **16**, 335–52.

Hemingway, H., Nicholson, A., Stafford, M., Roberts, R., and **Marmot, M. G.** (1997). The impact of socio-economic status on health functioning as assessed by the SF-36 questionnaire: The Whitehall II study. *American Journal of Public Health*, **87**, 1484–90.

Hobfoll, S. E., Schwarzer, R., and **Chan, K. K.** (1998). Disentangling the stress labyrinth: Interpreting the meaning of the term stress as it is studied in the health context. *Anxiety, Stress and Coping*, **11**, 181–212.

Israel, B. A., House, J. S., Schurman, S. I., Heaney, C. A., and **Mero, R. P.** (1989). The relation of personal resources, participation, influence, interpersonal relationships and coping strategies to occupational stress, job strains and health: a multivariate analysis. *Work and Stress*, **3**, 163–94.

Ivancevich, J. M. and Matteson, M. T. (1987). Organizational level stress management interventions: A review and recommendations, in J. M. Ivancevich and D. C. Ganster (eds.), *Job stress: From theory to suggestion*, pp. 229–48. New York: Howarth Press.

—— —— (1988). Promoting the individual's health and well-being, in C. L. Cooper and R. Payne (eds.), *Causes, coping and consequences of stress at work*, pp. 267–99. New York: John Wiley.

—— —— Freedman, S. M., and Phillips, J. S. (1990). Worksite stress management interventions. *American Psychologist*, **45**, 252–61.

Kobassa, S. C., Maddi, S. R., and Courington, S. (1981). Personality and constitution as mediators in the stress–illness relationship. *Journal of Health and Social Behavior*, **22**, 368–78.

—— —— and Kahn, S. (1982a). Hardiness and health: A prospective study. *Journal of Personality and Social Psychology*, **62**, 168–77.

—— —— and Puccetti, M. C. (1982b). Personality and exercise as buffers in the stress–illness relationship. *Journal of Behavioral Medicine*, **4**, 391–404.

—— —— and Zola, M. D. (1983). Type A and hardiness. *Journal of Behavioral Medicine*, **6**, 41–51.

Koeske, G. F., Kirk, S. A., and Koeske, R. D. (1993). Coping with job stress: Which strategies work best? *Journal of Occupational and Organizational Psychology*, **66**, 319–35.

Latack, J. C. (1986). Coping with job stress: Measures and future directions for scale development. *Journal of Applied Psychology*, **71**, 377–85.

—— and Havlovic, S. J. (1992). Coping with job stress: A conceptual evaluation framework for coping measures. *Journal of Organizational Behavior*, **13**, 479–508.

Lazarus, R. S. (2000) Toward better research on stress and coping. *American Psychologist*, **55**, 665–73.

—— (1999). *Stress and emotion: A new synthesis*. New York: Springer.

—— (1993). Coping theory and research: Past, present and future. *Psychosomatic Medicine*, **55**, 234–47.

—— and Folkman, S. (1984). *Stress, appraisal and coping*. New York: Springer.

Leiter, M. P. (1991). Coping patterns as predictors of burnout: The function of control and escapist coping patterns. *Journal of Organizational Behavior*, **12**, 123–44.

Maddi, S. R. and Kobassa, S. C. (1984). *The hardy executive: Health under stress*. Homewood, Ill: Dow Jones-Irwin.

Marmot, M. G., (1997). Social inequalities in health: Next questions and converging evidence. *Social Science and Medicine*, **44**, 901–10.

—— Davey Smith, G., Stansfeld, S., Patel, C., North, F., Head, J. *et al.* (1991). Health inequalities among British civil servants: The Whitehall II study. *Lancet*, **337**, 1387–93.

—— Bosma, H., Hemingway, H. Brunner, E., and Stansfeld, S. (1997). Contributions of job control and other risk factors to social variations in coronary heart disease. *Lancet*, **350**, 235–9.

—— Kogevinas, M., and Elston, M. A. (1987). Social economic status and disease. *Annual Review of Public Health*, **8**, 111–35.

—— Siegrist, J., Theorell, T., and Feeney, A. (2000). Health and the psychosocial environment at work, in M. Marmot and R. Wilkinson (eds.), *Social determinants of health*, pp. 105–31. Oxford: Oxford University Press.

Menaghen, E. G. and Merves, E. S. (1984). Coping with occupational problems: The limits of individual efforts. *Journal of Health and Social Behavior*, **25**, 406–23.

Murphy, L. R. (1988). Workplace interventions for stress reduction and prevention, in C. L. Cooper and R. Payne (eds.), *Causes, coping and consequences of stress at work*, pp. 301–39. New York: John Wiley.

—— (1996). Stress management in work settings: A critical review of the health effects. *American Journal of Health Promotion*, **11**, 112–35.

—— Hurrell, J. J. Jr., Sauter, S. L., and Keita, G. P. (1995). *Job stress interventions*. Washington, DC: American Psychological Association.

Parkes, K. R. (1990). Coping, negative affectivity, and the work environment: Additive and inter-active predictors of mental health. *Journal of Applied Psychology*, **75**, 399–409.

Pearlin, L. I. (1991). The study of coping, in J. Eckenrode (ed.), *The social context of coping*, pp. 261–76. New York: Plenum Press.

Peterson, C. (2000). The future of optimism. *American Psychologist*, **55**, 68–78.

—— (1988). Explanatory style as a risk factor for illness. *Cognitive Therapy and Research*, **12**, 119–32.

—— and Bossio, L. M. (1991). *Health and optimism*. New York: Free Press.

—— and Seligman, M. E. P. (1984). Causal explanations as a risk factor for depression: Theory and evidence. *Psychological Review*, **91**, 347–74.

—— —— and Valiant, G. F. (1988). Pessimistic explanatory style as a risk factor for physical illness: A thirty-five year longitudinal study. *Journal of Personality and Social Psychology*, **55**, 23–7.

Ptacek, J. T., Smith, R. E., Espe, K., and Raffety, B. (1994). Limited correspondence between daily coping reports and retrospective coping recall. *Psychological Assessment*, **6**, 41–9.

Salovey, P., Rothman, A. J., Detweiler, J. B., and Steward, U. T. (2000). Emotional states and physical health. *American Psychologist*, **55**, 110–21.

Scheier, M. F. and Carver, C. S. (1985). Optimism, coping, and health: Assessment and implications of generalized outcome expectancies. *Health Psychology*, **4**, 219–47.

—— —— (1992). Effects of optimism on psychological and physical well-being: Theoretical overview and empirical update. *Cognitive Theory and Research*, **16**, 201–28.

—— Weintraub, J. K., and Carver, C. S. (1986). Coping with stress: Divergent strategies of optimists and pessimists. *Journal of Personality and Social Psychology*, **51**, 1257–64.

Schoenpflug, W. and Battmann, W. (1988). The costs and benefits of coping, in S. Fisher and J. Reason (eds.), *Handbook of life stress, cognition and health*, pp. 699–713. New York: Wiley.

Schwarzer, R. and Schwarzer, C. (1996). A critical survey of coping instruments, in M. Zeidner and N. S. Endler (eds.), *Handbook of coping: Theory, research, applications*, pp. 107–50. New York: John Wiley.

Schwartz, J. and Stone, A. (1993). Coping with daily work problems: Contributions of problem content, appraisals and person factors. *Work and Stress*, **7**, 47–62.

Segerstrom, S. C., Taylor, S. E., Kemeny, M. E., and Fakey, J. L. (1998). Optimism is associated with mood, coping and immune change in responses to stress. *Journal of Personality and Social Psychology*, **74**, 1646–55.

Seligman, M. E. P. and Czikszentmihaly, M. (2000). Positive psychology: An introduction. *American Psychologist*, **55**, 5–14.

Shinn, M., Rosario, M., Morch, H., and Chestnut, E. E. (1984). Coping with job stress and burnout in the human services. *Journal of Personality and Social Psychology*, **46**, 864–76.

Smith, R. E., Leffingwell, T. R., and Ptacek, J. T. (1999). Can people remember how they coped? Factors associated with discordance between same day and retrospective reports. *Journal of Personality and Social Psychology*, **76**, 1050–61.

Stansfeld, S. A., Fuhrer, R., and Shipley, M. J. (1998). Types of social support as predictors of psychiatric morbidity in a cohort of British Civil Servants (Whitehall II study). *Psychological Medicine*, **28**, 881–92.

Stansfeld, S. A., Fuhrer, R., Head, J. Ferrie, J., and Shipley, M. J. (1997). Work and psychiatric disorder in the Whitehall II study. *Journal of Psychosomatic Research*, **43**, 73–81.

Stone, A. A., Schwartz, J. E., Neale, J. M., Shiffman, S., Marco, C. A., Hickcox, M. *et al.* (1988). A comparison of coping assessed by ecological momentary assessment and retrospective recall. *Journal of Personality and Social Psychology*, **74**, 1670–80.

Stone, A., Greenberg, M., Kennedy-Moore, E., and Newman, M. (1991). Self-report, situation-specific coping questionnaires: What are they measuring? *Journal of Personality and Social Psychology*, **61**, 648–58.

Sommerfield, M. R. and McCrae, R. R. (2000). Stress and coping research: Methodological challenges, theoretical advances and clinical applications. *American Psychologist*, **55**, 620–5.

Sutton, R. I. and Kahn, R. L. (1987). Prediction, understanding and control as antidotes to organizational stress, in J. Lorsch (ed.), *Handbook of organizational behavior*, pp. 272–85. Englewood Cliffs, NJ: Prentice-Hall.

Taylor, S. E., Kemeny, M. E., Reed, G. M., Bower, J. E., and Gruenewald, T. L. (2000). Psychological resources, positive illusions, and health. *American Psychologist*, **55**, 99–109.

—— and Brown, J. D. (1988). Illusion and well-being: A social psychological perspective on mental health. *Psychological Bulletin*, **103**, 193–210.

Tennen, H., Affleck, G., Armeli, S., and Carney, M. A. (2000). A daily process approach to coping: Linking theory, research and practice. *American Psychologist*, **55**, 626–36.

Terry, D. J. and Callan, V. J. (2000). Employee adjustment to an organizational change: a stress and coping perspective, in P. Dewe, M. Leiter, and T. Cox (eds.), *Coping, health, and organizations*, pp. 259–76. London: Taylor & Francis.

Zeidner, M. and Endler, N. S. (1996). *Handbook of coping: theory, research and applications*. New York: John Wiley.

CHAPTER 6

POSITIVE PSYCHOLOGY AND HEALTH: SITUATIONAL DEPENDENCE AND PERSONAL STRIVING

KATHLEEN A. MOORE

> I'm not coping, I'm living
>
> Anonymous Australian paraplegic

The excitement and anticipation of a new century during the last months of 1999 were contagious. To be one of those to welcome in a new millennium provided many people with a sense of optimism and well-being, of planning and forward-thinking. People everywhere were engaged in elaborate discussions and plans for where they might be at the 'specific moment in time' when the year 2000 rolled in and what they might do in the new and dynamic future that would follow. Such a reappraisal and optimistic process was apparently universal, at least for those of us living in the Western World.

Leaders in the field of psychology were not immune to this optimistic, forward-looking challenge for the future. In fact, the *American Psychologist* devoted its first issue of the new millennium to what it termed 'positive psychology'. That issue is comprised of papers that discuss subjective well-being, happiness, optimism, and self-determinism. Seligman and Csikszentmihalyi (2000) in their introductory paper provided a series of personal insights that, to a large extent, reflect their own surprise at their realizations of the positive, adaptive, and challenging profiles, held by some people close to them. They go on to review briefly some philosophical and theoretical views, ranging from an evolutionary perspective, trait theories, to a brief discussion of authenticity, and they conclude with the observation 'that positive psychology is not a new idea. It has many distinguished ancestors. . . . However, these ancestors somehow failed to attract a cumulative, empirical body of research to ground their ideas' (p. 13).

Both these claims are indisputably true. In fact, I would go so far as to suggest that the fervour associated with a new century, the sense of change and even the anticipation of a fresh start that seemed to pervade much thinking and feeling at that time, provided the zeitgeist for the recognition of positive psychology and striving and its empirical validation which had been lacking previously. The role of positive psychology can be seen across a range of life domains, for example, in areas of performance, motivation, and achievement, in the workplace and in relationships, and in its impact on health and well-being. In this last respect, positive psychology is particularly important for its role in promoting attitudes to health and in dealing with ill-health and other threats to well-being and to a lesser extent its success in predicting health behaviours. It is essential also, to understand the context in which these changes occur as, with the emergence of positive psychology this century, the time and context may be highly influential.

In this chapter, I will illustrate the beneficial effects of positive psychology on health and well-being, by drawing together many of the positive factors that have been shown to contribute to health and well-being and by providing examples of their health benefits. Many of the positive factors shown to contribute to health and well-being will be synthesized into a model of health adapted from my own work and that with colleagues, from the recent literature, and this will, to some extent, reflect the framework provided by Abraham Maslow.

Maslow (1954) was one of the early, yet unrecognized as such, writers in the arena of positive psychology. He proposed a hierarchy of human needs. In this chapter, Maslow's concept of a hierarchy of needs will be used as a metaphor for biopsychosocial health. Furthermore, people's ability to experience challenge and to strive in times of adversity will be used to illustrate Maslow's belief in the innate goodness and potential for growth which, he argued, are present in all human beings.

Brief history of the path to positive psychology

Modern psychology's early underpinnings were focused on the understanding of self (James 1892) and to this end, on introspection (e.g. Galton 1883). Psychology soon shifted from this inward focus to a concentration on overt and measurable behaviours (e.g. Watson 1913) during which period psychology was said to have 'lost its mind' (Dember 1974). During the 1960s, introspection, imagery, and the like again achieved respectability. This resurgence of interest was driven by the context of the time. That time included drug problems, the hallucinogenic effects of drugs such as lysergic acid diethylamide (LSD) and mescaline (Holt 1964; Richardson 1983) as well as the experience of hallucinations reported by long-distance truck drivers, astronauts, and jet pilots flying straight and level at high altitudes (Holt 1964). In parallel with this evolution, was the difficulty behaviourists were experiencing in developing methods that were not contaminated by instructions of the type: 'Tell me what is going on in your mind?' Moreover, despite behaviourists' well-known contempt for introspective methods, they were at a loss to explain the rationale behind their widespread use of techniques such as systematic desensitization (Wolpe 1954, 1958) and to a lesser extent implosive therapy (Rachman 1968; Stampfl and Lewis 1967) both of which involve an inward focus. These therapies require the client to identify a hierarchy of feared situations and the level of associated angst. Systematic desensitization also requires the practice of relaxation and the ability of the client to look inward and answer the question: 'Tell me, how anxious are you now?'

This time was ripe, too, for the emergence of cognitive-behavioural theories and therapies (e.g. Beck 1970; Ellis and Harper 1975). The utility and supremacy of these theories, in the present day context, to explain the aetiology of and maintenance factors contributing to mental ill-health and to mental distress remains largely undisputed. Negative schema, frequently formulated in childhood, and the accompanying cognitive distortions have been implicated in depression, anxiety, and low levels of self-esteem (Beck 1970). Cognitive therapy for these disorders is based upon challenging the person's negative or distorted cognitions and replacing them with a more realistic, or positive, perspective (e.g. Beck 1970; Ellis and Harper 1975). Since the 1970s and more particularly the 1980s, people's cognitions and their attributions, have been related also to physical health and well-being especially with respect to these as stress outcomes (e.g. Pearlin and Schooler 1978; Lazarus and Folkman 1984).

The 1980s onwards also saw the development of models to explain health behaviours. For instance, the Health Beliefs Model (HBM; Becker 1974), the Theory of Reasoned Action (TRA; Ajzen and Fishbein 1980), the Theory of Planned Behaviour (TPB; Ajzen 1985), Protection Motivation Theory (PMT; Rogers 1975, 1983) and more recently the Transtheoretical Model (TTM; Prochaska and DiClemente 1982) and the Health Action Process Approach (HAPA; Schwarzer 1992). While successive models have attempted to address the weaknesses in earlier models, they are subject still to criticism, empirical support remains equivocal and, with the exception of the TTM these models are linear, and the outcomes are typically specific behaviours rather than a generic or an wholistic approach to a healthy lifestyle. While these models variously examine perceived susceptibility to and severity of an illness, a balance of the pros and cons—where the decision to engage or not engage in the behaviour typically rests on the level of cons (e.g. Gee and Moore 1998)— and past experiences, they fail to assess the context in which the individual experiences this decision. So, while it is important to explain the motivating forces behind specific behaviours, it is also necessary to appreciate that these behaviours, or decisions relevant to them, occur within the context of the individual's life, and therefore a broader perspective may be more informative.

In considering such breadth, it is important to re-consider earlier generalist theorists whose work has provided the foundations and framework upon which much of what is subsequent has been built, whether we consciously acknowledge that scaffolding or not. To this end, I would like to revisit the work of Abraham Maslow, which, though formulated during the 1950s, foreshadows the spirit of the present time. In doing so, I will discuss his theoretical model in terms of health and I will use the sense of striving, of challenge that he described, as a metaphor for the positive strategies people use to avoid, solve or adjust to demands and to factors affecting health. A series of examples from different contexts will be used to show how such positive strategies enable us to deal better with the experience or perception of threats, losses or stress, with respect to our health. It is important also to consider the way that the conceptualization of health has changed across the course of the last century and how context has also influenced this change.

Health: a positive perspective

Health is considered by many people to be the absence of illness. However, a more positive paradigm replaced this limited and limiting approach when, in the immediate post Second World War years, the World Health Organization (WHO) reconceptualized health as: 'not only the absence of infirmity and disease but also a state of physical, mental, and social well-being' (WHO 1947). While this shift can be attributed partly to the recognition that the causes of death post the early twentieth century had changed, from diseases related to lack of hygiene, overcrowding, poor nutrition, and inadequate or polluted water supply, to those that involve *lifestyle factors*, this shift also occurred in the context of its time. This context involved the realignment that was taking place after the Second World War, the sense of new order and social responsibility. In addition, the insights from physicians, surgeons, and nurses working with the wounded on the battle fields and therapists involved with many of these same wounded in rehabilitation hospitals far from the site of battle presented a new perspective on the terms health and well-being. Interestingly, it was Goldstein, a neuropsychiatrist working during the First World War, who was among the first of modern practitioners to conclude that any particular symptom displayed by a patient could not be understood alone, rather it had to be considered in terms of the whole organism. In other words, the context albeit a physiological one was important here too.

This reframing of health constituted a radical shift in several ways. Among these was the move from a unidimensional construct of illness/health to a unified construct where not only the mind and body are considered together, but also one's sense of emotional and social well-being. This wholistic approach which incorporated the social self or *the sense of self and the world* was particularly relevant at this time. The war and its aftermath had, as indeed do most traumas, emphasized the social needs and particularly, the need for inter-connectedness among people. To many, the world had become *smaller* than ever before as people, especially soldiers, travelled from one side of the world to the other. People identified with each other through the presence of common threats and they drew together to gain a sense of solidarity, and to maintain their sense of hope and well-being in such times of turmoil. In Hobfoll's terms (see Chapter 4) such traumas or losses would serve to draw us together in a sense of communal coping.

This era also involved a time of reconstruction, of rebuilding economies, families, and of countries and citizens moving forward. Women had entered the workforce during the war and were not about to leave it, the baby boomers were being born and they would inherit and advance a new order. It was, in fact, a time ripe for social, political, and philosophical change: a time to accept the challenge to promote one's future well-being, including one's own health and that of the family, workplace, and nation.

In this context, Maslow (1954) upbraided members of the psychological community for their focus on a 'pessimistic, negative, and limited conception' of humanity. He argued that psychology had focused on people as attempting to avoid pain rather than as people taking active steps to gain pleasure and happiness. In contrast to what he considered the prevailing mood among psychologists although it might be said not the world in general, Maslow presented his hierarchy of needs. In this, he described individuals as striving to attain *self-actualization*. Self-actualization or self-realization, although different for everyone and not necessarily achieved by everyone, is the attainment of one's inherent potential.

Maslow's hierarchy of needs and health

Maslow's hierarchy of needs can be conceptualized in terms of physical, social, and psychological (mental) needs and, as such, reflects the WHO's definition of health (see Fig. 6.1). The hierarchy is built upon the foundation that individuals must first satisfy their physical needs: hunger, thirst, and warmth; these needs are followed by security needs such as

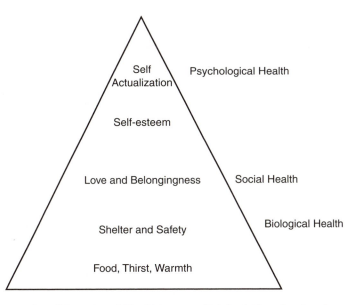

Figure 6.1 Representation of biopsychosocial health in terms of Maslow's hierarchy of needs.

shelter and safety. Together, these physical and security needs can be considered the base elements essential to a healthy individual or, more particularly, one's physical well-being. In terms of the WHO (1947) definition of health, satisfaction of needs at these levels would contribute to one's biological health.

The higher order social needs are next in Maslow's hierarchy and these are expressed in terms of belongingness and love, and social or self-in-the-world esteem. Fulfilment of these needs can be interpreted as contributing to social health. Finally self-esteem, which embraces being respected and approved of by others, but more importantly, one's own sense of dignity and self-regard, together with self-actualization which is the freedom for the fullest development of one's talents or aspirations, can be described as the elements of psychological health.

Individuals who have fulfilled their needs at these levels would in Maslow's terms be those who are self-actualized or who have achieved their potential, but in the terms of this chapter, they also are biopsychosocially healthy. Of course, these overarching terms are applied somewhat loosely as threats or losses at any level of the hierarchy may result in damage to one or more of these biopsychosocial systems. Yet, in sum, the satisfaction of these needs—to whatever individual degree—can be said to represent healthy individuals who have achieved their goals and, in Maslow's terms, who would be striving to achieve the goals further up the hierarchy. Such a positive, forward-moving approach is congruent with the basic survival motivation of human beings that is accompanied by their innate desire to achieve more for themselves and their families. However, much literature has focused on how people *cope* rather than how they *strive* forward and the assessment devices mostly are similarly limited in their focus.

Categories of coping strategies

From a psychodynamic perspective, coping with problems, with life, has been conceptualized as a series of defence mechanisms (e.g. denial, repression, humour, intellectualization) (Freud 1966) which are said to allow one to accept or cope with life's realities, and where the discharge of anxiety concerning these is seen as psychologically adaptive (Carr 1990; Raphael 1981). The cognitive-behaviourist's approach is directed more towards whether coping efforts are problem-oriented or emotion-based (e.g. Folkman and Lazarus 1980; Lazarus and Folkman 1984). There is much discussion in the literature about when each of these types of strategy are used. For instance, emotion-based strategies are said to be used when the situation is unchangeable (such as a terminal illness) or when the event first occurs (e.g. in the initial stages of being retrenched from work) but when the individual overcomes this initial shock, or in situations where change is possible, then problem-oriented strategies are said to be advanced. Yet, in a large community sample, Folkman and Lazarus (1980) found that in 98 per cent of cases people used both emotion-focused and problem-oriented strategies. Despite this, the real perplexity, remains in the lack of the assessment of what this situation means to the person facing the problem. This is particularly concerning in light of Lazarus and Folkman's description of an appraisal process that is said to occur in relation to potential and actual stressors. In order to overcome this operational deficit, we conducted interviews with people from a range of occupations and from these data developed a scale which incorporated four independent factors.

The Deakin coping scale

The scale we developed has 19 items which load onto four factors which together explain 57 per cent of the variance. These four factors are an appraisal component (7 items, e.g. I try to work out why it is a problem to me; Identify the source of the problem), a second factor which considered the level people were challenged by the problem (5 items, e.g. Take a positive approach and see it as a challenge; Take control of the situation), and a third factor which assessed the level of resources or, more specifically, social resources (4 items, e.g. Discuss it with my friends and colleagues; Seek help from others), sought to help overcome the issue (Moore and Greenglass 1997; Moore in press). In addition, there is a fourth factor labelled avoidant (4 items, e.g. Keep my fingers crossed that it will go away; Hope for a solution to appear). These four factors were internally reliable ($\alpha = 0.68$ to 0.88). A second-order confirmatory factor analysis was conducted and showed that these factors all loaded significantly onto a second-order factor which was labelled Striving to Achieve (χ^2 (147) 501.81, $p \leqslant 0.001$, Normed χ^2 3.41; Goodness of fit 0.91; Adjusted Goodness of Fit 0.89; Comparative Fit Index 0.90, Root Mean Squares Approximation (RMSEA) 0.06, $p > 0.05$). In addition, the single-sample expected cross-validation index (ECVI) suggested by Browne and Cudeck (1989) was 1.05 (90 per cent confidence intervals 0.93 : 1.17) indicating the potential stability of this model in further samples. As a further test of this model, a simultaneous confirmatory factor analysis for males and females was conducted to test for equivalence. This test revealed that the same factor model held true for both genders ($\chi^2 = 666.01$, $p \leqslant 0.001$, Normed $\chi^2 = 2.26$, RMSEA 0.04, $p = 0.74$).

The positive factors challenge and use of resources, together with the appraisal component loaded positively onto striving to achieve. Challenge demonstrated the highest loading (0.88). The avoidant factor, while loading significantly onto striving to achieve, was by far the lowest loading and negative (-0.19). Clearly, the use of avoidant strategies was divergent in effect to that demonstrated by the other factors. We have subsequently used this scale in several studies where the results have demonstrated that these positive approaches contribute to better health and well-being. However, when the use of avoidant strategies was dominant, the effects on health were negative.

One threat to people's well-being, that is, to their sense of esteem and psychological health which often has a ripple effect further down the hierarchy onto one's sense of belongingness, one's security, and also one's basic needs for food and shelter is unemployment and the associated loss of income. Unemployment results in the loss of a major role-identity, harm to psychological health and, beyond these, the resultant loss of income prompts people to reduce their expenditure on luxury items and leisure activities (Clarke 1982; Kessler *et al.* 1987) and this affects their social health. These financial reductions reduce the individual's sense of self-esteem and self-in-the-world. As unemployment continues, many unemployed people may have limited funds to spend on essential items and they may be forced to engage in subsistence living (Clarke 1982; Kessler *et al.* 1987). This last threatens even the basic needs described in Maslow's hierarchy.

Challenge strategies reduce impact of threats on health

Unemployment and health

Much research has shown that unemployment leads to poor health outcomes particularly in terms of depression and loss of self-esteem (Feather and Bond 1983; Wanberg *et al.* 1997). In our work, we have looked at the moderating role of positive and negative coping strategies on the relationship between income loss and psychological health during unemployment (Waters and Moore 2001). We found a significant interaction between whether people were employed or unemployed and their use of avoidant/affective coping strategies. High levels of avoidant/affective coping, which consists of blaming self, wishful thinking, and feeling miserable, were associated with poorer health outcomes as indicated by high levels of depression ($\beta = 0.46$) and low levels of self-esteem ($\beta = -0.34$). Those unemployed people who were significantly more depressed also used avoidant coping strategies more often while those not depressed used fewer avoidant coping strategies. The converse was true for positive strategies, that is, for strategies that were aimed at challenging the situation, finding a solution to the problem, and where persons actually reflected upon why the situation was a problem for them. Such a positive and challenging style can also be considered as approach-oriented efforts (e.g. Lazarus and Folkman 1984) but in addition, it involves an attitudinal component that will be addressed later in this chapter.

The interaction effects found in our study suggest also that when people were more challenged, the impact of income loss (when assessed separately for both material necessities and meaningful leisure activities) on depression was reduced. Furthermore, the impact of income loss on self-esteem was moderated when people used positive strategies in attempts to deal with or overcome this loss. These findings can be interpreted to suggest that people who adopt a position of challenge and the use of solution-oriented strategies or, in Maslow's terms, the concept of striving to maintain or increase one's base, are demonstrating an adaptive response during unemployment. That is, positive strategies mediated the impact of income loss upon psychological health, in this case, depression and self-esteem.

Restructuring changes and health

Depression and loss of self-esteem have been significant factors among nurses experiencing hospital-restructuring initiatives over the past decade or so (e.g. Greenglass and Burke 2000; Greenglass *et al.* in press). These initiatives have involved closure of beds, reductions in staffing levels, and reduced availability of resources for nurses, with little or no open consultation with the nursing staff involved. In addition to the significant levels of nurse distress following these radical changes, there has also been a marked intention by nurses to quit the profession (Moore 2001). In Maslow's terms, the health impact of these changes can be viewed in several downward spiralling ways. First, they have an impact on nurses' psychological health with respect to their sense of esteem (e.g. unworthy of being consulted, lack of resources to perform duties effectively). Second, for their effect on nurses' social health as they effect nurses' sense of belonging (e.g. reduced sense of being a meaningful part of the organization). Finally, under conditions of reduced shifts and therefore pay conditions, these initiatives also constitute a major threat to nurses' survival needs (e.g. food, shelter).

In a recent study of 200 Australian nurses, we used structural equation modelling to determine the impact of nurses' use of challenge strategies in response to hospital restructuring initiatives on a series of outcome variables (Moore 2002). Structural equation modelling is a statistical technique that allows for causal relationships to be inferred if the observed data fit the theoretical model and reveal the presence of significant paths among the variables in the model (Jöreskog and Sörbom 1989). It was found that where nurses reported that they were challenged by the changes, for instance, they 'took control of the situation' or 'tried to eliminate problems and carry on despite them', this sense of challenge contributed directly to their concurrent reports of professional self-efficacy ($\beta = 0.56$). For these nurses, this finding was interpreted to mean that they would and could do their jobs, that is, caring for their patients, despite the cutbacks. The use of challenge strategies also indirectly reduced nurses' intention to quit ($\beta = -0.13$) through their effect on professional efficacy while high levels of professional efficacy also led directly to a decrease in nurses' intention to quit ($\beta = -0.23$) (Moore 2002). In this same study, the high perceived impact of the restructuring changes (e.g less time for patient care, poorer working conditions) contributed to nurses' reported use of challenge strategies ($\beta = 0.41$). This predictive (and arguably causal) relationship suggests that nurses' sense of being challenged in response to the impact of restructuring was heightened and, as reported above, such challenge strategies contributed positively to nurses' well-being. This effect was in contrast to the direct relationship between high levels of restructuring and intention to quit ($\beta = 0.26$).

Overall, these findings can be used to suggest that nurses perceived the increase in demands and the deterioration in conditions as a challenge to be overcome. In this study, challenge was assessed as nurses' level of trying to eliminate problems and taking control of the situation, which clearly, they rated highly despite the demands upon them. In Maslow's terms, they were striving to maintain their position despite threats to their well-being.

Interestingly, nurses' perceptions of social support from their co-workers in response to hospital restructuring led to a concomitant increase in the use of challenge strategies. While the reasons for this relationship are unclear from the design of that study, many other researchers have suggested that social support exerts either a direct or a buffering effect against stressors (e.g. Bloom 1990). It is suggested here that nurses' sense of 'self-in-the-world' or, in Maslow's terms a sense of *belongingness* among their peers and in the ward/hospital, may have contributed to their use of positive strategies and hence their continued striving. In this same study, we found that social support was related also to decreases in nurses' sense of burnout and indirectly, to decreases in their intention to quit. The findings from this study support the positive role of striving, as described by Maslow, as the nurses strove to provide the best patient care despite the perception and, indeed reality, of a changed context and the conditions in which they worked. Their positive approach had implications for improved or maintained patient care. It also had implications for the nurses' own mental (reduced levels of burnout and intention to quit), social (social support, belongingness), and physical (the impact of actual quitting on nurses' resources and provision of basic needs) health and well-being in a context of change and stress.

Clearly, challenge strategies often involve pragmatic actions. These actions not only reduce or remove the stimulus or, in some situations maintain or achieve the individual's objectives but, according to Bandura (1977), would if successful, serve to increase one's sense of self-efficacy. The positive effect of efficacy on nurses' well-being was clearly evident among the nurses who formed this sample and there is much evidence from other researchers to suggest the utility of efficacy and related variables on health generally.

Mediators

Self-efficacy and control

Self-efficacy relates to 'people's judgments of their capabilities to organize and to execute courses of action required to attain designated types of performances' (Bandura 1997, p. 391). According to Bandura, the most potent source of self-efficacy is *enactive mastery experience*. This means that successes and failures are the most authentic and re-enforcing criteria in terms of demonstrating one's ability to perform a task or achieve one's goals. However, information from enactive mastery experiences is not all that is reflected in future performances. Both ability and non-ability factors are weighted so that people account for their perceived level of capability against the effort to be expended, as well as the difficulty and content of the task (Bandura 1997).

Moreover, it may be that people will choose not to engage in positive or challenge or fight strategies if they do not perceive value in the probable result for the effort and resources required to be expended or, in some cases, risked. It might be assumed that, in the studies mentioned above, nurses see value in caring for their patients; unemployed people see value in obtaining re-employment, and therefore, the use of positive strategies in their striving to maintain their health and meet their needs is appropriate. The literature on coping and coping strategies has failed to consider this important criterion of the object's *value* to the individual. Lazarus and Folkman (1984) did refer to primary and secondary appraisal processes where the individual appraises the situation as stressful or not (primary appraisal) and if appraised as stressful, then a secondary consideration follows which is basically an evaluation of: Do I have the resources to cope? While these processes do acknowledge that individuals relate the event to themselves, there is still no consideration of the value of the threatened resource or the event for the person and, aside from our scale items (see above), this aspect is lacking in most assessments.

The literature is also largely silent on those who have failed in their striving to solve demands or to deal with threats to their well-being in the past. These people would, in Bandura's (1977, 1997) terms, be said to lack self-efficacy or, in Seligman and Maier's (1967) terms, to have developed a sense of learned helplessness. Such a lack of efficacy would seem to act to reduce further striving and may be accompanied by the depressive affect common in situations of learned helplessness. The concept of learned helplessness is associated with a lack of control and a resultant lack of striving.

My own work has shown that those persons who were low in their use of challenge-oriented strategies but high in the use of avoidant strategies, rated the control influence of powerful others and chance significantly higher than those persons low in their use of avoidant strategies and high on challenge-oriented strategies (Moore 1999). This pattern occurred despite the fact that both groups rated themselves similarly on the internal control subscale. The control dimensions in that study were rated using Levenson's (1974) three-factor Locus of Control Scale.

This result can be extrapolated to suggest that efficacy may be multidimensional rather than unidimensional. That is, it is not only one's previous history of success or failure (in this case the level of internal control) but rather one's perceptions of external factors, in this case the influence of others and chance within the context of the particular scenario, that impacts on perceived efficacy. These detrimental effects on efficacy would, in turn, act to increase negative affect and reduce the use of positive, solution-oriented strategies. Of course, such a proposition has links with the notion of the need to assess specific self-efficacy indicators as advocated by Bandura (1997) among others and this may help explain the sometimes weak effects for efficacy reported in the literature. An indirect example of this effect, although not specifically couched in terms of internal or external control or indeed, self-efficacy, is Sharpley and Gardner's (2001) finding that 94 per cent of managers they interviewed related stress to a lack of physical, emotional, or behavioural control. The qualitative data they collected indicated that respondents' reports of lack of control were related to work outcomes, their amount of work relative to time limits, the quality of work produced, and their levels of job security. Another early theorist in this area, Karasek (1979) proposed an interaction between demands (as a stressor) and control (over that demand) and health outcomes and some research since has provided support for this concept. For instance, Tinker and Moore (2001) found that the higher the level of perceived control academics and teachers reported they had over the number of hours they worked, the less negative was the impact on their psychological and physical health. However, as Lazarus and Folkman (1984) pointed out, it is not only actual threats to, or loss of, our hierarchical needs or potential that affect our sense of striving and achievement; it is also our perceptions of threat or loss and, in more recent terms, dispositional factors (e.g. Kobassa 1979; Scheier and Carver 1985) that affect health and well-being.

Perceptions and goals

Lazarus and Folkman (1984) incorporated a perceptual or cognitive component into their definition of stress. Accordingly, it is when the *perceived* demands exceed the *perceived* resources that Lazarus and Folkman argued that stress occurs or, using Maslow's hierarchy when elements of self are perceived to be compromised, the individual's well-being is affected. However, if one considers the appraisal components that Lazarus and Folkman described in relation to stress, their definition would be more embracing if it were to include the word may: that is, when the perceived demands exceed the perceived resources stress *may* occur. The word *may* is italicized here for two reasons. One is because people will vary in the value they place on a construct under threat and secondly, because for some people high levels of demand or threat, whether they have or do not have resources available, will be considered by them to be a challenge. Rather than being disabled by high levels of demands or threat, they will be energized and take steps to assume control over the situation.

Kobasa (1979) referred to such people as having a hardy personality. More specifically, she described the hardy person as having a sense of challenge, control and commitment. People who exhibit a hardy personality have a lower risk of becoming ill following stress than people who are less hardy (Kobasa 1979; Kobasa *et al.* 1982). In fact, other research has shown that people with a *hardiness profile* have lower physiological reactivity to stress (Lawler and Schmeid 1992) and decreased susceptibility to stress related phenomena such as burnout (Sciacchitano *et al.* 2001). This image of a committed, in charge, and challenged personality type also conveys a sense of striving, of goals to be attained, and is congruent with Maslow's (1954) process of self-actualization. In the terms of this chapter, the ultimate goal would be the striving for and maintaining biopsychosocial health. More recently Scheier and Carver (1985) argued that practically all of human activity could be understood in terms of goal-directed behaviour. But not everyone has the same goals or the same profile to achieve. It may be that, in addition to the context and the value the individual places on the goal, it is individual differences in personality or ways of being in the world that determine whether one reacts negatively or is challenged. This personality dimension may be optimism.

Optimism, positive strategies, and health outcomes

Tiger (1979) for instance, conceptualized optimism as 'an attitude associated with an expectation about the social or material future—one which the evaluator regards as socially desirable, to his advantage, or for his pleasure' (p. 18). In Scheier and Carver's (1985) terms, optimism is the global expectation of positive outcomes. They termed people who generally have expectations of favourable outcomes 'optimists' and people who generally expect unfavourable outcomes 'pessimists'. These two definitions of optimism can be used to support an argument proposed earlier in this chapter. That is, if individuals *value* the object to be attained or maintained under threat of loss, and they have a sense that they can deal with powerful others, in combination these factors will lead to a positive forward-looking approach and strategies to deal with the threat. Findings from previous research lend support to this contention.

Research has found that optimism is associated with adaptation to stressful events because optimists use more action-oriented and have positive strategies to cope with stress

(Scheier *et al.* 1986; Vitaliano *et al.* 1987). Among the strategies shown to be associated with optimism and better outcomes are solution-oriented coping, seeking social support, emphasizing positive aspects, and acceptance when a problem is unavoidable. This last brings to mind the literature which states that emotion-focused strategies are used when situations are unchangeable and problem or solution-oriented strategies when the situation can be changed (e.g. Lazarus and Folkman 1984). However, in times of loss (e.g. death of a loved one) or diagnosis of a chronic or terminal illness, it needs to be acknowledged that distress following such an event is natural: it is to be expected among human beings. However, even in such circumstances, people's resilience, their goal-directed intentions and behaviours do rise to the fore with time. It is imperative, furthermore, to acknowledge the context of the loss and that some time is essential to grieve, but that this grief also needs to be time limited or health will be compromised.

Indeed, people will, in their own time, comment that they need to move forward, to move on. 'Their loved one would have wanted it'. 'They have to take sole responsibility now for the children and therefore they have to be strong'. This scenario is somewhat akin to Scheier and Carver's (1985) proposal that optimism, in this case of life without the loved one or with/despite the illness, drives goal-directed behaviour through a belief in the positive consequences of future behaviour and the potential for happiness. This last is similar also to Bandura's (1997) concept of self-efficacy where previous task success, whether real or perceived, encourages a sense of success in future behaviours. Kelly and Cross (1985) are among those who have provided empirical support for this proposition as they found that drawing on past experiences, one aspect of self-efficacy, was a major coping behaviour among nurses. Both the optimism and efficacy constructs suggest that people have a sense of empowerment. By extension, as was suggested earlier, empowered people would not perceive others to be more powerful than them or, at least, not so powerful as to disempower themselves in the attainment of their goals. Or, as the person who made the remark which opened this chapter stated 'I'm a paraplegic, but I'm not coping, I've got other things to focus on, I'm living not coping'. The time required for adjustment, to regain homoeostasis, will differ across people and across occasions, but for optimum health and well-being, it is an essential adaptation. This adaptation requires individual effort but it is generally enhanced by the support of others in our social world—a major component of health and well-being.

More recently, Adams *et al.* (2000) reported that optimism was related to life purpose ($r = 0.55$) and to perceived wellness ($r = 0.53$). Interestingly, they defined perceived wellness in terms of 'living in a manner that permits the experience of committed, balanced growth in the emotional, intellectual, physical, psychological, social, and spiritual dimensions of human existence' (p. 172). This definition has considerable overlap with Maslow's paradigm that people are engaged in growth, in striving for the attainment and advancement of their needs. Earlier in this chapter, these needs were conceptualized as physical, social, and psychological. However, it is arguable that the spiritual and intellectual domains proposed by Adams *et al.* are inherent in the domains of Maslow's hierarchy.

Challenge, optimism, efficacy, and physical health

There is much literature to suggest that positive, namely solution-oriented strategies are related to better health outcomes across a wide range of domains and illnesses. For example, Pakenham *et al.* (1997) found that avoidance strategies predicted levels of depression, distress, and low social adjustment among people with multiple sclerosis (MS) while problem-focused strategies typically predicted better adjustment. Conversely, the use of emotion-focused strategies, including avoidance and wishful thinking, have consistently been associated with poorer health outcomes among people with MS (e.g. Aitkens *et al.* 1997; Jean *et al.* 1999; McCabe *et al.* 2001). Building on findings such as these, Mohr and Goodkin (1999) found that intervention programmes designed to improve positive coping skills of people with MS were more effective at improving mood than were insight therapies.

As well as such training providing practical skills, such as identifying for self what the problems are and why, then developing the use of assertive skills to confront issues appropriately, such programmes may also involve, overtly or covertly, a change in levels of efficacy and optimism. Certainly, it would be expected that efficacy would be enhanced directly by rehearsal and role-plays and vicariously also by observation of others within the group. Increased efficacy would surely be related to increased expectations of positive future events or outcomes and, in terms of the life orientation test (LOT; Scheier and Carver 1985), such positive future beliefs would reflect optimism and such optimism would itself be reflected in purposeful striving. Both optimism and striving would be related to an increased sense of control of self, *vis a vis* powerful others or chance. The interactions among these factors are proposed in the following model.

Proposed model of biopsychosocial health

A model is proposed in the following figure (Fig. 6.2) that shows the direct impact of threats, demands, or stressors, on health where health is operationalized as a composite of biopsychosocial domains in accordance with the WHO (1947) and Maslow's hierarchy of needs. However, such a model takes no account of individual differences that have been shown to be important mediators of this relationship. It is necessary therefore to theoretically account for these in an extended model.

The discussion in this chapter has focused on the importance of positive strategies when dealing with threats or demands. It has been argued that a positive approach where the individual's perception and approach is one of *challenge* rather than avoidance or a sense that things are chores, leads to better health outcomes and is, moreover, innately part of the human condition. However, it was also argued that these relationships would only prevail if the actor valued the issue or outcome, if the context facilitated or inspired the individual

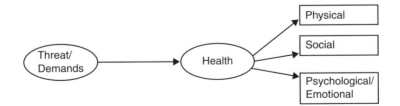

Figure 6.2 Direct impact of threats or demands on health.

to act or change, and if there were positive efficacy and outcome expectations. Therefore, the context is important. Figure 6.3 models these interrelationships. The complexity of the interactions and the feedback loops within such a nonrecursive model are more complex than can be discussed here and, for the sake of parsimony, the discussion of the model has been limited to those argued in this chapter as the main protagonists.

The arrows in the model indicate a direct relationship between threats or stressors and values. If the object under threat is not valued then the individual might take no further action. A feedback loop from values to threat acknowledges the presence of threat without any further action. If the threatened object is valued, then the person who has an optimistic bias and a sense of efficacy will also have a sense of control in this situation. Based upon these dispositions of optimism, efficacy, and a sense of control, they will be challenged by the demand or threat and will engage in the use of solution-oriented strategies to deal with it. These positive strategies contribute also to better physical, mental, and social health which of itself, also enhances the ability to deal with the perceptions or reality of the initial threat.

There are also dynamic feedback loops operating between feeling challenged and using solution-oriented strategies, optimism, and efficacy, and between health and threats/stressors. These loops indicate that the individual is continually challenging threats, re-enforcing levels of well-being and thus maintaining homoeostasis while, at the same time, allowing for growth and greater achievement and movement towards self-actualization and an wholistic concept of health.

The proposed model is reflective of the overall aim of any organism, that is, its survival. In order to survive or maintain homeostasis, the organism has to be positive and meet challenges or demands as appropriate. Moreover, as resources are limited, people have to achieve this in a manner that preserves those things that are of value to them while at the same time, conserving energy by ignoring those things that are not valued. Perceptions of value may vary inter- and intrapersonally as the context varies and as the context is dynamically influenced by the other factors in the model.

As with clinicians when a client first presents for treatment, researchers in the future needs to be cognisant of the context in which loss, threat, and demands occur. This context will be multidimensional and will include personal factors such as mood, motivation, expectations, age, and gender; social and cultural indicators such as peers, media, religion, laws, and world and community indicators such as the economy, and the states of peace or turmoil. It is also important, as in the present time, to heed Maslow's credo that people are innately good and positive.

Indeed, such an innate positive approach can be seen in everyday life. This positive response is not confined to major traumas but can be seen as an approach to everday life. An everyday example serves to illustrate what is, in Maslow's terms, human beings inherent positivity. Friends, colleagues, even strangers, ask us 'How are you?' and the reply is typically 'I'm well, thank you' no matter how we may be feeling. Is such a response simply a function of our socialization, that is, a sign of politeness; does it reflect a lack of thought about, or desire to reveal, any other status, or is it part of an inherently positive approach to life and living?

In this chapter I have argued in support of the last premise where such a premise is congruent with a survival process that also moves us forward to achieve our goals. These goals

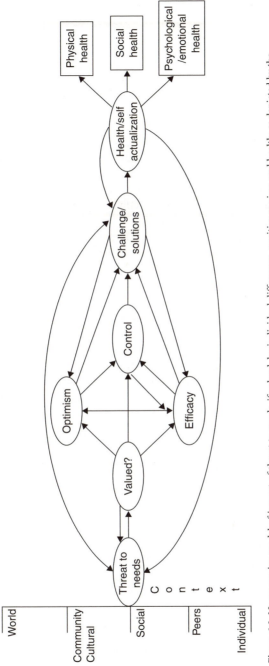

Figure 6.3 Nonrecursive model of impact of threat to needs, if valued, by individual differences, positive coping, and health: as depicted by the maintenance or attainment of Maslow's hierarchical needs profile within a multifaceted context.

relate to our biopsychosocial health. Biological and mental health may be considered to be more individually determined but social health, that is, the concept of belongingness, love and esteem, are inextricably linked to the concept of *self in and part of the world*. Just as all three elements of health are required for individual fulfilment, so too the place of self in the world is an essential component of this sense of well-being.

Conclusions

In this chapter I have argued that if one values an object that is under threat, then a positive attitude which involves a sense of optimism, self-efficacy, and a sense of control, will lead to the perception of that threat as a challenge. This evaluation will be contextual so that what is valued at some stages may not be at others. Such positive processes contribute to better health and, via the dynamic feedback loops proposed in the model, to enhanced strategies to deal with subsequent threats.

Maslow's hierarchy of needs model was used as a metaphor to describe the positive striving that individuals undertake in order to maintain homeostasis and to attain further needs. I do not suggest that there is an absence of impact for example from loss, however, it is proposed that the positive management of demands and resources and the successful resolution of these are both rewarding and efficacious. Furthermore, such a positive approach should not be characterized as coping, but more appropriately as striving and living.

While it may be argued that a simplistic and highly positive perspective has been presented one must ask what are the costs of not being positive. The costs, at least in Maslow's terms and those of the current milieu, are poorer biopsychosocial health. I respectively suggest that Abraham Maslow would agree with this premise.

References

Adams, T. B., Bezner, J. R., Drabbs, M. E., Zambarano, R. J., and Steinhardt, M. A. (2000). Conceptualisation and measurement of the spiritual and psychological dimensions of wellness in a college population. *Journal of American College Health*, **48**, 165.

Aitkens, J. E., Fischer, J. S., Namey, M., and Rudick, R. A. (1997). A replicated prospective investigation of life events, coping, and depressive symptoms in multiple sclerosis. *Journal of Behavioural Medicine*, **20**, 433–45.

Ajzen, I. (1985). From intentions to actions: A theory of planned behavior, in J. Kuhl and J. Beckman (eds.), *Action-control: From cognition to behavior*, pp. 11–39. Heidelberg: Springer.

—— and Fishbein, M. (1980). The prediction of behavior from attitudinal and normative beliefs. *Journal of Personality and Social Psychology*, **6**, 466–87.

Bandura, A. (1977). Self-efficacy: Towards a unifying theory of behavioral change. *Psychological Review*, **84**, 191–215.

—— (1997). *Self-efficacy: The exercise of control.* New York: W. H. Freeman.

Beck, A. T. (1970). Cognitive therapy: Nature and relation to behavior therapy. *Behavior Therapy*, **1**, 184–200.

Becker, M. H. (ed.) (1974). The health belief model and personal health behavior. *Health Education Monographs*, **2**, 324–508.

Bloom, J. R. (1990). The relationship of social support and health. *Social Science in Medicine*, **30**, 635–37.

Browne, M. W. and Cudeck, R. (1989). Single sample cross-validation indices for covariance structures. *Multivariate Behavior Research*, **24**, 445–55.

Carr, V. H. (1990). Managing the psychosocial responses of the transplant patient, in K. M. Sigardson-Poor and R. M. Haggerty (eds.), *Nursing care of the transplant recipient*, pp. 53–87. London: W.B. Saunders.

Clarke, R. (1982). *Work in crisis: the dilemma of a nation*. Edinburgh: The Saint Andrew Press.

Dember, W. N. (1974). Motivation and the cognitive revolution. *American Psychologist*, **29**, 161–68.

Ellis, A. and Harper, R. A. (1975). *A new guide to rational living*. New York: Prentice-Hall.

Folkman, S. and Lazarus, R. S. (1980). An analysis of coping in a middle-aged community sample. *Journal of Health and Social Behavior*, **21**, 219–39.

Freud, A. (1966). *The ego and mechanisms of defence*. New York: International Universities Press.

Galton, F. (1883). *Inquiries into human faculty and its development*. Reprinted 1973. New York: AMS Press Inc.

Gee, D. L. and Moore, K. A. (1998). Situational, dispositional and motivational factors in promoting health behaviour (Exercise behaviour), in R. Schwarzer (ed.), *Advances in Health Psychology Research*, CD ROM Vol. 1. Berlin: Freie Universitat.

Greenglass, E. R. and Burke, R. L. (2000). Hospital downsizing, individual resources and occupational stressors in nurses. *Anxiety, Stress and Coping: An International Journal*, **13**, 371–90.

—— Burke, R. J., and Moore, K. A. Nurse reactions to increased hospital workload: Effects on professional efficacy following hospital restructuring. *Applied Psychology: An International Review* (in press).

Holt, R. R. (1964). The return of the ostracized. *American Psychologist*, **19**, 254–64.

James, W. (1892). *Psychology: Briefer course*. New York: Henry Holt & Company.

Jean, V., Paul, R. H., and Beatty, W. W. (1999). Psychological and neurological predictors of coping patterns by patients with multiple sclerosis. *Journal of Clinical Psychology*, **55**, 21–6.

Jöreskog, K. G. and Sörbom, D. (1989). *Lisrel 7: A guide to the program and applications*. SPSS: Chicago.

Karasek, R. A. (1979). Job demands, job decision latitude and mental strain: Implications for job redesign. *Administrative Science Quarterly*, **24**, 285–308.

Kelly, J. G. and Cross, D. G. (1985). Stress, coping behaviors, and recommendations for intensive care and medical surgical ward registered nurses. *Research Nursing and Health*, **8**, 321–28.

Kessler, R. C., Turner, J. B., and House, J. S. (1987). Intervening processes in the relationship between unemployment and health. *Psychological Medicine*, **17**, 949–61.

Kobasa, S. C. (1979). Stressful life events, personality and health: An inquiry into hardiness. *Journal of Personality and Social Psychology*, **37**, 1–11.

—— Maddi, S. R., and Kahn, S. (1982). Hardiness and health: A prospective study. *Journal of Personality and Social Psychology*, **42**, 168–77.

Lawler, K. A. and Schmeid, L. A. (1992). A prospective study of women's health: The effects of stress, hardiness, locus of control, type A behavior, and physiological reactivity. *Women & Health*, **19**, 27–43.

Lazarus, R. S. and Folkman, S. (1984). *Stress, appraisal and coping*. New York: Springer.

Levenson, H. (1974). Activism and powerful others: Distinctions within the concept of internal-external control. *Journal of Personality Assessment*, **38**, 377–83.

Maslow, A. H. (1954). *Motivation and personality*. New York: Harper and Row.

McCabe, M. P., McDonald, E., and McKern, S. (2001). Coping and psychological adjustment among people with multiple sclerosis. Paper under review.

Mohr, D. C. and Goodkin, D. E. (1999). Treatment of depression in multiple sclerosis: Review and meta-analysis. *Clinical Psychology: Science Practice*, 6, 1–9.

Moore, K. A. (1999). A two-axis-model of coping: Impact on health. Paper presented at the *13th European Health Psychology Conference*, Florence, 1–3 October.

—— (2002). Hospital restructuring: Impact on nurses mediated by social support and a perception of challenge. *Journal of Health and Human Services Administration* (in press).

—— The Deakin Coping Scale: Strategies successful in striving to achieve. *The Journal of Interpersonal Relationships: Work, Social and Family* (in press).

—— and Greenglass, E. (1997). Development and applications of the Deakin Coping Scale. *Paper presented at the 5th European Congress on Psychology*, Dublin, 5–9 July.

Pakenham, K. I., Stewart, C. A., and Rogers, A. (1997). The role of coping in adjustment to multiple sclerosis-related adaptive demands. *Psychology, Health and Medicine*, 2, 197–211.

Pearlin, L. I. and Schooler, C. (1978). The structure of coping. *Journal of Health and Social Behavior*, 19, 2–21.

Prochaska, J. O. and DiClements, C. C. (1982). Transtheoretical therapy: toward a more integrative model of change. *Psychotherapy: Theory Research and Practice*, 19, 276–88.

Rachman, S. (1968). *Phobias: Their nature and control*. Ill: Charles C. Thomas.

Raphael, B. (1981). Personal disaster. *Australian New Zealand Journal of Psychiatry*, 15, 183–98.

Richardson, A. (1983). Imagery: Definition and types, in A. A. Sheikh (ed.), *Imagery: Current theory, research, and application*, pp. 3–42. New York: John Wiley and Sons.

Scheier, M. F. and Carver, C. (1985). Optimism, coping, and health: Assessment and implications of generalized outcome expectancies. *Health Psychology*, 4, 219–47.

—— Weintraub, K. K., and Carver, C. S. (1986). Coping with stress: Divergent strategies of optimists and pessimists. *Journal of Personality and Social Psychology*, 51, 1257–64.

Schwarzer, R. (1992). Self efficacy in the adoption and maintenance of health behaviours: Theoretical approaches and a new model, in R. Schwarzer (ed.), *Self efficacy: thought control of action*, pp. 217–43. Washington, DC: Hemisphere.

Sciacchitano, M., Goldstein, M. B., and DiPlacido, J. (2001). Stress, burnout and hardiness in R.Ts. *Radiologic Technology*, 72, 321–9.

Sharpley, C. F. and Gardner, J. (2001). Managers' understanding of stress and its effects in the workplace. *Journal of Applied Health Behaviour*, 3, 24–30.

Seligman, M. E. P. and Csikszentmihalyi, M. (2000). Positive psychology. *American Psychologist*, 55, 5–14.

—— and Maier, S. G. (1967). Failure to escape traumatic shock. *Journal of Experimental Psychology*, 74, 1–9.

Stampfl, T. and Lewis, D. (1967). Essentials of therapy: A learning theory-based psychodynamic behavioral therapy. *Journal of Abnormal Psychology*, 72, 496–503.

Tiger, L. (1979). *Optimism: The biology of hope*. New York: Simon & Schuster.

Tinker, S. and Moore, K. A. (2001). The impact of long work hours on the family-work relationship and health. *Paper presented at 1st Annual Conference—Relationships Interest Group of the Australian Psychology Society*, Melbourne, 17–18 November, 2001.

Vitaliano, P. P., Russo, J., Carr, J. E., Maiuro, R. D., and Becker, J. (1987). The ways of coping checklist: Revision and psychometric properties. *Multivariate Behavior Research*, 20, 3–26.

Waters, L. and Moore, K. A. (2001). Coping with economic deprivation during unemployment. *Journal of Economic Psychology*, 22, 461–82.

Watson, J. B. (1913). Psychology as a behaviorist views it. *Psychological Review*, 20, 158–77.

Wolpe, J. (1954). Reciprocal inhibition as the main basis of psychotherapeutic effects. *Archives of Neurology and Psychiatry*, 72, 205–26.

—— (1958). *Psychotherapy by reciprocal inhibition*. Stanford, CA: Stanford University Press.

World Health Organization (1947). The constitution of the World Health Organization. *WHO Chronicle*, 1, 29.

YOUNG PEOPLE'S WORLDS

CHAPTER 7

MEETING CHALLENGES IN A CLASSROOM CONTEXT

MONIQUE BOEKAERTS

Learning according to the principle of positive psychology

In the March issue of the *American Psychologist*, Sheldon and King (2001) argued that a negative bias, which seems to pervade much of theoretical psychology, may limit psychologists' understanding of typical and successful human functioning. These authors argue that researchers should focus on the virtues and strengths of individuals rather than on their weakness and impediments. In the same issue, Fredrickson (2001) also posited that researchers should cultivate a more appreciative perspective on human nature. She proposed a new theoretical perspective on positive emotions within the emerging field of positive psychology.

This article is written from the perspective of positive educational psychology. Within this sub-field of psychology, major shifts have been noted in the last decade. A first shift pertains to motivation research. In the 1990s motivation researchers recognized that student motivation is domain-specific. Research evidence in relation to different subject-matter areas convinced motivation researchers that the study of motivation as a stable personality characteristic should be supplemented. Later research (for review, see Järvela and Volet 2001) showed that it is not sufficient to study student motivation as a domain-specific trait. Domain-specific information about students' motivation and strategy use should be supplemented by their appraisals of the context within which a learning activity takes place (situation-specific motivation). In this respect, Boekaerts (2001*a*) argued that what students intend to do in an actual classroom situation (goal setting) depends largely on how they give meaning to the learning task and its context. What they subsequently do to achieve those goals (goal striving) depends on the quality of their self-regulatory skills and on their ongoing appraisal process. Today, many research instruments are available to study the goal-setting and goal-striving processes in detail. Data accumulated with these experience sampling methods (e.g. Boekaerts 1999*a*; Krapp 2001; Turner and Meyer 2000; Volet 1997) allow us to conclude that the unique way in which students assign meaning to a learning activity determines, to a large extent, how much effort they are prepared to invest to reach a curricular goal.

A second major shift that was noted in the psychology of education pertains to the new roles assigned to students and teachers. At present, teachers are making massive changes in their teaching practice. Direct teaching is replaced or supplemented by teaching according to the principles of social constructivism. This implies that teachers invite their students to adopt a new learner role (be active, constructive, self-regulative, and responsible learners). In order to help students to fulfil the new learner role, teachers adopt various complementary teacher roles. They first explain or demonstrate new knowledge, adopting the role of expert model. Subsequently, they change to the role of supportive and understanding coach. As a coach, teachers share the responsibility for learning with their students. It is the understanding of both students and teachers that teachers will gradually withdraw their instructional support while students progressively take on more responsibility for further learning. Research evidence as well as classroom observation show that students who are encouraged to adopt the new learner role learn in a fundamentally different way compared to students who passively listen to the teachers' presentation. Furthermore, they acquire a set of self-regulatory skills that prepare them for life-long learning (Boekaerts 1997; Pintrich 2000; Shuell 1988; Weinstein *et al.* 2000; Zimmerman 2000). Self-regulated learning includes the setting of appropriate goals, planning to reach these goals, time and effort management, evaluating whether the goals have been reached.

How can positive psychology and the major shifts in the psychology of education influence researchers and teachers' understanding of how students create meaning in their school life by striving for ambitious goals? How do students mobilize forces to turn complex learning tasks into a series of challenges that lead to the achievement of these ambitious goals? As Sheldon and King explained, positive psychology focuses again on the average person with an interest in what is working. It aims at understanding the strengths and virtues of individuals who function effectively. Its target is to describe what these persons actually do to improve their functioning. From the point of view of positive psychology, it is becoming increasingly clear that the functioning of students who make the grade cannot be accounted for within a framework that takes misunderstanding, misconceptions, misregulation, and coping with stress as a starting point. In the past, educational and instructional psychologists studied the content, structure, and sequence of various types of learning activities. Meticulous task analyses were set up to help teachers promote learning environments where mistakes could be prevented and students could achieve success. For their part, school psychologists focused on the impediments, threats, losses and failures of students, and asking many questions about the antecedents of failure. This research focus has provided us with shelves of books on student drop-out, repeating the grade, anxiety, fear of failure, and demotivation. Due to their concern with mistakes, errors and bugs, and their eagerness to prevent stress in the classroom, researchers devoted the majority of their attention to how students deal with the negative aspects of learning. The message these researchers gave to teachers is that students who are not successful in school lack something. They may lack intelligence, prior knowledge, adequate cognitive strategy use, favourable motivational beliefs, and even a favourable family background. This negative approach is not very helpful to teachers for two main reasons. First, it affects teacher self-efficacy and outcome expectation (cf. Bandura 1986). Research has yielded evidence that teachers obtain better results, when they believe that they can teach their students the basic skills necessary to pass the grade despite individual differences in intelligence and family background. These teachers promote a learning orientation in the classroom and persist longer in the face of obstacles (Gibson and Dembo 1984; Turner *et al.* 1998). Second, focusing on what can go wrong encourages teachers to adopt a remedial approach. Teachers with such an approach set out to help their students to compensate for lack of ability or lack of resources or to alleviate symptoms of anxiety, uncertainty, and frustration.

Positive psychology takes a different perspective by looking primarily at teachers and students who succeed in school, because they approach problems and obstacles in a positive way. They use the new context-sensitive measurement instruments to tap into the cognitive and motivational processes that students use in actual learning situations to turn it into a challenging experience. My aim in this article is to explore what students think, feel and do when they meet with problems in the classroom, yet appraise them as a challenge? The main question that I will address in this article is: 'What determines students' decision to invest effort in complex and difficult tasks?'

Goal setting and goal striving as part of the self-regulation process

Most teachers can identify students who maximize opportunities for learning and contrast them to students who minimize opportunities for learning. For an illustration of students who maximize opportunities for learning, I turn to a learning situation that was set up according to the principles of social constructivism.

In the beginning of the school year, I visited Leone's classroom. She is teaching fifth grade students. At the moment I entered her classroom she was informing her students that they were going to use the brand-new computer room. The students were informed that by the end of the year, they would be able to put their own texts and pictures on the World Wide Web. All of the students were enthusiastic about this message. They seemed very interested in what Leone told them about the web and they enjoyed watching how two of their peers were actually helping Leone find interesting sites. My attention was caught by Loraine's behaviour. It was immediately obvious that she did not have a clue as to what was required to manipulate the keys on the keyboard. However, she was fascinated when the screen turned into a succession of multi-coloured pictures and interesting stories. I knew from Leone's information that Loraine and most of her peers were passive students in the language lessons. These immigrant students still had difficulty with the Dutch language and disliked all kind of language exercises, primarily because they felt they did not have sufficient skills.

Two months later, I visited Leone's classroom again. Leone quickly informed me that her students were now able to write a short text in Word and illustrate it with some pictures she had scanned in herself. Currently they were learning to print their own messages and integrate this new skill with previously learned skills (write a message to a friend in Word and illustrate it with a picture). I watched how Loraine started enthusiastically, but somehow could not print her message. She tried to get the teacher's attention after several unsuccessful attempts. However, Leone was busy helping other students. Loraine, looked around and noticed that some students were already printing. She asked them for help. Interestingly, she was not satisfied when her text was printed. Before she checked the text and admired the pretty pictures, she asked the student who had helped her: 'Show me again how to do it so that I can do it myself, the next time'. She then continued working till she actually succeeded in printing her own message.

What this example shows us is that students who are usually passive in language class may show completely different behaviour when they are invited to pursue a learning goal that is in accordance with their own need and value system. There is plenty of anecdotal evidence that students who have established their own goalposts keep moving toward these goalposts, even when obstacles are apparent and the teacher is not present to encourage them to keep striving. In other words, students like Loraine, who are usually not committed to do language tasks, seem able to self-regulate their learning process and show responsibility for their learning. What can we learn from this example? What do students, who are able and willing to self-regulate their own learning process, do differently compared to students who seem to have difficulty in regulating their learning? In what way is their goal-striving process different from the goal-striving process of students who decline to take responsibility for the learning process? In the next few paragraphs, the self-regulation process will be described in some detail, focusing mainly on motivational, volitional, and affective aspects of self-regulation.

Self-regulation of the learning process

Many definitions of self-regulated learning have been given. These definitions all share the understanding that students who can regulate their own learning process have access to cognitive and motivational strategies that are necessary and sufficient to reach the goals set by the teacher or the curriculum. These students have built up conditional knowledge that will help them select specific cognitive strategies from their repertoire that are appropriate for the task or activity at hand. This knowledge is traditionally referred to as 'metacognitive' knowledge. Moreover, students who can self-regulate their learning process can also coordinate these strategies in the service of the learning goal. These skills are traditionally referred to as 'metacognitive skills' and include orienting, planning executing, monitoring, repairing, reflecting, and evaluating. Boekaerts (1997) proposed a heuristic six-component model to illustrate that self-regulated learning consists of several interacting sub-systems. This model describes various types of knowledge as well as the cognitive and motivational strategies that operate on that knowledge. Zimmerman (2000) described self-regulated learning as a cyclical process. He proposed three cyclic phases, namely forethought, performance and volitional control, and self-reflection. In each of these three phases metacognitive skills and motivational and volitional skills are intertwined. An inherent limitation of many current models of self-regulated learning is that learners are conceived as regulating themselves, after the goals for learning have been set by somebody else. What researchers, and by implication teachers who are involved in collaborative research, consider self-regulated learning seems to be a mixture of external regulation and self-regulation.

In the last two decades, researchers have described various self-regulatory skills that students use in a classroom context. Students' flaws in self-regulatory skills and in their beliefs about themselves as a self-regulated learner have also been described. For example, De Corte et al. (2000) reported that students' self-regulation of mathematical problem solving is poorly developed. Compared to the expert approach, 60 per cent of the students who solved complex mathematical problems in class seemed to rely heavily on two strategies. They read the problem and immediately selected one specific solution strategy to solve it. These students did not analyse the problem adequately. Neither did they consider any alternative strategies nor plan alternative actions, even when it was evident that they had not been making any progress. De Corte et al. (2000) described several intervention programmes in which students could improve their self-regulatory skills in relation to realistic mathematical problem-solving. They identified a set of principles for the design of powerful learning environments that promote the development of these skills. These authors also invited teachers to set up their mathematics teaching according to these principles. Positive results were reported. Other researchers have made similar attempts in relation to other subject areas, designing principles for volitional strategies (for review, see Randi and Corno, 2000), learning strategies (see Weinstein *et al.* 2000) and self-efficacy development (see, Schunk and Ertmer 2000). Overwhelmingly positive results were reported by researchers, teachers and by the students themselves (Masui 2001; Schunk 1994; Zimmerman and Martinez-Pons 1986; Volet 1997; Elliot *et al.* 1999) causing a tidal wave in education, worldwide. At the turn of the century, the construct of 'self-regulated learning' has been embraced by researchers, policy makers, teachers, students, and parents alike. The main reason for the interest in self-regulated learning is that the construct has the power to provide major insights into the various cognitive and motivational self-regulatory processes that should be promoted in students in order to help them become their own teacher. (Boekaerts 1997).

Lack of self-regulation: what do you mean?

At this point, I would like to make some cautionary comments. Most of the research on self-regulation in the context of the classroom was set up in accordance with a specific self-regulation model, focusing on distinct sub-skills of the self-regulation process. Although most researchers agree that self-regulation is a multi-level, cyclic process made up of a number of interacting sub-processes, they focus on a specific set of sub-skills. The decision to focus on specific sub-skills is based on the principle that a 'manageable' subset of the processes involved in self-regulation should be studied. The advantage of such careful and systematic analysis is that detailed descriptions can be given about the rules governing specific beliefs, procedures and strategy use. An important drawback of dissecting the self-regulation process into component skills is that the sub-processes are studied in isolation and that the interaction between the sub-processes is overlooked. This may lead to distortion, particularly because the overall regulation system that coordinates several subsystems (e.g., metacognitive processes, motivational/volitional processes, coping processes) is not taken into account. Does this mean that the findings that have been reported so far are suspect? No it does not. It simply means that there are still many gaps in our knowledge that are currently bridged by speculation or by assumptions based on incomplete evidence.

The point I want to make here is that the small spectrum models that are available at present are very useful for teachers and counsellors because they have provided guidelines for the design of powerful learning environment and for helping students to improve their self-regulatory processes. Yet, there are many dangers in providing teachers, curriculum designers and counsellors with an incomplete set of self-regulatory strategies. One danger is that teachers may regard students who show strategies that are different from the preferred set as 'deficient' or 'lacking' in some basic self-regulatory skills, whereas these students are regulating their behaviour according to a different set of principles.

In his influential lead article on self-regulation, Winne (1995) argued that it is incorrect to speak about students who cannot regulate their own behaviour or who lack self-regulatory skills. All people make attempts to self-regulate their cognitions, affects, and behaviour in such a way that important personal goals are set (goal setting), strived for (goal striving) and achieved (goal achievement). However, problems of definition arise when self-regulation is defined from the perspective of the dominant school culture. In school, students are supposed to adopt the goals set by the teacher or the curriculum and to strive to attain these goals. Teachers, who observe that their students are not using self-regulatory skills in the service of these goals, may state that their students lack self-regulation. Yet, from an objective point of view, they show a great deal of self-regulation. My argument is that, from the perspective of the students, many forms of behaviour are considered to be adaptive, in the sense that an attempt is made to align their own goals with the teacher's. For example, a student's goals may be to stay out of trouble in school and invest minimal effort to achieve the teacher-set goals. This student's goal setting may be translated into passive behaviour in class. From the perspective of the teacher (or the educational psychologist), passive behaviour is viewed as maladaptive or dysfunctional behaviour, mainly because it leads to underachievement. Put into plain terms: students who are satisfied with a mere pass and consequently do not adhere to the teacher's regimen (e.g. rely on surface level processing despite encouragement to use deep level processing strategies) are described as having 'flaws in self-regulation' (cf. De Corte *et al.* 2000).

In my view, researchers have to define self-regulation more precisely. An explicit distinction has to be made between students, who are not yet capable of self-regulating their learning process in relation to a specific subject matter area, and those who are not willing to comply to the teacher's demands at a specific moment in time, because they have other, more salient goals to attend to. For example, students who do not display the set of self-regulatory skills described by De Corte *et al.* (2000) in the math classroom may not have access to these skills or may not be able to coordinate them yet. On the other hand, they may have access to the necessary cognitive self-regulatory skills (metacognitive skills), but lack motivation or volition to apply these skills in the current context. In this article, I am most concerned with the latter interpretation. In the next section, I will address the following questions: Why are some students inclined to use their self-regulatory skills in the service of a whole host of learning tasks whereas other students feel that they deplete their resources and are not prepared to invest effort?

Self-regulation versus self-control

In school, students cannot pursue their own goals. They have to accept the goals teachers and curriculum designers set for them. They are constantly being urged to invest effort to achieve these goals. However, investing effort is a serious business, particularly if it relates to daily activities and to lengthy periods of time. Indeed, we are not talking about spontaneous involvement in interesting activities, but about long-term commitment to curricular targets that require constant effort management. In order to understand these volitional processes it is essential to realize how different students regulate their information processing in a classroom context.

Information processing in or outside the classroom requires the parallel input from different operating systems, including the cognitive, motivation/volition, and emotion system. Students have access to a repertoire of cognitive, motivation, and emotion strategies that they preferentially use to deal with specific learning situations. In other words, students' preferential regulation strategies may be distinct in different learning contexts.

In naturally occurring learning situations outside school or in easy, familiar learning situations in the classroom, there is no clear-cut distinction between an orientation stage, an execution stage, and an evaluation stage and not much conscious self-regulation is required to select and coordinate various subprocess (metacognition, volition, and emotion control). However, self-regulation becomes necessary when ambiguity and complexity increases or when a coherent structure is lacking. Self-regulation is also appropriate as soon as a specific internal or external cue calls forth specific action tendencies that may disturb the flow of the information process that is going on. For example, an important personal message may be communicated, an obstacle may occur, students may anticipate positive or negative consequences of their actions, or a conflicting goal demands attention.

Evidence from research has led to the conclusion that internal or external cues, which elicit emotions signal to the learner that the content or context of the learning process is changing or has changed. These cues have high priority, interrupting the flow of information processing (Frijda 1986). Fredrickson (2001) demonstrated that cues that elicit positive emotions, such as joy, contentment, satisfaction, anticipated pride or interest, temporarily broaden the scope of attention, cognition, and action. In contrast, cues that elicit negative emotions (e.g. anxiety, fear, frustration, irritation, shame, or guilt) temporarily narrow the scope of attention, cognition, and action. It is evident that these changes in the quality of the information process have serious consequences for the quality of the learning process.

At this point, I would like to revert to Loraine's example. Her motivation and persistence in computer class was an exception if we compare it with her previous behaviour in language class. However, it was not an isolated case since the behaviour of most of her peers had changed equally. When I interviewed the students in Loraine's class on my second visit, they told me that they wanted to become experts in using the World Wide Web. The main reason for their changed motivation in relation to the language class was that they *valued* the long-term learning goal communicated by the teacher (surfing the World Wide Web and putting your own information on the web) and adopted it as a long-term personal goal. In other words, the teacher-set goals were no longer in disharmony with the students' psychological needs (need-incongruent goals). Clearly, Loraine and her classmates experienced positive emotions (joy, interest, challenge, pride) which means that their habitual way of dealing with language exercises had changed: a broader mind set was created (an urge to explore, be creative, pushing themselves to the limits, expand the self, share information with others). Fredrickson *et al.* (in press) studies can shed some light on this phenomenon. These authors suggested that positive emotions experienced during the learning process fuel psychological resilience. Their research showed that resilient students who had to prepare a time-pressured speech entitled 'Why you are a good friend' experienced just as much anxiety as the non-resilient students did, and their cardiac activation was also considerable. However, these students reported many positive emotions as well (interest, anticipated pride, and contentment) and their cardiac activation returned much faster to baseline level. These authors suggested that the experience of positive emotions during a learning task may undo the detrimental effect that negative emotions have on the learning process and the learning product (see also the literature on interest, Boekaerts and Boscolo in press).

I am proposing here, that students who view a teacher-set goal as need-congruent will experience more positive cognitions and affects than students who see it as need-incongruent. As I explained elsewhere (Boekaerts 1998, 1999*b*) need-congruent goals are different from many goals that are imposed by the teacher on a daily basis (e.g. 'you have to finish your assignment in time', 'you have to refrain from talking with your peers about task-irrelevant topics'). Many teacher-imposed goals are not need-congruent and require constant conscious effort on the part of the students to keep them going. They are supposed to monitor their intention and their effort expenditure by controlling impulses to engage in other, more interesting activities, even when they view effort invested to reach the teacher-imposed goal as to no avail.

The distinction that Kuhl and Fuhrman (1998) made between self-regulation and self-control is highly informative when discussing goal setting and goal striving in the context of the classroom. They explained that both self-regulation and self-control are beneficial to learning, in the sense that students who use either form of action control are protecting their learning intention from competing action tendencies. To the casual observer, students using either of these two modes of action control seem to be engaged in learning and may even seem highly committed. However, knowledge of the students' goal structure would inform teachers which of their students are using self-regulatory strategies and which students are using self-control strategies. Kuhl and Fuhrman explained that self-regulation denotes students' ability to generate learning goals from their own need structure (goal hierarchy) and that pursuit of these personal goals is different from implementing goals imposed by others. Examples of self-regulatory strategies are attention control, motivation control, emotion control, and decision control. These authors further argued that using self-regulatory strategies to pursue personal goals activates the reward system, which is accompanied by positive emotions. Individuals who use self-control strategies to pursue goals imposed by others also demonstrate the ability to maintain a learning intention. However, their behaviour is characterized by avoiding, neglecting, denying, suppressing competing goals, even those that are congruent to their own need structure. Kuhl and Fuhrman suggested that individuals who pursue goals that they consider alien to their own goals basically activate the punishment system. Examples of self-control strategies are intention control, impulse control, and over-control.

Kehr *et al*. (1999) tested Kuhl's assumption that self-regulation refers to a higher form of volitional competence in the sense that it serves a *self*-maintenance function rather than a *goal*-maintenance function. Kehr *et al*. identified students (trainees in a management course) who were characterized as either 'self-regulators' (i.e. control their attention, motivation, and emotion and can swiftly initiate an activity) or 'self-controllers' (i.e. control their intention and impulses and tend to over-control). Three hypotheses were raised: first, that self-regulators remember their personal training intentions (assessed three months earlier) better than self-controllers; second, that self-regulation is associated with positive emotions and self-control with negative emotions; and third, that self-regulation promotes training transfer in terms of realization of the set goal(s) and in terms of the achievement of set criteria. These authors found that self-regulation increased intention memory, generated positive emotions during goal striving, and promoted training transfer. Interestingly, self-control was associated with negative emotions, providing further evidence for Kuhl's hypothesis that self-control activates the punishment system.

Effort-management signals commitment, involvement, and volitional control

Kuhl and Gotschke (1994) argued that good intentions that were strong in the pre-decisional phase (goal setting) do not necessarily lead to goal striving in the post-decisional phase. Many learning goals need active goal striving on the part of the learner in order to be accomplished, meaning that involvement and commitment should be translated into effort investment. Effort refers to an intentional act to amplify or reduce task engagement when the demand–capacity ratio increases or decreases. What determines whether students will invest more effort when perceived task demands increase? Carver and Scheier (2000) argued that in most models of effort there is a point beyond which effort seems fruitless and individuals reduce effort or disengage from the task. Nonetheless, there seems to be marked inter and intra individual differences in this cut-off point. Is there research evidence that reveals the factors that yield effort expenditure? In this section, I will refer to empirical studies, including some of my own studies, which conceptualized and operationalized aspects of students' effort investment.

Effort seen as a personal resource

Nichols (1990) argued that young children do not differentiate between ability and effort. They think that all children who put in effort will perform well. Paris (1988) demonstrated that children's theory of effort develops gradually over the middle childhood years. The unrealistic belief that persistence, good work habits, and good conduct are sufficient to succeed in school, independent of ability, is gradually unmasked. By the age of ten, children come to realize that putting in effort cannot compensate for low ability. Dweck (1986) demonstrated that older children who are learning oriented have a different perception of effort than ego-oriented children. The former students focus on effort, using it as an explanation of success and failure. They view effort as a sign of involvement and commitment and use it as a personal resource that they can use to improve their performance. The latter students focus on ability or lack of ability and consider effort as a sign of low competence and compliance.

Cain and Dweck (1995) and Smiley and Dweck (1994) set up some studies to investigate emerging aspects of children's theory of effort. More specifically, they measured very young children's tendency to persist with activities situated in the zone of proximal development. Preschoolers aged between three-and-a-half and five years old were told that there was additional time and that it would be fun to continue with some of the colourful puzzles. They were given the choice of continuing with puzzles that they had already solved or trying a new one. Thirty-seven per cent of the children chose to redo a puzzle that they had already successfully completed. The others wanted to continue with the unfamiliar puzzles. When asked why they chose the familiar puzzles, the children said they selected them because they were easy and because they already knew how to do them (in other words, the cognitive strategies necessary to do the puzzles were familiar to them). The reasons that were given by the children who chose the new puzzles were that they liked the challenge, they wanted to try a harder puzzle, or they wanted to see whether they could do a harder one. Similar answers were given when the same children were asked the same questions on a later occasion. These authors further examined children's spontaneous statements about the puzzles and reported that children who volunteered to improve their puzzle solving skills made significantly fewer negative statements about themselves and their performance than did the children who did not show interest in further improving their puzzle solving skills.

Dweck and her colleagues (see Dweck 1998) asked children to predict their future puzzle performance. Sixty-four per cent of the children who opted for skill improvement believed that they would be able to complete the puzzles, given adequate time. Only 29 per cent of the children who were mainly interested in using familiar skills believed that they would be able to finish any of the puzzles, even if they had all the time in the world. Another interesting finding reported by Dweck and her colleagues (Dweck 1998) was that children reacted differentially to criticism and that their reaction was associated with their theory of self and their persistence on later occasions. Of the children, who were quite satisfied with their performance, 39 per cent changed their judgment about their performance after criticism. This reaction shows two things. First, that they were uncertain whether their performance was up to standard. Second, that criticism acted as a signal that triggered negative emotions. By contrast, 61 per cent of the children, who were quite satisfied with their performance before the teacher levelled criticism at their work, stuck to their positive view of their performance. Compared to the children who reduced their self-assessment after criticism, these children showed higher persistence into continuing with activities in the zone of proximal development, more constructive solutions to the problems, lesser self-blame, and negative evaluations.

An interesting question that still needs further testing is whether the adaptive coping pattern seen in the latter group of children is due to these children's lower sensitivity to criticism or to their ability to use conditional knowledge. Children need conditional knowledge to assess their own performance and compare their own judgment with that of others. Several researchers have argued (e.g. Efklides et al. 1999) that students who have access to conditional knowledge find it easier to cope with interruptions of plan. In light of our present discussion, in combination with findings reported by Turner et al. (1998) and Boekaerts (2001a), I would like to make the following suggestions. Students who have access to conditional knowledge about a task or activity can attenuate the impact that obstacles, bugs, and unfavourable feedback have on cognition and action. This leaves room for alternative interpretations, positive emotions, and positive expectations. In other words, having access to and using domain-specific conditional knowledge is reflected in the coping strategies these students use.

Boekaerts (1999b) proposed that students who have access to relevant conditional knowledge use either one of two basic adaptive coping patterns, namely mindful action or disengagement. Mindful action is used when students consider increased effort or persistence to be fruitful. Students disengage when they consider further effort to be to no avail at that specific moment in time. Boekaerts contrasted these two coping patterns with mindless action and avoidance. She explained that students who do not have access to metacognitive knowledge (explained above, p. 132) or to incomplete knowledge also persist, but that their effort is largely undirected. In the literature on coping with stress, many coping strategies reflect mindless (undirected) action, providing evidence that persistence is not necessarily a virtue. Leventhal (1980) illustrated that individuals who are uncertain and experience a great deal of anxiety when they are faced with danger have two options. They may focus on their anxiety or on the danger itself. Students who use anxiety control as a coping strategy try to reduce their anxiety by ignoring the source of stress or by attenuating it. Students who use danger control focus on the danger itself and the changed demand–capacity ratio. They try to restore the balance by increasing effort. However, their focus in on re-allocating resources to control the danger and this produces rumination that interferes with the activity itself (undirected effort). Both mindless action (danger control) and avoidance (anxiety control) are rigid coping strategies that reflect the students' difficulty in interpreting the situation and allocating resources effectively. By contrast, mindful action and disengagement are adaptive coping strategies because these strategies reflect the student's understanding that involvement and commitment are necessary but not sufficient to achieve a learning goal. In the next section, I will explore which factors influence effort investment in relation to coursework.

Effort management presupposes action control

At the conceptual level, Kuhl's action control theory has been instrumental in making a clear distinction between low effort investment that is the result of low motivation and low effort that is contingent on failing volitional skills. In line with Kuhl's reasoning, several educational psychologists theorized that students have to activate action control strategies when they are requested to perform learning activities that they find unpleasant, of low importance or personal relevance, or unmanageable.

Following Kuhl and Goschke (1994) who found a moderate association between disengagement and initiative, Boekaerts (1994) theorized that students who are generally high on initiative are also high on disengagement. Such an association signals that individuals who swiftly generate meaning when faced with a complex activity and start the goal-striving process without further ado (high volitional efficiency) do not ruminate when they cannot achieve the goal. Instead, they disengage swiftly from the activity because they judge that effort will no longer make any difference. By the opposite logic, an association between these two aspects of action control implies that individuals who lose a lot of time in indecision before they initiate an activity tend to ruminate when they cannot achieve the goal. Kuhl and Goschke reported non-significant associations between persistence and both initiative and disengagement. This result can be interpreted in light of the different meaning that persistence may have for different individuals (e.g. those who do and do not ruminate about the results of their actions).

In our studies with ninth grade students (Boekaerts 1994), initiative was positively associated with disengagement (0.45), persistence was not associated with disengagement (0.03) but persistence was moderately correlated with initiative (0.32). This finding suggests that ninth grade students who are high on initiative in the orientation stage, tend to persist during the execution stage and that those who lose a lot of time in indecision in the orientation stage tend to be volatile in the execution stage. We also studied the effect of the three measures of action control on reported effort after doing a reading comprehension task. It was evident that ninth grade students who did well on the reading comprehension task had high scores on initiative, reflecting their volitional efficiency. High initiative was combined with either of three persistence-disengagement patterns (as an indicator of commitment): (1) high persistence–high disengagement, (2) high persistence–low disengagement, or (3) low persistence–high disengagement. Interestingly, the highest effort score was recorded for students who were high on the three aspects of action control. The lowest effort score was reported by students, who displayed an incongruent initiative-commitment pattern, and, who also showed an incongruent relation between persistence and disengagement. These results, taken in connection with the outcomes of our studies featuring mathematics tasks, suggest that students try to obtain an optimal balance between Initiative, Persistence, and Disengagement in order to create context-sensitive action control. In all learning situations, students profit from the capacity to select action plans swiftly. Hence, the capacity to initiate learning activities is an important aspect of effort management. In addition, students need the capacity to straddle the divide between (1) continuing with a selected action plan long enough to achieve the current goal, and (2) giving up the action plan without being hindered by intrusive thoughts when a false start or a slip in strategy is noticed, or when failure is unavoidable.

Effort management presupposes motivation control

So far, I have highlighted various aspects of action control as determinants of effort investment. It is important to note that apart from these traits, situation–person interactions may also enter into the picture. In another study, I explored the extent to which effort investment is determined by the value students attach to a task (context-sensitive appraisal of the content of the learning task). Students were asked to keep a diary and record their cognitions and affects in relation to their homework for different school subjects. More specifically, they were asked to complete the online motivation questionnaire before they started with their homework (math and history, respectively) and again after they had completed their homework assignment (for a more detailed description of the online motivation questionnaire, see Boekaerts 2001b). They had to keep the diary for three periods of two weeks at three data collection points. At the first data collection point, students were two months into the eighth grade. The second data collection point was at the end of the eighth grade and the third data collection point was two months after the start of the ninth grade. A complete set of data was obtained from 562 students for history and from 529 students for mathematics. These students followed any of three streams: either the academic stream, the higher non-academic stream, or the lower non-academic stream. There were slightly more girls than boys in the samples. The students also completed a series of tests and questionnaires, including an intelligence test (analogy test, Evers and Lucassen 1991), a learning style test (Vermunt 1992) and Kuhl's action control scale (Kuhl and Goschke 1994).

Inspection of the association between students' scores on the three subscales of the action control scale revealed that students who are high on disengagement, and hence do not ruminate much, showed more initiative (0.37). There was only a modest positive correlation between the students' score on initiative and persistence (0.17) and a modest negative correlation between persistence and disengagement (−0.17). This is further evidence that persistence is a complex construct that can only be interpreted in connection with rumination and initiative (mindful and mindless action).

MANOVAS were conducted, separately for the data collected at each of the three data collection points. The three aspects of action control were the dependent variables and gender and class type were the between variables. A significant gender effect was noted

($F = 24.83$; Wilks $= 0.91$; $p < 0.0001$) as well as a significant class type effect ($F = 2.64$, Wilks $= 0.98$; $p < 0.05$). Boys scored significantly lower on persistence than girls but did not show as much rumination. There was a trend for boys to show more initiative than girls. These findings suggest that girls persist longer because they are more pre-occupied. The students in the academic stream scored higher on initiative and persistence than those in the non-academic streams. The interaction effect 'class type $\times$ gender' also yielded significance ($F = 2.20$, Wilks $= 0.98$; $p < 0.05$), meaning that the girls in the lowest and highest streams were more persistent than the boys.

ANOVAS with reported effort as the dependent variable and gender and class type as the between variables were conducted for the data collected at the three time points, separately for math and history homework. There were no class-type effects. Gender yielded a significant effect for history in the beginning of the eighth and ninth grades, but not at the end of the eighth grade. In each case the girls reported more effort than the boys. The interaction effects were not significant. The data for mathematics homework showed two significant interaction effects. In the highest and the lowest streams, the girls reported more effort than the boys. In the middle stream this picture was reversed.

Correlations between two aspects of action control (i.e. initiation and persistence) and reported effort were modest to moderate. Correlations between disengagement and reported effort were weak to non-existent, implying that rumination as such does not affect effort investment. We wanted to explore the effect of action control in relation to other person variables. Also, we wished to examine whether context-sensitive measures of task value would add to the variance explained in effort investment, independent of action control.

In order to study these effects, hierarchical multiple regression analyses were conducted with reported effort as the criterion variable. The effect of four blocks of variables on reported effort was examined. Intelligence was entered first, because it was assumed that students who are more intelligent need less time to do their homework and hence report less effort than students who are less intelligent. Intelligence made a significant contribution to reported effort in the predicted direction. As can be seen in Table 7.1, it explained between 0.5 and 5 per cent of the variance in reported effort in the various homework conditions. The students' learning style explained an additional 6–16 per cent of the variance, when intelligence had been controlled for. Inspection of the beta weights revealed that students who preferred the surface-level processing mode invested more effort than students who used either the deep-level processing mode or the concrete learning style. After having controlled for cognitive aspects of information processing (intelligence and learning style), students' volitional strategies were entered into the equation. This additional block explained between 4 and 10 per cent extra variance. Examination of the beta weights suggests that students, who tend to lose a lot of time in indecision before starting an activity, invest less effort in their homework than students who initiate tasks and activities swiftly. Being persistent did not predict effort very well, expect at the second measurement point for the history task. Interestingly, being preoccupied when a goal cannot be achieved increased effort in relation to four of the six homework tasks. Clearly, cognitive and volitional strategies that students preferentially use are good predictors of effort for homework. Together they explain between 10 and 29 per cent of the variance in reported effort for homework. However, more than double this percentage was accounted for when students' appraisals of the homework assignment were entered into the equation as a last

Table 7.1 Summary of hierarchical multiple regression analyses with reported effort as criterium variable and four predictors. Results are provided for the three data collection points, separately for mathematics and history

Grade	Intelligence	Learning style	Action control		Motivation control		R^2 (%)
Math							
8	1.1	10.6	3.6	0.08	16.3	0.22	32.6
				0.09		−0.13	
				−0.02		0.30	
8	5.1	16.8	7.0	0.16	32.6	0.13	61.5
				0.02		0.05	
				−0.11		0.51	
9	2.5	7.2	9.7	0.19	31.9	0.21	51.3
				0.04		−0.19	
				−0.18		0.52	
History							
8	0.4	6.2	3.4	0.13	18.0	0.20	28.0
				0.01		−0.01	
				−0.14		0.29	
8	0.2	17.7	8.3	0.08	30.6	0.28	56.8
				0.18		0.12	
				−0.05		0.31	
9	0.4	8.8	9.0	0.21	20.9	0.23	39.1
				0.09		−0.15	
				−0.16		0.35	

Each row gives percentage variance explained per predictor and total variance.

For Action Control the three beta weights are printed (*I,P,D*) and for motivation control the beta weights for the three appraisals are provided (tasks attraction, perceived competence, perceived relevance).

block. As can be seen from the table, the amount of variance accounted for by motivation control is minimally 16 per cent and maximally 32 per cent. The beta weights inform us that students who valued the homework task consistently invested more effort. Judging the homework task as attractive yielded beta weights ranging between 0.13 and 0.28. Judging the task as important and personally relevant produced beta weights ranging between 0.29 and 0.51. Students who judged their competence for the mathematics homework task as low tended to report more effort than those who expressed high competence. Subjective competence seemed to be related to effort investment for history homework in a task-specific way. It did not yield a significant beta weight in the beginning of the eighth grade, had a positive beta at the end of the eighth grade, and a negative beta in the beginning of the ninth grade. Further research is necessary to determine which aspects of a history task signal to students that they are competent or not and how this judgement affects their effort investment. A cautionary comment is in order here. Since the design was cross-sectional, alternative causal interpretations have to be considered as well.

What do these results tell us about effort management? Firstly, action control or the students' capacity to initiate, persist, and disengage makes a significant contribution to effort management, independent of the cognitive aspects of self-regulation. In other words, investing effort in history and mathematics homework depends largely on the students' volitional efficiency or their capacity to initiate activities swiftly. In addition, students will profit from the capacity to judge whether a chosen action plan will lead to goal accomplishment, thus demanding increased effort (persistence). They also profit from the capacity to give up an action plan when it proves to be inadequate to achieve the goal, without too much rumination. Secondly, motivation control, or the students' skill to motivate themselves to invest effort by taking into account the value of the homework activity and their own competence to do the task, has a strong impact on effort investment, independent of cognitive and volitional aspects of self-regulation.

These results are in line with the results of studies with college students. For example, Volet (1997) reported that students at the college level showed most effort for their coursework when both motivation control and action control were high. Action control was not associated with learning style, meaning that both students with a surface- or deep-level processing style may be low or high on action control. Volet explained her finding as follows: University students have the potential to regulate their performance cognitively. (whatever learning style they have, it has proved adequate to pass exams at the secondary school level.) Yet, they may lack the skill to motivate themselves in the goal-setting stage and to protect their intention from competing action tendencies in the goal-striving stage. Mastering academic subjects requires students to constantly motivate themselves to invest effort and to set non-academic goals aside in favour of curricular goals. Effort allocation presupposes motivation control in the goal-setting stage and action control in the goal-striving stage.

Elliot and her colleagues confirmed these results in a recent study. Elliot *et al.* (1999) predicted and found, at the college level, that willingness to invest effort (motivation control) and persistence when difficulties are encountered during task performance (action control) mediated between students' study goals and their exam performance. These authors also found that a positive goal orientation (learning orientation or performance-approach goals) was positively linked to motivation and volition control whereas performance-avoidance goals were not.

Conclusions

This chapter began with a reference to positive psychology. It was argued that psychologists are interested again in the strengths and virtues of individuals who function effectively. This led to new questions, such as: 'What do students actually think, feel, and do when they are willing to regulate their own behaviour in relation to schoolwork and take on responsibility for their own learning?' and also 'According to which principles are they regulating their behaviour?'. This changed research focus coincides with a major shift in the teaching methods used in school. Indeed, at present, school life is more diverse than it was before the social constructivist perspective to teaching invited students to become self-regulated learners. This changed school scene inevitably altered the set of skills that students need to succeed in school and beyond. I have presented the conceptual elements of one possible approach to addressing some of the questions that are currently asked about self-regulated learning as a form of proactive coping.

I argued that in order to self-regulate one's own learning process, students need to have access to relevant declarative and procedural knowledge, as well as to the conditional knowledge that helps them to determine how, why, and when to use that knowledge. I also explained that students do not necessarily use this knowledge in the service of teacher-imposed learning goals. They also need motivational, volitional, and affective strategies. I have tried to specify how researchers currently think about these strategies. Loraine's example was used to illustrate that teacher-imposed goals which are in harmony with the students' goal structure have a better chance of being adopted (i.e. a learning intention is formed). These goals also have a better chance of being remembered (intention memory) and being achieved (active goal striving, reflected in the quality of the information process).

Various data sets were reviewed with the aim of gaining a better understanding of the descriptors of effort investment. Several researchers reported that positive affect has a beneficial effect on what students think and do in the classroom. The main reason underlying the beneficial effect is that a broader mindset is created. This mindset gives rise to an urge to explore, to be creative, to push oneself to the limits, to expand the self, and to share information with others. Another important reason is that the detrimental effect of negative emotions is attenuated or undone by positive emotions.

I believe that positive affect experienced in relation to coursework is closely aligned with the two dimensions that underlie effort management in the classroom, namely motivation control and action control. In line with Kuhl's theorizing, Kehr et al. (1999) measured students' action control, making a distinction between self-regulators and self-controllers. They found that self-regulating students remembered their personal learning intention better than self-controllers did, and they also experienced more positive emotions and fewer negative emotions during course work. These different cognitions and affects impacted on the realization of the set goals. Other researchers (e.g. Volet 1997; Boekaerts 1999a) noted explicitly that motivation control predicts effort for coursework and that this effect is strengthened by action control. It remains unclear how the various aspects of action control are linked to motivation control and to emotions experienced during learning.

In closing, I would like to say that the conceptual analysis in this chapter was intended to be applicable to all goal-directed behaviour in the classroom, including coping with goals that are imposed by the teacher and create an internal conflict. Many goals that are communicated by the teacher are poorly specified, are interpreted by the students as 'irrelevant' or 'boring', or worse, as alien to their own hierarchy of goals. Nevertheless, these learning goals are mandatory and recur across the curriculum. To the extent that students are successful in appraising these goals as 'meaningful' and 'valuable for their own development', positive affect will be elicited and exert its beneficial effects on coping processes.

References

Bandura, A. (1986). *Social foundations of thought and action: A social-cognitive theory*. Englewood Cliffs, NJ: Prentice Hall.

Boekaerts, M. (1994). Action control: How relevant is it for classroom learning?, in J. Kuhl and J. Beckmann (eds.), *Volition and personality*, pp. 427–35. Seattle: Hogrefe and Huber Publishers.

—— (1997). Self regulated learning: A new concept embraced by researchers, policy makers, educators, teachers, and students. *Learning and Instruction*, 7(2), 161–86.

—— (1998). Boosting students' capacity to promote their own learning: A goal theory perspective. *Research in Dialogue*, 1(1), 13–22.

—— (1999*a*). Motivated learning: Studying student * situation transactional units. *European Journal of Psychology of Education*, 14(4), 41–55.

—— (1999*b*). Coping in context: Goal frustration and goal ambivalence in relation to academic and interpersonal goals, in E. Frydenberg (ed.), *Learning to cope: Developing as a person in complex societies*, pp. 175–97. Oxford: Oxford University Press.

—— (2001*a*). Context Sensitivity: Activated motivational beliefs, current concerns and emotional arousal, in S. Volet and S. Järvelä (eds.), *Motivation in learning contexts: Theoretical and methodological implications*, pp. 13–27. New York: Pergamon Press.

—— (2001*b*). The online motivation questionnaire: A self-report instrument to assess students' context sensitivity, in M. L. Maehr and P. Pintrich (eds.), *Advances in motivation and achievement: Vol. 12. Methodology in motivation research*. New York: Pergamon Press.

—— and **Boscolo, P.** (2002). Interest in learning: Learning to be interested. [Special Issue]. *Learning and Instruction*, 12(4), 375–82.

Cain, K. M. and **Dweck, C. S.** (1995). The development of children's achievement motivation patterns and conceptions of intelligence. *Merrill-Palmer Quarterly*, 41, 25–52.

Carver, C. S. and **Scheier, M. F.** (2000). On the Structure of Behavioural Self-Regulation, in M. Boekaerts, P. R. Pintrich, and M. Zeidner (eds.), *Handbook of self-regulation*, pp. 41–84. San Diego, CA: Academic Press.

De Corte, E., Verschaffel, L., and **Op 't Eynde, P.** (2000). Self-Regulation: A characteristic and a goal of mathematics education, in M. Boekaerts, P. R. Pintrich, and M. Zeidner (eds.), *Handbook of self-regulation*, pp. 687–726. San Diego, CA: Academic Press.

Dweck, C. S. (1986). Motivational processes affecting learning. *American Psychologist*, 41, 1040–8.

—— (1998). The development of early self-conceptions: Their relevance for motivational processes, in J. Heckhausen and C. S. Dweck (eds.), *Motivation and self-regulation across the life span*, pp. 257–80. Cambridge: Cambridge University Press.

Efklides, A., Papadaki, M., Papantoniou, G., and **Kiosseoglou, G.** (1999). Individual differences in school mathematics performance and feelings of difficulty. *European Journal of Psychology of Education*, 14(4), 461–76.

Elliot, A. J., Mc Gregor, H. A., and **Gable, S.** (1999). Achievement goals, study strategies, and exam performance: A mediational analysis. *Journal of Educational Psychology*, 91(3), 549–63.

Evers, A. and **Lucassen, W.** (1991) *Differential Ability Test*. Lisse: Swets & Zeitlinger

Fredrickson, B. L. (2001). The Role of Positive Emotions in Positive Psychology. *American Psychologist*, 56(3), 218–26.

—— **Mancuso, R. A., Branigan, C.,** and **Tugade, M.** (2000). The undoing effect of positive emotions. *Motivation and Emotion*, 24, 237–58.

Frijda, N. H. (1986). *The Emotions*. Great Britain Cambridge: Cambridge University Press.

Gibson, S. and **Dembo, M.** (1984). Teacher efficacy: A construct validation. *Journal of Educational Psychology*, 76, 569–82.

Järvela, S. and **Volet, S.** (eds.) (2001). *Motivation in learning contexts: Theoretical and methodological implications*. New York: Pergamon Press.

Kehr, H. M., Bless, P., and **Von Rosenstiel, L.** (1999). Self-regulation, self-control and management training transfer [Special issue]. *International Journal of Educational Research*, 31, 487–93.

Krapp, A. (2001). Structural and dynamic aspects of interest development: Theoretical considerations from an ontogenetic perspective. Interest in Learning, Learning to be Interested [Special Issue]. *Learning and Instruction,* **12**(4), 383–409.

Kuhl, J. and Gotschke, T. (1994). State orientation and the activation and retrieval of intentions on memory, in J. Kuhl and J. Beckmann (eds.), *Volition and personality,* pp. 127–53. Seattle: Hogrefe & Huber Publishers.

—— and Fuhrmann, A. (1998). Decomposing self-regulation and self-control: The volitional components inventory, in J. Heckhausen and C. S. Dweck (eds.), *Motivation and self-regulation across the life span,* pp. 15–49. Cambridge, Cambridge University Press.

Leventhal, H. (1980). Towards a comprehensive theory of emotion, in L. Berkowitz (ed.), *Advances in experimental social psychology,* Vol. 3, pp. 140–208. New York: Academic Press.

Masui, C. (2001). Het bevorderen van Metakennis en Zelfregulatievaardigheden in het Academisch Onderwijs (Promoting meta knowledge and self-regulatory skills in academic education), Unpublished Doctoral Dissertation, Louvain, Louvain University.

Nichols, J. G. (1990). What ability and why are we mindful to it? A developmental perspective, in R. J. Sternberg and J. Kolligan Jr. (eds.), *Competence considered,* pp. 11–40. New Haven, CT: Yale University Press.

Paris, S. (1988). *Fusing skill and will: The integration of cognitive and motivational psychology.* Paper presented at the American Educational Research Association. Annual meeting, New Orleans.

Pintrich, P. R. (2000). The role of goal orientation in self-regulated learning, in M. Boekaerts, P. R. Pintrich, and M. Zeidner (eds.), *Handbook of self-regulation,* pp. 452–502. San Diego, CA: Academic Press.

Randi, J. and Corno, L. (2000). Teacher Innovations in self-regulated learning, in M. Boekaerts, P. R. Pintrich, and M. Zeidner (eds.), *Handbook of self-regulation,* pp. 651–85. San Diego, CA: Academic Press.

Sheldon, K. M. and King, L. (2001). Why positive psychology is necessary. *American Psychologist,* **56**(3), 216–17.

Shuell, T. J. (1988). The Role of the Student in Learning from Instruction. *Contemporary Educational Psychology,* **13**, 276–95.

Shunk, D. H. (1994). Self-regulation of self-efficacy and attributions in academic settings, in D. H. Schunk and B. J. Zimmerman (eds.), Self-regulation of learning and performance: issues and educational applications, pp. 75–99. Hillsdale, NI: Erlbaum.

Schunk, D. H. and Ertmer, P. A. (2000). Self-regulation and academic learning: Self-efficacy enhancing interventions, in M. Boekaerts, P. R. Pintrich, and M. Zeidner (eds.), *Handbook of self-regulation,* pp. 631–49. San Diego, CA: Academic Press.

Smiley, P. and Dweck, C. S. (1994). Individual differences in achievement goals among young children. *Child Development,* **65**, 1723–43.

Turner, J. C., Thorpe, P. K., and Meijer, D. K. (1998). Students' reports of motivation and negative affect: A theoretical and empirical analysis. *Journal of Educational Psychology,* **90**, 758–71.

—— and Meyer, D. K. (2000). Studying and understanding the instructional contexts of classrooms: Using our past to forge our future. *Educational Psychologist,* **35**(2), 69–85.

Vermunt, J. D. H. M. (1992). *Leerstijlen en sturen van leerprocessen in het hoger onderwijs (Learning styles and steering learning processes in higher education).* Academic dissertation, Tilburg University.

Volet, S. E. (1997). Cognitive and affective variables in academic learning: the significance of direction and effort in students' goals. *Learning and Instruction,* **7**(3), 235–54.

Watson, D., Wiese, D. Vaidya, J., and **Tellegen, A.** (1999). The two general activation systems of affect: Structural findings, evolutionary considerations, and psychobiological evidence. *Journal of Personality and Social Psychology*, **76**, 839–55.

Weinstein, C. E., Husman, J., and **Dierking, D. R.** (2000). Self-regulation interventions with a focus on learning strategies, in M. Boekaerts, P. R. Pintrich and M. Zeidner (eds.), *Handbook of self-regulation*, pp. 727–47. San Diego, CA: Academic Press.

Winne, P. H. (1997). Experimenting to bootstrap self-regulated learning. *Journal of Educational Psychology*, **88**, 397–410.

Zimmerman, B. J. and **Martinez-Pons, M.** (1986). Development of a structured interview for assessing students use of self-regulated learning strategies. *American Educational Research Journal*, **23**, 614–28.

—— (2000). Attaining self-regulation: A social cognitive perspective, in M. Boekaerts, P. R. Pintrich, and M. Zeidner (eds.), *Handbook of self-regulation*, pp. 13–39. San Diego, CA: Academic Press.

CHAPTER 8

POSITIVE EMOTIONS IN EDUCATION

REINHARD PEKRUN, THOMAS GOETZ, WOLFRAM TITZ, AND RAYMOND P. PERRY

Positive emotions are essential for human behaviour and adaption. They help to envision goals and challenges, open the mind to thoughts and problem-solving, protect health by fostering resiliency, create attachments to significant others, lay the groundwork for individual self-regulation, and guide the behaviour of groups, social systems, and nations. In spite of their many functions, however, positive emotions have been neglected by psychology. Until recently, psychology has focused on the dark side of human life. Psycho-pathological behaviour, negative emotions emanating from stress, and coping with stress and negative emotions have been studied extensively, whereas adaptive behaviour, positive emotions, and proactive coping did not receive that much attention (cf. Frydenberg 1997; Fredrickson 2001). Furthermore, traditional theories addressing the functions of positive emotions for cognition and behaviour have focused on negative effects of positive emotions, instead of their regulatory benefits (cf. Aspinwall 1998).

Educational settings are of specific importance for shaping human self-regulation and development, and students' and teachers' positive emotions can be assumed to be central to attaining these educational goals. However, educational psychology and educational research in general were no exception in neglecting positive emotions. Specifically, whereas students' test anxiety has been studied extensively, positive emotions related to learning and achievement have rarely been analysed. This seems to be true, in spite of the fact that anticipatory hope and pride relating to success and failure were deemed key determinants of achievement motivation and task behaviour by traditional theories of achievement motivation, along with anticipatory fear and shame (cf. Atkinson 1964; Heckhausen 1980). Studies on achievement motivation included items pertaining to these emotions in global measures of achievement motives, but rarely studied emotions in their own right. Specifically, this pertains to the positive emotions of hope and pride which were only regarded as components of the motive to achieve success. The motive to avoid failure, on the other hand, has often been equated with test anxiety on an operational level, having been assessed by test anxiety questionnaires in many studies (Atkinson 1964). Concerning positive emotions relating to learning, instruction, and achievement, the only major tradition of research addressing such emotions directly was attributional theory originating from Bernard Weiner's programme of research on achievement emotions (cf. Weiner 1985). This research produced a sizable number of studies analysing links between causal attributions of success and failure, and a variety of positive achievement-related emotions.

Table 8.1 Literature Search 1974–2000: studies linking emotions to learning and achievement

	[1974–1990]	[1991–2000]	Research tradition
Joy	32	29	Mood research
Enthusiasm	9	7	Teacher enthusiasm
Hope	0	9	
Relief	2	1	
Pride	17	10	Achievement motivation
Gratitude	2	1	
Admiration	0	0	
Sadness	10	5	Mood research
Anger	31	33	Type A personality
Anxiety	>700	>500	Test anxiety
Hopelessness	2	12	Hopelessness theory
Shame/guilt	24	20	Achievement motivation
Disappointment	2	0	
Boredom	27	16	Job monotony
Envy	5	1	
Contempt	0	0	
Surprise	6	1	Attributional theory

Beyond attributional research, we lack studies on positive emotions in education, and in learning and achievement generally. This is evident from a review of the literature by Pekrun and Frese (1992) updated recently (Pekrun *et al.* in press; cf. Table 8.1). Concerning positive emotions, this search pertained to all studies linking any of the emotions listed in Table 8.1 to the topics of learning, work, performance, test, and achievement, thus extending well beyond the educational domain and including achievement-related emotions at work and in sport as well. Apparently, whereas more than 1000 studies addressed achievement-related anxiety to date, and more than 200 studies other negative achievement emotions (like anger, shame, or boredom), the total number of studies addressing positive achievement-related emotions was less than 10 per cent of those addressing negative emotions.

In our own research on students' academic emotions, we therefore made an attempt to pay no less attention to positive emotional experiences in education than to negative emotions. Positive emotions are important for both students and teachers. In this chapter, however, we focus on the student side of educational settings. More specifically, we give an overview of our research addressing students' academic emotions, that is, their emotions relating to learning, instruction, and achievement in academic settings associated with attending class, studying, and taking tests and exams (Pekrun *et al.* in press). In so doing, we address the following problems in turn: (1) How frequently are positive emotions experienced by students at school and university, and which positive emotions play a role in academic settings (*occurrence*)? (2) How can students' positive emotions be assessed (*measurement*)? (3) How do these emotions influence students' learning and achievement (*effects*)? (4) What are the origins of these emotions in students' personality, classroom instruction, and social environments, and what can be done to foster them (*antecedents and intervention*)? In conclusion, we will stress the importance of strengthening research on positive emotions as well as positive emotion-based intervention in general, and in education specifically.

The occurrence of positive academic emotions: exploratory studies

Learning and achievement are among the most important topics across the life span today. This implies that they should be major sources of emotion, since by definition, emotions are reactions to important events and states. Academic settings of learning and achievement can thus be assumed to produce a variety of intense emotions, including both negative and positive emotions, and task-related as well as self-related and social emotions (see Table 8.2 for examples). However, the extent to which students' affective life is characterized by positive emotions has not yet been determined. There is converging evidence that motivational experiences relating to positive emotions tend to decline throughout the school years. This seems to be true for students in North America, as well as for Australian and European students. Examples are decreasing average values for students' self-concepts of academic abilities, interest in academic subject matters, and intrinsic motivation (cf. Pekrun and Fend 1991; Gottfried *et al.* 2001). To which extent do students, nevertheless, experience positive emotions?

To date the evidence to answer this question seems to be lacking. In a series of five qualitative studies, we explored university and secondary school students' emotions experienced in academic settings. In the first of these studies, university students were requested to recollect academic situations and emotions experienced in these situations from their autobiographical memories. The other four studies used a less retrospective format by asking students for their emotional experiences immediately after they had attended a class, finished a period of studying, or taken a test or exam. In all of these studies, oral or written narratives were gained by asking students a series of fixed questions, without providing any more formal prescriptions on how to answer them. Three of the studies did so by using interviews which were recorded and transcribed, the other two by questionnaires (cf. Pekrun 1992*a*; Spangler *et al.* in press; Titz 2001).

Table 8.2 The Domain of academic emotions: examples

	Positive	*Negative*
Task- and self-related		
Process	Enjoyment	Boredom
Prospective	Anticipatory joy	Hopelessness
	Hope	Anxiety
Retrospective	Joy about Success	Sadness
	Satisfaction	Disappointment
	Pride	Shame/guilt
	Relief	
Social		
	Gratitude	Anger
	Empathy	Jealousy/envy
	Admiration	Contempt
	Sympathy/love	Antipathy/hate

Data were analysed by using qualitative and quantitative methods. For purposes of quantitative analysis, a system for classifying emotional experiences was developed and used to integrate the narratives which our subjects had delivered. This descriptive classification system was based both on the accounts which our subjects had given, and on theoretical considerations derived from the literature. Originally, it contained a rather exhaustive set of 44 different categories of emotional experiences. However, it turned out that many of these categories pertained to different intensities and qualities of one and the same underlying emotion (e.g. fear and panic, both pertaining to the primary emotion of anxiety), such that 14 summary categories of academic emotions could be used to integrate most of the results.

The findings of the first study were typical for the other investigations as well. In this study, we had asked for experiences in three major types of academic situations: attending class, studying, and taking tests or exams. Interviews were conducted in such a way that the number of reports was balanced across situations. Overall, anxiety was the one emotion which was reported most often by the 50 university students interviewed, accounting for 19 per cent of all 414 emotional episodes reported. This finding corroborates assumptions about the prevalence of students' anxiety (Zeidner 1998).

However, in spite of the importance of anxiety and other negative emotions, it turned out that positive emotions were reported no less frequently than negative emotions. Concerning major categories of emotion, 37.5 per cent of all reports pertained to negative emotions, but no less than 40.5 per cent to positive emotions. The other 22 per cent of the reports related to affectively more neutral emotions like surprise, and to emotions which were reported less frequently or proved not to be classifiable by our system. Positive emotions reported most often were enjoyment (13.7 per cent), relief (8.6 per cent), satisfaction/contentment (6.0 per cent), hope (5.0 per cent), curiosity/interest (4.1 per cent), and pride (3.1 per cent). In addition to these major categories of positive emotions, a number of less frequently reported positive emotions played a role as well. Specifically, this applied to social positive emotions like sympathy and admiration.

The frequency of positive emotions depended on the type of situation addressed, however. For situations related to studying, attending class, and taking tests or exams, frequencies of positive emotions reported were 57.2, 52.3, and 31.2 per cent, respectively. Structural and functional differences between these situations can probably be made responsible for different profiles of frequencies. Specifically, university students' positive emotions may depend on the relative autonomy given to students, and on opportunities for success. Normally, there are more opportunities for autonomy and self-regulation in situations of studying, compared to attending class or taking tests, and, for many students, better chances for experiencing success while studying and attending class, compared to taking tests and exams.

Beyond giving accounts of emotions *per se*, the narratives our subjects delivered also described the experienced sources and effects of academic emotions. Specifically, the questions we asked covered cognitive and motivational processes experienced in the respective situations, as well as subjective experiences of physiological processes, and of social interactions. Contingency analysis showed that emotions were systematically connected to cognition, motivation, physiological changes, and interaction patterns.

For example, the contingency coefficient for relations between emotions and frequencies of specific cognitive appraisals within academic situations was 0.60 (χ^2 (196) = 476.69, $p < 0.001$; Pekrun 1992a). Concerning the three often reported positive emotions of enjoyment, satisfaction/contentment, and relief the following patterns of cognitive appraisals appeared to be typical. Enjoyment was systematically related to two different types of cognitions: thoughts about the learning material, on the one hand, and appraisals of mastery and success, on the other. Apparently, academic enjoyment can take process-related forms pertaining to learning activities, or outcome-related forms pertaining to resulting achievement and its consequences. Satisfaction and contentment, on the other hand, turned out to be outcome-oriented emotions. One primary source were appraisals of mastery and success. Another relevant type of appraisal was the perceived usefulness of academic learning (e.g. for instrumental purposes pertaining to one's anticipated future job). Relief, finally, was characterized by a pattern of appraisal correlates parts of which might seem counterintuitive at first sight. Generally, relief is an emotion which is triggered by the cessation of aversive circumstances. In our data, relief was related to appraisals of success and mastery in some cases, but to appraisals of non-mastery and failure in others. In any case, however, it pertained to the end of an aversive phase of studying, the end of taking a stressful test or exam, or a reduction of stress experienced during the course of a test or exam.

In sum, our exploratory studies corroborated the assumption that positive emotions may be no less characteristic of students' affective life than their negative emotions. Concerning situations of attending class and studying, they were reported slightly more often than negative emotions. Even concerning exams, however, positive emotions accounted for more than one-third of the emotions reported. This was true not only for samples of university students, but for secondary school students' academic experiences as well (cf. Holzwarth 1997; Rapp 1997; Titz 2001). The ubiquitous frequency of positive academic emotions implies that it should prove fruitful to examine them empirically, and to address them when designing instruction and educational interventions.

Measurement of positive academic emotions: the Academic Emotions Questionnaire (AEQ)

Whereas exploratory, qualitative methods are well suited to gaining preliminary insights into phenomena which have not been investigated thoroughly, quantitative measurement is needed for the more precise analysis of effects and causes. Instruments measuring positive academic emotions are lacking to date. Previous research addressing such emotions has either used more global measures of human emotions not pertaining to the academic domain, or single rating scales using one item per emotion (see Puca and Schmalt 1999; Turner and Schallert 2001). However, global measures of emotion may be less predictive of academic learning and achievement than more specific instruments, as may be seen, for example, from the fact that students' general trait anxiety correlates less with achievement than their test anxiety (Hembree 1988). Single-item scales, on the other hand, may lack reliability, and cannot capture the internal structures of academic emotions in adequate ways.

We therefore developed a quantitative self-report instrument measuring a number of more important academic emotions by multi-item scales (Academic Emotions Questionnaire, AEQ; for an overview, see Pekrun *et al.* in press). This instrument comprises 24 scales measuring nine emotions (enjoyment, hope, pride, relief, anger, anxiety, shame, hopelessness, and boredom) in three different academic settings (attending class, studying, and taking tests and exams).

Theoretical considerations and scale construction

The selection of emotions to be included was based on criteria relating to frequency and theoretical relevance. Specifically, we wanted to measure emotions which were reported frequently in our exploratory research, and can be assumed to be important for students' learning and achievement. The resulting set of emotions comprises four positive emotions, namely, enjoyment, hope, pride, and relief. In addition, the AEQ measures five negative emotions (anger, anxiety, shame, hopelessness, and boredom). Concerning positive emotions, our choice of emotions implied that four of the six most often reported emotions were included (see last section). Pride was included instead of the more often reported emotion of contentment since pride can be assumed to be of primary relevance for students' motivation (Heckhausen 1980).

However, whereas there is no dispute that enjoyment, pride, and relief are human emotions, the construct of hope is considered to be more problematic. Specifically, hope is viewed as a cognitive construct instead of an emotion by some authors. For example, Snyder's theory conceptualizes hope as a set of cognitive expectations relating to pathways and agency in the pursuit of goals (cf. Curry *et al.* 1997). There are two main reasons why we conceptualized hope as an emotion.

First, concerning anticipatory emotions relating to future events, hope can be considered the one positive emotion which is complementary to the negative emotion of anxiety. Both hope and anxiety imply subjective uncertainty about future events, in contrast to anticipatory joy and hopelessness implying subjective certainty. Whereas anxiety involves an amalgam of negative feelings and appraisals of uncertainty, hope involves a combination of feeling positive about a future event, wanting the event to happen, and appraising this as being uncertain. Second, consistent with such a view, subjects in our exploratory research had reported about hope as an emotional experience implying 'hot' expectations instead of cold cognition, implying that the experience of hope was not restricted to affectively neutral cognitive appraisals.

We decided to construct separate scales measuring the emotions listed above for situations of attending class, studying, and taking tests and exams. These situations differ with respect to their functions and social structures, implying that related emotions can differ as well. For example, enjoying studying at home may be quite different from enjoying the challenge of an exam. However, we also decided not to measure all emotions with respect to all three types of situations. Specifically, relief is measured for test situations only, and boredom for situations of attending class and studying. The other seven emotions are measured for all three types of situations. Accordingly, there are eight scales per situation, and a total of 24 scales in the instrument.

Concerning the internal structures of academic emotions, we adopted component process views conceptualizing emotions as sets of interrelated psychological processes (e.g. Scherer

Table 8.3 Academic Emotions Questionnaire (AEQ): reliability of the trait scales

| | Scales | | | | | |
| | Learning-related emotions | | Class-related emotions | | Test emotions | |
Emotions	α	Items	α	Items	α	Items
Enjoyment	0.90	14	0.89	15	0.90	23
Hope	0.86	9	0.84	9	0.89	16
Pride	0.84	9	0.86	9	0.92	16
Relief	—[a]	—	—	—	0.89	14
Anger	0.89	14	0.85	11	0.89	17
Anxiety	0.92	18	0.89	13	0.94	31
Hopelessness	0.93	13	0.88	10	0.94	21
Shame	0.90	14	0.91	15	0.93	19
Boredom	0.93	17	0.93	14	—[b]	—

[a]Relief scale for test emotions only.
[b]Boredom scale for learning-related and class-related emotions only.

1984), including affective, cognitive, physiological, as well as motivational processes. For example, important component processes of task-related enjoyment can be to feel excited when tackling the task, appraise the task as challenging, experience physiological arousal, and be motivated to work at the task. Such a view is in line with contemporary conceptions of students' test anxiety (cf. Hodapp and Benson 1997), although we regard motivational components as no less important than affective-physiological and cognitive components traditionally considered by test anxiety research.

Based on these considerations, we developed an initial item pool, extracted items for preliminary versions of the scales, tested these preliminary versions, and selected items for the final scale versions (see Table 8.3 for an overview). The items are worded such that the scales can be used with alternative instructions pertaining to trait academic emotions, course-related academic emotions pertaining to a specific course or class, and state academic emotions experienced within single academic episodes. Also, there are short eight-item versions of the scales. Recently, the short versions of the scales have been translated into the English language (Götz *et al.* 2001).

Reliability and structural validity

Table 8.3 provides an overview of the reliabilities of the trait versions of the scales, which turned out to be quite satisfactory ($N = 230$ university students for the learning-related and class-related scales, and $N = 222$ for the test-related scales; Molfenter 1999; Titz 2001). The reliabilities for the short trait versions, English-language short trait versions, course-related versions, and state versions proved to be sufficiently high as well (average Alphas were 0.86, 0.86, 0.87, and 0.86, respectively; cf. Titz 2001; Pekrun *et al.* in press; Goetz *et al.* 2001).

Confirmatory factor analysis was used to analyse the internal structures of the scales. Results implied that the scales show sufficient homogeneity, but nevertheless consist of differentiated internal structures pertaining to different components of emotions (i.e. affective, cognitive, physiological, and motivational components). For most of the scales, hierarchical latent factor models comprising separate first order factors for different emotion components, and one second-order factor representing the whole emotion, proved to have a better fit to the data than simple one-factor models. For learning-related enjoyment, a more complicated structure emerged, since this scale pertains both to enjoyment of learning activities, and to enjoyment of mastery and success resulting from learning (for a summary of confirmatory factor analyses, cf. Titz 2001).

The interrelations between learning-related, class-related, and test-related emotions proved to be moderate (average $r = 0.61$), thus corroborating that academic emotions pertaining to these three types of academic situations can be differentiated. Within each of these three groups, several clusters of emotions emerged. The positive emotions of enjoyment, hope, and pride constituted one such cluster for each of the three types of academic situations. This cluster did not represent all relevant positive emotions, however. Specifically, relief separated out by constituting a cluster on its own (Molfenter 1999). Enjoyment, hope, and pride showed close intercorrelations, though well below the respective reliabilities (average $r = 68$; Molfenter 1999; Titz 2001). Correlations between these three emotions and relief, on the other hand, were weaker ($r = 0.28, 0.03$, and 0.26 between test-related enjoyment, hope, and pride, on the one hand, and test-related relief on the other; Molfenter 1999).

From a theoretical perspective, this pattern of interrelations makes perfect sense. It is conceivable to regard enjoyment, hope, and pride as specific variants of one primary positive emotion, namely, joy. Hope can be considered a future-oriented variant of joy implying subjective uncertainty of upcoming positive events, and pride a more retrospective variant of joy implying internal attributions of past or present positive events which are interpreted as a person's own accomplishments. Furthermore, enjoyment, hope, and pride share activating properties. In contrast, relief is a tension-reducing, deactivating emotion which is tied to the cessation or avoidance of a negative state. In the academic realm, one important case in point relates to negative states of test-related stress and anxiety, thus explaining why the positive emotion of test relief correlated positively with the negative emotion of test anxiety ($r = 0.39$; Molfenter 1999).

In sum, this evidence shows that the AEQ is a multidimensional self-report instrument which measures students' emotions in reliable and factorially valid ways. Moving beyond reliability and structural validity, we also assessed the functional construct validity of the AEQ scales concerning relations to students' learning, achievement, personality, and social environments. These relations will be addressed in the next two sections. It should also be noted, however, that the domain of positive academic emotions is not exhaustively covered by the AEQ, and probably cannot completely be measured by any single instrument. Whereas the four positive emotions included may be of specific importance, there are further positive emotions which can play a role in academic situations as well (e.g. contentment, sympathy, and admiration).

The impact of positive emotions on students' learning, self-regulation, and achievement

Many traditional conceptions of human emotions attributed negative functional properties to positive emotions, postulating that positive emotions induce unrealistic appraisals, lead to shallow, superficial processing of information, and reduce motivation to become more deeply involved with the pursuit of challenging goals (cf. the cogent overview given by Aspinwall 1998). Do such accounts represent reality? Are positive emotions detrimental to students' academic learning, self-regulation, and achievement?

In order to obtain preliminary answers to these as yet largely unanswered questions, we first provide short accounts of previous theories and research on the impact of positive mood and positive emotions. We then present a summary of assumptions deduced from a cognitive-motivational model of the achievement effects of emotions (Pekrun 1992*b*), and discuss findings derived from a series of cross-sectional and longitudinal field studies on students' positive emotions which tested parts of these assumptions.

Research on effects of positive mood

Theories and research on the impact of positive affect have focused on positive mood, whereas discrete positive emotions have received much less attention. Over the past twenty years, a multitude of theories have been formulated which address effects of positive and negative mood on cognition and behaviour. These theories relate mood to specific cognitive processes like social perception, attitudes, memory, judgement, problem-solving, decision-making, and health-related appraisals (cf. Aspinwall 1998), and use assumptions on specific mediating processes to give accounts of mood effects within these areas. As a result, there are many theories today, some of them addressing rather specific combinations of mood effects and mediating processes. Although most of these theories seem to be substantiated by some body of research, they are often conflicting, and a more comprehensive theoretical framework reconciling them seems not to be in sight. Four more general approaches, however, can be differentiated, each of which seems to attribute negative functional properties to positive emotions. In summarizing this work, we necessarily have to give a simplified account of each of these approaches (for more detailed reviews, see e.g. Aspinwall 1998; Forgas 1995; Isen 1999; Schwarz and Clore 1996).

Mood-congruent effects. Following the pioneering work by Bower (1981) on mood and activation in semantic memory networks, mood has been postulated to serve as a cue for encoding and retrieving mood-congruent material from memory, thus enhancing storage and retrieval of positive material in positive mood states, and of negative material in negative mood states. Mood-congruent retrieval effects have consistently been found in experimental research. Recently, mood congruent retrieval effects have also been shown for emotion-specific mood states (Levine and Burgess 1997). Mood congruency has been postulated to interfere with effective self-regulation. Specifically, it has been assumed and corroborated empirically that positive mood can lead to an overestimation of chances to obtain positive outcomes due to mood-congruent retrieval of positive outcome-related probability judgments, and to an underestimation of the likelihood of negative events such as failure and illness (cf. Schwarz and Bohner 1996). Unrealistic appraisals of present circumstances and future events, however, can be detrimental to efficient self-regulation and goal pursuit, implying that positive mood can be dysfunctional.

Mood as information serving motivation. In safety-signal and mood-as-information approaches, the informational properties of mood and the motivational effects of these properties have been addressed (cf. Clore *et al.* 1994). Specifically, these approaches have assumed that negative mood signals unsafe conditions, thus inducing motivation to engage in elaborate cognitive problem-solving and effortful action. Positive mood, on the other hand, signals safe conditions, thus allowing for relaxation and counteracting any more systematic and careful processing of information. Again, this would imply that positive mood should be detrimental to efficient self-regulation, since relaxation and superficial information processing may compromise any long-term, effortful goal pursuit.

Mood as a goal of motivation. In this group of approaches, it is assumed that humans are motivated to maintain positive mood (mood maintenance), and to reduce or avoid negative moods (mood repair; cf. Schaller and Cialdini 1990). Motivation to maintain positive mood, however, is supposed to induce avoidance of negative thinking and of taking risks. Avoidance of thinking about negative aspects of the self, present, and future, however, can also be quite maladaptive from the perspective of cautionary, proactive long-term goal pursuit.

Mood effects on cognitive resources. Finally, from a variety of theoretical perspectives, it has been postulated that mood can distract attention, which would lead to superficial information processing. Specifically, the resource allocation model put forward by Ellis and Ashbrook (1988) assumes that mood draws on working memory resources, since working memory resources are finite. This would imply that mood diminishes the resources available for task purposes. Assumptions of the model have primarily been tested for negative mood (specifically, depressed and anxious mood), but have recently been corroborated for positive mood as well (cf. Meinhardt and Pekrun in press).

Alternative views: Positive effects of positive mood. The assumptions of these four approaches would imply that 'our primary goal is to feel good, and feeling good makes us lazy thinkers who are oblivious to potentially useful negative information and unresponsive to meaningful variations in information and situation' (Aspinwall 1998, p. 7). However, there are divergent views as well. Specifically, the work by Isen and colleagues has shown that positive mood can facilitate divergent thinking and creative, flexible thinking, thus serving efficient problem-solving in many situations, instead of compromising it (cf. Isen 1999). Furthermore, it has been shown that positive mood can facilitate performance at secondary tasks (Bless *et al.* 1996). Finally, recent experimental evidence shows that positive mood can generally enhance elaborate processing, even of negative information, when the subject has the goal of solving a problem, rather than the goal of just maintaining present positive mood (cf. Aspinwall 1998). This latter finding may be of specific importance in helping to deduce assumptions on self-regulation in real-life educational settings. A student's life is typically characterized by the pursuit of many goals, instead of just being oriented toward maintaining momentary good mood.

Limitations of experimental mood research. Generally, it seems that traditional mood research has suffered from a number of limitations which reduce the generalizability of results to real-life field settings. Three limitations may be of specific importance. First, with few recent exceptions (e.g. Levine and Burgess 1997), experimental mood research has focused on generalized positive versus negative mood states, at the expense of analysing more specific moods and emotions which may be more characteristic of human everyday life. Also, in many experimental procedures traditionally used, the specific profile of mood states which was triggered by mood induction procedures remained somewhat unclear, thus making interpretations of results ambiguous. Specifically, both positive and negative mood may comprise mood states implying different degrees of activation (e.g. frightened versus sad negative mood, excited versus relaxed positive mood; cf. Watson *et al.* 1999). The degree of activation implied by mood, however, can make quite a difference in terms of cognitive and behavioural effects. Second, due to methodological and ethical constraints, the mood effects of experimental induction procedures are relatively mild, thus undermining generalizability with respect to more intense emotional states.

Finally, many results of experimental mood research have been weak, lacked robustness, and remained inconsistent, which may in part be due to the two first-mentioned limitations. In some relevant traditions of research, even if findings consistently proved to be replicable within one specific laboratory, they proved not to be replicable in others (a case in point is research on affective priming; cf. Klauer 1998).

The usefulness of experimental mood research for explaining students' agency and performance thus seems to be limited. The results of this research are in danger of lacking ecological validity. Because of its inherent limitations, many studies of experimental mood research can be regarded as primarily being of an exploratory nature. They can provide valuable hypotheses, but cannot substitute the more direct analysis of real-life effects of affective states on students' learning, achievement, and self-regulation.

Lack of research linking positive emotions to learning and achievement

Whereas effects of positive mood have been studied extensively, the impact of discrete positive emotions on learning and performance has been analysed much less often (see Pekrun and Frese 1992). However, there are some exceptions as well. Specifically, there are a number of studies which have investigated relations of task-related enjoyment to various kinds of performance (e.g. Ferris and Gerber 1996; Helmke 1993; Larson *et al.* 1985; Puca and Schmalt 1999). In contrast to assumptions of experimental mood research, these studies consistently found that enjoyment had a positive influence on performance. For example, Larson *et al.* (1985) reported that high school students' enjoyment experienced while pursuing scholastic projects correlated significantly with the grade they received upon finishing the project ($r = 0.44$). In the study by Helmke (1993), elementary school children's enjoyment of learning at school correlated positively with academic effort, attention, grades, and achievement at scholastic tests. In longitudinal causal analysis, it turned out that these correlations were produced both by effects of enjoyment on achievement, and by reverse effects of achievement on enjoyment (however, the latter effects proved to be somewhat stronger than emotion effects on achievement).

The evidence of these studies suggests that positive emotions and students' performance are related in positive ways. However, since the number and range of studies are limited, no firm conclusions can be drawn to date. Before generalizations can be made, more research is needed which should investigate the relationship of different positive emotions to various facets of learning and performance in student populations ranging in age, ethnicity, and cultural background.

Assumptions of a cognitive-motivational model

In line with some of the approaches of mood research, we formulated a cognitive-motivational model which assumes that the effects of discrete emotions on learning and achievement are mediated both by cognitive processes and by motivational mechanisms (Pekrun 1992*b*; Pekrun *et al.* in press). Specifically, it is assumed that motivation and effort, strategies of learning and problem-solving, cognitive resources, and self-regulatory processes are primary mechanisms mediating the impact of emotions on learning and achievement.

Concerning the impact of mood and emotions on mediating processes and resulting achievement, it is important to distinguish between positive and negative affective states, as has been done by traditional mood research. However, it should prove fruitful to add a second traditional dimension differentiating affective states, namely, activation (cf. Watson *et al.* 1999). These two dimensions can be regarded as largely orthogonal, implying that four basic categories of emotions can be distinguished: positive activating and deactivating emotions, and negative activating and deactivating emotions. Examples of positive activating emotions are enjoyment, excitement, hope, and pride, and of positive deactivating emotions relief, relaxation, and contentment.

Furthermore, a third distinction should be important from an educational perspective as well. This distinction implies that there is a differentiation between emotions relating to inherent properties of task activities, and emotions relating to the outcomes of these activities. Borrowing terms from motivation research, activity-related emotions can be considered as intrinsic emotions, and outcome-related emotions as extrinsic emotions (Pekrun 1998). Intrinsic emotions like enjoyment of learning are based on interest in the process of learning, or in the objects of learning, whereas extrinsic emotions pertain to outcomes like success, failure, career consequences, etc.

The model assumes that positive emotions of these different categories influence mediating processes and resulting achievement in the following ways.

Motivation. Students' goal pursuit in academic settings is probably less characterized by goals of momentary mood maintenance, and more by goals of attaining mastery and achievement, avoiding failure, obtaining positive social reactions, etc. This implies that academic approach and avoidance goals pursued at school and university should be more important for students' positive emotions than goals of mood maintenance or mood repair. More specifically, concerning activating positive emotions, it can be assumed that such emotions enhance the action readiness (Frijda 1986) to perform academic task activities, and to pursue outcome-related academic goals. For example, both intrinsic enjoyment of learning and extrinsic joy and pride relating to success should strengthen the motivation to continue learning. This process can be facilitated by mood congruency effects implying that positive emotions enhance attention to and retrieval of positive task- and self-related appraisals from memory, like positive self-efficacy expectations further strengthening motivation (cf. Olafson and Ferraro 2001).

The situation may be more complex for deactivating positive emotions, however. Emotions like relief and relaxation can reduce any momentary motivation for effortful task engagement. On the other hand, these emotions can serve as reinforcers after task completion, thus strengthening motivation to engage in the next phase of learning. This would imply that deactivating positive emotions can be detrimental from a short-term perspective, but beneficial in the long run.

Learning strategies. Since activating positive emotions can strengthen motivation and the effortful pursuit of academic goals, they can also be assumed to benefit the elaborate processing of relevant information, including metacognitive and cognitive strategies of learning. In addition, generalizing from the evidence on mood and problem-solving, it can be assumed that creative, flexible, and holistic strategies are fostered by activating positive emotions.

Furthermore, since emotions serve functions of directing attention towards the object of emotion, intrinsic activating emotions like enjoyment of learning can focus attention on the learning task at hand. Task enjoyment should thus be a primary source of activity-related flow experiences (Csikszentmihalyi and Csikszentmihalyi 1988).

In contrast, the effects of deactivating positive emotions can again be equivocal and less easy to predict. These emotions can also be assumed to create a broadened mindset facilitating creative ways of thinking. On the other hand, they may be counterproductive for any more elaborate processing of information, producing more shallow, superficial information processing instead, in similar ways as has generally been assumed for positive mood by experimental mood research (as outlined above). However, there is a caveat here as well. Creative, divergent thinking may sometimes require one to loosen one's mind to such an extent that there is no longer any conscious pursuit of task goals at all. This would imply that phases of creative thinking needing elaborate, complex recombination of information may well be fostered by temporary emotional deactivation as implied by relaxation and contentment, even if this recombination of information does only in part take place at the level of conscious elaborate processing.

Cognitive resources. Mood research has shown that positive mood can reduce attention and working memory resources. It would be misleading, however, to simply generalize this finding to positive emotions in academic settings. Specifically, intrinsic task enjoyment serves functions of directing attention toward the task, thus allowing one to make full use of cognitive resources instead of reducing them. Extrinsic positive emotions, on the other hand, can indeed distract attention away from the task. For example, pride can focus attention on the self, and admiration on another person, thus reducing working memory resources available for task purposes.

Self-regulation of learning. Setting goals, planning, monitoring, and evaluating learning requires flexible information processing which adapts behaviour to goals and task demands. As argued above, this type of information processing should be fostered by positive emotions, although more so by activating than by deactivating positive emotions. By implication, emotions like enjoyment, hope, and pride should foster students' self-regulation of learning.

Academic achievement. The above assumptions imply that intrinsic activating positive emotions enhance motivation, facilitate elaborate information processing, benefit creative and flexible ways of thinking, direct attention towards task performance, and help self-regulation, implying that they should be beneficial for resulting academic achievement.

Extrinsic and deactivating positive emotions, on the other hand, can exert positive as well as negative effects on different mediating processes, implying that their achievement effects should be more complex. In these emotions, achievement effects can depend on specific interactions between mediating processes and task demands which determine the relative importance of mechanisms benefitted or undermined by the respective emotion. Nevertheless, concerning extrinsic activating emotions like hope and pride, positive motivational and processing effects should be stronger in most cases than any distraction of attention induced by them, implying overall beneficial effects as well. The effects of deactivating positive emotions, however, may remain more equivocal since these emotions can reduce immediate motivation and distract attention, but can also strengthen long-term motivation to pursue academic goals.

In sum, a realistic theoretical account of positive emotions' effects on academic learning and achievement implies that beneficial effects of positive emotions may far outweigh their potential costs under most conditions. One more general implication of such a theoretical analysis is that it would be misleading to assume that findings from experimental laboratory research could be generalized to real-life academic field settings in any simple ways, without taking the specific goal structures of these settings into account.

Empirical findings

We tested parts of the above assumptions in a series of seven cross-sectional, three longitudinal, and one diary-based study. The samples of these studies consisted of university and school students (cf. Pekrun *et al.* 1996, in press; Pekrun and Hofmann 1999; Titz 2001). In these studies, we used trait or state versions of the AEQ scales to measure students' emotions. German versions of the Study Interest Scale (Winteler *et al.* 1991) were used for assessing students' academic interest, trait and state versions of a German adaptation of the Motivated Strategies for Learning Questionnaire (MSLQ) to measure learning strategies and effort (Winteler *et al.* 1991; based on Pintrich *et al.* 1993), scales assessing task-irrelevant thinking when learning and taking tests as (negative) indicators of the availability of cognitive resources (adapted from Sarason 1984), and grades as well as performance at written exams as indicators of academic achievement (Perry *et al.* 2001).

The results showed that students' positive emotions do in fact relate in signficant ways to their learning and achievement. This was true of trait positive emotions as well as of course-related and state positive emotions. By and large, relations proved to be equivalent for university and secondary school students, and for German and Canadian students. Specifically, the following findings on mediating mechanisms and academic achievement emerged.

Motivation and effort. As expected, the activating positive emotions of enjoyment, hope, and pride correlated positively with students' interest, intrinsic academic motivation (i.e. motivation to learn because the material is interesting and learning is enjoyable), extrinsic academic motivation (motivation to learn in order to attain outcomes), total motivation to learn, and self-reported academic effort. These relations were somewhat stronger for learning-related and class-related emotions than for test emotions. Correlations with interest and intrinsic motivation were higher for enjoyment, whereas relations with extrinsic motivation were higher for the extrinsic emotion of pride. For example, correlations of learning-related enjoyment, hope, and pride with intrinsic academic motivation were $r = 0.61, 0.41$, and 0.30 ($p < 0.001$) in a study with $N = 230$ university students (Titz 2001), whereas correlations with extrinsic academic motivation were $r = 0.20$ ($p < 0.01$), 0.30, and 0.43 ($p < 0.001$). Correlations with resulting effort were $r = 0.43$, 0.49, and 0.34 ($p < 0.001$), thus pointing to the importance of both enjoyment and hope.

Concerning deactivating positive emotion, there is one relevant scale in the AEQ, namely, the test relief scale. As expected theoretically, correlations between relief and motivational variables were much less strong, most of them being non-significant and close to zero (cf. Molfenter 1999). This is in line with expectations relating to equivocal motivational effects of deactivating positive emotions. On the other hand, relations between relief and motivation could in part be epiphenomena of relations between anxiety and motivation, since relief is a tension-reducing emotion which can be tied to preceding negative affective states (as noted above, test relief and anxiety correlated positively in our studies; Molfenter 1999).

Learning strategies. Enjoyment, hope, and pride related positively to students' meta-cognitive strategies at learning, and to the flexible cognitive strategies of elaboration, organization, and critical thinking (e.g. $r = 0.44$, $p < 0.001$, between enjoyment of learning and elaboration in Titz 2001). This suggests that activating positive emotions can in fact facilitate flexible, creative modes of thinking and learning. However, an alternative interpretation would be that creative learning is more enjoyable. Concerning more rigid ways of learning, correlations of activating positive emotions with rehearsal strategies were also positive, but most of them were near zero and not significant. Finally, the correlations between relief and rehearsal were near zero as well. This pattern of relations implies that there is a strong, specific relationship between activating positive emotions and flexible strategies of learning, which is consistent with our theoretical expectations.

Cognitive resources. As expected, the relations between enjoyment and irrelevant thinking during learning and test taking were consistently negative (e.g. $r = -0.38$, $p < 0.01$, for learning-related enjoyment and irrelevant thinking during learning in Titz, 2001), which is in line with the assumption that intrinsic positive emotions can focus attention on the task. However, somewhat contrary to our expectations, relations for hope and pride proved to be negative as well. One possible interpretation is that positive motivational effects of these emotions on attention are stronger than any attention-diverting effects of implied cognitions about the self and the future. Relief, finally, did not relate significantly to task-irrelevant thinking.

Self-regulation versus external regulation of learning. Motivation, learning strategies, and attention can be regarded as key components of students' self-regulated learning. To regulate one's learning, however, involves more than being motivated, using learning strategies, and deploying cognitive resources. We used two newly developed scales to measure students' perceptions of self-regulation versus external regulation of their learning (Titz 2001). These two scales pertain to self-regulation versus external regulation by others concerning the goals of learning, the material used, the strategies of learning employed, and the monitoring and evaluation of outcomes. The two scales are moderately positively correlated, implying that self-regulation and external regulation need not be contradictory.

Enjoyment, hope, and pride correlated positively with self-regulation, which conforms to our assumptions (e.g. $r = 0.43$, 0.46, and 0.37, $p < 0.001$, in Titz 2001). These emotions were essentially unrelated to external regulation. Relief related positively to both types of regulation, but correlations were low (Molfenter 1999). Again, the pattern of relations suggests that there is a special relationship between activating positive emotions, on the one hand, and flexible ways of handling one's learning, on the other.

Academic achievement. Activating positive emotions related positively to students' academic achievement, whereas relief was essentially unrelated (cf. Pekrun *et al.* 1996; Pekrun and Hofmann 1999; Titz 2001). Typical correlations between learning-related, class-related, and test-related enjoyment, hope, and pride, on the one hand, and university grades, on the other, were in the range of $0.30 < r < 0.50$ (Molfenter 1999; Titz 2001). Correlations between secondary school students' positive emotions and their scholastic grades were of the same magnitude (Goetz 2002). These coefficients imply that positive emotions explain up to 25 per cent of the variance in achievement scores, a percentage of variance which is notably larger than the 10 per cent of variance typically explained by the well-researched emotion of test anxiety (Hembree 1988). Finally, from a longitudinal perspective, university students' enjoyment, hope, and pride measured early in the semester predicted grades as well as final course exam scores at the end of the semester (e.g. Pekrun *et al.* 2000).

Taken together, these findings imply that students' activating positive emotions relate in positive ways to academic motivation, effort spent at academic tasks, use of flexible strategies, availability of attentional resources, self-regulation of learning, and academic achievement. They are essentially unrelated to rehearsal strategies and to external regulation of learning, implying that they neither foster nor undermine more rigid approaches to learning. The deactivating emotion of relief proved to be unrelated to all of these variables of learning and achievement. However, it would be premature to generalize from relief to other deactivating positive emotions, since emotions like relaxation and contentment can relate to learning and achievement in a different way.

In sum, it turns out that enjoyment, hope, and pride relate to students' academic goal pursuit and outcomes in much more positive ways than might have been inferred from some of the findings of experimental mood research. However, the limitations of this evidence should be noted as well. Specifically, even predictive, longitudinal evidence does not imply that emotion effects on learning and performance are the only relevant direction of causation. Rather, it may be assumed that positive emotions, learning, and achievement are linked by reciprocal causation, positive emotions fostering achievement, but feedback of positive achievement in turn enhancing positive emotions. It is this kind of positive feedback loop which has been found by Helmke's study of learning-related enjoyment in school students cited above (Helmke 1993).

In addition, on a more general level, it can be quite misleading to infer from the sample statistics normally derived from correlational and experimental studies that the implied relations between variables do in fact apply to all subjects under study. Rather, correlational studies of the kind addressed here imply an analysis of relationships between individual differences in two or more variables. To ensure generalizability to intraindividual psychological functioning requires the more direct analysis of within-person functional relations (cf. Schmitz and Skinner 1993).

This is what we did in an idiographic–nomothetic diary study analysing the development of daily exam-related emotions of $N = 72$ students over a period of six weeks before and during final university exams. In this study, we calculated intraindividual correlations between daily emotions and variables of exam-related learning for each individual student, and analysed if these correlations were generalizable across the students of the sample. One main result was that, by and large, relations of positive emotions to learning proved to be similar for different students and equivalent to the respective interindividual correlations, thus indicating functional homogeneity of positive emotions across students. For negative emotions, a more complicated picture emerged (Pekrun and Hofmann 1999; cf. Pekrun *et al.* in press). Concerning positive emotions, the evidence of this study strengthens the conclusions reached on the basis of interindividual relations as outlined above.

Cognitive and social origins of students' positive emotions: implications of control-value theory

The assumptions and findings presented in the last section imply that positive emotions in education can make a big difference. Consequently, it would pay to attend to their antecedents, and to make an attempt to enhance them by educational intervention and in ordinary classroom instruction. To date, the sources of students' positive emotions are largely unexplored, in contrast to the antecedents of negative emotions like test anxiety (Hembree 1988; Zeidner 1998). Attributional research on the role of causal attributions in positive achievement emotions is the only major exception (Weiner 1985). The studies which are available seem to converge concerning the importance of two classes of individual antecedents inducing positive emotions, namely, (a) students' academic expectations, causal attributions, and self-evaluations of abilities, and (b) their interest in academic tasks and task-related goals (e.g. Ferris and Gerber 1996; Helmke 1993; Larson *et al.* 1985).

Academic expectations, causal attributions, and self-concepts relate to students' perceived control over academic actions and outcomes, and interest and goals to the values they attach to these actions and outcomes. In a recent control-value theory of achievement emotions, we made an attempt to integrate theoretical formulations addressing these two classes of antecedents (cf. Pekrun 1998, 2000; Pekrun *et al.* in press). Implications of this theory for antecedents of students' positive emotions, reciprocal linkages of emotions and antecedents, and educational applications will be discussed in turn.

Individual antecedents of students' positive emotions

Beyond genetic dispositions and physiological processes, cognitive appraisals can be regarded as main sources of human emotions. Control-value theory of achievement emotions posits that control-related and value-related appraisals are main determinants of achievement-related emotions. Examples of control-related cognitions are retrospective causal attributions, prospective causal expectancies (e.g. self-efficacy and action–outcome expectations), and state-related control cognitions relating to the present situation. Important value-related types of appraisals are intrinsic values and goals relating to inherent properties of activities, and extrinsic values and goals pertaining to their outcomes. In taking these different types of control and value cogitions into account, the theory attempts to integrate assumptions of expectancy-value and attributional theories of achievement-related emotions (Weiner 1985; Pekrun 1992*c*).

Consistent with basic assumptions of expectancy-value models of affect and motivation, the theory postulates that subjective control and values interact in such ways that both of them are necessary for academic emotions to arise. For example, it is assumed that enjoyment of learning presupposes that the student expects to be able to master the material, and is sufficiently interested in learning this material. Pride about success in a specific domain is assumed to be induced when the student attributes success to internal causes making achievement controllable (the causes as such can be controllable or uncontrollable, as with controllable effort and uncontrollable dimensions of ability), and sufficiently values success in this domain. However, control and value cognitions need not be processed each time an emotion emerges. In habitualized emotions, situational perceptions and emotions can be short-circuited (Pekrun 1988). In any case, however, they are supposed to be crucial when the emotion is learned initially (one specific exception is automatic processes of emotional contagion in classroom interactions; cf. Hatfield *et al.* 1994).

In some of our field studies on academic emotions, variables of students' academic control and values were included. In these studies, it turned out that academic self-efficacy, academic control of achievement, subjective values of learning activities, and subjective values of academic success and failure correlated positively with students' enjoyment, hope, and pride (cf. Pekrun 1998, 2000; Molfenter 1999; Titz 2001). Also, academic control measured early in the semester predicted enjoyment of university courses and related intrinsic motivation throughout the semester, thus corroborating the affective importance of academic control in longitudinal ways (cf. Pekrun *et al.* 2000; Perry *et al.* 2001).

Moving beyond main effects, a recent study by Barrera (2001) considered whether interactions of academic control and values can explain university students' emotions pertaining to statistics courses, including the enjoyment of such courses. Statistics is a subject which causes academic worries and undermines motivation in many of our students today. The results of this study implied significant interactions. In line with assumptions of control-value theory, enjoyment was high when both academic control in the domain of statistics and the subjective importance of this domain were high, whereas enjoyment was low when either control or value or both were low. By implication, any intervention making an attempt to ameliorate our students' approach to statistics should profit from paying attention both to students' sense of mastery and control in this domain, and to the value and usefulness they attribute to this subject.

Instructional and social antecedents of students' positive emotions

In line with social cognitive theories of affect and personality, control-value theory assumes that the impact of social environments on emotions is mediated by subjective appraisals. This implies that the theory's assumptions about cognitive antecedents of emotions can also be used to deduce hypotheses on their environmental origins. Environmental factors of specific importance should be those variables which influence control and value appraisals initially, thus indirectly affecting students' emotions as well. This can be assumed for the following groups of variables (Fig. 8.1; Pekrun 1998, 2000).

1. The *quality of classroom instruction* can be assumed to exert direct effects both on students' mastery and perceived academic control (Perry 1991), and on subjective values of academic learning, thus also affecting their emotions. Probably, there are different mechanisms underlying these effects. Modeling effects of teachers' behaviour, including teachers' expressed emotions, and the impact of quality instruction on students' mastery of learning may be of specific importance.

2. *Autonomy support* can meet students' needs for self-regulation, thus creating positive experiences of learning which can induce positive values as well. In addition, autonomy support can benefit the development of mastery and, therefore, the emergence of subjective control.

3. *Social achievement expectancies and values* conveyed by significant others, by educational goal structures, and by classroom interaction structures (like cooperation versus competition; see Chapter 10 in this volume) imply messages about aspiration levels and probabilities of success and failure, and about the importance of achievement, thus influencing students' achievement-related expectancies and values.

4. *Feedback and consequences of achievement* underly the formation of students' achievement expectancies, of outcome expectancies relating to parents' and teachers' social reactions, career opportunities etc., and of related perceptions of the instrumental value of achievement. Causal attributions can be of specific importance in mediating these effects (Weiner 1985).

5. Finally, *support and social relatedness* with parents, teachers, and peers in learning contexts can help students to deal with failures, thus strengthening positive expectancies, and to meet their needs for affiliation, which can foster the development of positive value perceptions pertaining to learning and achievement.

Consistent with these assumptions, findings of our field studies showed that teacher enthusiasm, positive feedback of achievement, as well as cooperation and affiliation within the classroom correlated positively with students' enjoyment of learning and hope for success. This evidence included both cross-sectional correlations and longitudinal prediction (cf. Pekrun 1998, 2000; Pekrun *et al.* 2000).

Reciprocal linkages between social environments and students' positive emotions

Control-value theory and the assumptions of our cognitive-motivational model on emotion effects imply that social environments influence students' positive emotions, and that emotions in turn affect academic learning and achievement. Taken individually, the assumptions of the two models would imply unidirectional causation. Taken together,

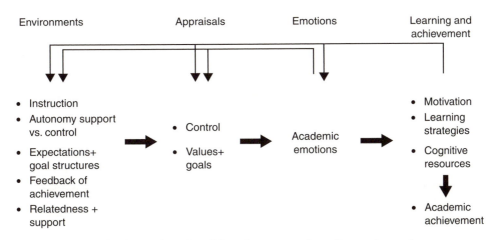

Figure 8.1 Control-value theory of emotions: linkages between emotions, effects, and antecedents.

however, they suggest that antecedents, emotions, and effects can be linked by reciprocal causation (Fig. 8.1).

For example, as outlined in the last section, positive emotions can foster students' achievement, but positive feedback of achievement is a major source of positive academic emotions (Weiner 1985), thus implying positive feedback loops between emotions and achievement. In a similar vein, the behaviour of significant others can influence students' academic control, values, and emotions, but students' can in turn affect the behaviour of educators. A case in point is teachers' enthusiasm which may be important for students' academic experiences, but can strongly be influenced by students' positive classroom emotions. Evidence on reciprocal linkages of this kind is largely lacking to date. One notable exception is the study by Helmke (1993). As cited above, this study found that elementary school students' enjoyment of learning positively influenced their academic achievement across the schoolyears, but was dependent on prior positive feedback of achievement, thus implying positive feedback loops between emotions, achievement, and feedback of achievement.

Implications for intervention and classroom instruction

Control-value theory can serve as a theoretical basis for designing measures of intervention and classroom instruction fostering students' positive emotions. Such measures can focus on students' appraisals underlying their emotions, or on instruction and social environments influencing appraisals and emotions. Concerning appraisals, the theory implies that methods influencing control and values should be of specific importance. An example is reattributional training which can help students to develop a feeling of control over important subjective outcomes by reshaping their causal attributions of success and failure. Reattributional training procedures can be used with individual students, but can be integrated into ordinary classroom instruction as well (cf. Foersterling 1985; Perry and Penner 1990; Perry *et al.* 1993).

As to the design of educational environments, the above assumptions on environmental influences suggest a number of ways to foster students' emotions (cf. also Astleitner 2000; Covington 1992). Improving the quality of instruction and being enthusiastically engaged in teaching can be a primary way of doing so. A second important method would be to give students autonomy to regulate their learning. However, a precondition would be sufficient competences for self-regulation by the students, implying that support by the teacher may be needed for younger students, and for students with regulatory problems (e.g. volitional problems like procrastination). Third, teachers and parents can foster students' affect by conveying achievement expectancies and values which challenge students without pushing demands beyond their capabilities. Fourth, concerning feedback of achievement, opportunities for success inducing positive emotions can be increased by using individual and criterion-oriented reference norms for giving feedback, instead of — or in addition to — social grading which seems to dominate scholastic feedback systems. Also, creating academic cultures of learning from errors and perceiving them as chances to improve, instead of being punished for them, can reduce negative emotions and thus lay the groundwork for positive affective experiences even in cases of non-mastery. Finally, creating reliable social bonds with students can help in conveying positive academic values and maintaining a mastery-oriented climate preventing the development of anti-achievement norms prevailing in many classrooms today.

Conclusions

As of yet, psychology as well as educational research have neglected the positive side of human affective life. One underlying implicit assumption seems to be that positive emotions should be less important for theoretical explanations of human agency and related practical applications than their negative counterparts (cf. also Fredrickson 2001). In this chapter, we argued that positive emotions are no less important than negative affect. We outlined theoretical assumptions and empirical findings of our programme of research into students' academic emotions, and in doing so, we focused on occurrence, measurement, effects, and antecedents of students' positive emotions.

Findings implied that students experience a great variety of positive task-related, self-referenced, and social emotions in academic settings when attending classes, studying, and taking tests and exams. Judging from the results of our exploratory studies, positive academic emotions are experienced no less often by students than negative emotions like test anxiety. In contrast to assumptions which might be deduced from experimental mood research, many of these positive emotions prove to be beneficial for students' learning and pursuit of challenging academic goals. Specifically, this is true for activating positive emotions like enjoyment of learning, hope for success, and academic pride. The control-value theory outlined here implies that perceived academic control and subjective values of academic mastery and achievement can be primary individual sources of these positive emotions, and classroom instruction as well as social environments important external sources. One implication is that there can be many ways of fostering students' positive emotions by addressing individual appraisals or instructional and social antecedents inducing such emotions.

However, there are also some limitations to the studies on students' positive emotions which have been conducted thus far, including our own studies. For example, even predictive evidence produced by longitudinal studies does not yet give an account of reciprocal linkages between positive emotions, effects, and antecedents, and of the relative importance of different causal directions. Even more importantly, intervention research testing assumptions on ways to foster students' positive emotions is still largely lacking.

Such limitations notwithstanding, the evidence presented in this chapter suggests that a realistic account of students' agency and goal pursuit requires us to take their positive emotions into account. Educational research should move beyond the analysis of test anxiety which has dominated in the past, and study the full range of students' academic emotions, paying no less attention to their positive affective experiences than to their negative emotions.

Acknowledgements

This research was supported by three research grants to the first author from the German Research Foundation (Pe 320/7–2, 320/7–3, 320/11–1) and by a grant to the first and fourth authors from the German American Academic Council.

References

Aspinwall, L. (1998). Rethinking the role of positive affect in self-regulation. *Motivation and Emotion,* 22, 1–32.

Astleitner, H. (2000). Designing emotionally sound instruction. *Instructional Science,* 28, 169–98.

Atkinson, J. W. (1964). *An introduction to motivation.* Princeton, NJ: van Nostrand.

Barrera, A. (2001). *Students' conceptions of intelligence, emotions, and achievement in university statistics courses.* Unpublished master's thesis, University of Munich, Germany.

Bless, H., Clore, G. L., Schwarz, N., Golisano, V., Rabe, C., and Wölk, M. (1996). Mood and the use of scripts: Does a happy mood really lead to mindlessness? *Journal of Personality and Social Psychology,* 71, 665–79.

Bower, G. H. (1981). Mood and memory. *American Psychologist,* 36, 129–48.

Clore, G. L., Schwarz, N., and Conway, M. (1994). Affective causes and consequences of social information processing, in R. S. Wyer and K. Skrull (eds.), *Handbook of social cognition,* 2nd edn, pp. 323–417. Hillsdale, NJ: Erlbaum.

Covington, M. V. (1992). *Making the grade: A self-worth perspective on motivation and school reform.* New York: Cambridge University Press.

Curry, L. A., Snyder, C. R., Cook, D. L., Ruby, B. C., and Rehm, M. (1997). Role of hope in academic and sport achievement. *Journal of Personality and Social Psychology,* 73, 1257–67.

Csikszentmihalyi, M. and Csikszentmihalyi, I. S. (eds.). (1988). *Optimal experience: Psychological studies of flow in consciousness.* New York: Cambridge University Press.

Ellis, H. C. and Ashbrook, P. W. (1988). Resource allocation model of the effect of depressed mood states on memory, in K. Fiedler and J. Forgas (eds.), *Affect, cognition, and social behaviour.* Toronto: Hogrefe International.

Ferris, J. and Gerber, R. (1996). Mature-age students' feelings of enjoying learning in a further education context. *European Journal of Psychology of Education,* 11, 79–96.

Foersterling, F. (1985). Attributional retraining: A review. *Psychological Bulletin,* 98, 495–512.

Forgas, J. P. (1995). Mood and judgment: The Affect Infusion Model (AIM). *Psychological Bulletin,* 117, 39–66.

Fredrickson, B. L. (2001). The role of positive emotions in positive psychology: The broaden-and-build theory of positive emotions. *American Psychologist,* 56, 218–26.

Frijda, N. (1986). *The emotions.* Cambridge: Cambridge University Press.

Frydenberg, E. (1997). *Adolescent coping: Theoretical and research perspectives.* London: Routledge.

Goetz, T. (2002). *Students' emotions in mathematics.* Unpublished dissertation. University of Munich: Department of Psychology.

—— Pekrun, R., Perry, R. P., and Hladkyi, S. (2001). *Academic emotions questionnaire: Codebook for English-language scale versions* (Technical report). University of Munich: Department of Psychology.

Gottfried, A. E., Fleming, J. S., and Gottfried, A. W. (2001). Continuity of academic intrinsic motivation from childhood through late adolescence: A longitudinal study. *Journal of Educational Psychology,* 93, 3–13.

Hatfield, E., Cacioppo, J. T., and Rapson, R. L. (1994). *Emotional contagion.* New York: Cambridge University Press.

Heckhausen, H. (1980). *Motivation und Handeln (Motivation and action).* Berlin: Springer.

Helmke, A. (1993). Die Entwicklung der Lernfreude vom Kindergarten bis zur 5. Klassenstufe (Development of affective attitudes towards learning from kindergarten to grade five). *Zeitschrift fuer Paedagogische Psychologie*, 7, 77–86.

Hembree, R. (1988). Correlates, causes, effects, and treatment of test anxiety. *Review of Educational Research*, 58, 47–77.

Hodapp, V. and Benson, J. (1997). The multidimensionality of test anxiety: a test of different models. *Anxiety, Stress and Coping*, 10, 219–44.

Holzwarth, A. (1997). *Emotionen in schulischen Prüfungssituationen: Eine explorative Interviewstudie* (*Emotions in exams at school: An exploratory interview study*). Unpublished master's thesis. University of Regensburg: Institute of Psychology.

Isen, A. M. (1999). Positive affect, in T. Dalgleish and M. J. Powers (eds.), *Handbook of cognition and emotion*, pp. 521–39. New York: Wiley.

Klauer, C. (1998). Affective priming. *European Review of Social Psychology*, 8, 63–107.

Larson, R., Hecker, B., and Norem, J. (1985). Students' experience with research projects: Pains, enjoyment and success. *High School Journal*, 69, 61–9.

Levine, L. J. and Burgess, S. L. (1997). Beyond general arousal: Effect of specific emotions on memory. *Social Cognition*, 15, 157–81.

Meinhardt, J. and Pekrun, R. Attentional resource allocation to emotional events: An ERP study. *Cognition and Emotion* (in press).

Molfenter, S. (1999). *Prüfungsemotionen bei Studierenden. Explorative Analysen und Entwicklung eines diagnostischen Instrumentariums* (*Test emotions in university students: Exploratory analysis and development of a diagnostic instrument*). Unpublished dissertation. University of Regensburg: Institute of Psychology.

Olafson, K. M. and Ferrraro, F. R. (2001). Effects of emotional state on lexical decision performance. *Brain and Cognition*, 45, 15–20.

Pekrun, R. (1988). *Emotion, Motivation und Persönlichkeit* (*Emotion, motivation and personality*). München: Psychologie Verlags Union.

—— (1992*a*). Kognition und Emotion in studienbezogenen Lern- und Leistungssituationen: Explorative Analysen (Cognition and emotion in academic situations of learning and achievement: exploratory analyses). *Unterrichtswissenschaft*, 20, 308–24.

—— (1992*b*). The impact of emotions on learning and achievement: Towards a theory of cognitive/motivational mediators. *Applied Psychology*, 41, 359–76.

—— (1992*c*). Expectancy-value theory of anxiety: Overview and implications, in D. G. Forgays, T. Sosnowski, and K. Wrzesniewski (eds.), *Anxiety: Recent developments in self-appraisal, psychophysiological and health research*, pp. 23–41. Washington, DC: Hemisphere.

—— (1998). Schüleremotionen und ihre Förderung: Ein blinder Fleck der Unterrichtsforschung (Students' emotions: A neglected topic of educational research). *Psychologie in Erziehung und Unterricht*, 44, 230–48.

—— (2000). A social cognitive, control-value theory of achievement emotions, in J. Heckhausen (ed.), *Motivational psychology of human development*, pp. 143–63. UK, Oxford: Elsevier.

—— and Fend, H. (eds.) (1991). *Schule und Persönlichkeitsentwicklung: Ein Resümee der Längsschnittforschung* (*Schools and personality development: Longitudinal studies*). Stuttgart: Enke.

—— and Frese, M. (1992). Emotions in work and achievement, in C. L. Cooper and I. T. Robertson (eds.), *International review of industrial and organizational psychology*, Vol. 7, pp. 153–200. UK, Chichester: Wiley.

Pekrun, R. Goetz, T., Titz, W., and Perry, R. P. Academic emotions in students' self-regulated learning and achievement: A programme of quantitative and qualitative research. *Educational Psychologist* (in press).

—— Hochstadt, M., and Kramer, K. (1996). Prüfungsemotionen, Lernen und Leistung (test emotions, learning, and achievement), in C. Spiel, U. Kastner-Koller and P. Deimann (eds.), *Motivation und Lernen aus der Perspektive lebenslanger Entwicklung*, pp. 151–62. Münster: Waxmann.

—— and Hofmann, H. (1999). Lern- und Leistungsemotionen: Erste Befunde eines Forschungs-programms (Emotions in learning and achievement: First results of a program of research), in R. Pekrun and M. Jerusalem (eds.), *Emotion, Motivation und Leistung*, pp. 247–67. Göttingen: Hogrefe.

—— Molfenter, S., Titz, W., and Perry, R. P. (2000). *Emotion, learning, and achievement in university students: Longitudinal studies.* Paper presented at the annual meeting of the American Educational Research Association, New Orleans, LA.

Perry, R. P. (1991). Perceived control in college students: Implications for instruction in higher education, in J. Smart (ed.), *Higher education: Handbook of theory and research*, Vol. 7, pp. 1–56. New York: Agathon.

—— Hechter, F. I., Menec, V. H., and Weinberg, L. (1993). Enhancing achievement motivation and performance in college students: An attributional retraining perspective. *Research in Higher Education*, 34, 687–720.

—— Hladkyi, S., Pekrun, R., and Pelletier, S. T. (2001). Academic control and action control in the achievement of college students: A longitudinal field study. *Journal of Educational Psychology*, 93, 776–89.

—— and Penner, K. S. (1990). Enhancing academic achievement in college students through attributional retraining and instruction. *Journal of Educational Psychology*, 82, 262–71.

Pintrich, P. R., Smith, D. A. F., Garcia, T., and McKeachie, W. (1993). Reliability and predictive validity of the Motivated Strategies for Learning Questionnaire (MSLQ). *Educational and Psychological Measurement*, 53, 801–13.

Puca, R. M. and Schmalt, H.-D. (1999). Task enjoyment: A mediator between achievement motives and performance. *Motivation and Emotion*, 23, 15–29.

Rapp, A. (1997). *Emotionen in schulischen Unterrichts- und Lernsituationen: Eine explorative Interviewstudie (School students' emotions in classroom instruction and studying: An exploratory interview study).* Unpublished master's thesis. University of Regensburg: Institute of Psychology.

Sarason, I. G. (1984). Stress, anxiety, and cognitive interference: Reactions to tests. *Journal of Personality and Social Psychology*, 44, 929–38.

Schaller, M. and Cialdini, R. B. (1990). Happiness, sadness, and helping: A motivational integration, in R. Sorrentino and E.T. Higgins (eds.), *Handbook of motivation and cognition: Foundations of social behaviour*, Vol. 2, pp. 265–96. New York: Guilford Press.

Scherer, K. R. (1984). On the nature and function of emotion: A component process approach, in K. R. Scherer and P. Ekman (Hrsg.), *Approaches to emotion*, pp. 293–317. Hillsdale, NJ: Erlbaum.

Schmitz, B. and Skinner, E. (1993). Perceived control, effort, and academic performance: Interindividual, intraindividual, and multivariate time series analyses. *Journal of Personality and Social Psychology*, 64, 1010–28.

Schwarz, N. and Bohner, G. (1996). Feelings and their motivational implications: Moods and the action sequence, in P. M. Gollwitzer and J. A. Bargh (eds.), *The psychology of action: Linking cognition and motivation to behavior*, pp. 119–45. New York: Guilford Press.

—— and **Clore, G. L.** (1996). Feelings and phenomenal experiences, in E. T. Higgins and A. W. Kruglanski (eds.), *Social psychology: Handbook of basic principles*, pp. 433–65. New York: Guilford.

Spangler, G., Pekrun, R., Kramer, C., and **Hofmann, H.** Students' emotions, physiological reactions, and coping at exams. *Anxiety, Stress and Coping* (in press).

Titz, W. (2001). *Emotionen von Studierenden in Lernsituationen* (*University students' emotions at learning*). Münster: Waxmann.

Turner, J. and **Schallert, D.** (2001). Expectancy-value relationships of shame reactions and shame resiliency. *Journal of Educational Psychology*, **93**, 320–9.

Watson, D., Wiese, D., Vaidya, J., and **Tellegen, A.** (1999). The two general activation systems of affect: Structural findings, evolutionary considerations, and psychobiological evidence. *Journal of Personality and Social Psychology*, **76**, 820–38.

Weiner, B. (1985). An attributional theory of achievement motivation and emotion. *Psychological Review*, **92**, 548–73.

Winteler, A., Schiefele, U., Krapp, A., and **Wild, K.-P.** (1991). *Skalen zu Studienintresse und Lernstrategien im Studium* (*Scales on study interest and learning strategies*) (Technical report). Neubiberg/Munich, Germany: University of the German Army.

Zeidner, M. (1998). *Test anxiety: The state of the art*. New York: Plenum.

CHAPTER 9

ADOLESCENT WELL-BEING: BUILDING YOUNG PEOPLE'S RESOURCES

ERICA FRYDENBERG AND RAMON LEWIS

This chapter considers the ways in which a theory of coping can be used as a platform from which to explore adolescent health and well-being. It outlines current conceptualizations and models of coping and puts forward an integrated model which takes into account many of the research paradigms that relate to coping. In doing so it moves attention from the conceptualization and study of coping *per se* as a response to stress, to emphasize instead the role that coping may play in enhancing the quality of life of young people.

Early research in the field of coping in the adolescent area has generally focused on coping without taking into account outcomes. Later research has more frequently addressed outcomes, but the interest has generally been on dysfunction. As the shift in psychology is moving to an emphasis on health and well-being there is an interest in resilience rather than dysfunction. Thus, more recent outcome studies consider well-being. Nevertheless, many of the definitions provided interpret well-being as the absence of dysfunction. This chapter reports later studies, including one just completed by the authors, which focus on the relationship between adolescents' coping strategies and various aspects of their general and academic well-being. It considers adolescent resources as important underpinnings for well-being, as well as the more direct relationship between well-being and coping. Finally coping skills programmes are considered. Programme outcomes generally indicate that it is possible to enhance coping skills in order to contribute to well-being.

To date much of the coping research in the child and adolescent area has been predicated on the theorizing of Folkman and Lazarus which emphasizes the context in which the coping actions occur, the attempt rather than the outcome, and the fact that coping is a process that changes over time, as the person and the environment are continuously in a dynamic mutually influential relationship (Lazarus and Folkman 1984; Folkman and Lazarus 1988). This is generally known as the transactional model of coping.

Folkman (1997) proposed modifications to the original theoretical model of stress and coping proposed by Lazarus and Folkman (1984), so as to accommodate positive psychological states. Transactions with the environment are appraised as threatening, harmful or challenging and, according to the model, stress is regulated by emotion-focused strategies, designed to reduce the distress, or manage the problem. These may lead to a favourable resolution, non-resolution, or an unfavourable resolution. According to this model, emotion is generated at three phases, at the appraisal phase, coping phase and at the outcome phase. There are three pathways. The first is directed by positive psychological states that give meaning to the situation and lead to 'revising goals and planning goal-directed problem-focused coping' (Folkman 1997, p. 1216). The second pathway is the response to the distress rather than the condition which created it. This accounts for the co-occurrence of both negative and positive states where the negative states, while they may be a result of enduring distress, may lead to the individual striving to find (consciously or unconsciously) positive meaning in the event, leading to the use of resources such as hope, social support, and self-esteem. The third pathway derives from the positive psychological states that result from the coping processes *per se* and can help the person remotivate, re-energize and re-engage in goal-directed activities. This formulation of stress and emotion is yet to be tested on young people but it would appear that, at least for adolescents, the search for meaning and the subsequent impact on mood state is likely to hold true. Muldoon (1997), following the analysis of interview responses of 9–10 year olds, found that primary appraisal, that is, assessing whether a situation is one of harm or loss, is an important determinant of children's coping, a factor that has been readily accepted, but rarely demonstrated in the literature relating to stress in childhood and adolescence.

Boekaerts (1996) in her model of coping delineates eight components of the coping process. The model depicts the relationship between the stress, the coping repertoire, coping goals, appraisals, and emotions as they impact upon coping intentions. Each contributes to the strategies which are utilized and subsequently incorporated into the coping repertoire through an evaluative process. Seiffge-Krenke (1995), describes her developmental model for adolescent coping as 'preliminary' in that it is based on a set of complex and interrelated variables which 'qualify' the stress–outcome association. In that model there is an emphasis on the stresses, internal resources, and external relationship resources that determine coping, which in turn determines outcome where symptomatology either continues or there is adaptation.

Building on her earlier work, Boekaerts (1999) offers a theory of coping which is particularly relevant to the learning context and which emphasizes the intentionality relating to goals, motivation, and task completion. Intentionality is a key feature of her conceptualization with an accompanying emphasis on goal frustration and goal ambivalence. Individual differences and temperament play their part. For some children a brief interruption to an action plan may be sufficient to produce destabilizing effects whereas it takes major obstacles to frustrate others. In any learning context students pursue multiple personal and social goals. Boekaerts' formulation illustrates an effective way of bringing coping theory and teaching and learning together. Furthermore, it emphasizes metacognitive knowledge and how one perceives oneself as a learner. Thus, goal theory has particular relevance for classroom situations. It is consistent with other theoretical frameworks of coping such as appraisal, and is particularly relevant in educational contexts.

Another recent conceptualization is Hobfoll's Conservation of Resources (COR) theory which is underscored by the wish to protect resources. The resource approach puts the emphasis on the fact that there is a 'commerce of resources' which accounts for the fact that some people manage to stay 'healthy' or adapt despite the circumstances they encounter. Early proponents of this theory were Antonovsky (1979) and Dohrenwend and Dohrenwend (1981).

Resource theories

A useful way of conceptualizing resource theories is to consider that there is a set of core resources that 'manage' or direct the resource pool. According to this framework, 'a key resource is depicted as being the prime vehicle controlling, promoting, or organizing the commerce of other resources' (Hobfoll 1988, p. 12). This model accommodates some major theorists whose work to date has not generally been associated with coping researchers. One such theory is Albert Bandura's (1982) concept of self-efficacy and the associated cognitions that are linked with people's inherent belief in their own capacity to cope. This belief in oneself underscores the capacity to 'centrally' organize and utilize the resources inherent within an individual and to draw upon resources from the environment. According to Bandura there is a 'construct' or fact of self-efficacy, which is akin to belief in one's capacities, rather than the mere perception that one has the resources.

Other key resource models have been offered by Antonovsky (1979), Kobasa (1979), Scheier and Carver (1987, 1993), and Seligman (1992, 1995). The tripartite resource model presented by Antonovsky (1979) has been seen both as a multiple resource model and a single resource model according to which the individual strives to achieve coherence. Essentially the sense of coherence (SOC) model emphasizes a personal feeling of confidence that can be broken down into three dimensions: comprehensibility, manageability, and meaningfulness. Comprehensibility assumes that life is structured and consequential: Manageability assumes that the person has the resources to meet the current demands, and meaningfulness is about the assessment of that challenge as being worthy of investment.

Scheier and Carver (1987, 1993) and Seligman (1992, 1995) see optimism as the major resource in dealing with stress. It impacts on how an individual perceives events, is motivated to deal with such events, the setting of goals and the initiating of actions. As Seligman moved from a conceptualization that emphasized 'learned helplessness' to that of 'learned optimism' he developed programmes to teach young people how to become optimistic as a form of 'stress inoculation' (Jaycox et al. 1994). Programmes such as those proposed by Seligman and his colleagues, and those discussed later in this chapter provide a means whereby young people can augment their coping resources.

In a somewhat different vein, Carol Dweck's emphasis on advancing student motivation in the classroom can also be regarded as a 'key resource' model. Dweck's work has focused most particularly on young people and how their perceptions of themselves are advanced or diminished through their interactions with adults (Dweck and Sorich 1999). For example, in a classroom context whether intelligence or one's own ability is seen as fixed or malleable may be determined by how a teacher responds to a students' failure to complete learning activities. This response then determines whether tasks are tackled again and has a subsequent impact on motivation. (see Chapters 7 and 11 in this volume). In the adult arena, Kobasa (1979) has put forward the theory of 'hardiness', a construct which is made up of control, commitment, and a sense of challenge (in contrast to one of threat), as a way of explaining motivation and task persistence.

Generally these theories of coping consider the match between resources and demands that are made on the individual. Where there is a mismatch between the demands and the resources there is likely to be stress (Van-Harrison *et al.* 1982). There are implications that resources are potentially malleable and individuals 'fit' their resources to meet the demands placed on them (Hobfoll and Lilly 1993). This would imply that ability to be flexible and accommodate resources to demands is a helpful commodity for coping and for moving beyond coping.

Aspinwall and Taylor (1997) distinguish between three types of coping, proactive, anticipatory (preparation for stressful consequences), and general coping. Current conceptualizations include proactive coping (see Chapters 2 and 3 in this volume). In the proactive stage informational and appraisal support are more important than social support. Nevertheless, social support has been described as the 'the building block for successfully mastering environmental demands' (Freedy and Hobfoll 1994, p. 320).

Holahan and Moos (1986, 1987) have offered models where there is an emphasis on the interaction between multiple resources. However, the multiple resource model of stress is arguably best illustrated by Hobfoll's (1988, 1989) COR theory. Hobfoll's COR theory rests on the assumption that stress occurs when resources are threatened, where there is a loss of resources or where there is an investment, and gains fail to materialize. The theory goes on to posit that where there is a loss of resources the resource pool is diminished for subsequent encounters. For example, if social support is a frequently utilized resource and a particular friendship is lost there is depletion in the individual's resource pool. The encounters may result in a loss spiral in that loss of friendship may lead to depression which in turn may account for poor school performance and subsequent failure to get into a training programme. In circumstances where there is a gain in resources, this can lead to a gain spiral, in that success in one sphere often leads to benefits in another area. For example, if a student is a good athlete he or she may become a popular figure amongst his or her peers. According to COR theory there are several principles at work. The first is that loss is the primary axis of stress. The second is that resources act to protect and preserve other resources and finally that there are loss and gain spirals (Hobfoll *et al.* 1996). Endler and Zeidner (1996) and Holahan and Moos (1986, 1987) point out that resources such as personality work in tandem with other resources such as social support. Hobfoll *et al.* (1998) refer to a 'caravan of resources which work in concert' in the service of the individual. Thus, when it comes to intervention it is both the contents of the caravan and the way the resources work together that need to be addressed.

The relationship between stress and the perceived threat to resources is in some measure accounted for in Folkman and Lazarus' concept of appraisal where a situation can be perceived to be one of challenge rather than of threat, harm, or loss. Where the above theories seem to differ is in the emphasis on the maintenance of the resources rather than the perceived challenge of a situation. There is some support from early longitudinal studies using a psychoanalytic framework (e.g. Haan 1974, 1977) in which students were categorized as 'copers' and 'defenders'. The latter group could be construed as 'conserving of resources'. Despite the fact that resources may or may not be the same from childhood through to adulthood there are, nevertheless, important resources for young people such as, attention, affection, self-worth, security in home, school, or friendship. It is a model that can be readily tested in the child and adolescent context.

Another aspect of Hobfoll's approach is that it emphasizes the notion that individuals attempt to conserve their resources (COR theory), that is, to maintain that which they value, and guard against loss when resources are threatened. Resources in this sense can be material, social, or esteem related. This model is currently being explored with populations of young people (Vanderzeil 2000; McKenzie 2001) and appears to have validity and utility for adolescents. The resources that Hobfoll identified as being valued by adults, such as objects (e.g. car, house), conditions (e.g. good marriage, good school), personal characteristics (e.g. self-esteem, mastery) and energy resources (e.g. money, credit) are not entirely the same resources that adolescents value such as peers and friendship, family, school, health, money, and possessions (Vanderzeil 2000).

According to Hobfoll *et al.* (1996) when it comes to losing or gaining resources the impact of loss is greater than the benefit of gain. This has implications for motivation. For example, where there is negative feedback about performance, the detrimental effect may in sum be greater than the approval or praise provided for some other accomplishment. Furthermore, childhood and adolescence are periods of major development and it is in the context of that development that potential expansion of the resource pool and the diminution of existing resources needs to be monitored.

The notion that individuals wish to hold on to that which they have seems to hold true for young people as much as for adults in that friendships, possessions, and pride are valued, particularly when they are under threat. A further promise of this model is its relevance for educators in that it includes a notion of values, and those principles and actions which might be included in the teaching of coping skills.

Models of coping, such as the multiaxial model of Hobfoll (1996) which is underscored by COR theory, hold promise for work with young people. Hobfoll's model differs from that of Folkman and Lazarus in that there are six axes which account for the prosocial and antisocial, the active and passive components of coping actions, and the direct and indirect dimensions of the response. This model attempts to shift the emphasis from an individualistic to a collectivist perspective. The importance of prosocial coping has relevance in relationship *to* adolescent happiness.

Frydenberg (1997) proposes a model that is consistent with that of Boekaerts (1996) and Seiffge-Krenke (1995), but which attempts to integrate the ever-increasing concomitants that are emerging in relation to coping. For example, within the model the person variable accounts for motivational factors. The fact that some children are more motivated than others is determined by situational factors, personality factors, and individual determinants based on family, school, and peer experiences. Similarly, it is possible to accommodate self-efficacy as a multidimensional phenomenon, for example, as general self-efficacy and self-efficacy in relationship to school based tasks (Zimmermann 1995; Bandura 1982, 1991). Similarly the conservation of resources theory can be partially accommodated in the coping intentions of the individual. Emotions cast a wide shadow in that they both affect the appraisal and the subsequent choice of response and also affect the outcome. This complex relationship is yet to be fully articulated, although there continue to be serious attempts to do so (see Lazarus 1991, Frydenberg Chapter 1 and Pekrun *et al.* Chapter 8 in this volume).

The model (Fig. 9.1) posits that coping is a function of the situational determinants and the individual's characteristics, perception of the situation, and coping intentions. The individual brings a host of biological, dispositional, personal, and family characteristics to the encounter. It is how these impact upon the perception of the situation and the response

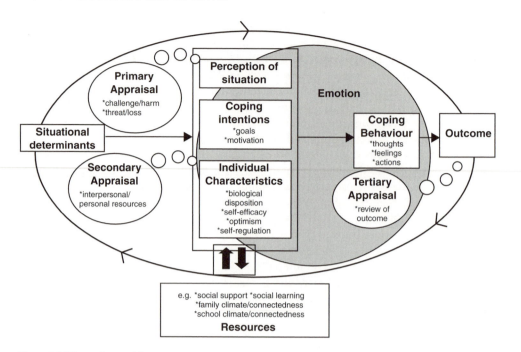

Figure 9.1 The coping model.

to the stress or concern that is of interest. Following an appraisal of the situation, the individual assesses the likely impact of the stress, that is, whether the consequences are likely to lead to loss, harm, threat, or challenge, and what resources (personal or interpersonal) are available to the individual to deal with it. The intent of the action, along with the action, determines the outcome. Following a response, the outcome is reviewed or re-appraised (tertiary appraisal or re-appraisal), and another response may follow. There may be a subsequent development in an individual's coping repertoire. There is a circular mechanism, or feedback loop, which determines whether the strategies are likely to be tried again or rejected from future use according to the effectiveness of the outcome after the deployment of a strategy, as judged by an individual. Coping intentions and beliefs about the self can both be accommodated within this model. Nevertheless, it has been pointed out that appraisal, as the central tenet of Lazarus and Folkman's theory, has been criticized because of the circularity or confounded nature of the construct (Hobfoll *et al.* 1998; Muldoon 1997). For example, if a circumstance is appraised as threatening, the appraisal *per se* may determine the coping response. To date the many instruments, both adolescent and adult, which have been developed to assess coping, have not succeeded in separating the appraisal of an event and the way in which an individual deals with it. What is not in dispute is that the ever expanding or diminishing body of resources is a key determinant of the coping process.

Resilience

Since the prevalence of depression amongst young people has became of major concern in some communities, the search for factors that are protective and which determine that one person is resilient to stress while another is not, has preoccupied researchers for some time. A transactional model of stress where the individual and the environment are in a reciprocal interaction posits that depression, for example, in children, results from the interplay between a number of factors which may be enduring such as strong family supports (protective factor) and transient circumstances such as changing schools (vulnerability factor). These may act as a buffer or may provide a challenge (see Harrington 1993). The co-occurrence of the predisposing characteristics of an individual along with circumstances that are externally determined may lead to depression. Vulnerability factors increase the risk of a disorder occurring. It has generally been accepted that there are several resiliency factors associated with positive personality disposition, supportive family milieu, and external societal agencies that function as a support system (Garmezy 1985).

The three major contexts which influence development, namely, family, school, and community exert their impact at times individually and on other occasions in concert. As Resnick *et al.* (1997) demonstrated in their study of 12,118 adolescents from 80 high schools in the United States of America, family connectedness and school connectedness were protective factors against health risk behaviours such as violence, suicidal thoughts, substance abuse (cigarettes, alcohol, marijuana), and early pregnancy. Furthermore, the combination of coping responses that are maximally associated with well-being involve the use of positive reappraisal and problem-solving and resigned acceptance. Adolescents who used less problem-solving, less positive reappraisal, more logical analysis, more cognitive avoidance, and more resigned acceptance, were more depressed and anxious. Thus, family and school connectedness can be construed as resources that come to the service of the individual.

The promotion of resilience does not lie in the avoidance of stress but the encountering of stress allows self-confidence to build up and competence to increase through a sense of mastery (Rutter 1985; Seligman 1995). The qualities are not constitutional or unmodifiable. Young people can be helped to develop adaptive qualities.

There is a suggestion that a lack of achievement (educational or physical) may lead to anxiety and/or depression (see Goodyer 1990). Goodyer points out that one implication of these findings is that it is not only environmental or constitutional factors but current outcomes may play a part in depression. Additionally, a transactional model of stress can be used to explain how age and developmental level determine what is perceived as a buffer or a challenge. For example, the buffering effect of a close same-sex or opposite-sex relationship may operate at a particular age and stage during adolescence, and may be dependent on maturational and other factors.

Efficacious outcomes

In addition to issues relating to resilience, and the minimization of dysfunction, there is the question of what makes young people function well. Adolescent happiness is one such index of well-being. It has been linked to young people's involvement with prosocial activities. For example there is emerging evidence that teaching prosocial behaviours has far reaching benefits (Roker *et al.* 1999).

Adolescent happiness

Magen (1998) set out to answer the questions, what makes adolescents happy, what makes them feel good about themselves and the world, and what invests their experience with meaning? She was intrigued by the young people who were engaged in activities benefiting social causes and/or individuals in need, and tried to ascertain what typified them, and whether they would experience life events as more inspiring and joyous.

The positive experience questionnaire (PEQ) was one of the research instruments used by Magen (1998) and her fellow researchers. It is an open-ended questionnaire designed to elicit adolescent's most joyful remembered experiences. It was used to evaluate depth or intensity of the life experience, on a four-point scale of intensity, ranging from shallow to peak intensity. The content area of the experience was assessed in relation to three major content categories: self-experiences, characterized by self-confidence and self-knowledge; external world experiences, characterized by love of the environment and the physical world, objects, and belongings; and interpersonal experiences, characterized by liking and compassion for others, and being prepared to take action on their behalf.

The life aspirations questionnaire (LAQ) (Magen 1998) her second research instrument, is a single open-ended question used to determine whether adolescents in fact had the desire to give of themselves. The responses were scored on the basis of the expression of commitment to others also on a four-point scale, from hedonistic and self-involved to fully expressing a desire for transpersonal or socially oriented commitment. Adolescents who had experienced a full year of helping those less fortunate than themselves demonstrated a higher level of verbally expressed transpersonal commitment and a stronger capacity to fully and intensely experience happy moments in life, as well as a greater sense of happiness.

In an earlier study examining adolescents' involvement in prosocial activities and its relationship to happiness, Magen and Aharoni (1991) found that young people who were involved in giving to others described joyous moments of a peak instensity, whereas none of the involved adolescents reported an experience that was just barely positive in nature. Magen's research demonstrates that even adolescents who have little or no access to positive and life affirming experiences can be helped to achieve self-actualizing, transpersonal commitment, and even happiness.

Well-being

Along with considerations about adolescent resilience and consideration of adolescent happiness it is helpful to determine other efficacious coping outcomes. Although some studies examine the relationship between coping and emotional or physical well-being, most studies which consider coping as a predictor of some outcome focus on negative outcomes such as depression, sickness, or some other forms of dysfunction. Additionally, well-being is generally seen as the absence of negative indicators of coping. For example, the adolescent component of a national survey of mental health and well-being, the largest study of child and adolescent mental health conducted in Australia, and one of the few national studies conducted in the world, appears to characterize well-being as the absence of 'mental disorders' (Sawyer et al. 2000).

Where the emphasis is not on the absence of a disorder, the interest is often on the avoidance of negative outcomes. For example, there is a demonstrated relationship between negative affectivity (anxiety, depression, and hostility) and adverse health outcomes such as alcoholism, depression, and suicidal behaviour (Dise-Lewis 1988; Patterson and McCubbin 1987).

While in the adult arena it is generally the individual who assesses the effectiveness of his or her coping, with children and young people objective outcome assessment can more readily be made through observer reports, gradings etc. There is a distinction that has been made in the child and adolescent arena between a coping response that is intentional and goal directed, and a stress response which represents a spontaneous emotional or behavioural reaction. This is because the former emphasizes the outcome of the response in relationship to adjustment. Consequently the transactional models have been replaced with those that emphasize the moderators (characteristics of child and the environment such as gender and development) and mediators (mechanisms linking stress and coping and adjustment such as appraisal and attentional deployment) and the relationship to outcome. For example such a model has been applied to studies which focus on young people who are dealing with illness and pain (Rudolph *et al.* 1995).

Ebata and Moos (1991) in their study of well-being compared 190 12–18 year-olds with behavioural, psychological, and physical problems with a control group of healthy adolescents. They used a 48-item instrument which they developed according to the broad-band dimensions that reflected active or approach (towards the threat) coping and passive or active avoidant (away from the threat) coping. Well-being was measured as an index of perceived happiness and self-worth. Greater use of approach coping (positive reappraisal, guidance/support, problem-solving, and alternate rewards) and less use of resigned acceptance was related to higher levels of well-being. Avoidance responses were generally associated with more distress. In general, they showed that adolescents who are able to engage in active problem-solving behaviour while being able to 'look at the bright side' and not get caught up in rumination and resignation are likely to be better adjusted.

Three studies which investigated facets of well-being using the adolescent coping scale (ACS) (Frydenberg and Lewis 1993a) are reported below. The scale consists of 79 questions which elicit ratings of individual's use of 18 coping strategies, plus provides a final open-ended question. Scores on the scales are standardized so that the respondent's self-reported preferred coping styles can be readily identified. The items on the ACS comprise 18 different scales, each containing between three and five items and each reflecting a different coping response. Each item, with the exception of the last one, describes a specific coping response, be it a behaviour or a mindset (e.g. 'Talk to others to see what they would do if they had the problem'). The last item, Item 80, asks students to write down anything they do to cope, other than those things described in the preceding 79 items.

In examining empirical relationships between the measures of coping provided by the ACS and theoretically related characteristics associated with adolescent well-being, the view adopted is a positivist one which examines correlations and other statistical indicators of association between a number of indicators of general well-being (such as self-concept, self-efficacy, and achievement) and coping scale scores.

One study examined the relationship between coping and self-efficacy. Jenkin (1997) surveyed 135 year-8 students (81 male and 54 female) who were participants in a school initiated Outward Bound (rugged, outdoor camping) programme. The instruments used were the specific long form of the ACS, a self-efficacy scale (Shever *et al.* 1982), and a physical self-efficacy measure (Ryckman *et al.* 1982). A discriminant function analysis found that the best predictors for distinguishing between high and low self-efficacy were the coping strategies, focus on the positive, focus on solving the problem, and work hard to achieve. A combination of these strategies accurately predicted low or high self-efficacy (top and bottom quartiles) for 70 per cent of the sample. Whereas 77 per cent of those in the bottom quartile of efficacy could be correctly identified by their lesser usage of these strategies, prediction of those in the high efficacy group appeared less successful (65 per cent). Therefore, although a relative absence of these productive strategies is predictive of low self-efficacy, students scoring higher on self-efficacy are not necessarily those who employ more of these strategies.

Academic well-being

Two studies which looked at the relationship between achievement and coping using the ACS were those of Parsons *et al.* (1996) and Noto (1995). In the former, 'capable' boys were compared with the regular student body of males using 374 boys in Grades 9, 10, and 11 at an independent boys' school in Melbourne. Capable students were less likely, than those less capable, to declare that they did not have the strategies to cope. It was also found that boys who achieved better than would be expected on the basis of ability alone ('over-achieved'), utilized more social support as a strategy for coping than did their peers.

In Noto's study (1995), a sample of 90 female adolescent students (years 9, 10, and 11) completed the ACS and the data were compared with that from the 374 boys included in the Parsons *et al.* (1996) study. IQ was measured by using the ACER Higher Test (ML/MQ), a pencil and paper group test of intelligence. A combined L and Q score was recorded for each person. Academic achievement scores were based on an average of all final end of year results from the previous year. While measuring the relationship between coping and achievement, Noto controlled for gender and IQ by using partial correlations. When the remaining relationship between coping and academic achievement was investigated, significant positive correlations were found for the problem-focused strategies, work hard and achieve, focus on solving the problem, seek social support, and focus on the positive. Significant negative correlations were reported for three non-productive strategies. These were, not cope, tension reduction, and ignoring the problem. It was also found that high usage of the strategy, invest in close friends, was negatively associated with achievement.

In reflecting on the discussion above which addressed the ways in which various authors have defined coping strategies, coping resources, and coping outcomes, it is important to note that the overlap in conceptualizations of certain aspects of adolescent experience has resulted in some measurement anomalies. For example according to the Folkman and Lazarus conceptualization, if students 'ring up a close friend' this behaviour is an indicator of a coping strategy identified as social support. Such a strategy is assumed to be a characteristic response to issues of concern. Hobfoll's model indicates that having friends is a component of an adolescent's personal resources, which are protected and then utilized in times of need. It is interesting to note that being with and sharing with friends has also been conceptualized as an outcome of coping. For example Ebata and Moos (1991) define 'having friends' as an aspect of efficacy and Reynolds (2001) uses the frequency with which an adolescent is having fun with friends as an aspect of well-being.

Clearly there is some overlap between the concepts underlying coping strategies, resources, and outcomes. For example, imagine an adolescent who is unable or unwilling to share his or her concerns, or even to communicate effectively. As a consequence of this characteristic response pattern, (this coping strategy), such an adolescent would have few friends, and could be described in Hobfoll's terms as having limited personal resources upon which to draw. One could argue in such a case that a coping pattern has affected resources. Alternatively, it could be argued that a child who has been raised in circumstances which provided limited access to other children, that is, a child who has limited resources, would be unlikely to customarily adopt social support as a preferred coping response. In such a situation, resources determine the coping strategy to be used.

As indicated earlier in this chapter, of all the outcomes that have been associated with coping and resources, most appear to be related to dysfunction. Most studies of coping therefore have sought to examine a direct link with indicators of dysfunction such as depression (Ebata and Moos 1994), low self-esteem (Brodzinsky *et al.* 1992), poor academic performance (Band and Weise 1988), suicidal ideation (Asarnow *et al.* 1987; Spirito *et al.* 1996), and substance abuse (Wills 1986). Others have stated that they are focusing on adolescent well-being but provide as their indicator an absence of dysfunction, for example, as mentioned earlier, a lack of mental disorder (Sawyer *et al.* 2000) or less inability to cope (Lewis and Frydenberg in press). Such studies appear to be predicated on the assumption that less dysfunction is equivalent to greater well-being.

Some studies have investigated the relationship between coping and indicators of well-being and, as indicated above, have reported the impact of coping on positive outcomes such as Achievement (Parsons *et al.* 1996; Skinner and Wellborn 1997). Very few have reported the relationship between coping and indicators of both dysfunction and well-being (see for example Ebata and Moos 1991). In the study that follows, coping strategies associated with dysfunction and those associated with well-being will be examined, as will the assumption that well-being and dysfunction are polar opposites of the one continuum.

To examine the relationship between general coping responses and states of well-being two questionnaires were administered to a sample of 1264 12–16-year-old secondary school students in Metropolitan Melbourne, Australia. Of these, 37 per cent were in year 7, 30 per cent in year 8, and 33 per cent in year 9. In general, half the sample were girls as the proportion of girls in years 7, 8, and 9 was 40, 45, and 56 per cent respectively. The first questionnaire administered was a slightly modified version of the short form of the ACS (Frydenberg and Lewis 1993*a*). The other was a 'state-of-being' scale (Reynolds 2001) which comprises 12 items. With regard to the ACS, the not cope item was omitted due to the overlap with the concept of dysfunction and the belong item (improve my relations with others) was also omitted due to perceived overlap with the friends item (spend good time with a friend). Three new strategies which have been derived from the responses to the open question, 'What else do you do to cope?', on the ACS in previous studies (Frydenberg and Lewis 1993*b*, 1994, 1996, 1999, 2000) were included. These assess acting out (act up), the use of humour (humour) and accepting that it was not possible to do more than had been done (accept). The state-of-being scale contained a mixture of two kinds of items. Approximately half appear to assess the likelihood of well-being (e.g. I felt good about myself, I felt that everything was OK in my life) and the other half indicated dysfunction (e.g. I felt depressed or sad, I had trouble concentrating). Students indicated how frequently, in the last six months, the item described them. The response alternatives were never, hardly ever, some of the time, most of the time, and nearly all of the time. For both the coping and the state-of-being items responses were coded 1–5 respectively. In total there were 23 items, each describing a coping behaviour. Students indicated whether, in response to their general concerns, they used the strategy hardly ever or never, or a few times, sometimes, often or nearly always.

To examine the structure of this state-of-being scale a factor analysis was performed. Because any potential factors would be likely to be related, an oblique rotation was performed (oblimin). Table 9.1 reports the factor pattern matrix. The solution provided two factors with eigenvalues greater than 1 that explain a total of 49 per cent of variance. All but two items load significantly (>0.3) on only one factor. The seven items loading positively on factor 1 refer to recent experiences which may be termed dysfunctional, and include reference to loneliness, tension, nervousness, depression and sadness, difficulty falling asleep, feeling like crying, and difficulty in concentrating. In contrast, the five items loading positively on factor 2 refer to well-being, for example enjoying the company of friends and family, being comfortable in the company of new people, and feeling good about oneself and life in general. It is interesting to note that the factor intercorrelation is a moderate 0.35 which supports the 2-factor structure and indicates that dysfunction and well-being are not polar opposites of the one continuum.

To test the reliability of the scales containing these two sets of items, Cronbach alpha coefficients of internal consistency were computed. For the seven well-being items the alpha was an acceptable 0.70 and it was 0.82 for the five dysfunctional items. Before considering the connection between these scale scores and the students' responses to the modified ACS, it was necessary to resolve a problem. As noted above, the well-being scale contained some items which noted how frequently in the last six months students 'enjoyed getting together with friends and family', 'had fun with friends' and 'felt comfortable meeting new people'. However some of the coping strategy measures referred to the frequency

Table 9.1 Facture structure of the well-being items

Item	Factor 1	Factor 2
I felt depressed or sad	0.803	−0.008
I felt like crying for no reason	0.748	0.003
I felt very tense	0.712	−0.067
I was very lonely	0.691	−0.089
I had trouble concentrating	0.657	0.089
I had trouble falling asleep	0.629	0.066
I felt nervous	0.582	0.033
I felt that everything was OK in my life	−0.475	0.368
I had fun with friends	0.032	0.759
I enjoyed getting together with my friends and family	0.046	0.750
I felt comfortable meeting new people	0.032	0.639
I felt good about myself	−0.340	0.496
Eigenvalue	4.43	1.42
Percentage of variance	37%	12%

with which students looked 'for support and encouragement from others' (social support strategy) and spent 'more time with a good friend' (friends). Such similarity in behaviour was consistent with the previous discussion about overlap between coping strategies and coping outcomes. It was recognized in this study that overlap of this kind may lead to tenuous conclusions when associations were sought between well-being and some coping strategies. Consequently, a scale was constructed from the two, more general, well-being items 'I felt that everything was OK in my life' and 'I felt good about myself'. This two-item scale had an alpha coefficient of 0.70 and was labelled general well-being.

To examine the relationship between coping and well-being and dysfunction Pearson correlations were computed between the 23 coping strategies and the measures of dysfunction, well-being, and general well-being. As mentioned earlier, correlations were utilized rather than regression analysis on the understanding that just as coping strategies may affect well-being, the opposite is also arguable. Table 9.2 reports these correlations. Because coping strategies co-exist in the repertoire of young people (Lewis and Frydenberg in press) a second computation was undertaken of partial correlations between each of the coping strategies and the three other measures while all other coping strategies were partialled out or controlled. The results of these analyses are also reported in Table 9.2. For this analysis scaling was converted to ensure a positive correlation reflected a positive relationship.

As has been noted elsewhere a number of coping responses reported in Table 9.2 are associated with dysfunction. These are generally avoidant or non-productive strategies

Table 9.2 Associations between coping scales and dysfunction and well-being

Scale	Raw correlations			Partial correlations		
	Well-being	General	Dysfunction	Well-being	General	Dysfunction
Soc. sup.	0.12	0.06	−0.01	0.06	0.01	−0.03
Work hard	0.18	0.17	−0.06	0.10	0.12	−0.05
Worry	−0.11	−0.17	0.30	−0.03	−0.05	0.14
Tens. red.	−0.13	−0.20	0.31	−0.05	−0.08	0.15
Wish think	−0.09	−0.17	0.21	−0.03	−0.07	0.02
Soc. act.	−0.00	−0.03	0.10	−0.07	−0.08	0.06
Self-blame	−0.31	−0.35	0.42	−0.22	−0.25	0.22
Keep self	−0.16	−0.15	0.24	−0.10	−0.07	0.13
Spirit	−0.04	−0.04	0.13	−0.02	−0.03	0.05
Fos. pos.	0.24	0.21	−0.14	0.11	0.10	−0.10
Prof. help	0.07	0.09	0.02	0.02	0.04	0.02
Phys rec.	0.20	0.18	−0.11	0.09	0.09	−0.04
Act up	−0.18	−0.17	0.20	−0.08	−0.05	0.09
Humour	0.11	0.10	−0.03	0.12	0.14	−0.04
Accept	0.20	0.21	−0.09	0.09	0.13	−0.07
Ignore	−0.16	−0.17	0.26	−0.06	−0.04	0.15
Friends	0.15	0.02	0.02	0.11	−0.02	−0.03
Solve. prob.	0.18	0.15	−0.05	0.02	0.02	0.07
Relax	0.18	0.14	−0.10	0.09	0.10	−0.09

$r = 0.1 \rightarrow p = 0.001$.

such as worry, tension reduction, self-blame, wishful thinking, keep to self, act up, and ignore. In contrast strategies such as focus on the positive, physical recreation, and acceptance are associated with well-being. As can be seen from the raw correlations in Table 9.2, only approximately half of the strategies share statistically significant ($p < 0.01$) variance with either dysfunction or well-being but not both. For example, although increased usage of problem solving is associated with greater well-being, less usage does not relate to increased dysfunction. Further, only two of the twelve items load substantially (>0.3) and positively on one factor and negatively on the other (refer to Table 9.1). Ten of the 12 items display a significant positive loading on one factor and an almost zero loading on the other. These results provide additional reason to question the bipolar characterization of dysfunction and well-being. When partial correlations in Table 9.2 are considered, only one strategy is capable of associating with both states of being. Young people who use more self-blame are in a significantly more dysfunctional state of being than those who use less, and those who use less are experiencing more well-being.

In summary, it can be argued that most of the relationships between coping strategies and state of being are statistically significant but very small in magnitude. The strongest relationships are those between coping strategies described as non-productive and a dysfunctional state of being. Nevertheless, due to the concurrent use of many of the strategies only the unique contribution of self-blame was worthy of note (with a partial correlation with well-being of -0.22 and a partial correlation of 0.22 with dysfunction. There is an implication that future preventive interventions should focus more on the reduction of maladaptive coping strategies, in particular the reduction of self blame, rather than the more common goal of increasing problem-focused coping.

Developing coping skills

As discussed earlier, appraisal is an important first step in the coping process. In recognition of the critical part that appraisal is seen to play, any programme that attempts to develop young people's coping skills through the development of positive cognitions also needs to teach skills of positive cognitive appraisal. Measurement also plays a major part in advancing our understanding of the coping process, in describing population trends, providing guidelines for educational programming, and facilitating clinical interventions. Since coping is largely a cognitive process, self-awareness can be raised through individuals examining their own coping profiles (such as the conceptual areas of coping identified by the ACS) and subsequently choosing to engage in self-directed behavioural change. That is, an individual may choose to change strategies that are not productive in particular encounters, and expand coping repertoires as a resource for the future.

Longitudinal studies indicate that in order to avert the development of non-productive strategies we need to consider both the sex of the person for whom the programme is being developed, as well as his or her age. For example, there appear to be indications that it is useful to intervene in the psychosocial development of adolescents of 14–16 years of age in order to attract their interest and commitment, and to capitalize on the particular developmental stage that they are traversing (Frydenberg and Lewis 2000). This is suggested because the greatest shift in coping occurs during these years. This would, therefore, appear to be the optimum time to engage adolescents in reflection on their coping behaviour and in discussion about the benefits of using particular strategies. Such an approach would appear to be particularly relevant for girls, who not only exhibit a greater shift in coping than do boys during the ages of 12–16, but whose expressed inability to cope increases significantly during that period.

There is a growing interest in the development of direct instruction programmes, that is, universal programmes provided to all young people in a school setting to prevent or alleviate depression by focusing on coping skills. Generally, researchers have focused on programmes aimed at children who are at risk rather than general prevention programmes for all children (Roberts 1999). There are resources for developing coping skills that rely on the clinician or instructor to compile a programme (e.g. Forman 1993). However, the benefit of coping skills programmes that are fully scripted to facilitate implementation is increasingly being recognized.

One example of a psycho-educational depression prevention programme with grade 7 students resulted in significant increases in coping skills, control over interpersonal and school relationships and problems (Rice *et al.* 1993). Similarly, the resourceful adolescent project (RAP) is aimed at preventing the development of depression disorders. The RAP uses a cognitive behavioural approach and aims to build resources and skills in adolescents and includes topics such as stress management, problem-solving, and cognitive restructuring (Shochet and Osgarby 1999). Another two Australian coping education programmes have also had positive impact on young people. The first, Bright Ideas, a cognitive-behavioural programme, effected positive changes in 11–12-year-old children's explanatory style (Brandon *et al.* 1999; Cunningham 2001; Cunningham *et al.* in press). The research highlights the fact that coping efficacy beliefs were stronger post programme and in particular students reported less use of self-blame. These changes were maintained at three-month follow-up. The pleasing outcome of teaching coping skills is the increased belief in young people's own capacities to cope.

The second programme, The Best of Coping (Frydenberg and Brandon 2002) was found to be most effective with adolescents at risk in the 16-year-old age group (Bugalski and Frydenberg 2000; Cotta *et al.* 2001). The Best of Coping was designed to help adolescents cope with daily stresses. Comprising ten sessions, the programme begins with a discussion of the meaning of coping and the different styles and strategies used to cope. Students are encouraged to think of strategies that are not helpful and to find alternative strategies. Other topics that are addressed include thinking optimistically, effective communication skills, steps to effective problem-solving, decision making, goal setting, and time management. The programme also includes a session for the practical building of those coping skills that have been learnt throughout previous sessions.

Evaluation of this programme notes participants' self-efficacy increases significantly when compared to non-participants (Bugalski and Frydenberg 2000; Cotta *et al.* 2001). This finding suggests that the programme is useful in developing a sense of psychological control for participants. A belief in one's sense of psychological control will direct whether or not one will attempt to cope with a situation (Bandura 1977). Once individuals have a sense of their own capabilities, it is more likely that they will approach their problems with the aim of solving them rather than avoiding them. In addition, self-efficacy has also been associated with a reduction in depressive symptoms and improvements in academic performance and health (Burger 1985). As a result, programme participants with higher levels of self-efficacy would be expected to utilize more productive coping strategies and use fewer avoidant strategies. These programmes highlight the value of teaching adolescents cognitive-based skills in coping and the use of their own interpersonal resources.

It is clear is that it is helpful to develop an integrated model of coping from which it is possible to examine, not only patterns of coping and resources but to take account of outcomes. This has implications as to what should be taught in a coping skills programme. Programmes which contribute to well-being need to be fostered. This can be done in the context of a direct curriculum where there is instruction to a 'universal' group or a particular targeted population, or it can be done in the context of an indirect curriculum where young people are engaged to consider their coping skills in the context of a range of school and leisure activities. In addition to what we know from other studies (e.g. Bugalski and Frydenberg 2000; Cotta *et al.* 2001; Frydenberg and Lewis 2000; Lewis and Frydenberg, in press) there are clear indications from the results reported in this chapter that whilst it is important to help young people to both increase their usage of productive coping strategies and decrease the use of non-productive coping strategies, it is important to emphasize the negative affects of dysfunctional strategies and highlight in particular the counterproductive impact of self-blame.

Furthermore, the factors that contribute to resilience over and above coping skills need to be acknowledged. For example, some exposure to stress, rather than the avoidance of it is likely to promote healthy development. The building of resources, in particular those that are valued by young people, is likely to be of benefit. Additionally, engagement in prosocial activities has potential benefits in promoting young people's happiness.

In summary, this chapter has provided the opportunity to examine issues of coping, in terms of its conceptualization and measurement. It has focused on how research in this field has progressed beyond simply documenting the coping behaviour of young people and has highlighted the progression from issues such as coping and resources to outcome studies focusing on the well-being of young people. In doing so a distinction has been drawn between definitions of well-being which focus on optimal levels of functioning and those which only emphasize lack of dysfunction. A study has been reported which empirically demonstrates the need for such a distinction. This study also has implications for programmes aimed at facilitating the well-being of our youth. The results support a recommendation that such programmes not only attempt to develop in adolescents a repertoire of problem solving and other positively regarded coping responses but also attend strongly to minimizing young people's use of non-productive strategies (in particular self-blame). However what is clear is that removing the bad, that is non-productive coping, does not necessarily promote the good (productive coping). Thus it is both the reduction of non-productive and the increase in productive coping that has to be addressed, with emphasis on the former.

References

Antonovsky, (1979). *Health, stress and coping.* San: Francisco: Jossey-Bass.

Asarnow, J. R., Carlson, G. A., and Guthrie, D. (1987). Coping strategies, self-perceptions, hopelessness, and perceived family environments in depressed and suicidal children. *Journal of Consulting and Clinical Psychology*, 55(3), 361–66.

Aspinwall, L. and Taylor, S. (1997). A stitch in time: Self-regulation and proactive coping. *Psychological Bulletin*, **121**(3), 417–36.

Band, E. B. and Weisz, J. R. (1998). How to feel better when it feels bad: Children's perspectives on coping with everyday stress. *Developmental Psychology*, **24**(2), 247–53.

Bandura, A. (1977). Self-efficacy: Toward a unifying theory of behavioural change. *Psychological Review*, **84**, 191–215.

—— (1982). Self-efficacy mechanism in human agency. *American Psychologist*, **37**(2), 122–47.

—— (1991). Self regulation of motivation through anticipatory and self-reactive mechanisms, in R. A. Dienstbier (ed.), *Nebraska symposium on motivation 1990: Perspectives on motivation*, Vol. 38, pp. 6–164. Lincoln NE US: University of Nebraska Press

Boekaerts, M. (1996). Coping with stress in childhood and adolescence, in M. Zeidner and N. S. Endler (eds.), *Handbook of coping*, pp. 452–84. New York: John Wiley & Sons.

—— (1999). Coping in context: Goal frustration and goal ambivalence in relation to academic and interpersonal goals, in E. Frydenberg (ed.), *Learning to Cope: Developing as a person in complex societies*. Oxford: Oxford University Press.

Brandon, C. M., Cunningham, E. G., and Frydenberg, E. (1999). Teaching optimistic thinking in pre-adolescence: Findings from a school-based program. *Australian Journal of Guidance & Counselling*, **9**(1), 149–59.

Brodzinsky, D. M., Elias, M. J., Steiger, C., Gill, S. J., and Hitt, J. C. (1992). Coping scale for children and youth: Scale development and validation. *Journal of Applied Developmental Psychology*, **13**, 195–214.

Bugalski, K. and Frydenberg, E. (2000). Promoting effective coping in adolescents 'at-risk' for depression. *Australian Journal of Guidance & Counselling*, **10**, 111–32.

Burger, J. M. (1985). Desire for control and achievement-related behaviours. *Journal of Personality and Social Psychology*, **48**(6), 1520–33.

Cotta, A., Frydenberg E., and Poole, C. (2001). Coping skills training for adolescents at school. *The Australian Educational and Developmental Psychologist*, **17**(2), 103–16.

Cunningham, E. (2001). *Developing coping resources in early adolescence: Mediational and latent curve analyses of program effects*. Doctoral Thesis, University of Melbourne, Melbourne.

—— Brandon, C. M., and Frydenberg, E. Developing the coping resources of preadolescents. *Stress, Anxiety, and Coping* Special Issue (in press).

Dise-Lewis, J. E. (1988). The Life Events and Coping Inventory: An assessment of stress in children. *Psychosomatic Medicine*, **50**, 484–99.

Dohrenwend, B. S. and Dohrenwend, B. P. (1981). Socio-environmental factors, stress, and psychopathology. *American Journal of Community Psychology*, **9**, 128–59.

Dweck, C. S. and Sorich, L. (1999). Mastery-oriented thinking, in C. R. Snyder (ed.), *Coping: The psychology of what works*, pp. 205–27. New York: Oxford University Press.

Ebata, A. and Moos, T. (1991). Coping and adjustment in distressed and healthy adolescents. *Journal of Applied Developmental Psychology*, **12**, 33–54.

Ebata, A. T. and Moos, R. H. (1994). Personal, situational, and contextual correlates of coping in adolescence. *Journal of Research on Adolescence*, **4**(1), 99–125.

Endler, S. N. and Zeidner, M. (eds.) (1996). *Handbook of coping*. New York: Wiley.

Folkman, S. (1984). Personal control and the stress and coping processes: A theoretical analysis. *Journal of Personality and Social Psychology*, **46**, 839–52.

Folkman, S. (1997). Positive psychological states and coping with severe stress. *Social Psychology Medicine*, **45**(8), 1207–221.

—— and **Lazarus, R. S.** (1998). Coping as a mediator of emotion. *Journal of Personality and Social Psychology*, **54**(3), 466–75.

Forman, S. G. (1993). *Coping skills interventions for children and adolescents*. San Francisco: Jossey-Bass.

Freedy, J. R. and **Hobfoll, S. E.** (1994). Stress inoculation for reduction of burnout: A conservation of resources approach. *Anxiety, Stress and Coping*, **6**, 311–25.

Frydenberg, E. (1997). *Adolescent coping: Research and theoretical perspectives*. London: Routledge.

—— and **Brandon, C.** (2002). *The best of coping*. Melbourne: Oz Child.

—— —— (1993*a*). *Manual: The adolescent coping scale*. Melbourne: Australian Council for Educational Research.

—— —— (1993*b*). Boys play sport and girls turn to others: Age gender and ethnicity as determinants of coping. *Journal of Adolescence*, **16**, 252–66.

—— —— (1994). Coping with different concerns: Consistency and variation in coping strategies used by adolescents. *Australian Psychologist*, **29**, 45–8.

—— —— (1996). The adolescent coping scale: Multiple forms and applications of a self-report inventory in a counselling and research context. *European Journal of Psychological Assessment*, **12**(3), 216–27.

—— —— (1999). Adolescent coping: The role of schools in facilitating reflection. *The British Journal of Educational Psychology*, **69**, 83–96.

—— —— (2000). Teaching coping to adolescents: When and to whom. *American Educational Research Journal*, **37**, 727–45.

Garmezy, N. (1985). Stress-resistant children: The search for protective factors. Recent research in developmental psychopathology, pp. 213–33. *Journal of Child Psychology and Psychiatry*, Book supplement No. 4, Oxford: Pergamon Press.

Goodyer, I. M. (1990). *Life experience, developmental and childhood psychopathology*. Chichester: John Wiley.

Haan, N. (1974). The adolescents ego model of coping and defence and comparison with Q-sorted ideal personalities. *Generic Psychology Monographs*, **89**, 273–306.

—— (1977). *Coping and defending. Processes of self-environment. Organisation*. New York: Academic Press.

Harringon, R. (1993). Similarities and dissimilarities between child and adult disorders: The case of depression, in C. G. Costello (ed.), *Basic issues in psychopathology*, pp. 103–24. New York: The Guilford Press.

Hobfoll, S. E. (1988). The ecology of stress. New York: Hemisphere.

—— (1989). Conservation of resources: A new way of conceptualizing stress. *American Psychologist*, **44**(3), 513–24.

—— (1996). Social support: Will you be there when I need you?, in N. Vanzetti and S. Duck (eds.), *A lifetime of relationships*. California: Brooks/Cole Publishing Co.

Hobfoll, S., Freedy, J. R., Green, B. L., and **Solomon, S. D.** (1996). Coping in reaction to extreme stress: The roles of resource loss and resource availability, in S. N. Endler and M. Zeidner (eds.), *Handbook of coping*. New York: Wiley.

Hobfoll, S. E. and Lilly, R. S. (1993). Resource conservation as a strategy for community psychology. *Journal of Community Psychology*, **21**, 128–48.

—— Schwarzer, S., and Chon, K. (1998). Disentangling the stress labyrinth. Interpreting the meaning of stress as it's studied. *Japanese Health Psychology*, **14**, 1–22.

Holahan, C. J. and Moos, R. H. (1986). Personality, coping and family resources in stress resistance. A longitudinal analysis. *Journal of Personality and Social Psychology*, **51**, 389–95.

—— —— (1987). Personal and contextual determinants of coping strategies. *Journal of Personality and Social Psychology*, **52**, 946–55.

Jaycox, L. H., Reivich, K. J., Gillham, J., and Seligman, M. E. (1994). Prevention of depressive symptoms in school children. *Behaviour Research and Theory*, **32**(8), 801–16.

Jenkin, C. (1997). *The relationship between self-efficacy and coping: Changes following an outward bound program*. Unpublished Master of Educational Psychology Project, University of Melbourne, Melbourne.

Kobasa, S. C. (1979). Stress life events, personality, and health: An enquiry in hardiness. *Journal of Personality and Social Psychology*, **37**, 1–11.

Lazarus, R. S. (1991). *Emotion and adaptation*. New York: Oxford University Press.

—— and Folkman, S. (1984). *Stress, appraisal and coping*. New York: Springer.

Lewis, R. and Frydenberg, E. Concomitants of failure to cope: What we should teach adolescents. *British Journal of Educational Psychology*, (in press).

Magen, Z. (1998). *Exploring adolescent happiness*. New York: Sage.

—— and Aharoni, R. (1991). Adolescents contributing towards others: Relationship to positive experiences and transpersonal commitment. *Journal of Humanistic Psychology*, **31**, 126–43.

McKenzie, V. (2001). *Young people and their resources*. Master of Education Thesis. University of Melbourne, Melbourne.

Muldoon, O. T. (1997). *Stress: Appraisal and coping in childhood. Descriptions and predictions*. Paper presented at the Annual Conference of the Northern Ireland Branch of British Psychological Society.

Noto, S. S. (1995). *The relationship between coping and achievement: A comparison between adolescent males and females*. Unpublished Master of Educational Psychology Project, University of Melbourne, Melbourne.

Patterson, J. M. and McCubbin, H. I. (1987). Adolescent coping style and behaviors: Conceptualization and measurement. *Journal of Adolescence*, **10**(2), 163–86.

Parsons, A., Frydenberg, E., and Poole, C. (1996). Overachievement and coping strategies in adolescent males. *British Journal of Educational Psychology*, **66**, 109–14.

Resnick, M. D., Bearman, P. S., Blum, R. W., Bauman, K. E., Harris, K. M., Jones, J. *et al.* (1997). Protecting adolescents from harm: Findings from the national longitudinal study on adolescent health. *The Journal of the American Medical Association*, **278**(10), 795–878.

Reynolds, W. M. (2001). Reynolds Adolescent Adjustment Screening Inventory. U.S.A: PAR—Psychological Assessment Resources, Inc.

Rice, K. G., Herman, M. A., and Petersen, A. C. (1993). Coping with challenge in adolescence: A conceptual model and psycho-educational intervention. *Journal of Adolescence*, **16**, 235–51.

Roberts, C. M. (1999). The prevention of depression in children and adolescents. *Australian Psychologist*, **34**(1), 49–57.

Roker, D., Player, K., and Coleman, J. (1999). Exploring adolescent altruism: British young people's involvement in voluntary work and campaigning, in M. Yates and J. Youniss (eds.), *Roots of civic identity: International perspectives on community service and activisim in youth,* pp. 56–72. New York: Cambridge University Press.

Rudolph, K., Dennig, M., and Weisz, J. (1995). Determinants and consequences of children coping in a medical setting: Conceptualisation, review and critique. *Psychological Bulletin,* **118**(3), 328–57.

Rutter, M. (1985). Resilience in the face of adversity: Protective factors and resistance to psychiatric disorders. *British Journal of Psychiatry,* **147**, 589–611.

Ryckman, R. M., Robins, M. A., Thornton, B., and Cantrell, P. (1982). Development and validation of a self-efficacy scale. *Journal of Personality and Social Psychology,* **42**, 891–900.

Sawyer, M. G., Kosky, R. J., Graetz, B. W., Arney, F., and Zubrick, P. B. (2000). The national survey of mental health and well-being: The child and adolescent component. *Australian and New Zealand Journal of Psychiatry,* **34**, 214–20.

Scheier, M. F. and Carver, C. S. (1987). Dispositional optimism an physical well-being: The influence of generalised outcome expectancies on health. *Journal of Personality,* **55**, 169–210.

———— (1993). On the power of positive thinking: The benefits of being optimistic. *Current Directions in Psychological Science,* **2**, 26–30.

Seiffge-Krenke, I. (1995). Conceptual approach for studying stress, coping and relationships in adolescence, in *Stress, coping and relationships in adolescence,* pp. 26–43. Hove: Erlbaum.

Seligman, M. E. (1995). *The Optimistic Child.* NSW: Random House Australia.

—— (1992). *Learned optimism.* NSW: Random House Australia.

Shever, M., Maddux, J. E., Mercadante, B., Prentice-Dunne, S., Jacobs, B., and Rogers, R. W. (1982). The self-efficacy scale: Construction and validation. *Psychological Reports,* **51**, 663–71.

Shochet, I. and Osgarby, S. (1999). The resourceful adolescent project: Building psychological resilience in adolescent and their parents. *The Australian Educational and Developmental Psychologist,* **16**(1), 46–65.

Skinner, E. A. and Wellborn, J. G. (1997). Children's coping in the academic domain, in A. Wolchik and S. A. Sandler (eds.), *Handbook of children's coping,* pp. 387–422. New York: Plennum Press.

Spirito, A., Francis, G., Overholser, J., and Frank, N. (1996). Coping, depression, and adolescent suicide attempts. *Journal of Clinical Child Psychology,* **25**(2), 147–55.

Vanderzeil, M. (2000). *Development of a version of the conservation of resources evaluation for use with adolescents.* Master of Education Thesis. University of Melbourne, Melbourne.

Van-Harrison, R., Caplan, R., French, J., and Wellons, R. (1982). Combining field experiments with longitudinal surveys: social research on patience adherence. *Applied Social Psychology Annual,* **3**, 119–50.

Wills, A. T. (1986). Stress and coping in early adolescence: Relationships to substance use in urban school samples. *Health Psychology,* **5**(3), 503–29.

Zimmermann, T. (1995). Psychosocial factores and chronic illness in childhood. *European-Psychiatry,* **10**(6), 267–305.

CHAPTER 10

TEACHING STUDENTS HOW TO COPE WITH ADVERSITY: THE THREE Cs

DAVID W. JOHNSON AND ROGER T. JOHNSON

Coping with stress and adversity

Everyone who is alive is under stress (Johnson 2000). The stress can be mild (such as when we are asleep) or severe (such as when we are under physical or psychological attack). Some level of stress, however, is always present. Stress cannot be avoided, and our stress level is never at zero. A certain amount of stress is necessary for providing the energy required for maintaining life, accomplishing goals, engaging in relationships, and adapting to constantly changing external influences. Stress is only damaging if it is too high or too low. Too high a level of stress for too long produces serious psychological and/or physiological problems. Too low a stress level for too long does likewise—that is why solitary confinement in the dark is so punishing. Not only is stress unavoidable and necessary, in many situations it is highly desirable. As a species, we are stress-seeking. We seem to long for new experiences and new challenges. Travelling to the North Pole, climbing mountains, living in deserts, and exploring the bottom of the oceans are all activities for which we are biologically and socially ill-adapted, but we do them anyway. Humans seek out certain types of stress and enjoy it.

Adversity is a different matter. Often at unforeseen, surprising times, individuals are faced with misfortune or a calamity, such as rejection by valued others, death of a loved one, or serious illness. *Adversity* is misfortune that taxes or exceeds the individual's resources. How stressful an adverse event is depends on an individual's ability to cope with stress. Coping is aimed at mastering, tolerating, or reducing the stress generated by adversity. To develop in healthy ways and to live productive and happy lives, children, adolescents, and young adults need to learn how to cope constructively with adversity and stress.

The independent-self or the interdependent-self

Based on social interdependence theory (Deutsch 1949*a*, 1962; Johnson and Johnson 1989), two approaches to teaching children, adolescents, and young adults how to cope with adversity and stress may be identified (i.e. the interdependent-self and the independent-self). The *interdependent-self approach to coping* views the person as being imbedded in networks of interdependent relationships such as family, friendships, church, community, country, and so forth and who, therefore, deals with adversity as a member of relational networks that provide resources above and beyond the individual's own (Johnson 2000). Interdependence may be positive (i.e. cooperation) or negative (i.e. competitive) (Deutsch 1949a, 1962; Johnson and Johnson 1989). The two types of interdependence are not mutually exclusive and most relationships are a mixture of both. In a network of inter-dependent relationships, the adversity of one person affects all other persons and becomes a joint issue. The assumption is that humans are innately social beings and when con-fronted with adversity a person faces it within networks of interdependent relationships that provide additional resources to help cope with the stress (see Chapter 4 by Hobfoll for additional support for this assumption). Coping is viewed as joint problem-solving, social support, social comparison, joint identity, intimate conversations, physical contact, and so forth. Thus, students need to be taught how to build and maintain interdependent rela-tionships within which individuals will receive the help and assistance they need to cope effectively with the adversity in their lives. This requires establishing a network of interde-pendent relationships, knowing how to manage conflicts constructively, and promoting the values underlying mutual support and assistance.

The *independent-self approach to coping* views the person as an independent, isolated individual separate and apart from all other individuals and who, therefore, deals with adversity on his or her own with only his or her own resources (Johnson 2000). Individualistic efforts reflect the absence of interdependence with others (Deutsch 1962; Johnson and Johnson 1989). This approach has had a powerful influence on the coping lit-erature (see Chapter 4 by Hobfoll). It emphasizes teaching each person a set of cognitive strategies (such as positive appraisal, problem-focus, noting positive events, appraisal of situational meaning, and others) that the person uses to cope with adversity. There is a dan-ger, however, that viewing coping as an individual activity leads to a self-orientation and a delusion of individualism that each person lives his or her life separate and apart from all other individuals and, therefore, one's own frustration, unhappiness, hunger, despair, and misery has no significant bearing on others' well-being and vice versa (Johnson 2000). Such social isolation may magnify the impact of adversity.

The importance of the interdependence-self approach to coping is illustrated in the research on depression. We are in an epidemic of depression, anxiety, and mental illness (Seligman 1988). Two major surveys of mental illness in the US, for example, showed that, contrary to expectations, younger people were much more likely to have had a depressive episode in their lives than were older people (Seligman 1988). The rate of depression over the last two generations has increased roughly tenfold. People experience much more depression now than they did two generations ago, feeling hopeless, giving up, being passive, having low self-esteem, and committing suicide. The reason may be found in the breakdown of cooperative, interdependent relationships with other people in our social networks (family, neighbourhood, community, work, church, and country) and commit-ment to larger social institutions. There has been a loss of faith in God, country, commun-ity, and family (Seligman 1988). Without faith in society's institutions, personal failures, and losses are often interpreted as catastrophic. When an individual's identity, hope, and meaning are no longer rooted in a relationship with God, when an individual no longer believes that his or her country and the organization he or she works for are powerful and benevolent, and when an individual no longer believes that his or her family or friends are a source of enduring unity and support, when faced with adversity the individual has to turn to a very small and frail being: the self. The result has been a 'huge increase' in the frequency and depth of depression and meaninglessness (Seligman 1988).

While there is almost no simple recipe for coping with stress, being isolated and detached from other people generally decreases coping and being involved in networks of supportive, caring, cooperative, and committed relationships generally increases coping (Johnson and Johnson 1989). Such relationships tend to lessen the impact of adverse events, provide opportunities for intimate and personal conversations and problem-solving, create opportunities for seeing adverse events from a variety of perspectives, and provide many other positive benefits. Building and maintaining supportive, caring, cooperative, and committed relationships requires cooperative experiences, resolving conflicts constructively, and establishing a mutual set of civic values. Within schools, this is known as the Three Cs Programme.

The three Cs programme

The Three Cs are essential conditions for coping with stress and adversity (cooperative community, constructive conflict, and civic values) (see Fig. 10.1). Working cooperatively with peers, resolving conflicts constructively, and internalizing prosocial values are experiences that all children, adolescents, and young adults need if they are to cope with adversity constructively. The Three Cs Programme is directly based on social interdependence and conflict theories, and the theories have been validated by a great deal of research on cooperation (Johnson and Johnson 1989), constructive controversy (Johnson and Johnson 1995c), and the peacemaker programme (Johnson and Johnson 1995a, 1996a, 2000). The Three Cs Programme, described below, has been implemented in a wide variety of schools throughout North, Central, and South America, Europe, Africa, the Middle East, and Asia. It has been used with inner-city, lower-class students and with upper-class private school

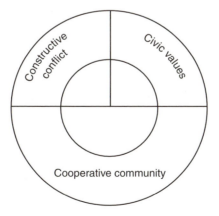

Figure 10.1 The Three Cs of effective schools.

students and with everyone in between. It has been used in schools in third world as well as industrialized countries. The widespread implementation of the Three Cs Programme gives it a generalizability not found in most educational programmes.

The first C: cooperative community

The nature of community and social interdependence

The interdependent-self approach to coping begins with ensuring the school is a learning community. Students need to learn how to build and maintain the interdependent relationships within which they will receive the help and assistance they need to cope effectively with adversity. In addition, within schools students establish a network of interdependent relationships that may last for the rest of their lives. Developing the interdependent relationships needed to provide the resources needed to cope with adversity is a product of a community and a culture. *Community* is a group of people who live in the same locality and share common goals and a common culture. The school community is made up of the faculty and staff, the students, their parents, members of the neighbourhood, and other stakeholders in the school (such as district administrators, government officials, college admission officers, and future employers). The heart of community is *social interdependence*, which exists when each individual's outcomes are affected by the actions of others (Deutsch 1949a, 1962, 1973; Johnson and Johnson 1989) (see Table 10.1). Social interdependence may be positive (cooperation), negative (competition), or absent (individualistic efforts). Positive interdependence (cooperation) exists when individuals work together to achieve mutual goals and negative interdependence (competition) exists when individuals work against each other to achieve a goal that only one or a few may attain. *Social independence*, where the outcomes of each person are unaffected by others' actions, is characterized by individualistic actions.

Table 10.1 Understanding cooperative efforts

Types of interdependence	Cooperative learning	Essential elements of cooperation	Outcomes of cooperation
Positive Cooperation	Formal cooperative learning	Positive interdependence	Effort to achieve
Negative Competition	Informal cooperative learning	Individual accountability	Positive relationships
None Individualistic	Cooperative base groups	Promotive interaction	Psychological health
		Interpersonal and small group skills	Social skills
		Group processing	Coping with adversity

Note: There are three types of interdependence, the most important of which is cooperation. The basic use of cooperation in schools is cooperative learning. There are three types of cooperative learning. Effective cooperation depends on five basic elements being structured into the situation. When the five elements are present, three types of outcomes tend to result.

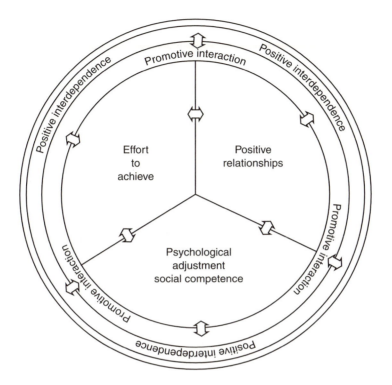

Figure 10.2 Outcome of cooperative learning.

Social interdependence theory assumes that the type of interdependence structured among individuals determines how they interact with each other which, in turn largely determines outcomes. Structuring situations cooperatively results in individuals promoting each other's success, structuring situations competitively results in individuals opposing each other's success, and structuring situations individualistically results in no interaction among individuals (see Table 10.1). These interaction patterns affect numerous variables, which may be subsumed within the three broad and interrelated outcomes (see Fig. 10.2) (Johnson and Johnson 1989).

The power of cooperation

Between 1897 and 1989, over 550 experimental and 100 correlational studies were conducted by a wide variety of researchers in different decades with different age subjects, in different subject areas, and in different settings (for a detailed review of the research on cooperative, competitive, and individualistic efforts, see Johnson and Johnson (1989)). In our own research programme at the Cooperative Learning Center (University of Minnesota) over the past 30 years we have conducted over 90 research studies to refine our understanding of the nature of cooperation and how it works. Many different researchers have conducted the research with markedly different orientations working in different settings, countries, and decades. Research participants have varied as to economic class, age, sex, nationality, and cultural background. A wide variety of research tasks, ways of structuring cooperation, and measures of the dependent variables have been used. The research on cooperation has validity and generalizability rarely found in the educational literature.

The research studies on social interdependence may best be summarized within a meta-analysis. A *meta-analysis* uses the statistically combined results of a set of independent studies that test the same hypothesis and using inferential statistics to draw conclusions about the overall result of the studies. Meta-analyses usually involve effect-sizes. An *effect size* is the standardized mean difference between the experimental and control groups or the proportion of a standard deviation by which an experimental group exceeds a control group (Glass *et al.* 1981).

Effort to achieve

Schools do not increase students' abilities to cope with adversity by being stress-free environments. Learning how to cope with adversity requires facing stressful challenges and successfully dealing with them. One of the arenas in which challenges are presented is academic learning. From Table 10.2 it may be seen that cooperation promotes considerably greater effort to achieve than do competitive or individualistic efforts. Effort exerted to achieve includes such variables as achievement and productivity, long-term retention, on-task behaviour, use of higher-level reasoning strategies, generation of new ideas and solutions, intrinsic motivation, achievement motivation, continuing motivation, and greater transfer of what is learned within one situation to another. Thus, more successful coping with academic challenges occurs within cooperative than within competitive or individualistic situations.

Interpersonal relationships

The degree of emotional bonding that exists among students has a profound effect on students' coping with adversity. There have been over 175 studies that have investigated the relative impact of cooperative, competitive, and individualistic efforts on quality of relationships (Johnson and Johnson 1989). From Table 10.2 it may be seen that cooperation generally promotes greater interpersonal attraction among individuals than do competitive or individualistic efforts (effect-sizes = 0.66 and 0.60 respectively).

In addition to friendly, caring, and committed relationships among collaborators, there has been considerable research on social support. Since the 1940s there have been 106 studies comparing the relative impact of cooperative, competitive, and individualistic efforts on social support. Cooperative experiences tended to promote greater social support from peers and from superiors (i.e. teachers) than did competitive (effect-size = 0.62) or individualistic (effect-size = 0.70) efforts.

It is difficult to overemphasize the importance of these research results. Children, adolescents, and young adults need supportive and caring friends. Friends give a person a developmental advantage. Students who do not have friends are at risk. Antisocial behaviour and rejection by the normal peer group are positively correlated (Cantrell and Prinz 1985; Dodge *et al.* 1982; Roff and Wirt 1984). Inappropriately aggressive behaviour leads to rejection by peers (Coie and Kupersmidt 1983; Dodge 1983). Rejected children tend to be deficient in a number of social-cognitive skills, including peer group entry, perception of peer group norms, response to provocation, and interpretation of prosocial interactions (Asarnow and Callan 1985; Dodge 1985; Putallaz 1983). Among children referred to child guidance clinics, 30–75 per cent (depending on age) are reported by their parents to experience peer difficulties (Achenbach and Edelbrock 1981). These difficulties are roughly twice as common among clinic children as among nonreferred youngsters. Moreover, referred children have fewer friends and less contact with them than nonreferred children, their friendships are significantly less stable over time, and their understanding of the reciprocities and intimacies involved in friendships is less mature (Selman 1981).

Psychological health

Asley Montagu (1966), a famous anthropologist was fond of saying that with few exceptions, the solitary animal in any species is an abnormal creature. Karen Horney (1937), a renowned psychoanalyst often stated that the neurotic individual is someone who is inappropriately competitive and, therefore, unable to cooperate with others. Montagu, Horney, and many others have recognized that the essence of psychological health is the ability to develop and maintain relationships in which cooperative action effectively takes place. With our students and colleagues, we have conducted a series of studies relating cooperative, competitive, and individualistic efforts and attitudes to various indices of psychological health. The samples studied included middle-class junior-high students, middle-class high-school seniors, high-school age juvenile prisoners, adult prisoners, Olympic ice-hockey players, and adult step-couples. The diversity of the samples studied and the variety of measures of psychological health provide considerable generalizability of the results of the studies. A strong relationship was found between cooperativeness and psychological health, a mixed relationship has been found with competitiveness and psychological health, and a strong relationship has been found between an individualistic orientation and psychological pathology.

More specifically, in our studies we found that the more positive a person's attitudes toward cooperating with others, the less likely they are to engage in antisocial behaviours such as drug abuse and criminal activities, the less their tension and anxiety, the less their depression and dejection, the less their anger and hostility, the less forceful and demanding they are, and the less rebellious and egoistic they are (see Johnson and Johnson 1989). In addition, the more cooperative individuals are, the more they use socially appropriate and approved ways of meeting environmental demands, the more they see reality clearly without distorting it according to their own desires and needs, the greater their emotional maturity, the greater their ability to resolve conflicts between self-perceptions and adverse information about oneself, the higher their self-esteem and self-acceptance, the greater their basic trust in others and optimism, the more aware they are of their feelings, the more they can control their anger and frustration and express them appropriately, the more they take into account social customs and rules in resolving interpersonal and personal problems, the more willing they are to acknowledge unpleasant events or conditions encountered in daily living, the more their thinking is organized and focused on reality and free from confusion and hallucinations, the greater their leadership ability and social initiative, the more outgoing and sociable they are, the greater their sense of well-being (which includes minimizing their worries and being free from self-doubt and disillusion-ment), the greater their common sense and good judgment, and the more conscientious and responsible they are (see Johnson and Johnson 1989). All of these qualities relate to coping successfully with stress and adversity.

Interpersonal and small group skills

An essential aspect of coping with adversity is the mastery of the interpersonal and small group skills needed to interact effectively with other people (Johnson 2000; Johnson and Johnson 2000). They include such skills as communication, trust-building, self-disclosure, leadership, decision-making, goal-setting, and social influence skills. Conflict resolution skills are highly important in both interpersonal and small group settings. Students master interpersonal and small group skills in a cooperative context (Johnson and Johnson 1989). Competitors tend not to interact in constructive ways and in individualistic situations no interaction takes place. Lew *et al.* (1986*a*,*b*) found that socially isolated and withdrawn students learned more social skills and engaged in them more frequently within coopera-tive than within individualistic situations, especially when the group was rewarded for their doing so. Slavin (1977) found that emotionally disturbed adolescents who experienced cooperative learning were more likely than traditionally taught students to interact appro-priately with other students, and this effect was still present five months after the end of the project. Janke (1980) found enhancing effects of cooperative learning on appropriate interactions among emotionally disturbed students and also found the programme improved these students' attendance. More generally, cooperation promotes more frequent, effective, and accurate communication than do competitive and individualistic situations (Johnson 1973, 1974). Within cooperative situations communication is more open, effective, and accurate, whereas in competitive situations communication will be closed, ineffective, and inaccurate (Bonoma *et al.* 1974; Crombag 1966; Deutsch, 1949*b*, 1962; Deutsch and Krauss 1962; French 1951; Fay 1970; Grossack 1953; Johnson 1971, 1973, 1974; Krauss and Deutsch 1966).

Basic elements of cooperation

These outcomes tend to result only when cooperation is effectively structured to contain five basic elements (Johnson and Johnson 1989, 1999) (see Table 10.2). First, there must be a strong sense of positive interdependence, so individuals believe they are linked with others so they cannot succeed unless the others do. Positive interdependence may be

Table 10.2 Mean effect sizes for impact of social interdependence on dependent variables

	Cooperative vs. competitive	Cooperative vs. individualistic	Competitive vs. individualistic
Achievement	0.67	0.64	0.30
Interpersonal attraction	0.67	0.60	0.08
Social support	0.62	0.70	−0.13
Self-esteem	0.58	0.44	−0.23

Taken from Johnson, D. W., and Johnson, R. (1989). *Cooperation and competition: Theory and research*. Edina, MN: Interaction Book Company.

structured through mutual goals, joint rewards, divided resources, complementary roles, and a shared identity. Second, each collaborator must be individually accountable to do his or her fair share of the work. Third, collaborators must have the opportunity to promote each other's success by helping, assisting, supporting, encouraging, and praising each other's efforts to achieve. Fourth, working together cooperatively requires interpersonal and small group skills, such as leadership, decision-making, trust-building, communication, and conflict-management skills. Finally, cooperative groups must engage in group-processing, which exists when group members discuss how well they are achieving their goals and maintaining effective working relationships.

To create a learning community within which students (a) learn how to build and maintain interdependent relationships and (b) establish a network of supportive and caring relationships that will continue throughout their schooling experience and beyond, positive interdependence must be structured at all levels of the school: learning group, classroom, interclass, school, school-parent, and school-neighbourhood.

Cooperative learning

Cooperative learning is the instructional use of small groups of students working together to maximize their own and each other's learning (Johnson *et al.* 1998*a*). Any assignment in any curriculum for any age student can be done cooperatively. There are three types of cooperative learning—formal, informal, and cooperative base groups (see Table 10.2).

Formal cooperative learning consists of students working together, for one class period to several weeks, to achieve shared learning goals and complete jointly specific tasks and assignments (such as decision making or problem-solving, completing a curriculum unit, writing a report, conducting a survey or experiment, or reading a chapter or reference book, learning vocabulary, or answering questions at the end of the chapter) (Johnson *et al.* 1998*a*). In formal cooperative learning groups teachers

1. *Make a number of preinstructional decisions.* Teachers specify the objectives for the lesson (both academic and social skills) and decide on the size of groups, the method of assigning students to groups, the roles students will be assigned, the materials needed to conduct the lesson, and the way the room will be arranged.

2. *Explain the task and the positive interdependence.* A teacher clearly defines the assignment, teaches the required concepts and strategies, specifies the positive interdependence and individual accountability, gives the criteria for success, and explains the expected social skills to be used.

3. *Monitor students' learning and intervene within the groups to provide task assistance or to increase students' interpersonal and group skills.* A teacher systematically observes and collects data on each group as it works. When needed, the teacher intervenes to assist students in completing the task accurately and in working together effectively.

4. *Assess students' learning and help students process how well their groups function.* Students' learning is carefully assessed and their performances evaluated. Members of the learning groups then discuss how effectively they worked together and how they can improve in the future.

Informal cooperative learning consists of having students work together to achieve a joint learning goal in temporary, *ad hoc* groups that last from a few minutes to one class period (Johnson *et al.* 1998*b*, 1998). During a lecture, demonstration, or film, informal cooperative learning can be used to focus student attention on the material to be learned, set a mood conducive to learning, help set expectations as to what will be covered in a class session, ensure that students cognitively process and rehearse the material being taught, summarize what was learned and precue the next session, and provide closure to an instructional session. The procedure for using informal cooperative learning during a lecture entails having three-to-five minute focused discussions before and after the lecture (i.e. bookends) and two-to-three minute interspersing pair discussions throughout the lecture.

Cooperative base groups are long-term, heterogeneous cooperative learning groups with stable membership whose primary responsibilities are to provide support, encouragement, and assistance to make academic progress and develop cognitively and socially in healthy ways as well as holding each other accountable for striving to learn (Johnson *et al.* 1998*b*, 1998). Typically, cooperative base groups (a) are heterogeneous in membership, (b) meet regularly (for example, daily or biweekly), and (c) last for the duration of the semester, year, or until all members are graduated. When students know that the base group will stay together for some time, they become committed to find ways to motivate and encourage their groupmates and solve any problems in working together. The procedure for using base groups is to assign students to base groups of three to four members, have them meet at the beginning and end of each class session (or week) to complete academic tasks such as checking each members' homework, routine tasks such as taking attendance, and personal support tasks such as listening sympathetically to personal problems or providing guidance for writing a paper.

Classroom interdependence

There are numerous ways to extend the positive interdependence within the learning groups to the classroom as a whole. Class goals may be established (criteria for students to reach, improvement goal for each student, total class score), class rewards or celebrations may be created (bonus points when class members achieve up to criterion, nonacademic rewards such as extra recess time or a class party), class roles may be structured (classroom government, class newsletter in which each cooperative group contributes one article), and class processing takes place in class meetings. Finally, a common class identity may be created through a class name, slogan, flag, or song.

Interclass interdependence

An interdisciplinary team of three to six teachers may organize their classes into a 'neighbourhood' or a 'school within a school.' Science and math, or literature and social studies, may be integrated and the classes combined. Students of different ages can be involved in cross-class 'reading buddies' that meet weekly throughout the year so they can jointly share and explore literature. Several classes can do periodic projects on learning specific social skills and values. In these and many other ways, interclass interdependence may be created.

School interdependence

School level positive interdependence is established in numerous ways (Johnson and Johnson 1994). The school mission statement may articulate the mutual goals shared by all members of the school and may be displayed on the school's walls and printed at the top of the agenda of every meeting involving faculty and staff. Faculty and staff can meet weekly in teaching teams and/or study groups. Colleagial teaching teams consist of two–five teachers who meet weekly and discuss how better to implement cooperative learning within their classrooms and colleagial study groups meet regularly to discuss a book or series of articles about cooperative learning. Teachers may be assigned to task forces to plan and implement solutions to school-wide issues such as curriculum adoptions and lunchroom behaviour and *ad hoc* decision-making groups during faculty meetings to involve all staff members in important school decisions.

School–parent interdependence

Parents may be involved in establishing school goals and the 'strategic plan' to achieve the goals, producing a school newsletter, publishing the school yearbook, volunteering in classes, helping conduct special projects, and serving on all school committees or the site council. The PTA may raise money for supplies and technology. A faculty–parent task force may be formed to deal with serious discipline problems.

School–neighbourhood interdependence

The school mission can be supported by local merchants through such programmes as giving a discount to students who have a card verifying that in the last grading period they achieved a 'B' average or above. Members of the neighbourhood could contribute resources to school activities such as playing in the school band. Classes could do neighbourhood service projects, cleaning up a park or mowing the yards of elderly residents.

The second C: constructive conflict resolution

For interdependent relationships to exist and be maintained over a long period of time, conflicts must occur and be managed constructively. In addition, much of the adversity in any person's life involves conflicts with others. If conflicts are managed in destructive ways, both the frequency and level of adversity increases. On the other hand, when conflicts are managed constructively, they can increase (a) individuals' energy, curiosity, and motivation, (b) achievement, retention, insight, creativity, problem-solving, and synthesis, (c) healthy cognitive and social development, (d) clarification of own and others' identity, commitments, and values, (e) quality of relationships, and (f) many other positive outcomes (Johnson and Johnson 1995*a,b*, 1996*a*, 2000).

Managing conflicts constructively depends on (a) clear procedures for managing conflicts, (b) individuals being skilled in the use of the procedures and value using them, and (c) community and organizational norms and values encouraging and supporting the use of the procedures. Faculty and staff need to teach students (and learn themselves) three

Table 10.3 Types of conflict

Academic controversy	Conflicts of interest
One person's ideas, information, theories, conclusions, and opinions are incompatible with those of another and the two seek to reach an agreement.	The actions of one person attempting to maximize benefits prevents, blocks, or interferes with another person maximizing their benefits.
Controversy procedure	*Integrative (problem-solving) negotiations*
Research and prepare positions	Describe wants
Present and advocate positions	Describe feelings
Refute opposing position and refute attacks on own position	Describe reasons for wants and feelings
Reverse perspectives	Take other's perspective
Synthesize and integrate best evidence and reasoning from all sides	Invent three optional agreements that maximize joint outcomes
	Choose one and formalize agreement

procedures for managing conflicts: academic controversy, problem-solving negotiation, and peer mediation procedures (see Table 10.3).

Academic controversies

To promote coping with adversity, teachers can structure academic controversies frequently and teach students how to resolve them. A controversy exists when one person's ideas, opinions, information, theories, or conclusions are incompatible with those of another and the two seek to reach an agreement (Johnson and Johnson 1995*b*). Controversies are resolved by engaging in what Aristotle called deliberate discourse (i.e. the discussion of the advantages and disadvantages of proposed actions) aimed at synthesizing novel solutions (i.e. creative problem-solving). Teaching students how to engage in the controversy process begins with randomly assigning students to heterogeneous cooperative learning groups of four members (Johnson and Johnson 1979, 1989, 1995*b*). The groups are given an issue on which to write a report and pass a test. Each cooperative group is divided into two pairs. One pair is given the con-position on the issue and the other pair is given the pro-position. Each pair is given the instructional materials needed to define their position and point them towards supporting information. The cooperative goal of reaching a consensus on the issue (by synthesizing the best reasoning from both sides) and writing a quality group report is highlighted. Students then do the following.

1. *Research, learn, and prepare position*: Students prepare the best case possible for their assigned position by researching the assigned position, organizing the information into a persuasive argument, and planning how to advocate the assigned position effectively to ensure it receives a fair and complete hearing.

2. *Present and advocate position*: Students present the best case for their assigned position to ensure it gets a fair and complete hearing.

3. *Engage in an open discussion in which there is spirited disagreement*: Students freely exchange information and ideas while (a) arguing forcefully and persuasively for their

position, (b) critically analysing and refuting the opposing position, (c) rebutting attacks on their position, and (d) presenting counter-arguments.

4. *Reverse perspectives*: Students reverse perspectives and present the best case for the opposing position.

5. *Synthesize*: Students drop all advocacy and find a synthesis on which all members can agree. Students summarize the best evidence and reasoning from both sides and integrate it into a joint position that is new and unique. Students are to write a group report on the group's synthesis with the supporting evidence and rationale and take a test on both positions. Groups then process how well the group functioned and celebrate the group's success and the hard work.

Benefits of controversy

We have conducted over twenty-five research studies on the impact of academic controversy and numerous other researchers have added to the literature (Johnson and Johnson 1995*b*, 1989) (see Table 10.4). The research indicates that intellectual conflicts create higher achievement, greater retention, more creative problem-solving, more frequent use of higher-level reasoning and metacognitive thought, more perspective taking, greater continuing motivation to learn, more positive attitudes toward learning, more positive interpersonal relationships, greater social support, and higher self-esteem (Johnson and Johnson 1985, 1995*b*). Engaging in a controversy can also be fun, enjoyable, and exciting.

Conflict resolution training

In addition to intellectual conflicts, conflicts based on individuals' differing interests within a situation must be resolved constructively. If students are to resolve conflicts constructively, they must learn how to resolve conflicts of interests. Conflict of interests exist when the actions of one person attempting to maximize his or her wants and benefits prevents, blocks, or interferes with another person maximizing his or her wants and benefits. The Teaching Students To Be Peacemakers Programme began in the 1960s (Johnson 1970; Johnson and Johnson 1995*a*) to teach students how to resolve conflicts of interests constructively. All students are taught how to engage in problem-solving negotiations and mediate their schoolmates' conflicts. The programme is then implemented and all students take turns in being a class or school mediator.

Problem-solving negotiations

Conflicts of interests are resolved through negotiation (when negotiation does not work, then mediation is required). There are two ways to negotiate: distributive or 'win–lose' (where one person benefits only if the opponent agrees to make a concession) and integrative or problem solving (where disputants work together to create an agreement that benefits everyone involved). In ongoing relationships, distributive negotiations result in destructive outcomes and integrative leads to constructive outcomes. The steps in using problem-solving negotiations are (Johnson and Johnson 1995*a*):

1. *Describing what you want.* '*I want to use the book now.*' This includes using good communication skills and defining the conflict as a small and specific mutual problem.

Table 10.4 Meta-analysis of controversy studies: Average effect size

Dependent variable	Mean	SD	*n*
Achievement			
Controversy/concurrence seeking	0.68	0.41	15
Controversy/debate	0.40	0.43	6
Controversy/individualistic efforts	0.87	0.47	19
Cognitive reasoning			
Controversy/concurrence seeking	0.62	0.44	2
Controversy/debate	1.35	0.00	1
Controversy/individualistic efforts	0.90	0.48	15
Perspective-taking			
Controversy/concurrence seeking	0.91	0.28	9
Controversy/debate	0.22	0.42	2
Controversy/individualistic efforts	0.86	0.00	1
Motivation			
Controversy/concurrence seeking	0.75	0.46	12
Controversy/debate	0.45	0.44	5
Controversy/individualistic efforts	0.71	0.21	4
Attitudes			
Controversy/concurrence seeking	0.58	0.29	5
Controversy/debate	0.81	0.00	1
Controversy/individualistic efforts	0.64	0.00	1
Interpersonal attraction			
Controversy/concurrence seeking	0.24	0.44	8
Controversy/debate	0.72	0.25	6
Controversy/individualistic efforts	0.81	0.11	3
Debate/individualistic efforts	0.46	0.13	2
Social support			
Controversy/concurrence seeking	0.32	0.44	8
Controversy/debate	0.92	0.42	6
Controversy/individualistic efforts	1.52	0.29	3
Debate/individualistic efforts	0.85	0.01	2
Self-esteem			
Controversy/concurrence seeking	0.39	0.15	4
Controversy/debate	0.51	0.09	2
Controversy/individualistic efforts	0.85	0.04	3
Debate/individualistic efforts	0.45	0.17	2

Source: Johnson, D. W., and Johnson, R. (1995*b*). Creative controversy: Intellectual challenge in the classroom, 3rd edn. Edina, MN: Interaclient Book company.

2. *Describing how you feel.* 'I'm frustrated.' Disputants must understand how they feel and communicate it openly and clearly.

3. *Describing the reasons for your wants and feelings.* 'You have been using the book for the past hour. If I don't get to use the book soon my report will not be done on time. It's frustrating to have to wait so long.' This includes expressing cooperative intentions,

listening carefully, separating interests from positions, and differentiating before trying to integrate the two sets of interests.

4. *Taking the other's perspective and summarizing your understanding of what the other person wants, how the other person feels, and the reasons underlying both.* 'My understanding of you is . . .' This includes understanding the perspective of the opposing disputant and being able to see the problem from both perspectives simultaneously.

5. *Inventing three optional plans to resolve the conflict that maximize joint benefits.* 'Plan A is . . ., Plan B is . . ., Plan C is . . .' This includes inventing creative options to solve the problem.

6. *Choosing one and formalizing the agreement with a hand shake.* '*Let's agree on Plan B!*' A wise agreement is fair to all disputants and is based on principles. It maximizes joint benefits and strengthens disputants' ability to work together cooperatively and resolve conflicts constructively in the future. It specifies how each disputant should act in the future and how the agreement will be reviewed and renegotiated if it does not work.

Peer mediation

When students are unable to negotiate a resolution to their conflict, they may request help from a mediator. A *mediator* is a neutral person who helps two or more people resolve their conflict, usually by negotiating an integrative agreement. In contrast, *arbitration* is the submission of a dispute to a disinterested third party (such as a teacher or principal) who makes a final and binding judgement as to how the conflict will be resolved. Mediation consists of four steps (Johnson and Johnson 1995a):

1. *Ending hostilities*: Break up hostile encounters and cool off students.

2. *Ensuring disputants are committed to the mediation process*: To ensure that disputants are committed to the mediation process and are ready to negotiate in good faith, the mediator introduces the process of mediation and sets the ground rules that (a) mediation is voluntary, (b) the mediator is neutral, (c) each person will have the chance to state his or her view of the conflict without interruption, and (d) each person agrees to solve the problem with no name calling or interrupting, being as honest as you can, abiding by any agreement made, and keeping anything said in mediation confidential.

3. *Helping disputants successfully negotiate with each other*: The disputants are carefully taken through the problem-solving negotiation steps.

4. *Formalizing the agreement*: The agreement is solidified into a contract.

Implementing programme

The peacemaker programme is implemented once students understand how to negotiate and mediate. Each day the teacher selects two class members to serve as official mediators. Any conflicts students cannot resolve themselves are referred to the mediators. The mediators wear official T-shirts, patrol the playground and lunchroom, and are available to mediate any conflicts that occur in the classroom or school. The role of mediator is rotated so that all students in the class or school serve as mediators an equal amount of time. Initially, students mediate in pairs. This ensures that shy or nonverbal students get the same amount of experience as more extroverted and verbally fluent students. Mediating classmates' conflicts is perhaps the most effective way of teaching students the need for the skillful use of each step of the negotiation procedure.

If peer mediation fails, the teacher mediates the conflict. If teacher mediation fails, the teacher arbitrates by deciding who is right and who is wrong. If that fails, the principal mediates the conflict. If that fails, the principal arbitrates. Teaching all students to mediate properly results in a school-wide discipline programme where students are empowered to regulate and control their own and their classmates actions. Teachers and administrators are then freed to spend more of their energies on instruction.

Continuing training and spiral programme

It takes years of training and practice to gain real expertise in resolving conflicts construct-ively. A few hours of training are clearly insufficient. Students' skills may be refined and upgraded through integrating negotiation and mediation training into academic lessons. Almost any lesson in literature and history, for example, can include role playing in which the negotiation and/or mediation procedures are used. Each year the Teaching Students to be Peacemakers training is repeated with increasing sophistication and complexity. The Peacemaker Programme is a 12-year spiral programme. The twelve years of training and practice will result in a person with considerable expertise in resolving conflicts con-structively.

Benefits of conflict resolution and peer mediation programmes

Between 1988 and 2000 we and our colleagues conducted seventeen studies on the effect-iveness of the Peacemaker Programme in eight different schools in two different countries (Johnson and Johnson 1995a,d, 1996a, 2000). Students involved were from kindergarten through ninth grades. The studies were conducted in rural, suburban, and urban settings. The benefits of teaching students the problem-solving negotiation and the peer mediation procedures are as follows (see Table 10.5).

First, students and faculty tended to develop a shared understanding of how conflicts should be managed and a common vocabulary to discuss conflicts. Second, students tended to learn the negotiation and mediation procedures, retain their knowledge throughout the school year and into the following year, apply the procedures to their and other people's conflicts, transfer the procedures to nonclassroom settings such as the playground and lunchroom, transfer the procedures to nonschool settings such as the home, use the pro-cedures similarly in family and school settings, and (when given the option) engage in problem-solving rather than win-lose negotiations. Third, students' attitudes toward conflict tended to became more positive. Students learned to view conflicts as potentially positive and faculty and parents viewed the conflict training as constructive and helpful. Fourth, students tended to resolve their conflicts without the involvement of faculty and administrators. Classroom management problems, in other words, tended to be signific-antly reduced. The number of discipline problems teachers had to deal with decreased by about 60 per cent and referrals to administrators dropped about 90 per cent. Faculty and administrators no longer had to arbitrate conflicts among students; instead they spent their time maintaining and supporting the peer mediation process. A teacher commented,

Table 10.5 Mean effect sizes peacemaker studies

Dependent variable	Mean	SD	Number of effects
Learned procedure	2.25	1.98	13
Learned procedure—retention	3.34	4.16	9
Applied procedure	2.16	1.31	4
Application—retention	0.46	0.16	3
Strategy constructiveness	1.60	1.70	12
Constructiveness—retention	1.10	0.53	10
Strategy two-concerns	1.10	0.46	5
Two-concerns—retention	0.45	0.20	2
Integrative negotiation	0.98	0.36	5
Quality of solutions	0.73	0	1
Positive attitude	1.07	0.25	5
Negative attitude	−0.61	0.37	2
Academic achievement	0.88	0.09	5
Academic retention	0.70	0.31	4

'Classroom management problems are nil as far as I'm concerned. We don't do a lot of disciplining *per se*. A lot of times, when a conflict occurs on the playground, they resolve it there and do not bring it back to the classroom. So there is a lot less I have to deal with in the classroom.'

Fifth, the conflict resolution procedures tended to enhance the basic values of the classroom and school. A teacher who emphasizes the value of 'respect' states, 'The procedures are a very respectful way to resolve conflicts. There's a calmness in the classroom because the students know the negotiation and mediation procedures'. Sixth, students generally liked to engage in the procedures. A teacher states, 'They never refuse to negotiate or mediate. When there's a conflict and you say it's time for conflict resolution, you never have either one say I won't do it. There are no refusals'.

Finally, when integrated into academic units, the conflict resolution training tended to increase academic achievement and long-term retention of the academic material. Academic units, especially in subject areas such as literature and history, provide a setting to understand conflicts, practice how to resolve them, and use them to gain insight into the material being studied.

The third C: civic values

Some historians claim that the decline and fall of Rome was set in motion by corruption from within rather than by conquest from without. Rome fell, it can be argued, because Romans lost their civic virtue. *Civic virtue* exists when individuals meet both the letter and spirit of their public obligations. For a community to exist and sustain itself, members must share common goals and values aimed at defining appropriate behaviour and increasing the quality of life within the community (Johnson and Johnson 1996b, 1999). These common values provide internal resources to cope with adversity constructively and effectively.

There are a wide variety of programmes to teach students values (Kohn 1997). Some of these programmes focus on listing values that should be taught and others on developing student character. Both approaches tend to be collections of exhortations and extrinsic inducements designed to make children work harder and do what they are told. Students are often drilled in specific behaviours rather than engaged in discussions that require reflection on how one should live. Kohn criticizes these approaches and concludes that a more generic approach is needed that (a) focuses on the overall organizational structure of the school, (b) assumes a positive view of human nature, (c) aims at developing individuals who are active advocates for democracy and social justice, (d) instills values (beyond selfishness) aimed at improving the quality of life for all societal members and the common good, and (e) utilizes cooperative learning as the primary means of instruction.

A learning community cannot exist in schools dominated by (a) competition where students are taught to value striving for their personal success at the expense of others or (b) individualistic efforts where students value only their own self-interests. Rather, students need to internalize values underlying cooperation and integrative negotiations. The value systems underlying competitive, individualistic, and cooperative situations as well as constructive controversy and integrative negotiations are a hidden curriculum beneath the surface of school life.

Whenever students engage in competitive efforts, for example, they learn the values of commitment to getting more than others, success depends on beating and defeating others, what is important is winning, not mastery or excellence, opposing and obstructing the success of others is a natural way of life, feeling joy and pride in one's wins and others' losses, and a person's worth (own and others) is conditional and contingent on his or her 'wins'.

The values inherently taught by individualistic experiences are commitment to one's own self-interest, success depends on one's own efforts, the pleasure of succeeding is personal and relevant to only oneself, other people are irrelevant, self-worth is based on a unidimensional view that the characteristics that help the person succeed are, and extrinsic motivation to gain rewards.

The values inherently taught by cooperative efforts are commitment to own and others' success and well-being as well as to the common good, success depends on joint efforts to achieve mutual goals, facilitating and promoting the success of others is a natural way of life, the pleasure of succeeding is associated with others' happiness in their success, other people are potential contributors to one's success, and own and other people's worth is unconditional, intrinsic motivation.

Participating in the controversy process teaches such values as (a) you have both the right and the responsibility to derive a reasoned position and advocate it, (b) 'truth' is derived from the clash of opposing ideas and positions, (c) insight and understanding come from a 'disputed passage' where one's ideas and conclusions are advocated and subjected to intellectual challenge, (d) issues must be viewed from all perspectives, and (e) you seek a synthesis that subsumes the seemingly opposed positions.

Problem-solving negotiations and peer mediation are closely related to cooperation. They inherently teach all the values associated with cooperation. In addition, problem-solving negotiations and mediation teach such values as being open and honest about what one wants and how one feels, understanding the other person's wants and feelings, striving to see the situation from all perspectives, being concerned with the other person's outcomes as well as one's own, seeking to reach agreements that are satisfying to all disputants, and maintaining effective and caring long-term relationships. In other words, constructive conflict resolution inherently teaches a set of civic values aimed at ensuring the fruitful continuation of the community.

Conclusions and summary

Stress is unavoidable, necessary, and desirable. It is only when it is too high or too low that stress becomes a problem. Adverse events create high stress with which individuals must cope. There are two views of coping presented here. The interdependent-self approach emphasizes building and maintaining networks of supportive and caring relationships within which individuals are committed to each other's well-being as well as their own. The independent-self approach emphasizes cognitive strategies to manage adverse events. While the latter approach has considerable value, the former approach is the most powerful and has the most data validating its effectiveness. Learning how to cope with adversity requires (a) creating a cooperative context in which the supportive and caring interdependent relationships may be built, (b) constructively managing conflicts in order to maintain and deepen the relationships over time, and (c) adopting a set of civic values that encourages concern for each other's well-being and the common good.

As the impact of family and community life has decreased, the school has become a more important place in which learn how to cope with adversity. Many if not most children, adolescents, and young adults spend more time interacting with others in school than in any other place. Schools, therefore, can either increase or decrease students' abilities to manage adversity constructively. This does not mean that schools should be stress-free environments. Coping is not facilitated by a stress-free existence. Rather, facing stressful challenges and successfully dealing with them facilitates coping.

It is within schools that students are confronted with academic challenges that require considerable effort and commitment to complete successfully. It is within schools that relationship challenges are presented in the process of forming and maintaining relationships with peers and developing constructive patterns of interaction with authority figures. It is within schools that students are challenged by a multitude of conflicts with schoolmates and authority figures. It is within schools that value challenges occur as students decide whether to commit themselves to either (a) egocentric or even antisocial concerns or (b) concerns involving other people's welfare and the common good.

For students to cope with these challenges successfully and to transfer the strategies they learn to nonschool situations, three important conditions need to be met. First and foremost, the school must be a cooperative place in which students, faculty, and administrators work towards mutual goals. Caring and supportive interdependent relationships develop when cooperation is carefully structured at all levels in the school. Cooperative learning is especially important as it teaches students how to work together and inculcates important civic values. Second, students must know how to resolve conflicts constructively and to recognize the potential positive outcomes of conflicts. Many of the adverse events in a person's life involve conflicts with others and to maintain and deepen interdependent relationships the constructive resolution of conflict is essential. The more experience they get with resolving conflict constructively, the better off they tend to be in many ways. Third, students need to adopt a set of civic values that underlie community and democracy. Civic values guide and direct the cooperation and constructive conflict resolution. While each of the Cs may be implemented separately, together they represent a gestalt in which each enhances and promotes the others. Together the Three Cs are a complete programme for creating effective and nurturing schools where children and youth learn and develop in positive and healthy ways.

Educational practices come and go, but cooperative learning, constructive conflict, and civic values will always be with us for many reasons. The amount and consistency of research demonstrating the effectiveness of cooperative efforts, constructive controversy, and integrative negotiations are staggering. In schools where practice follows knowledge about effective teaching, the Three Cs are foundational. In addition, cooperative learning and constructive conflict are easily integrated with (and are in some cases a requirement for) other instructional practices such as mastery learning, effective elements of instruction, whole language, and critical thinking. Finally, the Three Cs Programme is an effective means of maximizing students' ability to cope successfully with stress and adversity and provides a foundation for other programmes aimed at doing so.

References

Achenbach, T. and Edelbrock, C. (1981). Behavioral problems and competencies reported by parents of normal and disturbed children aged four through sixteen. *Monographs of the Society for Research in Child Development*, **46**(1), Serial No. 188.

Asarnow, J. and Callan, J. (1985). Boys with peer adjustment problems: Social cognitive processes. *Journal of Consulting and Clinical Psychology*, **53**(1), 80–87.

Bonoma, T., Tedeschi, J., and Helm, B. (1974). Some effects of target cooperation and reciprocated promises on conflict resolution. *Sociometry*, **37**, 251–61.

Cantrell, V. and Prinz, R. (1985). Multiple perspectives of rejected, neglected, and accepted children: Relation between sociometric status and behavioral characteristics. *Journal of Consulting and Clinical Psychology*, **53**, 884–9.

Coie, J. and Kupersmidt, J. (1983). A behavioral analysis of emerging social status in boys' groups. *Child Development*, **54**, 1400–16.

Crombag, H. (1966). Cooperation and competition in means-interdependent triads: a replication. *Journal of Personality and Social Psychology*, **4**(6), 692–5.

Deutsch, M. (1949a). A theory of cooperation and competition. *Human Relations*, **2**, 129–52.

——— (1949b). An experimental study of the effects of cooperation and competition upon group processes. *Human Relations*, **2**, 199–231.

——— (1962). Cooperation and trust: Some theoretical notes, in M. R. Jones (ed.), *Nebraska symposium on motivation*, pp. 275–319. Lincoln, NE: University of Nebraska Press.

Deutsch, M. (1973). *The resolution of conflict*. New Haven, CT: Yale University Press.

Deutsch, M. and Krauss, R. M. (1962). Studies of interpersonal bargaining. *Journal of Conflict Resolutions*, **6**, 52–76.

Dodge, K. (1983). Behavioral antecedents of peer social status. *Child Development*, **54**, 1386–89.

——— (1985). The over-negativized conceptualization of deviance: A pragmatic exploration. *Deviant Behavior*, **6**, 17–37.

Dodge, K., Coie, J., and Bakke, N. (1982). Behavior patterns of socially rejected and neglected pre-adolescents: The roles of social approach and aggression. *Journal of Abnormal Child Psychology*, **10**, 389–409.

Fay, A. (1970). *The effects of cooperation and competition on learning and recall*. Unpublished master's thesis, George Peabody College.

French, J. (1951). Group productivity, in H. Guetzkow (ed.), *Groups, leadership and men*, pp. 44–55. Pittsburgh: Carnegie Press.

Glass, G., McGaw, B., and Smith, M. (1981). *Meta-analysis in social research*. Beverly Hills, CA: Sage Publications.

Grossak, M. (1953). Some effects of cooperation and competition upon small group behavior. *Journal of Abnormal and Social Psychology*, **49**, 341–48.

Horney, K. (1937). *The neurotic personality of our time*. New York: Norton.

Janke, R. (1980). Computational errors of mentally-retarded students. *Psychology in the Schools*, **17**, 30–2.

Johnson, D. W. (1970). *Social psychology of education*. New York: Holt, Rinehart, & Winston.

—— (1971). Role reversal: A summary and review of the research. *International Journal of Group Tensions*, **1**, 318–34.

—— (1973). Communication in conflict situations: A critical review of the research. *International Journal of Group Tensions*, **3**, 46–67.

—— (1974). Communication and the inducement of cooperative behavior in conflicts: A critical review. *Speech Monographs*, **41**, 64–78.

—— (2000). *Reaching out: Interpersonal effectiveness and self-actualization*, 7th edn. Boston: Allyn & Bacon.

Johnson D. W. and Johnson, F. (2000). *Joining together: Group theory and group skills*, 7th edn. Boston: Allyn & Bacon.

—— Johnson, R. (1979). Conflict in the classroom: Controversy and learning. *Review of Educational Research*, **49**, 51–61.

—— —— (1989). *Cooperation and competition: Theory and research*. Edina, MN: Interaction Book Company.

—— —— (1994). *Leading the cooperative school*, 2nd edn. Edina, MN: Interaction Book Company.

—— —— (1995*a*). *Teaching students to be peacemakers* 3rd edn. Edina, MN: Interaction Book Company.

—— —— (1995*b*). *Creative controversy: Intellectual challenge in the classroom*, 3rd edn. Edina, MN: Interaction Book Company.

—— —— (1995*c*). Teaching students to be peacemakers: Results of five years of research. *Peace and Conflict: Journal of Peace Psychology*, **1**(4), 417–38.

—— —— (1995*d*). Why violence prevention programmes don't work—and what does. *Educational Leadership*, **52**(5), 63–8.

—— —— (1996*a*). Conflict resolution and peer mediation programmes in elementary and secondary schools: A review of the research. *Review of Educational Research*, **66**(4), 459–506.

—— —— (1996*b*). Cooperative learning and traditional American values. *NASSP Bulletin*, **80**(579), 11–18.

—— —— (1999). Cooperative learning, values, and culturally plural classrooms, in M. Leicester, C. Modgill and S. Modgil, (eds.), *Values, the classroom, and cultural diversity*. London: Cassell PLC.

Johnson D. W. and Johnson, R. (2000). *Teaching students to be peacemakers: Results of twelve years of research*. Paper presented at the Society for the Psychological Study of Social Issues Convention, June (Submitted for publication).

—— —— and Holubec, E. (1998*a*). *Cooperation in the classroom*, 6th edn. Edina, MN: Interaction Book Company.

—— —— —— (1998*b*). *Advanced cooperative learning*, (3rd edn.) Edina, MN: Interaction Book Company.

—— —— Smith, K. (1998). *Active learning: Cooperation in the college classroom*, 2nd edn. Edina, MN: Interaction Book Company.

Kohn, A. (1997, February). How not to teach values: A critical look at character education. *Phi Delta Kappan*, 428–40.

Krauss, R. and Deutsch, M. (1966). Communication in interpersonal bargaining. *Journal of Personality and Social Psychology*, **4**, 572–77.

Lew, M., Mesch, D., Johnson, D. W., and Johnson, R. (1986*a*). Positive interdependence, academic and collaborative-skills group contingencies and isolated students. *American Educational Research Journal*, **23**, 476–88.

—— —— —— —— (1986*b*). Components of cooperative learning: Effects of collaborative skills and academic group contingencies on achievement and mainstreaming. *Contemporary Educational Psychology*, **11**, 229–39.

Montagu, A. (1966). *On being human*. New York: Hawthorn.

Putallaz, M. (1983). Predicting children's sociometric status from their behavior. *Child Development*, **54**, 1417–26.

Roff, J. and Wirt, R. (1984). Childhood aggression and social adjustment antecedents of delinquency. *Journal of Abnormal Child Psychology*, **12**(1), 111–26.

Seligman, M. (1988). Boomer blues. *Psychology Today*, **22**, 50–5.

Selman, R. (1981). The development of interpersonal competence: The role of understanding in conduct. *Departmental Review*, **1**, 401–22.

Slavin, R. (1977). *A student team approach to teaching adolescents with special emotional and behavioral needs*. Johns Hopkins University, Center for Social Organization of Schools, Report #227.

IMPACT OF CHILDHOOD ON ADULTHOOD

CHAPTER 11

SUCCESS AND ACHIEVEMENT: FACTORS THAT CONTRIBUTE TO POSITIVE OUTCOMES

ERICA FRYDENBERG

My interest in the type of success and achievement that is often linked to exceptional people was spurred on by a chance meeting with Atti,[1] a surgeon who was a distinguished medical professor and international philanthropist. He was the keynote speaker at a conference that I was attending as an accompanying spouse. Having been a researcher in the field of coping I was fascinated by his story. Born in Ethiopia, in 1942 in Chevo, Atti came from an isolated traditional village, 150 km from Addis Ababa, where there was no electricity or tap water. This village has a 'religious culture' with monasteries and churches in abundance. Atti stayed there until the age of seven, when he was sent to Addis Ababa to live in an uncle's home and to attend the French school for a few hours each day. When his mother came to visit some months later, he begged to return to be with his brothers and sisters. Back home he took care of sheep and cattle, travelling for two–three days at a time to tend the herds. At the age of eleven, he returned to Addis Ababa, to restart his schooling and moved through two grades at a time until he completed his Baccalaureate. When he was 20 his older brother died after a six-month illness. Not knowing why he died Atti decided to study medicine 'to help people escape death'. In Europe, he became an internationally eminent professor of surgery. He is guided by his father's philosophy 'don't try to move the mountain', that is, do something that you can really do. When one of his sons, a medical student, committed suicide, one of the ways he dealt with his loss was through forging further ahead in medicine and by producing a new medical invention in his field of specialization.

The lingering question for me was how unique was Atti's capacity to rise above circumstance to achieve success on the world stage? In an attempt to answer that question, and to understand how individuals attain exceptional heights in their fields of endeavour, be it in the arts, sports or commerce, a series of interviews[2] were conducted with a wide range of

---

[1] All names have been changed.

[2] The 1–2 hour interviews were conducted in the interviewee's setting of choice, home or workplace.

people deemed 'successful achievers'. The participants, ranging from early adulthood to mid-life, were generally known to the researcher, and were recruited to represent a wide range of endeavours. The interviews centred around the subjects' life experiences, and the coping strategies they used. Additionally, the aim was to understand how these achievers set goals and met challenges. Questions centred around their life histories, including their journey to success, their family and school life, the ways in which they coped, and how they dealt with obstacles and setbacks. The purpose of this chapter is to see how both the theories of human behaviour, along with the stories of high achievers contribute to our understanding of the factors that contribute to success. Coping and related theories are presented, followed by exerts from the life stories of the high achievers which explicate the theory.

The question whether exceptional achievement and the successful response to challenge is a matter of circumstance, ability, or a combination of factors, has fascinated psychologists for a long time. No single theory holds all the answers, but collectively they explain much of what can be gleaned from the life histories of high achievers. While theories of development help in our understanding of life stage transitions, the concept of coping provides many insights into the responses of individuals to their environment. Coping is a conceptual framework or heuristic device that allows us to explore the relationship between persons and their environments. From early psychodynamic theorists such as Haan (1977) who characterized people as 'copers' and 'defenders', through appraisal theorists such as Folkman and Lazarus (1988) to more recent resource theorists such as Hobfoll (1988, 1989, 1998) it has been possible to examine the qualities of human adaptation. Generally, this has been done by reviewing the coping actions of a set group of people, often those suffering from illness or disability, stress or depression, to see how they cope. A less frequently used approach is to examine those who are doing well, achieving beyond expectation, to see what are the characteristics of these people. Furthermore, how do these qualities inform us about the interplay between personal characteristics, such as ability and talent, and resources such as those amassed by the individual or available in the environment?

In addition to the most widely cited theories of coping such as the transactional model of Richard Lazarus, and the Conservation of Resources Model of Stevan Hobfoll, there are a range of theories that help us to understand how people achieve beyond what is expected on the basis of ability alone. First, there are our understandings about temperament and the interaction between nature and nurture (Rutter 1996; Prior 1992). Second, there is the concept of emotional intelligence (Goleman 1998; Salovey et al. 1999) and third, the concept of 'flow' (Csikszentmihalyi 1997), explains how people remain engaged in activities that become satisfying in their own right. Finally, there is the work of Carole Dweck (Dweck 1998) which explains how people become mastery oriented, seeing their abilities as malleable rather than becoming helpless and defeated.

Temperament

The major debate in human development has been the issue of the relative impact of heredity and environment. As Rutter (1996) pointed out, people act on their environments to shape and select their experience. They develop models rather than just react. But individual characteristics involve differences in reactivity to the environment. There is a two-way interplay between persons and their environments. People are both affected by their environments and in turn affect their environments. All behaviour has a biological base, much of which is genetic. However, genetic factors may not be a direct cause but provide potential risk factors, just as environmental aspects of a supportive milieu, coupled with positive personality characteristics, can provide the resiliency factors. Temperament refers to observable, stable, individual characteristics of behavioural style. These characteristics, or dispositions, are present from early in life; they are at least in part biologically driven and genetic in origin; and they persist over time and across situations. They are the foundations of what is later called personality (Prior 1992).

A study of Australian young people tracked 2000 subjects through a survey at each developmental stage of their life (Prior *et al.* 2000). The best predictors of coping were easy temperament as rated by teachers, the warmth of the mother–child relationship and the level of stress as perceived by the child. The temperament characteristics which emerged in a study of Prior *et al.* (2000) as predictors of easy coping were social responsiveness, lower levels of reactivity and distress, even-temperedness, and the capacity to draw people to them. These temperament characteristics were similar to those identified in other studies (Felsman and Vallant 1987; Rutter 1978; Werner and Smith 1982). Emotional responsiveness is a feature of emotional intelligence which in turn explains the capacity to be aware of one's emotions and that of others.

Emotional intelligence

According to Goleman (1998) emotional intelligence includes self-awareness and impulse control, persistence, zeal, self-motivation, empathy, and social expressiveness. He points out that IQ accounts for only 20 per cent of factors that determine success in life. Likewise, he asserts that academic intelligence has little to do with emotional life. A whole host of factors, including what he describes as emotional intelligence, account for the greater part of an individual's successful transition through life. He points out that there are different ways of being smart and emotional intelligence is one of them. The price of what he calls 'emotional illiteracy' is too high and can be seen in the levels of depression and despair experienced by people. Emotional intelligence is not fixed at birth, it can be nurtured and strengthened. While there is no emotional centre of the brain there are several systems or circuits that disperse regulation of a given emotion.

Emotional competence is made up of two major components, personal competence, and social competence, (Goleman 1998). The former includes self-awareness, self-regulation, and motivation. Motivation consists of achievement drive commitment, initiative, and optimism which involves pursuing goals despite setbacks. Personal competence includes emotional awareness or the recognition of how our emotions are affecting our performance; accurate self-assessment, a sense of our strengths and limits, and self-confidence that provides the courage to move forward based on 'certainty about capabilities, values and goals'. People with this type of competence 'know which emotions they are feeling and why, realize the links between their feelings and what they think, do and say, realize how their feelings affect their performance, and have a guiding awareness of their values and goals (p. 54)'.

Martin—property developer. Martin, a successful property developer in his late fifties, who has shaped the landscape of many urban communities, was born in a country town in moderately comfortable circumstances. He proudly describes his father's accomplishment as a shire engineer who succeeded in replacing all 101 wooden bridges in the town with steel ones. Nevertheless, there was never any pressure from either his father or his mother to succeed academically or commercially. 'Our happiness was always at the top of the list so there wasn't a lot of pushing.' He sees that an important element of his success is the ability to select people and to trust them, that is, people skills.

People will follow me. I've got guys around here who are getting their gold watches because they've been around that long. I'm the sort of person that wakes up when a guy's not getting enough and he's unhappy. I give him a raise before he has to come and ask you.

The social component of emotional competence determines how we handle relationships. This requires empathy, or the ability to recognize other's feelings or concerns. It also requires social skills which include conflict management and the ability to work with others and an ability to build bonds and nurture instrumental relations to achieve goals and objectives.

Andrew—indigenous doctor. Andrew, a 27-year-old indigenous Australian doctor (there were only 50 in the country when he graduated) grew up in an industrial city, completed medicine and has taken up a position in a Central Australian community with a large indigenous population and very scarce medical resources. Growing up as an indigenous Australian meant that he was at times confronted with injustice and racism. He describes the racism he has met as often being covert.

My skin's white. The racism that I experience is when people say whatever they want because they don't think that I'm Aboriginal. When I say that I am Aboriginal it completely turns on its end. The racism is not overt. People are trying to hide exactly what they're saying but I can see straight through it which is even more frustrating. I have come across racism on both sides in that I'm caught halfway between two cultures and sometimes I'm not accepted by either; other times I am. Often, I don't bring up my Aboriginality.

Emotional intelligence is evident in his handling of difficult situations. He demonstrates a capacity to be insightful and read the cues from others' reactions towards him, and respond appropriately. There is a different response to racial slurs depending on the setting. If Andrew is by himself he would say 'cut that out'. When he is with other people he would think about it first. He is inclined to 'switch off'. 'There's only so much you can hear, and sometimes it's easy enough to turn away.' He has never been in a fight in his life, something completely 'unheard of' in the working class environment in which he grew up. Generally, he can argue with the best of them. He has always been able to deal with situations verbally. He considers the capacity to have the language to respond when challenged is a major asset.

The concept of flow

Why it is that some gifted and talented people pursue their goals and others fall by the way-side is further explained by the concept of 'flow' (Csikszentmihalyi 1997). The exceptional moments when what we feel, wish, and think are in harmony has been labelled 'flow'. It is an effortless action which stands out as best, such as an award winning performance for an athlete or artist. Flow and complexity are regarded as sustaining talent and providing an 'optimal experience' (Csikszentmihalyi 1990). Flow is a subjective state that people report when they are completely involved in something to the point of total engrossment, where time may appear to 'stand still' and the activity becomes all important, such as being engrossed in a novel, playing sport, having a conversation and so on (Csikszentmihalyi *et al.* 1993). It is the depth of involvement that is intrinsically rewarding. Flow usually begins when a person takes on tasks or challenges just above his or her skill level. This leads to complexity and the individual needs to find new challenges and perfect new skills in order to avoid anxiety. The duality between actor and action disappears. When one does what needs to be done without conscious effort this can distort the sense of time. The activity becomes autotelic, that is, worth doing for its own sake. (See also Chapter 5 in this volume.)

IQ alone is no guarantee of achievement. While gifted young people often display a single-minded perseverance with which they pursue their talents, Albert and Runco (1986), Bloom (1985), and Rimm (1991) have shown that without 'dedicated parents, savvy coaches and mentors, good schools and challenging opportunities to express their gifts' (Csikszentmihalyi *et al.* 1993, p. 2), it is very difficult for teenagers to persist in the demanding discipline that the cultivation of talent requires.

Martin, the developer, went to boarding school. His brother who was six years older, succeeded in school and subsequently become an academic. At school Martin was neither successful academically nor was he successful at sport. He left school at 16 but never saw himself as a failure. 'My mother gave me belief in my self, by treating me as special every day of my life. I got from her a real belief in myself.'

The questions that are often asked are, to what extent do events interfere with the discipline that any talent eventually entails? How do young people become committed to their talent and why do some young people disengage from their talent?

Attention as psychic energy is a limited resource; we can only deal with one demanding task at a time (Csikszentmihalyi 1990). Thus, it has been suggested that gifted people need to reduce daily hassles. The individual has clear goals and needs to receive unambiguous feedback. Self-esteem is the ratio of expectation to success. Csikszentmihalyi *et al.* (1993) provide a summary of factors associated with talent development based on extensive research with this population of young people. Gifted young people have skills considered useful in their culture; they have personality traits conducive to concentration (e.g. achievement and endurance), openness to experience (e.g. awareness or sentience), and understanding. Their habits are conducive to cultivating talent (e.g. less time socializing and hanging out with friends). Finally they generally have families that provide both support and opportunities to enhance the development of talent.

Both of the high achievers so far mentioned, Martin and Andrew, have skills that are valued in their culture, personality traits exemplifying endurance and perseverance, and families who support the development of their talent.

Robyn—concert pianist. Another remarkable achiever, Robyn, an Australian born concert pianist, was acclaimed as a child prodigy at the age of three. She has personality characterisitcs conducive to talent development, along with having the support of her family and teachers. After performing for Arthur Rubenstein at the age of five, Rubenstein proposed that an American philanthropist support her American and European education.

She studied at the Curtis Institute of Music in Philadelphia (gaining her Bachelor's degree at 17 as well as the Festorazzi award, the Institute's highest award for Outstanding Pianist). She subsequently attended the Juillard School in New York, where she received her Masters degree by age 21. Robyn made her American debut with the Detroit symphony at age 10 and performed with the Philadelphia Orchestra at 11. She has since performed with many of the leading orchestras and conductors and given recitals in most countries of Europe, North and South America, Canada, China, and Australia. She has performed twice for presidents of the US.

Robyn sees her Romanian mother as the 'key person' in her life. Her Polish father met her mother during the Second World War and they lived together in Russia, where her sister was born. Her parents separated before she went to the US. Her brother was born in Austria, in the post war refugee camps and Robyn was born in Australia. There are twelve years between the siblings. Her entire family is musical. Her brother is a conductor and a violinist, and her sister a pianist. Music was constant in the home and it was regarded as 'normal'. Her lessons began when she was two-and-a-half. She gave her first public performance on the ABC [Australian Broadcasting Commission] at three-and-a-half years of age. She describes herself as being precocious academically, having skipped two grades during her primary school years.

She describes the music culture in the US as a high pressured 'hot house' environment which was both competitive and demanding. Students felt that they were on probation from the day they were accepted into the school until the day they left. They could be expelled until the day before graduation if it was not thought that you were up to the standard. Of the 160 applicants who were chosen to audition, two were accepted. While she felt 'privileged', she also felt 'pressured'. One of her mother's sayings helped her to cope, 'How do you eat an elephant—a bite at a time'. She learned to tackle each new score bit by bit. Her mother gave her the message that she should enjoy her music. 'Play was a four letter word', according to her mother who was her piano teacher in her early years. There was an emphasis on taking responsibility for one's own life and work.

She describes herself as having '*slogged* through every lesson, every day, every performance, every expectation'. When she did not feel that a performance had been a success she said to herself , 'Next time it'll be better, someone else will understand what I'm trying to achieve'.

In her adolescence and beyond, successes were more frequent than setbacks.

As a child prodigy, whatever you do, if you're doing it well, it's accepted as being wonderful because you're young. As an adult one starts to compete with people, 50, 60, 70 who have a world of experience. People expect you to fizzle out as a child prodigy, and don't expect you to make the transition. It's only the mentally tough and healthy who make that transition.

Robyn utilizes her positive self-talk and has a capacity to retain confidence even after a bad performance. She has experienced setbacks in her musical career and in her life in general. Post Julliard she fought for 'musical independence', that is, to establish her own approach and to express her own ideas. She was invited to record with a major symphony orchestra but a week after the audition she put her hand through a window and cut it badly. The recording was to be five weeks later. She was determined, and took a risk by taking her cast off to practice within a week. This, she says, turned out to be good fortune, because, if the cast had been left on longer, there would have been adhesions.

She recorded with one symphony orchestra and was asked to do another recording with another major orchestra. Because of the excessive hours of practice, she developed carpal tunnel syndrome that required three operations as part of the treatment. She was not going to let operations be a setback. When a tram hit the back of her car she suffered a severe back injury. While in hospital, the orchestra asked her to play Gershwin's Rhapsody in Blue and she accepted, despite having only three weeks to prepare.

I didn't tell them that I was flat on my back in hospital and that I had learnt it on an electronic keyboard with headphones while lying on my back. The concert went really well. I just slogged through things. I am very determined, and always find ways around things.

Mindset

The impact of mindset on achievement is demonstrated by Dweck. Dweck (1998) gives clear guidelines as to the experiences that develop helplessness rather than a sense of mastery with a belief that abilities are changeable (see also Chapters 7 and 11 in this volume). She points out that it is the rewarding of effort rather than labelling of talents or abilities that determines motivation and how goals are achieved. Perception of the self is determined by feedback after completing tasks. Rather than praise for speed and perfection, there needs to be acknowledgement of effort (see also Chapters 7 and 11 in this volume).

Tania—marathon swimmer. Tania, a marathon swimmer in her early thirties, who has had many successes, including swimming Manhattan, Loch Ness and the English Channel,[3] described her plans for the Murray River swim,[4]

I'll give it my 'best shot'. There are no real failures, there are just new learning experiences. If I don't make this Murray swim I'll reassess and look at where I went wrong. I might even look at doing it again, seeing what I can do to make myself better. It's all about *improving* yourself.

She also talks about knowing when to give up and does not see herself as a loser. When she swam Port Phillip Bay she was stuck 5 km away from the finish.

I wasn't moving because of the tide and had to pull out of that swim, but I went back the following day and I completed the last 5 km for my own peace of mind. There are no failures. You just go back and give it your best.

....

[3] In 1998 she broke a record by swimming 40 laps at Bondi Beach (a 40 km swim). The following year she swam across Cook Strait in New Zealand setting a new world record. Followed by another swimming race in Manhattan, New York in which she was placed second. She was planning the Murray river swim. The 2400 km would take about three months. Her longest previous swim was when she circumnavigated Port Phillip Bay, a swim of 144 km taking 21 h.

[4] Now successfully completed after several setbacks and delays to the start because of the weather.

She was disappointed, but described how one could swim the same stretch of water four or five times and each time it can be different. She construes these variations as 'nature throwing up challenges'. After a loss or setback there is no self-recrimination or self-blame.

I always have to be prepared for something to happen that's out of my hands. That swim was taken out of my hands because the tide had changed and we hadn't anticipated that. At the end of the day I'm very happy because it was the longest swim I've ever done. The longest I had done before was 90 km, so I had extended myself to 144 km.

Tania learned to set goals, review progress and accept failure through her training programme. When she was 13 she had a coach who was a former Olympic water polo player. Learning to deal with failure was a gradual process. The swimmers had to keep a logbook which in which they recorded and gave a rating of their own performance in the training session. They would record how they felt and what they wanted to improve. There were swimming competitions and the swimmers would write down their comments to the coach and the coach would write a response.

When there were losses, parents were waiting with open arms to say 'You gave it your best, let's look at what you're going to do next'. When she first learnt to swim she did not want to go to the pool, because she was overweight, which made her the butt of teasing at school. Although the successful achievers never describe themselves as victims, she describes the teasing as having left a scar. She had to make adjustments, such as getting her mother to make her clothes, because she was self-conscious about going shopping. In contrast, at the swimming pool she found a good atmosphere where the teachers were positive. She never felt 'put-down', nor did she have any negative comments directed towards her. People were positive because they saw that she had the desire to do it. Although initially she did not like to be there, she said to herself, 'I'm here: I may as well make the most of it'. Her teachers saw that she was always willing 'to give it a go'. 'Give it the best shot' is her prevailing motivational and self-affirming expression. Because she was willing to give it a go, she found the teachers to be very encouraging.

Perseverance is a feature of how she deals with setbacks. She joined the surf life-saving club to find new challenges. She thrived on the new opportunities to develop her skills in the water. She made it a goal to be able to paddle a Malibu board because she described herself as having 'no balance'. She remembers the first season when she competed in the iron woman competition.[5] Throughout the year she had won that competition when the conditions were calm and she was able to stay on the board. The day of the Victorian championships turned out to be rough. She fell off the board so many times that she ended up coming last. Everyone said, 'You haven't mastered the Malibu'. She was there the entire winter 'getting on that board' and practising in rough water to help her overcome the failure of not being able to stay on.

---

[5] An ironwoman competition is a combination of three water events. There is a swim leg which is about 400 m, followed by a Malibu board leg and finally a ski leg. The Malibu and the ski leg are about 800 m of paddling and in between you have to run along the beach, pick up your next piece of apparatus. So it takes probably about 15–20 min to complete the event. It is quite a gruelling event which is in the upper echelon of competition in surf lifesaving.

Stress and coping

Along with the theories of talent development two major theories of stress and coping help explain how people deal with their environments. The first is the transactional model of stress. For Lazarus and his colleagues, who have remained at the forefront of stress and coping research for several decades, the theory of stress and coping is predicated on the person–environment interaction model that posits that the individual is in an ongoing interaction with the environment. Thus, in any encounter, the person and the environment are in a dynamic relationship and the demands upon the individual change during the course of the encounter (Folkman and Lazarus 1985, 1988). This model recognizes that people both shape and respond to their environments. Strategies that are often identified in the coping literature such as working hard, focusing on the positive, and dealing with problems directly, are generally adopted by the successful achievers in many spheres of endeavour. In contrast, the nonproductive strategies such as self-blame, tension reduction, and keeping to oneself are not a feature of their lives. There is generally a move away from self-blame and an ability to see positive outcomes despite adverse circumstances. (see also Chapter 9 for the impact of self-blame).

Doug—a business man. Doug, a successful business man who was not a high academic achiever in school, accepted the presidency of a football club that quickly reached the top of the league. Like others interviewed, Doug described himself as having more opportunities than setbacks. When he described a business failure, he did not blame himself for the outcome. He used positive reframing and externalized the event. He described a setback from the early 1990s when he became Executive Chairman of a meatwork business and appointed a CEO who had worked for the family for many years to operate the business. When that did not work out he had to run the business with his brother. When that also was not a success he did not blame himself, but rather the economic and industrial circumstances that surrounded the failure.

The whole industry was going through a rough time, with unions, the dollar was down, it was just all bad. It didn't work. It was a setback in terms of my own pride that it wasn't a success.

Responding to challenges requires a positive mindset. When the 'gauntlet is down' there is a keenness to take up the challenge. Doug did that when he accepted the presidency of the ailing football club, which was then at the bottom of the league.

Why would any sensible fellow put his hand up to take control, or take the number one job in a club that was about to fold? It was my willpower, my own challenge, pushing myself to say 'let's go and give it a go'. When someone said to me 'Club x, no players, no money, no hope' those words are very vivid in my mind. I'm going to prove that we do have players, hope etc. So in some ways I do react to comments or challenges made. I may not disclose it at the time but I do respond to challenging words.

Risk and resilience

The question as to why some people cope despite adversity and others do not, is explained in part by the way the risk factors and protective factors work together to facilitate or inhibit adaptation. There are both risk and protective factors inherent in adaptation. Risk factors are those things that threaten well-being and their capacity for continuing adaptive development. Risk factors include: parental conflict, separation and divorce, chronic illness in child or parent, poverty and social disadvantage, and race. It is clear from the stories of successful achievers that each had been subject to some risk factors. However, it is the protective factors that appear to play a significant part in achieving success. Two classes of protective factors have been studied. There are the intrinsic or intrapersonal factors, believed to be constitutional in large part, such as personality, temperament and intelligence, and extrinsic or environmental influences such as a caring family, the availability of social supports, or caring mentors, positive school experiences, and strong attachments. The interaction of these factors has been demonstrated as an important element of coping and resilience (Rutter 1983, 1990). Each of the high achievers has both intrinsic and extrinsic resources to help them deal with setbacks.

Support, often spiritual and generally social, can be construed as a key protective factor. For example, Martin describes his mother as 'incredibly Christian'. She would leave soup for poor people in the neighbourhood. Church and Sunday school was part of his childhood.

Doug relies on the family's input, saying that 'two heads are better than one'. The support network amongst the family was evident when the family sat down and talked about issues and achieved solutions 'even when not setting out to do that'. He saw the opportunities to sit and talk about what was happening in the business as a source of 'mental strength'. Since running his own business he misses 'the sitting around and talking and sharing'.

An additional source of support for Doug is the Forum group which emerged from the Young Presidents organization.[6] The group was made up of seven men who had been together for nearly 12 years. They meet every six weeks and there is complete confidentiality. It provides an opportunity to 'take your mask off, to take off the veil, to talk about your own issues, your own self, and talk about your real feelings and thoughts.' He went on to explain that at first they would meet 'just to talk' and that was invigorating without being threatening.

With men there's a lot of frustration built up simply because we can't sit down and talk about the issues. I draw on the values I've been brought up with and then go and talk to the Forum group. I might say 'it's not my problem, it's the organization's problem so I'm going to share it with everyone'. It gets back to fundamental values. At the football club, or with my own investment company, the buck really stops with me. I do have people there who can share the load, so I'm learning. 'Don't take it on yourself, share the issues around'.

I believe in the glass table. If you have an issue and you keep it under the table you can't see it or touch it so it can't be deal with. I say at every meeting 'put the issue on the table because then we can all see it and deal with it and move it. You're not going to get rid of it by ignoring it'.

Given that both risk and resiliency factors have featured in the lives of the remarkable achievers, it seems helpful to look to other paradigms that may explain how they cope and

---

[6] An international organization of business and coorporate achievers who reach heights of success at an early age.

why they are not stopped in their endeavours through adversity. The Conservation of Resources (COR) model (Hobfoll 1989) is one such model.

Resource theory

COR theory is based on a single motivational tenet that individuals strive to obtain, retain, and protect that which they value. Stress occurs when resources are actually lost, threatened or when the individual invests resources without getting adequate returns. When there is adequate return for investment the resource pool is built up, self-esteem, and confidence are boosted.

Resources are defined as objects such as possessions which are valued for their physical nature, but they can often be associated with socio-economic status or status in general. There are personal characteristics such as, seeing things as predictable and happening in one's best interest, being optimistic, having mastery, conditions such as, marriage, employment, tenure, or promotion. Finally, there are resources associated with energy, such as networks, power, money, time, and knowledge that allow you to obtain other resources. COR theory posits that people do not wait for disaster to strike, they invest in resources, that is, take out insurance. For example, people purchase future protection by investing time and energy in relationships.

People strive to develop a resource surplus to offset the possibility of future loss. Resource surpluses are likely to be associated with eustress (positive well-being) rather than distress. Self-protection is about trying to protect against resource loss. We invest time and energy and love and affection in the expectation of the return of the same. Power and money are important resources that allow us to accumulate other resources. The concept of loss is central to COR theory. It posits that gain is important, but secondary to loss. Most severe stress events are loss events. However, with COR theory there is the notion that individuals can shift the focus of attention from loss by reinterpreting threat as a challenge.

This is essentially a ledger view of stress and coping which has its basis in existential and biological theories of human adaptation. It is the resource side of the ledger that needs to be monitored so that it can be augmented to a level that provides protection and enables advancement (see also Chapter 9 in this volume).

We have emphasized the homeostatic aspect of coping and the attempt to remove the discomfort or feeling of turbulence and restore the individual's sense of well being or equilibrium (Frydenberg and Lewis 1993). While it is true that it is difficult to predict or identify that which is going to restore the equilibrium for an individual, nevertheless, it seems clear that there are efforts to remove the discomfort and these efforts can be called coping. The attempts are made up of thoughts, feelings, and actions. In the same way, the efforts to conserve resources could be regarded as attempts to maintain the equilibrium for the individual, as is the search for meaning or the attempts to retain coherence.

It is interesting to consider whether there is a point on the balance sheet which indicates whether a person has enough credits in the resource pool to render them resilient. The expectation is that it is a matter of appraisal, whether we see our resources as adequate or not. Thus, temperament and personality characteristics play an important part. All those interviewed felt that they had a strong support system in the form of a parent, teacher, or coach. They also had an enthusiasm and passion for their pursuits which in turn was determined both by environmental opportunities and personality traits. They tended to see fortune rather than misfortune. Not all were successful at school, nor did all of them have their talents recognized and nurtured by an external other. Over and above, their opportunities and circumstance they demonstrated a capacity to maintain momentum and move forward despite adversity.

Tania, the long distance swimmer, had to deal with many setbacks out of the water. Her mother and sister were involved in a car accident which placed her mother in hospital for several months 'with her kneecap smashed in 20 pieces and her ankle obliterated'. Her father was critically ill while she was training to swim around Manhattan Island, but he encouraged her to do the swim. After her father's death, which came shortly after her swim, she reflected on all the things she should or shouldn't have done, but tried to stop herself by thinking 'well you can't change anything, it's over and it's gone'. Rather, she focuses on the positive. There is a general reframing of events to produce helpful outcomes.

The two things I look at are: we had that time together, and that I was able to get my brother and sister on the phone and get them to the hospital, and Dad acknowledged the fact that we were all there. Generally I try and look at things and see that there are always people in worse situations than myself. We tend to get caught up in our own problems. There are always inspirational people around us and I try and draw on people around me and look at different things, watching TV, reading, and seeing people who have overcome difficulties.

Justin—tennis player. Similarly, Justin, a tennis player, used the strategy of comparing himself to others who are worse off. Having spent his early years in a north Queensland country town, Justin's ambition was to move on to escape 'the dullness' of his hometown. His tennis prowess took him to the Australian Institute of Sport in Canberra at the age of 15, where he concentrated on singles competitions until he was 20. His parents divorced during that time. In doubles he was ranked in the top two on the international circuit. He learned to deal with losses early in his career.

As a tennis player you are guaranteed to lose every week of the year. You always look to the tournament next week. It makes you more motivated if you have setbacks early in your career. I try and turn it around and make myself more determined. I was probably more hungry[7] when I was younger; my livelihood depended on it. If I didn't win I wasn't going to be really able to travel and do what I loved doing. I had a lot of negativity stored up inside me, and I just used that to try and succeed by just reminding myself of where I've come from and where I really wanted to be, just trying to get out of that whole negative circle of life that I was in. I kept saying 'I don't want to go back to town X'. I knew there was a lot more out there and I really wanted to see it and get out there.

He has a capacity to reframe his threats as challenges. When talking about his involvement in the share market he describes the challenge of clawing his investment back.

The only way you're going to get the most out of yourself is by putting yourself on the line. For example when I play golf I have to be playing for big things to challenge me. When I was 18, my

---

[7] An expression associated with motivation in the tennis world.

coach said 'why don't you put $50 in and winner takes all'. It was a great way to learn how to handle pressure. In tennis you get into many situations when you just don't think you can do it and at the end of the day you can. When you're doing something you really love you give it 100 per cent.

While theories of stress generally focus on how an individual reacts to environmental demands, according to COR theory people assert themselves proactively. There is a capacity to be both proactive and to externalize. That is, people can anticipate the future and externalize the negative outcomes of the present.

Raima—visual disability. Raima, 34, was born with a visual impairment and lost all her sight at the age of 25. She spent her childhood in the Western suburbs of Sydney where the family lived in public housing. Her father, who died when she was nine years of age, was Sri Lankan, and her mother Australian. After several positions as a telephonist–receptionist in the government sector, she went to university at the age of 25, and graduated with Honours. She now has her 'dream job' teaching Braille at an Institute for the Blind.

When looking for employment she applied for many positions in the government sector and explains her lack of success as partly discrimination, because she had a disability, partly because she was a woman, and partly because she was 'uneducated'. By aspiring for higher educational goals she saw herself as working towards something that she could change, whilst she could not change her gender or disability.

She was sexually abused between 11 and 15 years of age. Following her realization that incest was wrong (after revealing the events to her boyfriend of the time) she went through a long period of guilt. Her search for a way to understand the situation helped her to overcome self-blame.

People were telling me there was no need to feel guilty. People who knew about it would say things like 'you don't need to feel guilty, you were just a child', but none of this convinced me. One friend just said 'you got yourself into a situation not knowing the circumstances and then you couldn't get out because you did know the circumstances'. And for me that just clicked. It was a good way of thinking about it and it made sense to me.

When describing how she coped with school and university it was evident that she had the capacity to be assertive whilst both utilizing and amassing resources. She found the work very easy at the primary school level because there was a 'lower expectation of the students' in the Special School that she attended. The idea was 'well you're blind, you'll probably finish school and go to a sheltered workshop or have a switchboard job'. It was easier to cater for the students who could not keep up. When she went to high school she was integrated into a regular high school and that was difficult at first because she had a lot of ground to make up. In a sighted classroom, with 30 sighted children, where teachers were writing on the blackboard and the text and handouts were in print, there was a lot to cope with. She would do her work in Braille and then the specialist teacher would write over it in print. She would then hand it back to the teacher for marking. There was a need to educate the teachers. They had to read what was on the board. She asked for assistance when stuck. For example, she asked teachers to draw the diagrams of the trigonometry exercises with her fingers. Although she found the teachers to be creative, she had to ask for assistance and give them suggestions.

Raima describes herself as a 'very determined' person who enjoys learning. Motivation and organizational skills are her key resources. To access information, such as printed handouts, text books, overheads, diagrams on the board, she arranged to meet with her lecturers beforehand and explained to them what her needs were and asked them to accommodate her by making adjustments. She told them that they could help her by reading what was on overheads, reading what they had written on the board, and giving them to her in advance so she could get them in Braille. She approached the disability liaison officer, who suggested getting a classroom support person who could whisper the content of the visual materials to her.

She'd whisper in English and then I'd have to have the Spanish knowledge to try and answer the questions. I arranged to get the literature in Braille, in subjects like Spanish and Linguistics. I arranged to get a lot of Philosophy lectures on cassette. Sometimes there was a delay because it took a long time to put things into Braille or on tapes so I had to be very organized. I had to rely on others to photocopy and have my readers read to me. I organized a network of readers. I asked the disability liaison officer if she could put up signs in the union building in different departments advertising for students. People responded to that. I had about 6–8 students as volunteer readers as well as the Institute for the Blind's volunteer reader. I would meet with my readers in a small room in the library and they would read the handouts onto tape or read it to me in Braille, depending on what the subject was. So I had to be very organized because I had 6–8 readers to keep to a detailed schedule, to know that I was meeting Ruth at 1 p.m. on Mondays, and Jane Tuesdays at 4 p.m., or whatever. I had to help them to know what to do, because some of them were very nervous. So I said 'sit down and read it and I'll tell you if you're being too detailed or not detailed enough'. So I made them feel comfortable and got from them what I needed.

Petra—entrepreneur. For others, self-protection was achieved by going on the offensive. When it comes to dealing with rejection or bullying which could be construed as a potential loss of resources, there is a guarding of one's esteem by avoiding becoming the victim. Petra, Young Australian of the Year, a business executive who had been on a much publicized roller coaster ride when at the age of 26 her business went into receivership, emerged again as a high profile corporate CEO. She described her days in the schoolyard.

The playground's pretty brutal from the point of view of self-esteem. It's very much a survival of the fittest and I was very aware of that. I really had to push myself. I felt that if I let go at any stage I would be the girl being teased. So I ended up being the teaser to make sure that I wasn't the one being teased.

Her father became sick when she was five and died two years later. She was asked to leave the girls' private school at the age of 12 and describes herself as being different in that school. Anytime she did something bad 'it was seen as ten times worse than anyone'. Eventually they just said, 'We'd prefer it if you weren't here'. Her mother, however, saw 'being different' as something to be proud of. She saw her daughter as a 12-year-old who was exhibiting signs of special qualities, and at other times was just being silly and naughty. Her mother told her that sometimes it is 'a badge of honour' *not* to fit in.

When it comes to dealing with disasters Petra says that she becomes 'hysterical', cries, rings her friends, digests the fact that her worst fear is going to happen' and then from that point everything seems to be an improvement on the situation. 'Any little win from that point, seems fantastic.'

I never understood how people could get through the Holocaust. What these stories made me understand is that you can adjust your quality of life. What became a good day during internment was just a day they weren't shot or gassed, and so they didn't have any more hope for anything beyond that. A good day during that receivership or that whole process was just a day where I'd find something to laugh about, or a day that the whole thing hadn't collapsed. There was still some hope. When things didn't collapse, that was a good day.

There is a personal capacity to rise to the challenge.

No matter how upset I am, or how hysterical, or how everything is caving in on me, I've never actually said 'no I can't do something'. I always find the strength to do whatever it is. In the middle of the receivership, I had journalists chasing me down lanes, business partners trying to get me bankrupted; at the same time I was launching the lingerie range. One of the people who'd been advising me about the process, ended up having a 'mental breakdown'. He had bipolar disorder which I wasn't aware of. I had to get him arrested because he was suicidal. On top of that it looked like my business was going to collapse and I was going to lose my house and have no money. I had been on the phone to the receiver and then to the police because of my adviser. At the same time his father was ringing up abusing me I had to go and compère a lingerie fashion parade in front of all these people at a large Department store and talk about lingerie. Even though I was hysterical before I went to compere the parade, absolutely hysterical in my office, bawling my eyes out, I went. When it really comes to it, I can do it; as long as I get it out, I can do it.

Resources are construed as things that are valued. However, under threat, an effective way of coping is to construe the loss as being of little value or replaceable. Petra describes the reason she coped during the period when her business was collapsing was due to the way she appraised the situation.

All I had on the line was financial risk, and my reputation, which are two things I felt I could always rebuild. I didn't really care about the idea of losing status, or fame, or money, and I think that gave me a feeling of freedom, because if you don't care about those things, they don't become such a pressure.

For some, like Andrew, the indigenous doctor, rather than being on the offensive it is a matter of turning a blind eye. For others there was some reproach for personal failing but it was never excessive and it was associated with a challenge to the self, leading to an increased effort.

Jason—script writer. Jason, a comedy script writer and journalist who has published pieces in the daily press, is at the age of 22 a producer of a commercial radio show, his first job after finishing a bachelor's degree. Jason describes himself as not having setbacks but rather as having 'opportunities'. As a burgeoning writer, however, there were always rejections of submitted work. To him a setback is 'just an opportunity to take a different path to maybe a different destination'.

His secondary school, had a heavy bias towards academic pursuits. But when it comes to something that is highly valued in the culture, such as sport, he describes himself as a failure. He sees his failure at sport as one of the banes of his existence, not having had the will or interest to pursue sport.

There's always the feeling that if other people are doing it, and if it's a bonding thing for them, then you're missing out if you're not doing it. I felt an outsider in terms of sports. It was a recurring troubling theme, a consistent source of concern, just a niggling thorn in my side.

His overriding emotion was reproach, along with 'dumbstruck fascination' with why it was important in the first place to be good at sport followed by a 'slight resentment' at the fact that sport is an important part of growing up and achieving one's identity. Nevertheless, he poured all the more effort into the things he was good at, to make them more notable. He focused on academic pursuits to fill the vacuum that the lack of sporting prowess had left.

Justin, the tennis player had a setback at 17 when he developed a major disorder.

When you're 17 you think you're invincible. I realized how fragile life can be. I was glad something like that happened to me because it put what I was doing in my life into perspective. It took about a year to come to terms with my illness. It changed my mood and personality. It put a lot of uncertainty about whether I would still be able to play tennis, or how it would limit my life. I dealt with it by talking to different people who had had the same illness and I went to seminars about it.

Optimism

Although Martin Seligman (1992, 1995) describes us as living in an age of melancholy in which depressed explanatory style has preoccupied our research efforts, he also points out that one third of the population are deemed to be resilient. It is clear that optimists do better than pessimists and optimism can be learned. Optimism and pessimism are defined by adaptive versus negative patterns of explanatory style. Optimists expect good outcomes, pessimists expect bad outcomes. Twin studies show explanatory style is subject to genetic influences (Plomin et al. 1992, Schulman et al. 1991). Nevertheless, studies with adolescents and preadolescents indicate that when young people are shown how they can develop a positive explanatory style they do so (Brandon et al. 1999; Bugalski and Frydenberg 2000; Cunningham et al. in press). Optimism and pessimism is a continuum. The constructs can be measured (Peterson and Seligman 1984) and are deemed to remain constant throughout the lifespan if there is no attempt at intervention (Burns and Seligman 1989).

There is convincing evidence that optimism is helpful under adversity. There is substantial evidence in the medical arena. For example, optimists recovering from coronary by-pass surgery, (Scheier et al. 1986) one day before and six months post surgery, reported lower levels of depression and hostility and more relief and happiness. In another coronary artery by-pass surgery study (Fitzgerald et al. 1993) one month before and eight months after, it was found that optimism was negatively related to presurgical distress and positively related to post-surgical life situation. A study of women in the early stages of breast cancer (data was collected at, diagnosis, on the day before surgery, 7–10 days after surgery and 3, 6, and 12 months later) showed optimism predicted lower initial distress and resilience to distress during the year following surgery (Carver and Gaines 1993). In a study of infertility (Scheier *et al.* 1986) pessimism was strongest predictor of distress on the second occasion.

Doug, the businessman describes seeing his glass as being half full rather than half empty. Justin, the tennis player, describes himself as learning to lose every day of his life and still going out to play the next match. Robyn, the concert pianist, who had been in and out of hospital with a back injury for several years, having received various treatments and epidurals, describes *in vitro* fertilization (IVF) which went on for nine years, as the most difficult to endure but was able to reframe it positively. When she miscarried at ten weeks she was really 'excited'. Everybody thought she must be really depressed. Instead, she said,

This is great, it's a sign of success! That is how I coped. The miscarriage was terrible for me, it was devastating, but it was also a sign of success. I could taste the possibility of success and it just spurred me further. When I'm low I work out how I'm going to come out, how it's going to be better.

Last year has been one of the worst of my life. I contracted a virus from my daughter that gave me rheumatoid arthritis which has just cut me flat for nine months. I use the same approach to get through performances, this virus, or IVF, I focus on positive outcomes. It's the projection of how it's going to feel when you've succeeded. Specifically, when I'm playing, and very nervous about it (you should be nervous to do it well, it's a normal part of it), I make myself as nervous as possible at the piano during the rehearsal so that on stage I do the reverse, I make myself as calm as possible. The piano looks the same, the music is the same. I flip it and it becomes normal and comfortable on stage, just as it became normal to be nervous at rehearsals.

Livia—a court judge. Livia, a 47-year-old judge, did not skip grades but progressed through her schooling at an early age and seemed to both make and benefit from the opportunities that led to her successful career as a court judge. Livia was 18 months younger than others in her class throughout her schooling. She went to university at 16 and became a lawyer at 20. She was a frail child during her first six years of school and she missed several months of schooling each year before reaching sixth grade. She describes herself as being regarded as 'bright but not exceptional'.

She has been a barrister and a prosecuting attorney in Hong Kong, and has spent ten years in the Magistrate's Court and the Children's Court, the Crimes Court and the Adult Criminal Courts. She describes herself as having a 'very fast paced career', which began when her parents 'pushed' her out of the house at the age of three or four. She is married, with two sons, 14 and 11.

I am very, very organized. If there's a problem with my work I get it done. I approached university very much like a working day. Even if I had one lecture in the day, I'd do a 9–5 day, and still have plenty of time for having a wild time. University was a wonderful time.

Her mother died of cancer at age 47. Although the youngest in the family, she felt a responsibility to look after everybody else, and keep managing.

I put on a very strong coping act. I was very worried that I was going to be the only one left at home to be with my father. I was 17. On the morning my mother died I was the one who organized the death notice and all those sorts of things. I coped by just getting on with things. Which I now say is not the best way of coping. That was all I had in my armoury at 17. We were all very close to her and I think that was all I could do to keep going.

When it comes to coping with a massive workload Livia sees things in bite-sized chunks.

It might have been that I had a particular goal for that year or for that term or that week because I notice now, that no matter how much everything is falling part around me domestically, if my goal is that I've got to write a particular judgement by a particular time, no one else can control it in the sense that I'm the judge. If I don't get it written then they have to wait. When I have a goal, I just do it.

She did not feel that there were high expectations on her because she shared her family's expectations. It was never a pressure.

I have one child who is incredibly like me. He's so self-motivated that he's not pressured by anyone except himself. I think that's the way it was for me.

She made the opportunities come her way. After six years as a barrister she wanted to move on, but it wasn't happening, so she applied for a Fellowship.

It brought me to the attention of the Chief Justice. I was looking for a solution. How can I fix this? And I was frustrated because for the first time in my life it didn't get fixed immediately. It took a few years and by that time I was seeing 'head hunters' (employment people) and looking at completely different careers. Lawyers would not normally see 'head hunters'. They would say, should I be doing an MBA [Master of Business Administration] or other form of study.

She describes her best achievement so far as being the children. It has been 'the best, the hardest, the most heartache, and the most joy'. Family life is where her coping resources are most challenged. While no one is invincible there is generally a resilience or capacity to cope effectively, albeit differently, under different circumstances.

Life's always a struggle. It is the first time ever that the children have gone back to school without me having everything in place. It's the one thing that undermines my peace of mind. There can be crises at work and it can upset me or agitate me or annoy me but I cope with it. If there is a minor crisis like that at home, I actually don't cope well. That's my soft spot. That's my vulnerable spot. Minor crises at work remain minor crises, minor crises at home become major in my mind.

Making success happen

Each of the remarkable achievers has both a talent and a circumstance that enables the talent to flourish. They have both internal resources such as a temperament which enables them to persevere and flourish, a capacity to reframe losses as opportunities, and the capacity to access external or communal resources in the form of support. A summary, Table 11.1 of the key features of their profiles provides a means of quick overview of resources and circumstances.

Those interviewed saw themselves as having more opportunities than setbacks and generally share an optimistic outlook. Nevertheless, each person has experienced 'failure' and loss. It is how they construe those losses in the context of their resources (external and internal) in a social setting that might be perceived as lenient, that is, forgiving or elastic that makes the difference. It enables their continued effective functioning. From the interviews it is evident that losses are reframed as gains, or at least externalized to leave the sense of self intact. For many, setbacks are seen as opportunities.

Table 11.1   Summary of the high-flyers

High-flyer	Resources					
	Success at School	Flow/passion	Emotional savvy	Support from parent/s	Support from coach/teacher	Reframe losses
Petra (business)		✓	✓	✓		
Doug (business)		✓	✓	✓		✓
Martin (developer)			✓	✓		✓
Andrew	✓		✓	✓	✓	✓
Miti (doctor)	✓				✓	
Livia (judge)	✓		✓	✓		
Jason (script writer)	✓		✓	✓		✓
Tania (swimmer)		✓	✓	✓	✓	✓
Justin (tennis player)		✓	✓	✓	✓	✓
Robyn (pianist)	✓	✓	✓	✓	✓	✓
Raima disability			✓	✓		✓

Many of the high achievers call upon a guiding principle or 'mantra'. These are messages imprinted in their minds, often from parents or significant others, and used as reminders of what is possible and what is not. These sayings are a support, and a comfort to which they return with regularity, especially when the going gets difficult. They may in some ways act as the invisible permanent presence of a support person. Each has a mentor, a coach, or a supportive parent who was with them through setbacks and victories, at least during the development years. It is not IQ that sets these people apart but rather each can be construed as possessing the elements of emotional intelligence. They have insight into their own lives and that of others. They generally rely on the support of trainers, crew, or workplace teams.

Many of the high achievers have been exposed to risk factors such as divorce in the family (Robyn, Raima, Justin), illness or loss of a parent (Tania, Petra, Livia) and experienced setbacks such as failed enterprises (Doug, Petra), sporting losses (Tania, Justin), or illness (Justin) which prevented them from pursuing their passions. Sports people learnt to cope with losses early in their careers, as have business people who have generally recovered from substantial losses. However, it is not the losses that dominate the present. There appears to be a capacity to recover and strengthen the resolve to amass additional resources to see them through the next challenge. Like gifted and talented people in all walks of life they have enthusiasm and passion in the pursuit of their main endeavours. Their pursuits are generally in their areas of interest, such as sport, music, writing, or commerce.

Awareness of time disappears in the pursuit of their goals. All their pursuits are valued in their community. They do not use the self-denigrating strategies of self-blame or excessive release of tension. Instead they have enough drive to reframe events in a positive way, acknowledge the part that circumstances play, and then they move on in pursuit of their goals.

While temperament and the interplay between heredity and environmental circumstances play their part, it is clear from the work of Dweck (1998) and others that the responses we give to young people following their performance determines the subsequent perceptions of their abilities and how they cope. Both emotional intelligence and optimism can be learned. While none of the high achievers had formal coping skills training they had role models in the form of parents, coaches and instructors. Nevertheless, in today's complex society, in order to ensure that young people thrive and reach their potential, we know that it is helpful to provide some direct instruction in coping. It is possible to teach young people how to cope (Buglaski and Frydenberg 2000; Cunningham *et al.* 1999, 2000 in press; Forman 1993; Shochet and Osgarby 1999) (see Chapter 9 in this volume). That is, coping skills programmes provided within the school curriculum or as extra curricular opportunities both for students and the adults with whom they interact, namely parents and teachers, is increasingly being demonstrated to be a worthwhile endeavour. Improving adolescent adaptation to stress is a most promising approach to preventing problems (Compas *et al.* 1989) and provides young people with the capacity to achieve their goals and meet challenges. All this augurs well for the future.

References

Albert, R. S. and Runco, M. A. (1986). The achievement of eminence: A model of exceptionally gifted boys and their families, in R. J. Sternberg and J. E. Dougson (eds.), *Conceptions of giftedness*, pp. 332–63. New York: Cambridge University Press.

Burns, M. O. and Seligman, M. E. P. (1989). Explanatory style across the lifespan: Evidence for stability over 52 years. *Journal of Personality and Social Psychology*, 56, 471–77.

Bloom, B. S. (1985). *Developing talent in young people*. New York: Ballantine.

Brandon, C. M., Cunningham, E. G., and Frydenberg, E. (1999). Bright ideas: A school-based program teaching optimistic thinking skills in pre-adolescence. *Australian Journal of Guidance & Counselling*, 9, 153–63.

Bugalski, K. and Frydenberg, E. (2000). Promoting effective coping in adolescents 'at-risk' for depression. *Australian Journal of Guidance & Counselling*, 10, 111–32.

Carver, C. and Gaines, J. (1993). Optimism, pessimism and post-partum depression. *Cognitive Therapy and Research*, 11, 449–62.

Compas, B. E., Phares, V., and Ledoux, N. (1989). Stress and coping preventive interventions for children and adolescents, In L. A. Bond and B. E. Compas (eds.), *Primary prevention and promotion in the schools*, pp. 319–40. Newbury Park: Sage.

Csikszentmihalyi, M. (1990). *Flow: The psychology of optimal experience*. New York: Harper and Row.

—— (1997). *Finding flow*. New York: Basic Books.

—— Rathunde, K., and Whalen, S. (1993). *Talented teenagers: The roots of success and failure*. New York: Cambridge University Press.

Cunningham, E. G., Brandon, C. M., and Frydenberg, E. (1999). Building resilience in early adolescence through a universal school-based prevention program. *Australian Journal of Guidance & Counselling*, 9, 15–24.

Cunningham, E., Brandon, C.M., and Frydenberg, E. (2000). *The development of coping resources in pre-adolescence within the context of the whole-school curriculum*. East Lansing, MI: Resources in Education (ERIC Document Reproduction Services No.CG029974).

—— —— —— Developing the coping resources of preadolescents. *Stress, Anxiety, and Coping* (in press).

Dweck. C. S. (1998). The development of early self-conceptions: Their relevance to motivational processes, in J. Heckhausen and C. S. Dweck (eds.), *Motivation and self-regulation across the life-span*. pp. 257–80. New York: Cambridge.

Felsman, J. K. and Vallant, G. E. (1987). Resilient children as adults: A 40-year study, in E. J. Anthony and B. J. Cohler (eds.), *The invulnerable child*, pp. 289–314. NY: Guilford.

Fitzgerald, T. E., Tennen, H., Affleck, G., and Pransky, G. S. (1993). The relative importance of dispositional optimism and control appraisals in quality of life after coronary artery bypass surgery. *Journal of Behavioural Medicine*, 16, 25–43.

Forman, S. G. (1993). *Coping skills interventions for children and adolescents*. San Francisco: Jossey-Bass Publishers.

Frydenberg, E. and Lewis, R. (1993). *The adolescent coping scale: Practitioners manual*. Australian Council for Educational Research.

Folkman, S. and Lazarus, R. S. (1985). If it changes it must be a process: A study of emotion and coping during three stages of a college examination. *Journal of Personality and Social Psychology*, 48(1), 150–70.

—— and Lazarus, R. (1988). The relationship between coping and emotion: Implications for theory and research. *Social Science Medicine*, 26(3), 309–17.

Goleman, D. (1998). *Working with emotional intelligence*. London: Bloomsbury.

Haan, N. (1977). *Coping and defending. Processes of self-environment organisation*. New York: Academic Press.

Hobfoll, S. E. (1988). *The ecology of stress*. New York: Hemisphere.

—— (1989). Conservation of resources: A new way of conceptualising stress. *American Psychologist*, 44(3). 513–24.

—— (1998). Stress, culture and community. New York: Plenum.

Peterson, C. and Seligman, M. E. P. (1984). Causal explanations as a risk factor for depression: Theory and evidence. *Psychological Review*, 91, 347–74.

Plomin, R., Scheier, M. F., Bergeman, C. S., Pederson, N. L., Nesselroade, J. R., and McClern, G. E. (1992). Optimism, pessimism, and mental health: A twin/adoption analysis. *Personality and Individual Differences*, 13, 921–30.

Prior, M. (1992). Childhood temperament. *Journal of Child Psychology and Psychiatry*, 33, 249–79.

—— Sanson, A., Smart, D., and Oberklaid, F. (2000). Pathways from infancy to adolescence: Autstralian temperament project 1983–2000. Melbourne: Australian Institute of Family Studies.

Rimm, S. B. (1991). Parenting the gifted adolescent: Special problems, special joys, in M. Bireley and J. Genshaft (eds.), *Understanding the gifted adolescent*, pp. 18–32. New York: Teachers College Press.

Rutter, M. (1996). Integrating nature and nurture: Implications for developmental psychopathology. American Psychological Association Conference.

Rutter, M. (1978). Family, area and school influences in the genesis of conduct disorders, in L. A. Hersov, M. Berger, and D. Shaffer (eds.), *Aggression and anti-social behaviour in childhood and adolescence*, pp. 95–114, Oxford: Pergamon.

—— (1983). Stress, coping and development: Some issues and questions, in N. Garmezy and M. Rutter (eds.), *Stress, coping and development in children*. pp. 1–41. NY: McGraw-Hill.

—— (1990). Psychosocial resilience and protective mechanisms, in J. Rolf, A. S. Masten, D. Cicchetti, K. H. Nuechterlein and S. Weintraub (eds.), *Risk and protective factors in the development of psychopathology*. pp. 181–214, Cambridge: Cambridge University Press.

Salovey, P., Bedell, B. T., Detweiler, J. B., and Mayer, J. D. (1999). Coping intelligently: Emotional intelligence and the coping process, in *The psychology of what works.*, 141–64. Oxford University Press.

Shochet, I. and Osgarby, S. (1999). The Resourceful Adolescent Project: Building psychological resilience in adolescents and their parents. *The Australian Educational and Developmental Psychologist*, 16, 43–64.

Seligman, M. (1992). *Learned optimism.* Australia: Random House.

Seligman, M. E. (1995). *The Optimistic child.* NSW: Random House Australia.

Scheier, M. F., Weintraub, J. K., and Carver, C. S. (1986). Coping with stress: Divergent strategies of optimists and pessimists. *Journal of Personality and Social Psychology*, 51, 1257–64.

Schulman, P., Keith, D., and Seligman, M. E. P. (1991). Is optimism heRobynble? A study of twins. *Behavior Research and Therapy*, 31, 569–74.

Werner, E. E. and Smith, R. S. (1982). *Vulnerable but invincible: A study of resilient children.* NY: McGraw-Hill.

CHAPTER 12

CONCLUDING REMARKS: WHAT IT ALL MEANS

ERICA FRYDENBERG

The preceding chapter, the last in this volume, on success and achievement, illustrates the fact that we can examine the life trajectories of successful achievers and see that it is more than talent and ability alone that places them well on the measures of success in their communities. Throughout the book we have identified theories that account for this, including the work of Goleman (1998) on emotional intelligence, Csikszentmihalyi and the concept of flow (1997) and Maslow's concept of self-actualization (Maslow 1954), along with the theories that have evolved from the field of stress and coping. Two areas of research that have emerged from the field of coping stand out, Conservation of Resources (COR) theory with its extension to communal coping, and proactive coping with its emphasis on goal management.

In his most recent work Hobfoll points out that COR theory 'considers both environmental and internal processes in relatively equal measure' (Hobfoll 2001). It perhaps best exemplifies that both aspects account for the successful outcomes as the individual interacts with his or her environment. He goes on to point out that the self derives from the attachments to intimate biological or intimate social groups and at the same time the individual is nested within a tribe or community which determines the cultural scripts that are brought into an encounter. The study of individual processes without reference to the cultural context is bound to fall short. Additionally, what helps us to move beyond the appraisal models of stress is the fact that the individual is able to be seen as proactive rather than reactive, that is, proactive coping is future oriented rather compensating for loss or alleviating harm.

The key argument of COR theory is the primacy of loss, that is it outweighs the benefit of gain. However, gain becomes important in the context of loss. To safeguard against loss there is an investment of resources which includes 'acquisition, maintenance, and fostering'. These in turn are motivational goals consistent with proactive coping. The way in which proactive coping is defined by Greenglass (Chapter 3 in this volume) and Schwarzer and Taubert (Chapter 2 in this volume) would imply that 'acquisition, maintenance, and fostering' are important strategies to achieve success. Similarly Boekaerts presents an educationalists' view of anticipatory or proactive coping in the context of goal attainment. The point is made by Boekaerts that the unique way in which students give meaning to learning activities determines how much effort they are prepared to invest to achieve a school related goal. That is, if the learning goal or task is in accordance with their need and value systems they are likely to succeed. It could be said that all the high achievers in the preceding chapter pursued goals that were congruent with their needs. Whether they were constructing a collection of buildings, playing the piano, or undertaking a long distance swim, the endeavour was consistent with their personal goals and values. According to Boekaerts, self-regulated learning is about having the metacognitive skills to orient, plan, execute, monitor, and repair. It requires forthright volitional control and self-reflection.

But to return to COR theory with its emphasis on conservation of resources, investment, and building up of a stockpile of personal, social, and economic resources points to the proactive aspects of coping. The emphasis on the 'individual-nested in family-nested in tribe' highlights the communal and collectivist aspect of coping. The focus on us as social beings is also taken up by Moore, in the adult context and by Johnson and Johnson in the educational context. Communal coping is underscored by support. The availability of support is vividly illustrated in the stories of high achievers. In the context of communal coping. Hobfoll presents communal mastery as a viable construct which provides an alternate way of dealing with life. Communal mastery was found to be associated with lower anger, depression, and physical symptoms in contrast to self-mastery. This points to the potential benefit of this approach to life management. But there is a cost, a social contagion related to being involved with others. That is, there is a cost in terms of emotional and social burden. Hobfoll also points out the that there is a value placed on self-mastery as providing inner strength. The path to success is likely to be made up of both self- and communal-mastery. He points out that the reliance on the study of personal agency limits our understanding about the role that attachment to others can play.

COR theory emphasizes the individual's approach to coping it is complemented by the concept of communal coping with its emphasis on interdependence. Proactive coping is another important development in the coping literature which emphasizes the individual's role in maximizing optimum outcome for future events

Chapter 2 reviews the field of stress and coping. Along with Chapter 3 it makes a distinction between anticipatory coping, where one anticipates that critical events are to occur and there is investment in risk management, and preventative coping, where there is an investment of effort to build up 'resistance resources' to minimize the severity of impact. Proactive coping, in contrast, is about building up resources to promote challenging goals and personal growth, that is, it is about 'goal striving'. In that sense it is both consistent with Hobfoll's COR theory and an extension of it. Proactive copers have vision and coping for them is about goal management. It is not self-defeating but self-initiating and about having a vision that gets transformed into action. This is just what the high achievers do (see Chapter 11 in this volume).

Following the work of Mashlach on burnout, Greenglass notes that those with personal goals and resources are less vulnerable to stress. Among the personal resources of affluence, health, optimism, self-efficacy, and hope are included coping skills. Greenglass makes four important points in relation to coping. First, coping can have multiple functions, only one of which may be to minimize stress. Functions that relate to maintaining relationships, keeping to task or beating a competitor can all be coping. Second, coping is multidimensional rather than bipolar as frequently represented by the dimensions of control/escape, active/passive, and problem-focused/emotion-focused. Third, it does not occur in a social vacuum. Fourth, the function of coping is not only to alleviate distress but also increase potential for growth, satisfaction, and quality of life. Chapter 3 illustrates how use of proactive coping can lead to lower burnout, lower anger and to positive outcomes such as professional efficacy.

Shwarzer and Taubert identify extensions of the coping construct to include positive strivings which were hitherto in the domain of motivation and action theorists. We have now moved beyond a reactive theory of coping to one where concepts such as mastery, optimization, and resources gain are consistent with proactive coping. Concepts such as benefit finding, sense making, the search for meaning, all broaden the coping concept. Chapter 2 also highlights the negative relationship between proactive coping and depression. Proactive teachers report less exhaustion, less cynicism, more personal accomplishments than their reactive counterparts. Highly proactive teachers regard their stressors as more challenging and less threatening or loss-based than their reactive counterparts. That is, proactive teachers have less burnout, more challenges, and less threat and loss. Proactive coping is about growth and taking responsibility for making things happen. Qualities of leadership are closely linked to proactive coping. It seems highly beneficial to develop skills of proactive coping.

The learning or schooling experience is all important in providing a basis for adult life. What is clear from the work of Dweck (see Chapters 1 and 7 in this volume) and others such as De Corte *et al.* (2000) is that it is possible to change students' perceptions of themselves in relationship to the learning task. Various cognitive and motivational self-regulatory processes need to be promoted to help students become their own teacher. Cues which elicit positive emotions, such as joy, contentment, satisfaction, anticipated pride or interest, temporarily broaden the scope of attention, cognition, and action. In contrast, cues which elicit negative emotions (e.g. anxiety, fear, frustration, irritation, shame, or guilt) temporarily narrow the scope of attention, cognition, and action. The consequences for the learning task are evident (see Chapter 7 in this volume). Not all children choose challenging tasks when given the opportunity, rather 37 per cent choose to do the familiar and easy puzzle. However, the response they receive at the completion of the task determines whether they persevere (Smiley and Dweck 1994).

Students profit from an increased capacity to judge whether a particular action will lead to goal attainment, that is, whether, increased effort and persistance will pay off. However, effort investment is related to perceived value of tasks and perceived competence of execution. In a diverse and changing school climate students are increasingly being called upon to be self-regulated learners. Additionally distinction is made between self-regulation and self-control in that the latter activates the punishment system while the former is associated with positive emotions. Educators need to foster skills for self-regulation.

The concept of proactive coping needs to be integrated into the world of young people. The link between self-regulated learning and proactive coping can be made. Goals which are in harmony with students' goal structure have a better chance of being adopted and achieved. As Resnick *et al.* (1997) demonstrated in their study of 12, 118 adolescents from 80 high schools in the US, school and parent connectedness are key factors in resiliency. It can generally be assumed that where goals in education are congruent with both the students' and their parents' objectives, the goals are more likely to be achieved, resulting in a situation where there is a strong sense of connectedness with both the school and parents.

Boekaerts also highlights that positive affect is helpful in fulfilling the activities which are important in the classroom. The 'broader mindset' with which positive mood state is associated, encourages exploration, extension of oneself, and the sharing of information. The Resnick et al. survey interviewed young people for emotional distress, suicidal thoughts and behaviours, violence, use of substances (cigarettes, alcohol, marijuana), and two types of sexual behaviours (age of sexual debut and pregnancy history). They found that 18.4 per cent of 9th through to 12th graders experienced significant distress. Thus, it can be expected that while the majority of young people go through their school years with a healthy positive affect, there are many for whom addressing their emotional well-being is an imperative. Furthermore, the idea of working in groups in an educational community (see Johnson and Johnson, Chapter 10 in this volume) should contribute in this regard. Johnson and Johnson are able to achieve a positive mindset. It is in the context of focusing on the three Cs (cooperative community, constructive conflict resolution, and civic values) that we need to encourage students to be self-regulators rather than self-controllers, since it is the former who experience more positive emotions.

Following the theme of positive psychology, proactive coping, motivation, and goal attainment, Pekrun et al. (Chapter 8 in this volume) consider the frequency of emotions reported in a number of learning related areas. They found that although anxiety, the negative emotion associated with stress was often experienced, positive emotions were experienced with similar frequency as the negative ones. These researchers established a measure of positive emotions in relation to students learning, achievement, personality, and social environments to determine whether positive emotions are helpful or not. The relative benefit of positive emotions in contrast to the often considered negative effect of emotions, including unrealistic appraisals, and shallow superficial processing of information, was considered. The researchers showed that positive mood can facilitate divergent and flexible thinking to enhance problem-solving. They formulated a cognitive motivational model that involves positive activating emotions such as hope and pride and positive deactivating emotions such as relief and relaxation. They go on to borrow terms from motivation research which relates to outcomes, such as where intrinsic emotions are related to enjoyment of the task, a concept somewhat like Csikszentmihalyi's (1990) concept of flow, and extrinsic emotions relate to outcomes such as success or failure. Generally the assumption is made that students' pursuit of their goals in an academic setting is more likely to be associated with gaining mastery and avoiding failure rather than mood maintenance.

They sum up their findings as showing that emotions like, enjoyment, hope, and pride relate to students academic goal pursuits and outcomes in positive ways. Since emotions can make a difference, a case can be made for attending to emotions in the classroom. There is a reciprocal relationship between students' environments and positive emotions. That is, social environments effect positive emotions and positive emotions in turn effect academic learning and achievement. There are implications for classroom practice such as attributional training and designing classroom environments which include cooperative learning. (See also Chapter 10 in this volume.)

Burke (Chapter 5 in this volume) focuses on coping and the workplace. He points out that stress and coping need to be seen as a field of endeavour that was found to be lacking in the 1980s. The point is made by Burke and others (e.g. Pearlin 1991) that little progress has been made in coping in the workplace by looking at individual factors, but rather we should be looking at organizational or group factors. This is consistent with Mashlach and Leiter's (1997) recent emphasis on workplace engagement (see Chapter 1 in this volume) where the emphasis is on what can the organization do to improve the coping outcomes of workers. Those in managerial roles come to an organization with resources. They are a generally highly educated, middle, or upper socio-economic group and hold values that support responsibility, discipline, and achievement. Generally they have a sense of confidence and good problem-solving skills. But some are hardy and resilient and others are not. When the hardiness concept of Maddi and Kobassa (1984) was applied to managers experiencing high stress and low illness, hardy managers were found to have low blood pressure, low anxiety, depression, and suspiciousness. The three components of hardiness, commitment, control, and challenge, are also the characteristics of the high achievers (see Chapter 11 in this volume) where those who are successful in their chosen endeavour display those qualities.

Concepts such as hardiness (Maddi and Kobassa 1984); sense of coherence (SOC) (Antonovsky 1987), flow (Csikszentmihalyi 1990), resonance (Clawson 1999), optimism and positive affect (Seligman 1992) (see Chapter 5) are used to explain how individuals thrive and succeed. For example, sense of coherence (SOC), is a way of making sense of the world, seeing things as comprehensible, manageable, and meaningful. Flow is a concept that has generally been applied to gifted and talented young people. However, here it is applied in the organizational context to managers. Managers experience more flow at work than do clerical or blue-collar workers. What is surprising is that men and women experience more flow at work than in their leisure. Those who cope effectively can transform a negative situation into one of flow where there is a focus outward towards the environment, accompanied by the discovery of new goals and solutions. The term 'resonance' (Clawson 1999) is used to describe peak performances, be it by athletes, musicians, or managers.

Change is a certainty with which we all need to cope. Coping with change is about feeling that one has personal control, tolerance of ambiguity, and ability to share worries. In a study of police officers Burke (1998) found that more escapist coping was associated with work–family conflict and had an effect on well-being measures such as job satisfaction and lack of psychosomatic symptoms. The negative relationship between control and escapist coping has been observed widely. For example, in their study of nurses Burke and Greenglass (2000) found greater use of control coping was associated with greater work satisfaction and fewer psychosomatic symptoms. Burke cites a study by Heaney *et al.* (1995) of 1375 managers and direct care staff who participated in a training programme in which the use of social support and perceived control was emphasized. The experimental group, in contrast to the control group, used more social support, which had the effect of increasing self-esteem, raising morale, and =providing a sense of connection.

Ultimately it is all about well-being. The point is made by Moore and Frydenberg and Lewis in Chapters 6 and 9, respectively, that well-being is not merely the absence of illness. Moore builds on the work of Maslow (1954) and looks at data from, for example, the world of the unemployed and nurses experiencing the impact of hospital restructuring. Those who felt challenged reported greater feeling of self-efficacy. Similarly, solution-focused strategies are related to better health outcomes for people with illness such as multiple sclerosis. In the adolescent arena, a clear link is found between self-blame and lack of well-being, causing the researchers to conclude that while we should be encouraging the increasing use of productive coping strategies and the decreasing usage of non-productive strategies it is the use of self-blame that is most strongly to be discouraged.

When it comes to change, it is possible to develop coping skills such as proactive coping, attributional training, and flow. Similarly, it is important to consider the collective and cooperative aspects of coping, along with approaches to change for which the organization can take responsibility in settings that relate to the workplace or in learning environments. In educational settings, for example, the focus can be on establishing a classroom climate which fosters positive emotions, goal attainment, and effective learning in a cooperative communal context. Such organizational changes contribute to the achievement of success. The life trajectories of high achievers illustrate how personal characteristics, along with opportunities for talent development account for the attainment of success. Individuals with strong psychosocial resources are likely to cope proactively to achieve their goals.

Communal and proactive coping, along with positive emotions and self-regulation contribute to our understanding of well-being and thriving. While it is possible to change individual behaviour and thinking, it is also helpful to change organizational settings in ways which assist individuals to achieve well-being and to contribute to their thriving and success.

References

Antonovsky, A. (1987). *Unraveling the mystery of health: How people manage stress and stay well.* San Francisco, CA: Jossey-Bass.

Burke, R. J. (1998). Work and non-work stressors and well-being among police officers: The role of coping. *Anxiety, Stress, and Coping.,* **14**, 1–18.

—— and **Greenglass, E. R.** (2000). Hospital restructuring and nursing staff well-being: The role of coping. *International Journal of Stress Management,* 7, 49–59.

Clawson, J. C. (1999). *Level three leadership: Getting below the surface.* Upper Saddle River, NJ: Prentice Hall.

Csikszentmihalyi, M. (1990). *Flow: The psychology of optimal experience.* New York: Harper & Row.

—— (1997). *Finding Flow.* New York: Basic Books.

De Corte, E., Verschaffel, L., and Op 't Eynde, P. (2000). Self-regulation: A characteristic and a goal of mathematics education, in M. Boekaerts, P. R. Pintrich, and M. Zeidner (eds.), *Handbook of self-regulation,* pp. 687–726. San Diego, CA: Academic Press.

Heaney, C. A., Price, R. H., and Rafferty, J. (1995). Increasing coping resources at work: a field experiment to increase social support, improve work team functioning, and enhance employee mental health. *Journal of Organizational Behavior,* 16, 335–52.

Goleman, D. (1998). *Working with emotional intelligence.* London: Bloomsbury.

Hobfoll, S. E. (2001). The influence of culture, community, and the nested-self in the stress process: Advancing conservation of resources theory. *Applied Psychology: An International Review,* 50(3), 337–421.

Maddi, S. R. and Kobassa, S. C. (1984). *The hardy executive: Health under stress.* Homewood, IL: Dow Jones-Irwin.

Mashlach, C. and Leiter, M. P. (1997). *The truth about burnout: How organisations cause personal stress and what to do about it.* San Francisco, CA: Jossey-Bass.

Maslow, A. H. (1954). *Motivation and personality.* New York: Harper & Row.

Pearlin, L. I. (1991). The study of coping, in J. Eckenrode (ed.), *The social context of coping.* pp. 261–76. New York: Plenum Press.

Resnick, M. D., Bearman, P. S., Blum, R. W., Bauman, K. E., Harris, K. M., Jones, J. *et al.* (1997). Protecting adolescents from harm: Findings from the national longitudinal study on adolescent health. *The Journal of the American Medical Association,* 278(10), 795–878.

Smiley, P. and Dweck, C. S. (1994). Individual differences in achievement goals among young children. *Child Development,* 65, 1723–43.

Seligman, M. E. (1992). *Learned optimism.* Australia: Random House.

INDEX